CW00924936

Beneath the Cloud Forests

For baby Marshall George William
Memories of his beauty will stay forever

Beneath
the
Cloud Forests

A History of Cave Exploration in Papua New Guinea

by Howard M. Beck

SPELEO
PROJECTS

Howard Beck was born in northern England in 1947 and has lived and worked in Papua New Guinea. With 34 years experience as an explorer, climber, potholer and extreme walker, he has had many opportunities for extensive travel throughout the world. He has led expeditions to an isolated region of Arctic Norway, to Spain and to the Gouffre de la Pierre St. Martin in the Pyrenées. He has caved throughout the United Kingdom and been involved with many important discoveries in his native Yorkshire Dales.

In 1975 he was an organiser and participant of the British Speleological Expedition to Papua New Guinea, where he spent eight months in the uncharted, central jungles as a part of the expedition to the Hindenburg Mountains.

He has been a freelance photographer and writer for almost 30 years but has only been seriously writing since the early 1980s. His work has been featured in many journals, magazines and books. His other caving title, *Gaping Gill, 150 Years of Exploration*, is now out of print.

Beneath the Cloud Forests
by Howard M. Beck
First Edition, 2003

© Speleo Projects, Caving Publications International, Switzerland.

Publisher: Urs Widmer
Text and Photo Editor: Melanie Alspaugh
Photos and maps individually credited.
Where not otherwise mentioned, maps redrawn by Howard Beck
Cover photograph: Kavakuna Doline by Gerald Favre
Back cover: Nare Doline by Dave Gill
Proofreaders: Ray Craig, Stefan Eberhard, Alan Warild
Layout Design: Til Ottlik
Prepress: Urs Widmer
Typefaces: ITC Garamond, Gill
Print: Druckerei Schüler AG, Biel
Jacket finish: Printlack, Schwadernau
Binding: Grolimund AG, Reinach

Contact:
Speleo Projects, Caving Publications International
Lettenweg 118, CH-4123 Allschwil, Switzerland
E-mail: info@speleoprojects.com

SPELEO
PROJECTS

Printed in Switzerland
ISBN 3-908495-11-3

CONTENTS

FIGURES IN TEXT

I will let loose against you the fleet-footed vines –
I will call in the Jungle to stamp out your lines!

Rudyard Kipling,
Mowgli's Song Against People, *The Second Jungle Book*

ACKNOWLEDGEMENTS

The research for this book has taken over four years and been aided by many organisations without which my task would not have been possible. I am deeply indebted to the following for their assistance:

John Fairfax (UK); *South Pacific Post*, Port Moresby; *Geographical Journal*; *Spelunca* Magazine; Ok Tedi Mining; Infoline Information Services, Sydney; Pacific Helicopters; *Sous Terre*, Canada; *Craven Herald* Newspapers, Yorkshire; Brisbane *Sunday Mail*; the Dept. Civil Aviation, PNG; Australian Speleology Federation; *New Zealand Herald*; *Wild* Magazine, Australia; *Niugini Caver* Magazine; Spelefilm Enterprise, Geneva; *The Sydney Sun*; *Descent* Magazine; Societé Suisse de Spéléologie; the London Office of *Sydney Morning Herald*; *Walkabout* Magazine, Australia; Pacific Publications; Sydney Speleological Society; Rotorwork Helicopters, Mount Hagen; University Queensland Speleological Society; Japan Office of Information, London; British High Commission, Port Moresby; Papua New Guinea High Commission, London; *Japan Caving* Magazine; Fédération Française de Spéléologie; *Telegraph* and *Argus* Newspapers (UK); Sheffield University Speleological Society; New Zealand Speleological Society; British Cave Research Association; Helicopter Association of Australia; Nanzan University of Nagoya, Japan; Meiji University, Japan; Spéléoclub de Schaerbeek, Belgium; Spéléoclub Troglodite and *Speleoc* Magazine (Midi-Pyrénées).

In addition to the above there are countless individuals who in no small way have helped with the production of this book. A special thank you is extended to Dr. Julia James for permission to abstract material from Muller expedition reports, including the Atea and Mamo Kananda surveys, Fred Parker and Ken Grimes, Eds. *Helictite* for permission to use the survey of Kara River Cave, Joe Buleka, Director & Chief Geologist of PNG for permission to base Fig. 3 on the 1973 1:250 000 series maps Blucher sheet, Gérald Favre and the Expédition Spéléologique Suisse 1979 for use of the Lemerigamus plan, Jean-Paul Sounier for the Muruk and Arcturus surveys and endless amounts of help and abstracted passages from his book *Muruk*, Prof. Ernest Löffler (University of Saarland, Germany), Captain Gareth Bean, Bernie Flanagan (Civil Aviation Authority of PNG), Mike Shepherd (Massey University, New Zealand), Dr. Rod Wells (Flinders University, Adelaide), Ross Ellis (Sydney Speleological Society), Luc-Henri Fage, Randall King, Dave Brook and Jean-François Pernette. For translations from the French I have to thank Doreen Claydon, Paul Everett and Andy Kaye, and from Japanese, Andrew Kynaston.

For taped self-interviews, advice and access to personal notes, diaries, letters, expedition reports, press cuttings and microfilms I am indebted to Ian Westwood, Steve Bunton, Al Warild, Brian Evans, Barry Were, Shane Wilcox, Tony White, Chris Pugsley, Dr. Tim Lyons, Steve Worthington, Chas Yonge, Mike Farnworth, Kevan Wilde, Henry Shannon, Dave Yeandle, Dick Willis, Dr. Phil Chapman, Major Jack Sheldon, Ernest Garza, Erich Delnatte, Andy Eavis, Carol Vesely,

Dr. Jon Buchan, Steve Crabtree, Noel Plumley, Norman Flux, Richard Bartrop, Allan Goulbourne, Mike Bourke, Tim Sprod, Dave Martin, Neil Hickson, Ian Miller, Tom Hayllar, Nick Hume, Rolan and Stefan Eberhard.

I must also thank Cathy and Trevor Worthy, Lex Brown, Mark Laurendet, Mark Wilson, Brian Carter, Geoff Francis, Dave Gill, Guy Cox, Rowan Emberson, Rob Kay, Neil Montgomery, Trevor Ford, Van Watson, Ashley Cody, Paul Seddon, Urs Widmer, Alfred Montserrat, Dave Bunnel, the late Philippe Rouiller, Keith Plumb, Karlin Meyers, John Hobson, Trevor Wailes, Atsushi Fugii, Dirk Stoffels, Daniel Caron, Roy Paulson, Hugh Blanchard (Ed. *Explorer*), Tony Karas, Dave Elliott, Stephen Gough, Ray Mansfield, Joan Devitt, Marie France Castagne, Dick Anderson, Simon Jolly, Peter Ackroyd and Karen McMillan. Last but certainly not least, I must thank my hard-working editor, Melanie Alspaugh, for her considerable input.

Howard M. Beck

INTRODUCTION

The early exploration of New Guinea came at a time when Europe had almost completely "discovered" the remainder of the world. Towards the close of the nineteenth century library shelves held rank upon rank of glowing reports penned by adventurers the world over and national museums were literally stuffed to bursting with all the spoils of exploration. Ah, yes, the 1800s. It belonged to the pioneers, the flamboyant entrepreneurs and rash adventurers. It was the era of the dawn of fulfillment, the age of the speleologist, and the cave explorer had yet to see the light of day.

New Guinea was a mysterious land indeed, sandwiched between the equator and the Australian continent. At the crossroads of Southeast Asia, it lay as if severed from the East, where the Indonesian archipelago melts away into the sun-kissed coral seas of the South Pacific. It was as isolated as one could imagine; romantic but remote, beautiful yet savage, and so often referred to as "The Last Unknown."

Compared with any similar sized region, New Guinea has the distinction of being blessed with great concentrations of mountainous terrain. By happy circumstance for speleologists, much of this terrain consists of pure limestones, massively bedded and cavernous. On the negative side, from sea level to around 3,700 metres in altitude, these mountains are densely covered in primary rain forest and mid-mountain moss forests, the latter often referred to as cloud forest because of the way wraith-like mists and vapours daily shroud the lofty mountain peaks and ridges. Just for good measure and as an additional impediment to travel, the country is located entirely within the equatorial wet zone. Consequently, the humidity is high and the land frequently deluged by a staggering ten metres of rainfall per annum. All these factors contrive to make overland travel downright unpleasant and cave exploration extremely hazardous.

Throughout the 1960s and early 1970s the search for the deepest cave in the world – the speleologist's "holy grail" – pushed the frontier of cave exploration virtually to every country with limestone deposits of any significance. The quest revealed many grails, for while only one mountain may rank the highest, the title for deepest cave may change year in and year out and even week by week. We can never be certain when the absolute deepest hole has been explored; new discoveries are continually being made and extensions added to existing caves.

Really deep caves were for a long time the preserve of French cavers. With the Pyrénées and the high Alps on their doorstep, they enjoyed a jealously guarded monopoly on 1,000 metre-deep caves. By the mid-1970s however, New Guinea was emerging as the best prospect for discovering record-breaking cave systems. To some it was the ultimate adventure, a speleological El Dorado.

Over the past 30 years cave exploration in New Guinea has progressed in leaps and bounds. A handful of the most extensive caves in the world have been explored, from the confusing labyrinths of Mamo Kananda to the beautifully decorated galleries of Selminum Tem and Lik-lik

Vuvu. Moreover, some of the most technically difficult river caves were by their very nature also the most voluminous in the world.

As expeditions grew in size and scope, aviation was to play a vital role in their ultimate success, just as in the post-war years it was instrumental in the rapid exploration of the High-lands. Fixed-wing planes filled a niche for air dropping essential supplies to some of the earliest administration patrols; in more recent times, they have fulfilled an identical function for caving expeditions. With the sudden upsurge in the number of foreign expeditions to New Guinea, helicopters too were to gain wider acceptance as a viable alternative to air drops or the endless carrier lines of tradition. While the introduction of aviation eased logistics, the latter still dictated resources that were beyond the scope of smaller, informal groups of resident expatriate cavers.

Nevertheless, the requirement in human terms was not diminished, and a willingness to strive under the most appalling conditions was always an essential ingredient in the recipe for success. Reaching the caves required a great deal of good old fashioned jungle bashing, and this was never free from difficulty. The explorer quickly develops a love-hate relationship with the all-embracing jungle, the "bush" as the Australians affectionately call it. This affinity with nature is an inescapable facet of jungle travel, which is to some a utopia and to others hell on earth.

Since 1965, over 30 international caving expeditions have been fielded throughout New Guinea. The story unfolds like a drama, a compelling narrative of survival both above and below ground. The fortunes of its principal characters – the speleologists, their native guides and por-ters, and the pilots who risked their necks in the cloud-shrouded mountains – are punctuated with a bittersweet mixture of success, disappointment, elation and disaster at the frontier of the known world. The following chapters record the fascinating details of these achievements, span-ning over a quarter of a century.

Though we are not particularly concerned with statistics, the nature of these explorations dictate a frequent reference to records. Nor is the purpose of this volume to present a guide to every known cave in New Guinea; to attempt this would be a colossal task, tedious to author and reader alike. Rather, this is a popular account of adventure and exploration in one of the world's last remaining wild places, the primordial jungles and the strange realm of the caverns which lie hidden beneath them.

Some of the lesser explorations have been included where I have deemed it desirable; for instance, when a more general overview of cave exploration is presented, or where discoveries might be seen as milestones along the road to success. These accounts also illustrate the wider history of pioneer cave exploration in this fascinating region.

The frequent use of the name New Guinea throughout the text refers solely to Papua New Guinea as distinct from Irian Jaya, the Indonesian-controlled western half of the island.

The megadoline of Minye viewed from beyond the first river crossing.

Chapter One

EVEREST LIES BELOW

Peering down through the cataract as it leapt out into space, Fernand could be seen silhouetted in the light from his lamp against the heavy spray that filled the continuing shaft. Initially this consisted of a 20-metre fall followed by an inclined slabby section separating it from a further vertical drop below. Teetering on the brink of this, he clung perilously to hope and the flimsy wire caving ladder. Whipped into a frenzy by eager zephyrs, the "rain" enveloped him with an enthusiasm of attachment that chilled him to the marrow. He strained to see what was below.

Waiting anxiously up above, his companions looked over the edge and could see him pull up where two waterfalls apparently merged, presenting a united front against further exploration. Directing the beam of his cap lamp downwards, Fernand could just glimpse through the falling water, a vague outline that gave a hint of a continuing passage. The noise of crashing water was deafening as it fell into a plunge pool below. He came up.

"What about it?" asked his colleagues.

Rather breathlessly he gave a brief account. "It will go…but not today. We shall need special gear as we did at the Claudine cascade."

This was back in September 1954, when a large French team under the leadership of Fernand Petzl reached a new world depth record of 903 metres in the Gouffre Berger. This exciting chasm had been discovered two years earlier by Jo Berger whilst investigating the high alpine karsts of the Sornin Plateau above Grenoble, in the French pre-Alps region of the Vercors.

After a long and tiring haul out, the cavers eventually emerged after 66 hours below ground, exhausted but elated that the magical 1,000 metres was now within their grasp. Two more years would pass before this dream became a reality. In 1955, they succeeded merely in adding a further 82 metres to the depth of the cave, and then only after a year's preliminaries were followed by an arduous struggle with the subterranean elements. During those ten days below ground the resources of the French cavers had been so overstretched that they decided the next year they would invite an international team for a fresh assault on the chasm.

Thus, it was on August 11, 1956 that a siphon pool was finally reached at 1,130 metres, the first cave ever to reach such a depth. The effect that this victory had on the caving world was to lend impetus to the aspirations of others: the French success had been a magnificent feat, the culmination of many years of painstaking work by members of the Club Alpin Français. Inspired by this achievement a number of countries, including France, fielded hopeful teams that attempted (but ultimately failed) to reach the bottom of the cave.

One British caver whose imagination had been kindled by news of these explorations was Frank Salt, a member of the Birmingham Cave and Crag Club. Together with John Gregory, he descended the Gouffre Berger in 1960 and again the following year, but bad weather on both occasions prevented them reaching even the site of the first French camp 494 metres down.

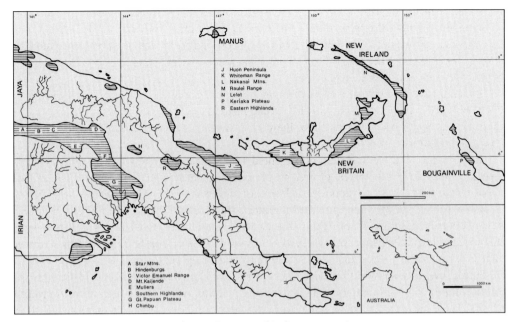

Fig. 1) New Guinea and its limestone regions

Frank's appetite was whetted, and from the first seed implanted by those encounters with the Berger sprang an ambitious plan for 1962: to put an all British 30-man team down the world's deepest cave. The venture involved cavers from the Midlands, Yorkshire and Derbyshire, with such familiar names as Dave Allsop, Ken Pearce and David Judson taking part. The success of this expedition proved a complete vindication of the team's determination and organisational ability, highlighted by the fact that of those participating, one third would reach the terminal sump. It was also the first wholly national team to reach the bottom.

The post-war years had of course seen French caving exploits organised on the grand scale, much publicised by colourful characters like Casteret. Graphic accounts of his exploits in works such as *My Caves* and *Ten Years Under The Earth* inspired adventurers the world over. Current feelings among the British intimated that their success in bottoming the Berger chasm would rapidly erode the hitherto unchallenged French supremacy in cave exploration, and there were some who yearned to look further afield. In 1962 the deepest known caves after the Gouffre Berger were the Antro della Corchia (805 m), Gouffre de la Pierre St. Martin (737 m) and the Grotto di Piaggie Bella (689 m), all of them located in Europe. During the last few days on the Sornin Plateau spirits were running high throughout the British camp. They were revelling in their success, riding a tide of wine and euphoria; talk frequently strayed to far-flung exotic places. What were the options for cave exploration outside Europe? Could a cave be found even deeper than the Berger?

Teams of cavers from Oxford University were already discovering spectacular systems in the Picos Mountains of northern Spain, but at that time the region did not appear to have the potential for great depth. Other groups of British cavers were also beginning to prospect abroad. Frank Salt had ideas of his own vaguely conceived in 1962 while in the Vercors.

At that time New Guinea had been mentioned briefly and dismissed. But not so easily ignored were the reports circulated by geologists undertaking aerial surveys in that wild land for British

Petroleum. While flying over the remote interior, pilots had reported seeing huge cave entrances in the sides of jungle shrouded mountains, occasionally with equally large rivers sinking into them to emerge…well, no one quite knew where. Pools of unfathomed darkness punctuated the all-embracing green of the tropical forest, betraying places where shafts descended into caverns beyond even the most vivid imagination.

Accounts such as these were more than any red-blooded caver could bear. Suitably inspired, Frank gathered together a small following of like-minded cavers drawn from the Cave and Crag Club and the South Wales Caving Club. Between them they were determined to find out more about this apparent cavers' paradise.

Research revealed that the country presented a geological structure with vast areas of virgin limestone surpassing the wildest of dreams. Moreover, geomorphologists seemed to agree that massive limestone (see fig. 1) deposits such as exist in New Guinea, when combined with the hot climate and high precipitation, provided the ideal conditions for caverns to develop on a vast scale. Cavers in Australia, if not Britain, already subscribed to this view. This was all very well, but the questions asked by cavers everywhere focused upon prospects for finding these caves. Was it the caver's El Dorado that the initial observations suggested?

Further evidence showed that much of mainland New Guinea and large areas of the principal islands of the group – New Ireland, New Britain and Bougainville, for example – are composed of pure and semi-pure limestone rising to 3,000 metres or more. These are massively bedded with classic features typical of the tropical karst landscape: reports came in of huge dolines, pinnacle, arête and tower karst, extended sink-to-resurgence distances, and mature cave development. Only time would tell whether beneath the dense forests lurked a cave more extensive than anything Europe had to offer.

When at last the 1962 British Berger expedition had become a fading memory, Frank's first inkling of an idea waxed into an ambitious concept: to sustain a team of at least 15 persons in the field for three to four months and, hopefully, to explore caves in one of the most uncompromising environments known. As more was gleaned about this distant isle, it became clear they were faced with the greatest challenge to exploration in modern times. Planning progressed well into 1963 with a departure date projected for June the following year. Logistically it was a nightmare.

The task of finding sponsors for the venture was not the simple matter it might have been, given the undoubted caving potential. However, it was not enough to know that extensive limestone existed, or that caves had been sighted. Backers wanted more substantial evidence, but beyond the reports of petroleum geologists, there was precious little upon which to state a case.

There had been a caving presence in New Guinea prior to 1960 but their activities were fragmented in the extreme. Indeed, if any explorations were undertaken then, there was no record of the fact beyond a few scant stories passed down by word of mouth. In 1937, an Administration Patrol Officer (also known as a *kiap* in pidgin English)[1] visited some caves at Henganofi in the Eastern Highlands. Ten years later, another *kiap* tracking the murderers of a policeman chased an armed group of suspects into Tefola Cave at Sonofi, in the Eastern Highlands. He set a guard at the cave entrance for three weeks while, unknown to him, his "captives" escaped from another exit!

It was no easy matter gleaning anything of the holes themselves. Cavers in the United States had showed an interest in New Guinea as early as 1957, when one person seeking information wrote to David Taylor, an Australian caver then domiciled in Port Moresby. His reply merely stated that the few people who had stumbled upon cave entrances were too pre-occupied with

---

[1] *See Appendix V on page 346 for the short glossary of pidgin English terms.*

survival to explore them or even record their existence. Such was the nature of New Guinea's untamed hinterland.

The British contact in New Guinea was Gordon Bain, President of the Port Moresby Speleological Society, an informal organisation formed four years earlier. Gordon was given the task of organising down-under and recruiting an Australian contingent to augment the British team. To this end he addressed the Australian Speleological Federation through the July 1963 issue of its newsletter. While this was going on, preparations back in the UK were painfully slow and sponsorship as easy to come by as a dodo egg.

Gordon had tendered his recommendations for likely target areas based upon available local knowledge and his own experience with the PMSS. The fortunes of the latter had necessarily ebbed and flowed with the somewhat transient nature of its widespread membership. Nevertheless, during the first three years of its history the club had run 46 field trips, principally to the Javarere Caves near Port Moresby. Out of these meets, there had been four to the Chuave district of the Eastern Highlands. Together with the Porgera area (in what was later to become the Enga District) and the Star Mountains, Chuave was billed as one of the most promising karst regions of New Guinea. Gordon therefore suggested that the expedition concentrate on these three areas.

Frank Salt approached the Royal Geographical Society for its support, but the board refused to recognise what it considered a gallant but unreasonable proposal, a stance it had also taken with the 1962 British Gouffre Berger Expedition. It could also be argued that in a country obviously lacking communications infrastructure, having three geographically isolated target areas was impractical, and not calculated to engender confidence in prospective backers. Frank had proved the Society wrong in 1962 and hoped he could do it a second time.

Matters were beginning to look as bleak as the tropical storms that lash New Guinea's mountains, when out of the blue the expedition acquired the patronage of General Sir Hugh Stockwell. He had enjoyed a colourful career with the British Armed Forces, having led them through the Suez Canal crises of the mid-1950s. As luck would have it he was able to pull a few strings. Although a final judgement on choice of caving area had still to be made, preparations now gathered impetus. Through the General, access to MOD equipment was generously arranged and UNESCO sponsorship followed soon afterwards, although this would later prove a mixed blessing.

More crucial to the success of the venture, concessionary transport to the antipodes now became a distinct possibility. British nuclear tests in Australia were still winding down, the Woomera trials on the Black Knight missile were very much in evidence and the RAF was still apparently making regular runs down-under with transport planes. The fortunes of the expedition quickly changed when it transpired that one of the general's social acquaintances held the rank of Air Vice-Marshall. Almost overnight, the expedition had a lift laid on to Australia.

The organisers eventually realized that the logistics of having three target areas would be far too complicated; a decision had to be made, and soon. Expedition members closely examined the available options. The Chuave area, and to a lesser degree that at Porgera, had excellent accessibility from the main Highlands Highway and a network of minor arterial tracks. Moreover, a Goroka branch of the PMSS had been formed in January 1963, and throughout that year they had under the guidance of Kevin Read partially explored a number of promising caves at Chuave and the Henganofi areas of the Eastern Highlands. Most notable of these was the investigation of Kaimomo Cave, surveyed by Gordon Bain and Chris Borough in 1963, and Murifinka Stream Sink (Hell's Gates) respectively.

Apart from field trips run by the Goroka group, caving elsewhere had been a sporadic affair involving a scattered population of expatriates often carrying out lone explorations. The year before, Laurie Bragge had looked at Batari Cave in the Obura region to the south of Kainantu.

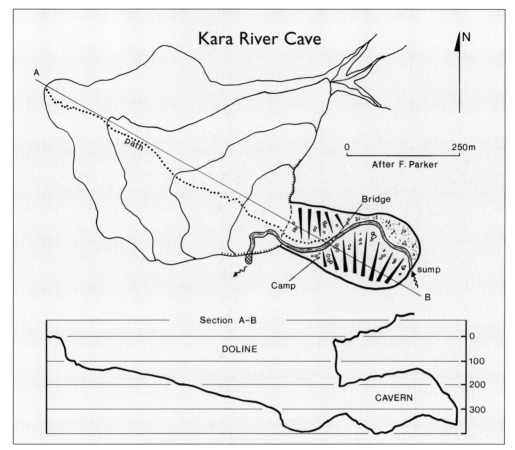

Fig. 2) Kara River Cave

May of 1963 saw Chris Borough organising a brief reconnaissance to the Baining Mountains of New Britain but no notable caves were discovered. Chris also looked at some minor caves in the Morobe District out of Lae during August and September. In the Western Highlands in early December of that same year, three other cavers from the PMSS accompanied Laurie Le Fevre to two small but flood prone caves at Baiyer River, some 30 kilometres west of Mt. Hagen township. These explorations gave a taste of things to come.

About this time another Australian, Fred Parker, was becoming active on Bougainville Island. He was a member of Sydney Speleological Society and had an inveterate interest in caves and reptiles. It was only natural for him to come to work in New Guinea where he could pursue both his passions. In September of 1963 while returning from a trek to the active volcanic craters of Mt. Balbi (2,461 m), his guide showed him an impressive doline on the Keriaka Plateau. The southeast aspect of this was dominated by a vertical cliff soaring 184 metres from the jungle-covered floor, and at its base a swift-flowing river emerged from a portal 107 metres wide and almost as high. Before sumping, this passage attained the impressive dimensions of 138 by 153 metres.

While exploring this incredible cavern, trees growing some 60 metres in from the entrance had to be felled to bridge the 20-metre wide river (see fig. 2). Moreover, the camp that was set up inside was rained upon from clouds that gathered in the roof! After emerging from the main

The Kara River Cave has an entrance to rival that of Deer Cave in Sarawak, being 107 metres wide and almost as high. Note the smoke rising from a campfire to the left of the river.

cave, the explorers followed the river across the southeast corner of the depression to where it slid into a somewhat diminished passage, sumping after only 30 metres.

The water was presumed to reappear as the Kara River close to the coast, at least three kilometres to the southwest. With the aid of a local guide, Fred also visited this site, where on a makeshift raft of wild banana "trees" he followed the sluggish river to its source. Laid out on the plantains and balancing as best he could, he used his hands to paddle beneath a lowering jungle canopy. Gliding silently upstream, creepers drooped lazily across the channel and aerial roots, lowered searchingly from epiphytic plants, brushed against his face and arms. He shuddered at their touch but dared not capsize, for didn't that log have eyes?

With some relief he drifted from the twilight of the living tunnel into the deepening night of the cave. Paddling still, he reached the end in a largish chamber 45 metres from daylight, where the deep green water welled up from beneath one wall. Although sorely tempted to leave his ramshackle craft to investigate, he resisted…local villagers had informed him that large estuarine crocodiles were frequently sighted cruising around near the entrance.

Although there was clearly some exciting caving to be had elsewhere, the areas that Gordon suggested appeared to offer the best scope for success. Access at Chuave was definitely a plus, with the Kaimomo Cave potentially a long but dangerous system. The postulated resurgence was over ten kilometres distant. On the other hand, the Star Mountains represented the last remaining blank on the map of New Guinea. Here was a vast tract of unexplored mountainous territory slap-bang in the centre of the island. Extending along the fifth parallel, it straddled the far western extremity of the border between British New Guinea and Papua, where this crossed into what was then Dutch New Guinea.

There was precious little information to be culled concerning the high-altitude limestone plateaux known to exist in this mountain wilderness. Once again through General Stockwell, access to air photographs, mostly of US military origin, gave a hint of what might be in store. Based upon photographic interpretation Gordon eventually decided to make the Stars their goal, although logistically it offered by far the greatest obstacles to exploration. Yet the thickness of limestone surely promised great depth for any caves that might ultimately be discovered.

If New Guinea was the "Last Unknown" then the Star Mountains were surely the final frontier of that land. They were of course uncharted; the only maps of the region had been reduced from aerial photographs and bore such useful annotations as "obscured by clouds," "unexplored" or "relief data incomplete." Few Europeans had even been within sight of them.

The world first became aware of these fabulous mountains just before the First World War. A Dutch military expedition had with great fortitude travelled inland through the vast swamplands of Dutch New Guinea south of the main ranges. From their most northerly position, they glimpsed a great barrier of jagged mountains ahead of them, some snow-capped, extending eastwards into Papua. They named the range the *Sterren Gebergte* (Star Mountains), calling the principal tops that they could see Capella, Scorpio, Orion and Sirius after first magnitude stars and constellations in the heavens.

The first explorer to come anywhere near them was a flamboyant Italian named Luigi D'Albertis, who in 1876 had encouraged his tiny vessel, *Neva*, 933 kilometres up the Fly River from its outfall in the Gulf of Papua. The peaks he saw were in fact not the Star Mountains, but their continuation east where they merge into the Hindenburg and what D'Albertis named the Victor Emanuel Range (see fig. 3).

He was followed in 1926 by an administration patrol led by Austen and Thompson. Reaching an upper tributary of the Alice River, known in those parts as the Ok Tedi, they encountered rough limestone country forming the southern foothills of the central range 968 kilometres from the sea. Any further progress northwards was prevented by the rugged nature of the terrain, here deeply dissected by the aggressive water of the Alice River and its tributaries. Later that same year and in 1927, Ivan Champion and Charles Karius led two patrols of exemplary conduct; after several months they discovered a route through the "devil country," the limestone barrier of the Victor Emanuel Range. This journey took them from the Fly headwaters in the vicinity of Bolivip to Telefomin on the upper Sepik. They made contact with many new tribes while completing this, the first south-to-north crossing of the central divide.

Further west the Star Mountains remained unknown territory until once again the Dutch took the initiative with a massive 75-man expedition. Pushing up the Digul River in April 1959, they navigated northwards through head-hunting country in the mosquito-ridden lowlands, and at last laid to rest the mystery of these cloud-shrouded peaks. After a journey lasting five months they eventually reached the Sobger River on the northern watershed having achieved the first crossing of the Star Mountains.

Back in the UK the British organisers turned up an article which gave an account of the Dutch expedition. In it the explorers reported seeing huge sinkholes, shafts and cave entrances in a region where the limestone reached altitudes in excess of 3,600 metres, surely confirmation of the great caving potential. As 1963 drew to a close, Frank was going all out to sell the "hard man" image of the British caver to likely sponsors, when the winds of change blew cold comfort for the proposed expedition. Only a few months earlier, the Dutch had been forcefully ousted from the western half of the island by Indonesian forces that had somehow secured the sanction of the

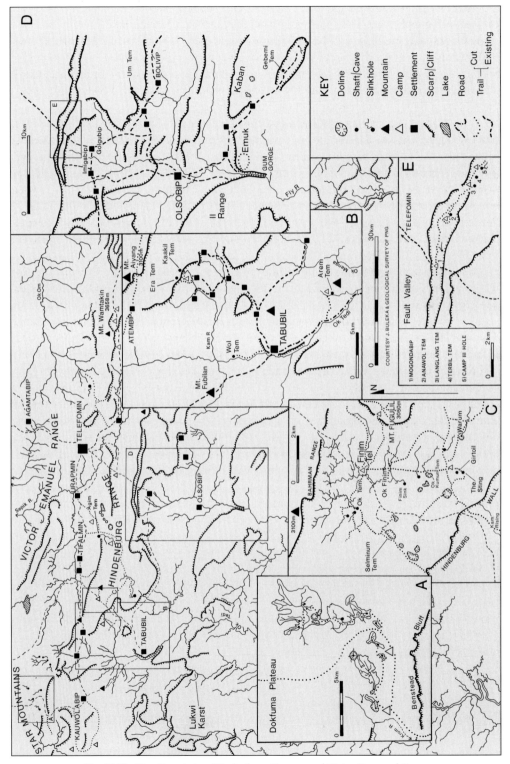

Fig. 3) The Star Mountains, Hindenburg Range, and Victor Emanuel Range

United Nations. The border region with West Irian, as the new "colonists" renamed Dutch New Guinea, suddenly became a sensitive issue with the Australian Administration.

Emotions were running high in both Canberra and Port Moresby. In the former there was understandable concern that the Indonesian Premier, Sukarno, might be setting out his stall as a Southeast Asian dictator. Meanwhile, officials in the New Guinea capital were held in disbelief that anyone would want to travel half way around the world and fight their way through some of the worst terrain known, merely to look at holes in the ground.

In the wake of a gathering political storm with suspected anti-British undertones, the expedition eventually began to disintegrate, and in early 1964 its ultimate fate seemed sealed when two of the team dropped out because of personal difficulties. This left a serious void in the scientific programme that lent the venture some semblance of respectability. The final death knell was sounded when the Australian officials denied the expedition access to territory within 80 kilometres of the border. Then in an act of unguarded suspicion, the organisers were asked to give a detailed account of the connection with the UN through their affiliation with UNESCO. Frank's disappointment was complete and unconcealed when it was finally agreed that the British venture be deferred for at least a year.

If the latter half of 1964 proved to be the undoing of expeditions to the Stars, caving elsewhere began to gather momentum. By mid-July the Goroka branch of the PMSS had coalesced into the Goroka Caving Club; the PMSS itself folded soon afterwards. Near Kundiawa, cavers started a systematic exploration of the Porol Ranges and the gorge of the Chimbu River where this bisected the escarpment. Many holes were recorded or partially explored in these areas, including Mebikombogo and a river cave named Yericongui. Perhaps the most significant exploration was in Irukunguai Cave, later named Queen's Cave (see fig. 4).

Irukunguai was first entered on Queen Elizabeth's birthday weekend and proved to be a regally decorated cavern developed on several levels. Investigation over a period of time was to extend it to at least three kilometres in length, making it the longest system in the country at that time. So richly decorated was one fossil gallery that the first explorers followed it barefoot to avoid destroying the pristine crystal floors, hence its name, the Passage of a Thousand Wounds.

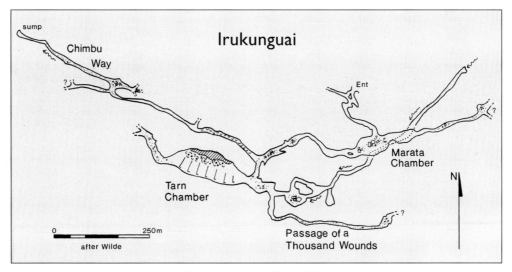

Fig. 4) Irukunguai (Irapui) Cave

Mebikombogo was a two-tier cave located near Irukunguai on the south bank of the Kwi River. Some 800 metres in extent, it was interesting from a cultural standpoint too, having been used as a refuge by the Gurema people when they attacked the first Government patrol into the area. The cave walls at the entrance still bear the scars of the fighting, where bullets apparently shattered the warriors' shields thus stopping the confrontation before lives were spent (though several warriors were in fact wounded).

Fred Parker had by that time moved from Bougainville to mainland New Guinea and started investigating caving areas of the Eastern Highlands and Chimbu. He visited Irukunguai cave in November of 1964 and also spent the remainder of that year and most of 1965 exploring the Porol Range, recording many new cave sites. While wandering about the region of the Sikuri Pass on Christmas Day, he chanced upon an obvious sinkhole. It was one that gave the impression it would go places. Many flatter only to deceive, yet this was somehow different. The find was to have a far-reaching effect on caving in New Guinea.

Meanwhile down in Sydney, the Australians were getting their act together. Strangely enough, all the difficulties with red tape experienced by the pommies seemed to dissipate into the muggy tropical air, and like the phoenix rising from the ashes: out of the failed British trip emerged the Australian Star Mountains Expedition. By July Gordon Bain had recruited two participants in Australia and a third in New Guinea. There was Tom Hayllar, a schoolteacher at Manly High School in Sydney, and David Cook, a palaeontologist working with Mt. Isa Mines. Both had eagerly accepted the invitation to participate in a caving expedition to New Guinea. The third man was Barry Craig, an anthropologist who had taken a teaching post at a mission school in Telefomin, the last government station before the border with West Irian.

When the weather is kind it is just possible to see the eastern-most peaks of the Star Mountains from Telefomin, a view which Barry had often contemplated with professional wonder. Were those distant peaks hiding a vast population as the earliest pioneers into the Eastern Highlands had found during the early 1920s? Only a few months before, a patrol led by Assistant District Officer Des Fitzer, out of Kiunga on the Fly River, had passed through Telefomin after exploring the southern foothills of the Stars. The area was sparsely populated and Fitzer believed that the region to the north was totally uninhabited.

The six-man Australian Star Mountains Expedition of 1965 became the first organised group to investigate the caving potential of New Guinea's wild interior. Back row left to right: David Cook, Paul Symons, Tom Haylar. Front row left to right: John Huon, Barry Craig, Mike Shepherd. Right: A tree-fern clad doline of the Dokfuma Plateau.

In December 1963, Craig indulged his curiosity with a chartered flight over the region to solve the mystery for himself. Fitzer was correct in his presumption, for the fly-past revealed no evidence of settlements. In his disappointment, Craig abandoned any thoughts of a patrol into those mountains – that is, until months later when news filtered through to Telefomin that an expedition was being planned. Without delay, he wrote to Hayllar and Cook in Sydney. They were quick to accept local expertise. He was on the doorstep, spoke fluent pidgin, and even offered to pay his way.

Shortly afterwards, correspondence with the authorities in New Guinea produced a daunting list of conditions that the Chief Administrator, Sir Donald Cleland, insisted expedition members comply with. Much of this focused upon the obvious need for peak physical fitness and non-violation of the border. The expedition also had to maintain daily radio contact while in the field and was asked to carry out some surveillance work for the army. Gordon Bain was considering the implications of this mandate when a transfer became imminent, dictating that he drop out.

As the new year was ushered in, so were two new members to the team. Paul Symons was a Western Australian working as a psychologist for the Department of Immigration. He had an inordinate taste for waspish poetry and excellence in tea, but also had much to his credit in the field of climbing and caving. Youngest to join the group was Michael Shepherd, an English student studying geomorphology under a scholarship at Sydney University. The first that Hayllar and Cook heard about Shepherd was a telephone message saying a man who had come second in a 50-mile walking race wished to enlist.

Finally, there was a Frenchman whose main claim to fame was being one of the founding members of the Club Martel de Nice. John Huon, or to give him his full and somewhat grandiose title of John Huon de Navrancourt, was stationed in New Britain and had 13 years medical patrol work behind him, experience that would be a great benefit to the expedition. There was an enthusiastic exchange of correspondence between Sydney and Rabaul, where he was stationed, but in the end he was to participate only during the first month.

Barry Craig now took over the responsibility for planning at the New Guinea end, whilst down south Hayllar, Symons and Shepherd began marshalling supplies and equipment there. By December matters were well in hand. Like the British, they decided that a scientific element was necessary to give credibility to the venture. Then as the call for "essential" supplies and creature comforts outgrew the group's contingency planning, the expedition began to waver beneath the weight of conflicting ideals.

There were those like Symons to whom Eric Shipton was a folk hero and therefore favoured the austere, "bare necessity" expedition. Arguing the opposite school of thought, Craig and then Cook became hell-bent on driving the venture the way of the massive journey of discovery for which the Victorians were famous. By the New Year they had reached a compromise, but not before the organisers in Sydney had finally agreed to employ 15 carriers. Only when calculations revealed the need for over seven tonnes of food over the three months did it become clear that, once in the field, they would be dependent upon at least two air drops.

THE STAR TREK

After many months of painstaking preparations, everything at last came together on Thursday, February 25, 1965, when Shepherd and Hayllar, accompanied by 14 porters, set off west from Telefomin. Huon planned to fly out and meet them at Tifalmin village two days hence; the remainder of the expedition was to follow at a later date. It was a fine day and for the first few

Andy Eavis crossing a delicate vine bridge over the upper Sepik river en route to the Feramin and Wamtakin regions.

kilometres they strolled through hamlets scattered haphazardly amid grasslands. As the afternoon melted into early evening, they arrived at a point where they could cast their eyes down onto the Sepik River flowing through an impressive limestone gorge. Beyond this ravine grassy regions merged into a blue haze where they could just make out distant forested mountains. A medley of grass huts straddling a spur on the far bank of the river was their immediate destination.

A beetling trail led steeply down to the Sepik at an abrupt narrowing where a vine suspension bridge had been audaciously slung across. Beneath this flimsy structure the turgid river groaned like a hundred angry water buffalo jostling to squeeze between walls only five metres apart. At the far side a steep climb led onto a manicured terrace high above the river where at Urapmin they endured their first night.

A flea-ridden night was relieved by yellow sunbeams winking through chinks in the hut walls. Rising to the smell of village fires and rancid pig fat they set off without delay into a warming dawn, eager to be on their way on the next stage of their journey. At the edge of the hamlet the trail plunged down a bank beneath the eaves of the darkling forest, and the group passed like shadows into a strange world of green twilight. Lianas trailed lazily from the boughs of southern beech, the hardwood kwila tree, and other tropical species, as they strolled through undergrowth that smelled a bit like gravy browning. The boles of huge buttress-rooted trees towered 50 metres above their heads, supporting the forest crown. Like itinerant jewels, multicoloured parrots flickered through the treetops.

Tifalmin was a good day's march further west. At times they wavered over stifling grassy knolls, parched by a sun borrowed from a spaghetti western, but always descended again into the welcome cool of the forest. The trail was often a nightmare underfoot, where forest giants shot out their lateral roots in response to the shallow tropical soils. High above them, a flash of red betrayed the presence of the leguminous D'Albertis creeper striving for light through the trees. The silence seemed unreal, for east of the Wallace Line there are none of the noisy primates and game animals found in neighbouring Malaysia. Apart from the raucous call of the shy bird of paradise and their own laboured breathing the only sounds were the occasional plaintive peeping of small reptiles lurking somewhere in the undergrowth, or the electronic hum of myriad insects.

Six hours out of Urapmin, they were wading up to their middles along the reedy margins of the Ilam (Dream) River. Shortly afterwards, they left the forest behind to cut a path across a number of creeks descending from the forested slopes to their left. Thirty minutes later, the trail slipped unceremoniously into Tifalmin, where John Huon awaited their arrival. Over dinner that evening, they discussed preparations for crossing the Hindenburg Range. The plan was to proceed west along the Tifalmin Valley, around the base of the 3,150 metre high Mt. Aiyang, before dropping to Atembip below the Hindenburg Wall, a journey of three days. From there, they estimated an additional two days' trek to Kauwolabip in the southern foothills of the Stars. If everything went according to plan, they hoped to receive air dropped supplies there before the advance north. They took on an old man called Kwetokim to be their guide over the mountains.

Early the following morning Shepherd and Hayllar awoke to Huon lighting the hurricane lamp and bellowing in pidgin, *"Kuk boi. Wokim tripela kap ti!"* Tea was considered the only civilised way to start the day.

From Tifalmin they climbed steadily for at least an hour. Descending at either side of them, dark fingers of forest searched the yellow "sea" of hot *kunai* grass through which they laboured. Though the Ilam River remained sequestered in its unseen gorge away to their right, a distant murmur reminded them of its presence.

The last hamlet of the upper Tifalmin Valley had receded to little more than a dot in the distance when the gradual transition into the bush provided welcome respite from the noon heat. As afternoon wore on, they trekked deeper into the cloud forest, eventually reaching a solitary bush hut where they decided to make camp for the night. Mike's altimeter read 2,153 metres. For the following week, they were to know little else but a strange world of stunted trees where every bough, living or otherwise, was bearded with dripping moss. The forest floor was littered with decaying vegetation and fallen trees, all carpeted in deep pile moss.

A cool dawn arose with wraith-like vapours and mists permeating the gnarled trees. Rain came ever more frequently as they vacated camp and continued to climb. At a height of 2,646 metres, they crossed into Papua before starting downhill again. The trail cut across the grain of the land in a frustrating manner, climbing up some ridge underpinning Mt. Aiyang, only to drop down the far side before repeating the process over other spurs. Breaks in the cloud allowed the occasional foreshortened glimpse of Benstead Bluff over five kilometres further west. After wading through a swamp with late afternoon chasing their heels, they reached Atembip, a marshy clearing with a single hut.

Another troubled night came abruptly to an end at 5:00 a.m. with the now familiar sounds of John scrabbling in the gloom as he organised brews. The atmosphere was a dank, dripping world of monotone green suffused with an acrid smell of decaying vegetation that they could almost taste. Camp was struck at 7:00 a.m. and they continued their struggle through the endless forest. In places, tall succulents spread their fleshy umbrellas over the track as if mindful of shielding the weary travellers from a downpour that left them contemplating building an ark.

The afternoon was well advanced when the rumour of turbulent water forewarned them that the Ok Tedi (upper Alice River) was somewhere below. Though it remained invisible, its approach was imminent. Here they met a man who in stature could almost be termed a pygmy. He was armed with a fine blackpalm bow and arrows, his only attire a phallic gourd. Gesturing that he was from Atemin, he indicated that they should follow. In cautious pursuit they took a trail that clung precariously to the side of a deep valley. At times, the way ahead crossed landslides or became merely a vague scar etched into crumbling cliffs that dropped perhaps 100 metres to the river.

More than once, a carelessly placed boot found some unexpected pitfall in the debris of the forest floor – a bottomless fissure, perhaps, hidden in waiting for the unwary. Once when they paused for breath, Hayllar was horrified to find their hands covered in blood, gorged upon by loathsome, writhing leeches.

At one point shrubbery growing tenaciously to the scarp had been stamped down, providing a precarious walkway; it was no place for the feint hearted. Sometimes they had to claw desperately at what moss and vegetation they could find, whilst they anxiously traversed upstream. Clods of red earth spun dizzily into the swirling waters below as their feet slipped, dangling through the branches. They swore inwardly at their fleet-footed guide who, they imagined, was silently mocking the stumbling white men.

When at last they reached the Ok Tedi, they faced 25 metres of whitewater tearing by at a terrifying pace. Boulders broke surface here and there, transforming the river into a swirl of angry confusion. They found little solace in the bundle of slender poles masquerading as a bridge, but they crossed without incident and soon reached Atemin.

The next two days continued through similar terrain: ridge upon ridge ran down through the foothills, between which rivers had carved precipitous gorges. In places, they scaled the sides of canyons on flimsy sapling ladders. They had been on the trail eight days when finally they turned southwards to climb almost 1,000 metres onto a divide separating the Kauwol and Tedi Rivers. Leaving the forest behind for a long grassy spur, they found the remains of one of Fitzer's camps and knew that Kauwolabip must be close. They unpacked the Vaughan transceiver and made radio contact.

"Star Mountains portable calling Telefomin. Star Mountains portable calling Telefomin. Do you copy?"

"Telefomin receiving SMP. Go ahead."

"We have just seen Fitzer's drop zone and the Benstead summits. Expect to arrive Kauwolabip within the hour."

Tom was relieved to hear from Telefomin that the remainder of the expedition team had departed Tifalmin that very day.

"Congratulations and good luck."

"Thanks. Star Mountains portable over and out."

They had not gone far along the trail before they were overwhelmed by a group of young boys who excitedly accompanied them to the hamlet. The first stage of the expedition was successfully completed without mishap.

On March 7, the whole team was once again together. For nearly three weeks Kauwolabip was home while they awaited the arrival of supplies. The location was magnificent. Northwards the great bluffs of Benstead and Benkwim rose another 1,500 metres, the marshalling grounds of fierce tropical storms. A dip in the forest marked where the two cliffs failed to meet and allowed the Beroro Pass between the limestone walls. It was through this break in the natural armour that they hoped to pick up Fitzer's old trail (see fig. 3).

Food was running dangerously low when on March 13, almost 30 packages finally rained from the sky. It was a moment for celebration: while some cans of food were badly damaged upon impact, three bottles of rum, inadvertently slipped into the same pack, landed miraculously unscathed! That same day, Huon set off north to locate Fitzer's old Beroro Pass base camp, clear the overgrown trail, and reconnoitre the ground beyond. The remainder took a round trip via Benkwim Bluff. They travelled through confusing terrain for four days, and although they were treated to fine views of the snow-capped Juliana across the border, they found no caves.

Two weeks later they had found the way through Beroro Pass and established the advance base camp on the Dokfuma Plateau, at an altitude of just over 3,000 metres. An unexpected bonus came when they discovered that Krom Creek was dry, providing an easier route onto the plateau. This had saved days, possibly weeks, of track cutting. They were at last in cave country, but still awaited the second air drop containing their equipment. This arrived a few days later.

They spent over a week prospecting the caving potential of the surrounding plateau region but found no significant underground development. A number of large grassy basins, or poljes, were pockmarked by large dolines. Into the latter some sizeable streams disappeared, but none could be followed into worthwhile cave passage. Disappointment was further exacerbated as supplies ran low yet again and they were forced to supplement their meagre diet with wild dog.

Mike and Tom investigated some small shafts and cave entrances down the Krom, but these either choked or pinched in. One of the most promising was found in a group of sinkholes where darkness beckoned from behind some stalactites in an alcove. Optimistically squeezing through these, Hayllar struggled to gain the caving ladder, his clothing rucking up around his armpits in the tight section. Stepping off the last rung, he lit his acetylene lamp and to his horror found several nasty looking spiders glaring at him from the walls. He stumbled as he lunged for one of these with a specimen jar, and fell into a narrowing of the rift. Feeling sure he had brushed the creatures down on himself, he glanced about with a hunted expression. The spiders had gone. The shaft merely closed in, and with no desire to linger he returned up the ladder as quickly as the dimensions would allow.

Although their scientific programme progressed well, caving was a continual disappointment. All the holes were immature or choked with glacial debris. With time advancing, plans were made for the first ascent to the summits of Capella and Sirius. Elsewhere, David and Barry ran a patrol further west to the Ban River and Lake Vivien, close to the border with West Irian, but once again the caves proved elusive. Following a third air drop, they spent the last month climbing the high limestone peaks before returning to Telefomin. They investigated a few enlarged grykes and shafts in the lapiaz karst high on Capella, but once again the area appeared speleologically barren.

From a caving standpoint, the poor results produced by the Star Mountains resulted in wide spread scepticism towards further expeditions to New Guinea. Elsewhere, the inspiration generated by the breaking of the 1,000-metre depth barrier in the Berger continued to spread throughout the caving world like ripples on a millpond. While the French seemed content in the knowledge that the world's deepest cave was safely tucked away in their own "backyard," other cavers, especially those from Britain and the USA, were gripped by an almost feverish quest to break the world depth record.

It is said that wherever caves are to be found the British will eventually turn up. Over the next few years, teams of cavers, many of them weaned on the restricted and often dangerous wet systems of Yorkshire, began probing ever eastwards for their thrills. In the Pindus Mountains of Greece the 400-metre deep Provatina Abyss fell to a British team over a three-year period from 1965. Elsewhere on the Astraka Plateau, the Epos Chasm found by Pete Livesey was descended to 136 metres. A return the following year reached the bottom of the great shaft at 447 metres.

Between 1964 and 1965, two expeditions from the South Wales Caving Club explored the Balinka Pit near the town of Karlovac, in northwestern Yugoslavia. Using a ludicrously cumbersome winch, they descended a 180 metre deep entrance shaft to follow a descending passage to an ultimate depth of 300 metres. British expeditions were also run to the Italian Antro della Corchia and Monte Cucco Abyss in 1967 and 1969 respectively.

The French reacted by finding the Tête Sauvage, a new upper entrance to the Gouffre de la Pierre St. Martin, giving the system a new overall depth of 1,165 metres and relegating the Gouffre Berger to second place. The Reseau Trombe (930 m) and the Splugga della Preta (879 m) followed a close third and fourth in the world depth stakes.

Expedition mania was also gripping the opposite side of the Atlantic. In the Xilitla region of eastern Mexico a number of promising cave systems were explored by ex-patriot British cavers and teams from MacMaster University.

The first of many American successes took place in 1965-1966, when cavers from Texas found and partially explored Sótano de San Agustín. Joined by Canadians in 1967, they descended the Sótano del Rio Iglesia to a new North American depth record of 535 metres. Later that same year and again with Canadian cavers, they pushed the Sótano de San Agustín to a sump and a new depth record at 612 metres after five days below ground. Again in 1967, Texans bottomed the huge shaft of Sótano de las Golondrinas (333 m low/376 m high), and five years later found and mapped the grand daddy of the great shafts, El Sótano de El Barro (410 m).[2]

About the time that Mexico fever was raging through the caving world, Van Watson met Julia James while caving in New Zealand's Mt. Arthur region. Julia had immigrated to Australia from England in 1965. Van and a few other prominent vertical cavers had at the time been considering the possibilities of running an expedition to New Guinea. Julia was already one step ahead of them. As soon as she arrived in Australia she had looked up the participants of the 1965 Star Mountains venture. Though they had little encouragement to offer she was nonetheless keen to field an expedition as soon as possible.

Formerly a member of Wessex Caving Club, "Jooles," as she was affectionately known to friends, had enjoyed an apprenticeship in the caves of Llangattoc in South Wales where she discovered her first new cave passage. Once smitten by the exploration bug, she rapidly established herself as something of a redoubtable speleologist who had become almost obsessive in her desire to explore deep caves. The relationship between Julia and Van was cemented: they would gather as much concrete evidence as possible in readiness for an expedition to New Guinea. In 1971 Van was fortunate in securing work for himself right on the "doorstep" as it were.

Meanwhile in the New Guinea Highlands, a small but dedicated group of expatriate cavers continued with explorations in the more accessible areas. Among his other explorations, Fred Parker returned in 1965 to the unexplored sinkhole he had found in the Porols near the Sikuri Pass. This large doline, populated by a colony of flying foxes, swallowed a strong creek that appeared to fall at least 50 metres. Following the streambed inside the cave, Fred reached a depth of 24 metres, beyond which the water leapt out into an enticing void. Frustrated by a lack of rope and manpower, he had to leave the echoing depths for "another day." It would be another seven years before anyone re-entered that significant cave.

Three years later, Australian Harold Gallasch began examining the caving potential on New Ireland, sowing the seeds for future expeditions there. Very soon afterwards, Chris Borough became interested in neighbouring New Britain, where the limestone regions were completely

---

[2] "A History of Mexican Speleology to 1992," AMCS Activities Newsletter, Number 22, May 1997, pp. 25-48.

unknown and access difficult. He had found some wartime maps that covered a limestone plateau in the Nakanai Mountains to the north of Pomio. Marked on these were two enormous
dolines. Notations on the sheets gave the largest as being one and a half kilometres across and
460 metres deep.

After Chris secured aerial photographs of the area the location of the holes was pinpointed
with greater reliability. Terrain was extremely rugged, consisting of endless dolines (technically
termed polygonal karst) separated by narrow ridges. This combined with the dense rain forest to
make overland travel in the area nearly impossible. To make matters worse, New Britain has
some of the highest recorded rainfall in Melanesia. People who had been there spoke of trackless, nightmarish country overrun with snakes and voracious insect life.

A helicopter flight over the area was arranged early in 1968 and after some anxious sweeping
across the treetops, Chris Borough eventually pinpointed the smaller of the two dolines. It was
just as described, with sheer or overhanging walls, in places clear of the jungle mantle. A large
whitewater river could be seen flowing out of and into unknown caverns below. Navigating with
the photographs it was determined that some way to the west a branch of the Pandi River
suddenly appeared from nowhere close to Tuke village. Another visit was planned for May.

On that occasion, Kevin Read and Chris Borough flew from Open Bay (again by helicopter)
and touched down at Tuke to spend a couple of days exploring. Since it was nearby, they opted

Aerial view of Minye's colossal doline, first visited in 1968 by Australian cavers
Mike Read and Chris Borough.

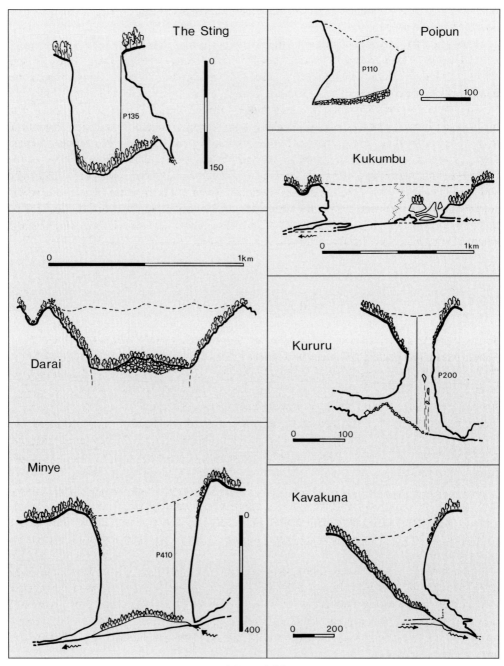

Fig. 5) Typical dolines

to examine the resurgence. Here the powerful Kanue River glided silently from a generous canyon passage overhung with vines (see fig. 24). The current was fierce however, and all attempts to follow the cave merely resulted in the explorers being washed downstream. After this undignified "retreat" they enquired after the huge doline situated on the plateau. The villagers called it Minye, but when plied to act as guides they blanched, refusing to have anything at all to do with the hole itself.

"*Ples nogut tru,*" they tendered in pidgin.

"*Bikpela puk-puk i stap insait,*" meant they feared the huge, ravenous crocodiles that village elders believed to lurk in the depths. Undeterred by local superstition, the cavers decided to see the hole for themselves.

After labouring for hours through terrain that contrived to break their sense of purpose, they finally reached the great pit (see fig. 5). Reeking in perspiration and close to collapse, they gazed in disbelief at the sheer size of the shaft. The ground they stood upon and the trees all about them seemed to reverberate to the noise rising from below, no doubt the "growling" of the hungry crocodiles sensing the approach of a meal. They scrambled down, swinging monkey-like and grasping at the near vertical vegetation as far as nerves and their only available rope would permit. When they reached a point 60 metres down where the sides fell sheer, they concluded that it was yet a further 300 metres to the floor. Ten years would pass before anyone learnt whether crocodiles really inhabited that mysterious cavern.

SOUTH OF MENDI

In 1969 Neil Ryan took up a posting as a patrol officer in the Southern Highlands Province and soon began prospecting for caves and shafts in the Kagua, Erave and Lake Kutubu areas. Working mostly alone over the next couple of years, he partially explored several amazing sites. In the Southern Highlands the limestone forms one of the most extensive areas of cavernous strata in New Guinea. Forming part of a wide band known geologically as the Darai Limestone, it stretches southeast from the Star Mountains, passes south of Mendi station and crosses the Great Papuan Plateau into the Gulf District near Kikori. Without doubt Neil's most exciting find was located two and a half kilometres northeast of Pulupare village between the Kagua and Pangia sub-districts.

Neil heard about Tobio, a large cave located deep in a gorge where the Iaro River surfaced from an underground course of almost two kilometres. From Pulupare Neil followed an old trading route that initially took him past scattered gardens and regrowth areas. Through the choking heat of kunai and wild cane grass he went, drawn onwards and downwards by a steepening trail.

After some time, the dimming forest closed in about him, strangling all sounds save the drone of insects and the splashy padding of his boots in the jungle ooze. He continued downhill. Occasionally, a raucous screech accompanied clouds of gregarious parakeets as they rocketed unseen through the forest canopy. Another sound caught his attention: a barely audible murmur rising from the forest depths was increasing to the unmistakable grumble of a large river. The trail grew rockier underfoot.

Near the bottom of the gorge the track fell away vertical, the only way forward being down sapling ladders secured with bush vines. Neil could sense a large void through the stifling trees, and after a final descent he dropped to a broad limestone shelf beside the river. He stood riveted by the sight of a colossal cave mouth that yawned in a somehow menacing way. It was fully 40 metres high and 25 metres wide; from within its unexplored recesses galloped the Iaro River like a stampede of white horses. In its impetuous, headlong rush towards the distant ocean, it roared off down a narrow, white-walled canyon, overhung here with prying vines and there

*In the high altitude bamboo forests of the Hindenburg Range, dense vegetation combined with tottering
tower karst and deep grikes made finding caves a treacherous operation.*
Right: A grotto in Irukunguai, until 1975 the longest cave in Papua New Guinea at just over 2 km.

with gangling lianas, shot through with a pallid green light filtering down through the overhanging jungle.

Some 45 kilometres upstream from the cave mouth, the Iaro is a respectable river even in
normal flow, 60 metres wide and an estimated two metres deep. At the downstream portal of the
gorge below the cave, it is literally squirted from between confining cliffs only three metres apart.
Thoughts of exploring the river cave must be tempered by these facts. Just beyond the entrance
zone, Neil could see huge tree trunks jammed in a submerged crevice. They waved about in the
current like ears of corn in an indolent breeze: to fall in the river was unthinkable, to explore the
passage, impossible.

During 1969 Chris Borough, Charles Legrady and David Nun made a determined attempt to
revive the caving activities of the PMSS. A number of field trips took place, including two to the
Highlands; however, it was a brief renaissance and the club never survived the year. Despite this,
the next biennial saw caving gathering momentum. In 1971, the Mendi region of the Southern
Highlands witnessed a flurry of caving activity among a highly motivated group led principally
by Kevan Wilde and John Van Amstel.

Panorama across the heavily dissected mountains of Enga Province.

Chas Yonge crosses a vine bridge over the upper Sepik River.

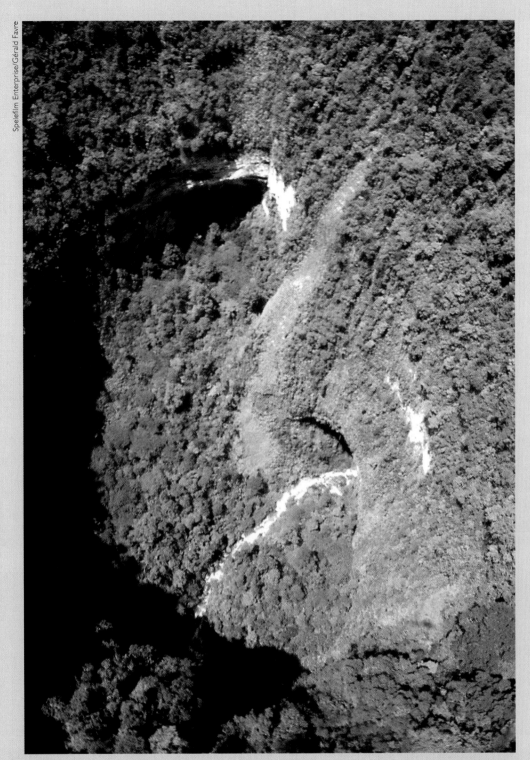

Aerial reconnaissances in New Guinea have always revealed breathtaking landscapes, as with the cone karst of the Southern Highlands (left) and the Minye's megadoline.

The Mount Hagen – Porgera Road, or Highlands Highway.

Typical stockaded village in the Mt. Elembari region of Chuave, Chimbu Province.

Typical dwelling of the Min-speaking people of the headwaters of the Fly and Sepik rivers.

The lower Iaro River gorge downstream from its efflux from the huge Tobio River Cave.

The Goura or crowned pidgeon is one of the most spectacular of birds endemic to Papua New Guinea.

Huli "wigman" in Southern Highlands. This mode of dress is commonplace among unmarried males in this region.

Primitive rock art found on a cliff at Nambayufa, Chimbu Province.

Decorated dancer from Poppendetta draped in "tapa'cloth" (beaten tree bark) cape.

40

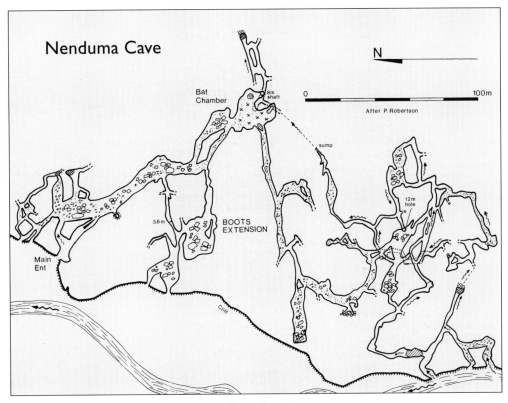

Fig. 6) Nenduma Cave

Later that year, two groups from the "Land of the Rising Sun" visited the New Guinea Highlands. The first expedition took place between June and September when a five-man team, fielded by the Komori-kai (Bat Club) and led by Kenro Hironaka, visited a number of caves in the Mendi region. They also looked at the Irukunguai Cave in the Chimbu, though this was more by way of a sightseeing trip. The second team came from the Explorers Group of Nanzan University in the town of Nagoya. This expedition was primarily archaeological in its aims; it visited and excavated four cave sites, two in the Chimbu, another in the Baiyer River valley north of Mt. Hagen, and a fourth southwest of Wapenemanda in the Enga District.

Pure exploration now continued apace through 1970 and 1971. Peter Robinson visited Nenduma Cave on Bougainville, which had been briefly examined by a Conzinc Riotinto field survey crew three years previous (see fig. 6). Throughout 1971 several trips to this multi-entrance cave system increased the surveyed length to 1,500 metres. Michael Bourke had arrived from Australia the year before to take up a posting in Rabaul. He soon took an interest in the caves on New Britain's Gazelle Peninsula, exploring a few holes in the Baining Mountains with Allan Keller and later teaming up with Hal Gallasch to look at the caving prospects of New Ireland.

The year 1972 was to prove quite fortuitous for New Guinea caving. Passing through the Chimbu, Van Watson chanced upon Kevan Wilde, who was working as a policeman in Kerowagi. Van was then a geological field assistant with Carpentaria Exploration at their Ramu base. Their interests were complementary, so they agreed to join forces in exploring caves in the nearby ranges. They were also instrumental in founding the Papua New Guinea Cave Exploration Group.

*Roy Blackham in a decorated chamber at -250 metres during the second descent of
494 metre-deep Bibima Cave.*

Soon afterwards, *Niugini Caver* was being published on a regular basis with Mike Bourke as its editor. These events and the revelations to follow were to act as a unifying force, drawing together the scattered kindred spirits of speleology.

Meanwhile, Mike Bourke was considering expeditions of his own, and the remote limestone regions in the Nakanai Mountains of New Britain especially intrigued him. He planned a solo reconnaissance to the Ora Doline about 30 kilometres north from the patrol post at Pomio. Ora was the larger of the two huge pits marked on the military map and was located northwest of Ora village at an altitude of 1,230 metres. To the southeast, the postulated resurgence manifested in a powerful jet of water emerging from a cave high up a 370-metre cliff flanking the Isis River.

In April, Mike spent eight days getting into the area, looking at the hole and returning to the coast. Stopped by cliffs, he failed to reach the bottom of the doline but by teetering on the brink of the chasm he could sneak a view of the river rumbling into a cave passage estimated to be 15 metres high. He also noted a possible route down at the northern end of the doline but lack of time dictated his return. Mike believed what he saw justified an expedition. Circulars were sent out via the publications of several Australian caving organisations.

On the New Guinea mainland, many interesting cave systems were being investigated during this period, mostly in the Chimbu and Eastern Highlands. Prime movers were the Wilde-Watson partnership. In many instances, caves were only partially explored because of either lack of equipment, lack of manpower, or the acute dangers from sudden flooding. In May 1972, Julia James travelled to the Highlands from Sydney to join Kevan and Van for three weeks of caving and to lay the groundwork for the expedition they had proposed for the following year. They visited Irukun-guai and carried out a more systematic investigation, mapping three kilometres of galleries.

Thoughts then turned to the sinkhole first entered by Fred Parker on the Porol escarpment. Bibima Cave was located at 2,100 metres in the vicinity of an east-west fault, about 20 kilometres northeast of Kundiawa township. Access was relatively easy from the Highlands Highway via the Mai loop road. Local geology promised some depth, though just where the water from the cave emerged was anyone's guess.

Kevan, Van and Julia once again teamed up for a first tentative exploration. By way of a six-metre electron ladder they reached the vertical drop that had repelled the original explorer. This proved to be a roomy 39-metre pitch in sound rock and could be rigged with the water crashing harmlessly to one side. At the bottom, a high rift passage led off at once with the stream burbling downhill through pools. At a depth of 180 metres the cave continued to descend at an angle of 30 degrees. Though it narrowed here and the roof had dropped to three metres, the passage gave them the impression of going on forever. At this point lack of time and rope forced their return to the surface.

Kevan was keen to accept the challenge of Bibima, so over the first weekend of August he and Van returned to the fray. Tony Maddern, a local government officer from Kerowagi and Bill Sanders, Assistant District Officer for the Chimbu, accompanied them this time. Reveille at the crack of dawn guaranteed them an "alpine" start on Saturday.

After struggling up to the Sikuri Pass beneath bulging packs, they gathered at the entrance to find a frantic traffic of fruit bats still returning to roost in the depths. The sight of their leathery wings flapping in the first glimmer of dawn gave a primordial feel to the scene before them. They mustered 280 metres of rope for the descent, a few lengths of electron wire ladder, lead acid batteries, acetylene lamps and a 40-hour supply of calcium carbide. After spending some time roping down and protecting the entrance pitch where it overhung, they were ready to continue the descent.

Quickly reaching the previous limit of exploration, they rigged a drop of nine metres with a length of Terylene and a short, level stretch took them to a chamber displaying some eccentric stalagmites with a unique blue hue. A brief photography interlude provided them a breather and the chance to take stock of the continuation. The explorers soon passed the next drop using a six-metre ladder, and were then forced into a crawl that became intimate with the stream. Following a rest, they continued to descend the relentless gradient.

A scramble on loose scree preceded a nine-metre drop followed by a tension traverse, the Swingletree. Faith and friction moves along the next section took them through a 15-metre high rift, and the world fell away abruptly at their feet. The cavers had stumbled upon a colossal chamber. The void around them heightened the feeling of isolation for they knew then that they were approaching a depth of 300 metres. Excitement mounted since the current Southern Hemisphere depth record stood at 357 metres, a distinction held by Harwoods Hole in New Zealand.

The beams from their lamps stabbed pathetically at the cave "night" but could not penetrate the vastness of Lucifer's Quarry. As if descending a mountainside on a moonless night, they cautiously picked their tortuous route downwards, their astonished comments echoed by unseen walls. The floor of the chamber dropped perhaps 100 metres to a blank wall. At first there appeared to be no exit, and after some ferreting about, they eventually located the way onwards, down a hole in the boulder choke forming the floor.

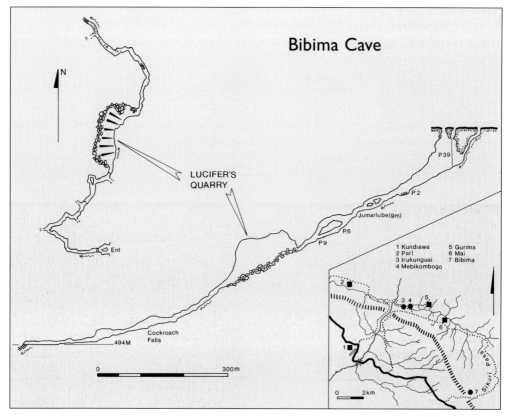

Fig. 7) Bibima Cave

The passage now descended more steeply and they noticed several inlet passages en route, but all were ignored in the cavers' pursuit for greater depth (see fig. 7). A short wet pitch – the Passion Cooler – led to another cascade within 50 metres, Cockroach Falls. Beyond this the gradient eased and a lowering passage loomed ahead, less inviting, ominous even. A gathering fog veiled the gloomy passage as they pushed on for a further 250 metres, negotiating a squeeze. This was merely the prelude to an ignominious end: a sump, where the muddy roof dived into the water. The pool was restricted, dark, gloopy, and quite definitely terminal.

They had been underground for eight hours when they finally turned to face the irksome return journey. Weariness was about them, but it was that languid feeling that accompanies the deep down satisfaction of a hard won success. After a short food break, they set off surveying out, each of them in his own mind attempting to calculate just how deep they had gone.

The ascent went smoothly until they arrived at the second nine-metre pitch above the Swingle-tree. Here a liberal covering of mud to the rope caused some anxiety when Kevan's jumars slipped alarmingly, dropping him half a metre at a time. With some difficulty he finally reached the top and draped a ladder down. They resumed their return to the entrance without further mishap.

With fatigue overtaking them, all their energy was marshalled for the ascent of the 37-metre entrance shaft. It was 3:00 a.m. About an hour later, the four cavers were finally on the surface, close to total exhaustion. With senses finely honed by almost 20 hours below ground, they rediscovered the full nuance of jungle aromas and sounds. How sweet the mountain air seemed in those chill hours before the Highland dawn. They were thankful to be back once more in the known world, and satisfied in the anticipation of broken records. When the survey data was computed they found that the bottom of Bibima was 494 metres, making it the deepest known cave system in New Guinea and snatching the record from New Zealand.

The descent of Bibima proved a milestone in New Guinea caving history, for it vindicated what some cavers around the world had long believed: the prospects for discovering deep caves was excellent. It reaffirmed the commitment of Van, Julia and Kevan who were now keener than ever to come to grips with the New Guinea underground, now irrefutably placed on the caving map of the world and soon to be visited by a plenitude of hopeful international expeditions.

Kevan Wilde descending a jungle-fringed entrance shaft.

The Ora Resurgence.

Chapter Two

JOURNEYS INTO HOPE

In the wake of Bibima, the eyes of the caving world were focused on New Guinea with renewed wonder. Were those explorations the precursor of greater triumphs to come? Some believed that tropical karsts were geologically immature, uplifted too recently for large caves to have developed, but this view would soon be shattered. Kevan Wilde and Van Watson were still highly involved in preparations for a New Guinea expedition, tentatively aimed at the Southern Highlands. Towards the close of 1972, they had settled upon the Lavani Valley, the fabled "Shangri-la," first entered on May 3, 1954 by an oil prospecting patrol amid a flurry of media attention.

An expedition prospectus seeking recruits with vertical caving expertise was being circulated throughout Australasia and beyond. Meanwhile, under the auspices of the University of Queensland Speleological Society, an expedition to New Britain was moving into its final stages with Mike Bourke its leader. In early December Mike, Hal Gallasch, and Derek Clark chartered a Cessna 172 and flew over the Nakanai Mountains for a final look before the arrival of the main team. During the flight the pilot thrilled his passengers by flying over the impressive Minye Doline. The sight was to haunt Mike's dreams for the next five years.

Like a blowfly on the windowpane of the world, the tiny plane droned on as the plateau unfurled beneath their wingtips. It was dramatic on a scale unimagined in Australian caving circles. The seemingly endless forest was pitted by countless dolines, a surreal landscape, like a huge table of badly laid green baize. Here and there the forest green merged with pockets of blackness that betrayed unexplored depths.

Though drainage was predominantly subterranean, the plateau was sometimes dissected where rivers, fuelled by rainfall had carved precipitous pathways to the coast. Huge limestone cliffs, possibly as much as 900 metres high, bounded the plateau to the north and east. It was breathtaking. They returned to Rabaul, suitably impressed and eager to tackle anything the Nakanai could throw at them.

On the 17th, John Webb arrived in Pomio with almost 500 kilos of gear. The team, comprising Alex "Lex" Brown, Mike Bourke, Lesley Lemon, Pauline McMahon and Harold Gallasch, arrived at Palmalmal Plantation two days later by Aztec charter. Using motor launches and tractors, they travelled on with the rest of the equipment to Pomio. By Wednesday the 20th, they had reached base camp at a mission station close to the outfall of the Isis River. Here they experienced some difficulty recruiting sufficient porters; however, two days later they had succeeded in backpacking most of their supplies along the trail north to Nutuve village. Conditions overland were appalling, and only Mike and Hal had ever experienced anything quite like it.

An early departure the next day saw them on the long and wearisome march northwards. The never-ending trail of mud and wayward tree roots was a shock to the uninitiated; it was nine hours before they dragged their sodden feet into Ora village at the eastern edge of the karst

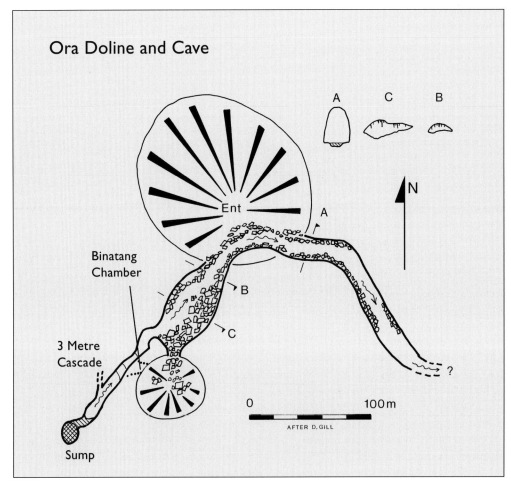

Ora Doline and Cave

Binatang
Chamber

3 Metre
Cascade

Sump

Ent

A

B

C

A C B

N

0   100 m

AFTER D. GILL

Fig. 8) Ora Doline and Cave

plateau. The voracious mosquitoes, the ubiquitous mud and the near-hundred percent humidity had taken its toll.

The Sabbath was spent examining the suspected resurgence for Ora Cave, a one and a half kilometre trek northwest from the village of Ora (see page 46). The volume of water emerging from the cave was a sobering sight and gave them their first inkling into the difficulties of exploring the rivers of New Britain, both above and below ground. Back in the village, the cicadas heralded dusk, their many voices uniting as one in an ear-piercing crescendo. The fanfare seemed somehow appropriate since the festive season was upon them. Lex and John spent Christmas Day walking to the Ora Doline with Mike. From the village, the chosen route took them steadily uphill to a cirque where a line of frowning cliffs guarded the approach to the doline country beyond.

The ascent proved easier than it had initially appeared and soon they were on the main limestone plateau travelling through increasingly difficult terrain. Progress was impeded on all fronts by the constant need to climb in and out of dolines. They slithered and tripped along the switchback trail. A hand extended in a desperate bid to arrest a stumble frequently found a stinging or spiny handhold. Adding insult to injury, every one of the dolines examined was choked with no visible cave entrances. At last they glimpsed the object of their aspirations, the Ora Doline, and any thought of resting or licking wounds was instantly forgotten.

They headed immediately around to the north side of the abyss to where on his reconnaissance Mike had thought there was a way down. Contrary to the predictions of the villagers, the descent followed without incident. Once at the bottom they stared open-mouthed at the wild river dashing from an arched entrance over twenty metres high. Like a whirling dervish, the river swept beneath an undercut section of the northeast wall, remained within daylight momentarily, then disappeared into the unknown down a slightly smaller exit.

The team decided to establish a camp within the doline itself. They found that the bottom supported a vegetation every bit as lush as that on the plateau above and included a rare species of wild banana. They felled trees and cut a terrace into a thirty-degree slope, upon which they built a hut from bush materials and plastic sheeting. As this was taking shape, the ground suddenly became mobile and trees shook violently as the shockwaves of an earth tremor passed through. Fearing the wrath of the *masalai*, the carriers bolted in all directions.

The next day Lex was confined to camp after being stricken by a mysterious bug. Perhaps there was some truth in the superstition that an evil spirit inhabited the hole? Later that morning John and Mike discovered a place where, half-swimming and half-wading, they could carefully ford the river. Exploring the southern half of the double doline, they entered and followed a well decorated upstream passageway at Binatang Chamber, where clouds of irritating insects flew into their eyes, mouths and noses.

The river was confined to a deep trench flowing on their left, but within a few metres it fanned out across the full width of the cave. The current slackened and a gloomy lake extended into the distance. At the limit of vision, about thirty metres ahead, the passage seemed to turn a corner. Did the cave sump? They could not be sure.

Returning now to the entrance, they focused their attention on the downstream section. With the obvious cave at the resurgence, thoughts dwelled upon the possibility of exploring open passage right through to emerge again at this point. Progress was frustrated once again however when a river crossing became unavoidable. With high hopes the cavers made plans. They rigged a rope across the river to aid entry into the downstream passage, while elsewhere on the plateau Hal, Leslie and Pauline walked to a multiple resurgence two kilometres down the Isis River from Ora village. Here several streams cascaded impressively from outlets fifty metres up a cliff, but only one dry cave nearby could be reached. This revealed a paltry 70 metres of uninspiring passage.

In Ora, Lex and Mike returned to the upstream lake and floated off into the unknown on air mattresses. They had gained little more than 60 metres when hopes of a vast continuation were dashed yet again. The roof suddenly angled downwards to meet the water in the inevitable sump. Not being equipped for cave diving they were forced to retreat. Allowing the current to carry them swiftly back to Binatang Chamber, they returned to camp. By noon the rest of the team had arrived from the village with the last of the equipment. They examined various schemes for river crossing and tested these in daylight before risking life and limb down the riverway.

Everyone went underground the next day. It was preferable to remaining in the camp, which had by then become a quagmire. John intended to take depth soundings in the lake while Hal busied himself with photography. Lex and Mike carried out stream flow measurements as the others prospected down the river, rushing off along a passage roughly triangular in cross-section. Enthusiastic as the explorers were they could only follow the passage a short way due to the volume of water.

Dawning like any other day on the plateau, Thursday was damp with the humidity and overnight rain. The team "enjoyed" a breakfast of eggs and cereal along with the obligatory ration of forest mud and ants. Les remained in camp, for two days earlier she had taken a fall and damaged her leg, which had swollen alarmingly. She had spent a troubled night in considerable pain and Mike was a little concerned.

Once underground, Lex and John led the downstream offensive, each in turn taking the initiative when it became necessary to ford the river. Progress was slow and hazardous, and the roaring of the river underlined their private anxieties. John made the first crossing to the far bank by simply leaping from rock to rock. Though he was lifelined, the manoeuvre was extremely hazardous so they sought a safer alternative. For the second crossing, Lex allowed himself to be swept across the current on a rope belayed fifteen metres upstream. He was attached to a second rope so that, in the event that he got into difficulty, he then could be hauled back. It was impossible to communicate except by using whistle signals.

Donning a life jacket, Lex stood on a prominent boulder and clipped into the fixed line. He made a quick check of his gear, blew twice on his whistle, then taking a deep breath launched himself into the flood, almost disappearing from view as huge waves swept over him. Fighting for air he eventually reached the far side, more by luck than judgement, shaken but not stirred. A tyrolean line was fixed so all could cross simply by clipping into the rope with a snaplink and hauling themselves over. Even so, there was no room for complacency. John was badly knocked about when twice he was flipped bodily around the rope by the sheer weight of water! The impressive tunnel beckoned.

The river seemed to gain momentum, its roar weighing heavily on the minds of the explorers. All too soon, they were brought to a halt when in a single impetuous leap, the river dropped two metres, beyond which the passage continued 18 metres high and wide. With gallant resolve, John and Pauline sought a way around the impasse by traversing along the near wall. With the exploration of such large cave rivers merely in its infancy and lacking suitable equipment, they had little hope of succeeding. Reluctantly, the attempt was abandoned.

By New Year's Day Lesley's leg had worsened. A spine was suspected of penetrating the flesh, causing internal infection. To the Kol people it was the work of the spirit Tuke; for Mike it was decision time. She could barely walk and if he delayed, he feared that her aggravated condition would dictate the use of a helicopter. The Civil Defence had loaned the expedition a transmitter but this was back at Ora village.

The cave had been surveyed and partly detackled. Although other entrances might have offered a bypass to the downstream waterfall, there was now little prospect of following the cave any further with their meagre resources and in the time that remained. It was decided that the following morning, Lex and Hal would accompany Les back to the village and radio Rabaul for medical advice. Because their feet were constantly wet, most of the team was by then suffering from mycosis, a sort of fungal infection that rots the skin, leaving raw exposed flesh. They were not looking forward to the walk out. A message was sent ahead asking for carriers.

The next day Les was strapped into a makeshift litter fashioned from bush materials, sacking and climbing tape and so began the evacuation. In Ora village Lex took to the radio.

"VJ8 Delta Tango calling Rabaul. VJ8 Delta Tango calling Rabaul. Do you read? Over."

They learnt that a chopper would cost them 1,200 Australian dollars. The next morning was a time of indecision. The helicopter airlift was ordered, then cancelled again. Though her leg was still badly swollen Les was feeling much better but still unable to bear her full weight. A few loose ends were cleared up underground and, after some deliberation, they decided to carry the patient to the coast starting early the next morning. For ten long hours that day Les' only view until they reached Nutuve village was the slow procession of the tree canopy overhead, as she was jogged and bumped along the jungle trail. The next day a haul of almost nine hours brought them at last to the mission station at the coast. The following day an Aztec lifted Les out of Palmalmal plantation airstrip.

So ended the first true caving expedition to New Guinea. Though it was a limited undertaking with modest results, it highlighted the need for good communications and medical backup in such remote locations. It was also the first exploration of an underground river in New Guinea. The experiences of the Ora Expedition were to prove of considerable benefit to Julia James and others planning the forthcoming Southern Highlands expedition.

A MULLER RECCE

In 1972 Kevan Wilde attended a lecture in New Zealand, where at the general meeting of the NZ Speleological Society he heard Prof. Paul Williams' talks on his brief visit to the dramatic limestones of the Lavani Valley. Two years later, Van Watson addressed the Ninth Biennial Caving Convention in Australia, where to a captivated audience he extolled the caving virtues of New Guinea. Since vertical cavers from throughout Australasia attended the function, it proved an ideal "shop window" for recruiting an expedition team. Cavers were at last warming to the idea of tackling the jungle caves and matters started to gain momentum.

Upon his return to New Guinea, Van immediately contacted British Petroleum, which was carrying out exploration of the Lavani region. Its geologists were openly pessimistic about the area and to prove a point, took Van for a helicopter ride over the Lavani and a neighbouring plateau in the Muller Range. Like a child in a toyshop Van gazed wide-eyed at a landscape of endless dolines and huge sinkholes. After the flight he sent a glowing report and some inspired photography back to Julia in Sydney.

Despite the obvious appeal of the Mullers, Julia had her reservations, until Van's aerial reconnaissance could be supplemented by a ground patrol. Kevan and Van were quick to offer their Easter break for this purpose, and Julia suggested they target the promising holes Van had seen. On Friday, April 13 – not the most auspicious of dates – a team consisting of Kevan, Van, and the geologist Keith Holmes flew into Koroba. They took with them sufficient rope to descend 150 metres into any cave they might discover. After travelling on to Kelabo, they set off the next morning, travelling over the northern slopes of the Muller Range and crossed the 3,000-metre Anu Pass.

The trail to Nomad patrol post led them through rough bush country with the occasional clearing. After three days they found themselves on the brink of a scarp where the Nali River emerged as a tributary of the Burnett 1,000 metres below them. Looking west they could see the swamplands of Papua fading into a blue heat shimmer. The continuing track was downwards to Nomad, so a camp was established. From this rudimentary base they began cutting trails.

Working without aerial photographs or maps, they headed off approximately northwards in search of Van's sinks. One of their Duna carriers found a very large depression measuring 400 metres across and about half as deep, to which they gave the rather prosaic title "The Largest Doline in the World." After thrashing a way to the bottom, zigzagging down between cliffs, bamboo and barbed vines, they were discouraged to see the stream vanish into an impenetrable jumble of mud, rocks and forest detritus.

Ten days after setting out from Kelabo, they still had no idea of their position in relation to the features seen from the air, and Van conceded that things looked somewhat different on the ground. It had rained most of the time, they had seen no caves, and it made little sense to try to penetrate further into trackless bush without some indication of direction. With time running out they reluctantly returned to civilisation. With the aid of aerial photographs, they later calculated that they had been at least three days short of the target area.

Some 225 kilometres east of the Mullers lies the Chimbu Province. The dramatic limestone scenery here has an intrinsic beauty that is no doubt enhanced by the year round spring-like climate. It was a complete contrast to the cloud forests of the Mullers. With its easy access, the area would prove magnetic to cavers. After the Muller reconnaissance Van and Kevan returned with Bill Sanders to the Porol Range, scene of their record-breaking descent at Bibima. Van had previoulsy found an interesting cave in late 1971, naming it in the local tongue simply Darua Muru (The Hole). The entrance, a muddy scramble with a permanent stream, was located at an altitude of 2,200 metres some 10 kilometres northwest of Kundiawa township. Van had already penetrated the cave for thirty metres and it looked a goer.

A short abseil rigged with 11 millimetre Terylene dropped them into a stinking grovel through black mud and bat guano. Two more drops in succession preceded a wet eight-metre pitch, also rigged with Terylene. This led them into a cleaner section of passage via a downhill scramble. They then reached a deep rift carved in sound, creamy-white limestone. Hurling the customary "henry" into the void produced a satisfying silence followed by a lingering "booOOM."

It was a clear indication of something deep. They found a belay for their 75-metre rope; Van tied a knot in the end and offered himself into the breach. Once through the narrow section Van's exclamations told his waiting friends that the hole had opened out into a fine shaft. He had to attach an additional length of rope to the end before reaching the bottom. The others joined him and together they scrambled to a five-metre handline pitch followed by a series of sporty cascades, at which point two of their electric lamps failed and emergency carbides had to be stoked up.

A further pitch swallowed the descending passage. After chimneying down this for 15 metres, Van reported that the cave continued to descend, but with no more tackle left they sounded the retreat. Suddenly an ominous rumbling noise rolled out of the depths, and for a moment they stood rooted to the spot. Not wishing to hang about to investigate the cause of the noise they turned tail and affected a hurried exit, having reached a depth of 170 metres.

An exchange of correspondence with Sydney conveyed the news about Darua Muru. Those in Sydney responded that despite the failure to reach the proposed expedition area in the Mullers or explore any encouraging spelological features, expedition planning would go ahead regardless. The Muller trip was on.

TO ULIWAPO AND BACK

On July 21, the advance team moved in, comprising John Cater, Van Watson, Kevan Wilde and ten Duna tribesmen acting as carriers and guides. An air drop of supplies had been made into a clearing at Geroro beyond the Anu Pass and upon arrival there, they found it had been 95 percent successful. Continuing west, they found it necessary to build bridges at two points where their trail crossed the Yu Atea (Atea River). They finally established base camp at Lumbi, a day's walk from Geroro, located on a ridge separating the Yu Atea catchment from the Nali cliffs.

The expedition area earmarked as having the best prospects for deep caving was centred upon a remote clearing beside the Yu Roripongo, eight kilometres to the northwest of Lumbi, at the northern-most extremity of the Mamo Plateau. This plateau appeared so honeycombed with dolines on the aerial pictures that it soon became known as "the cheese." An advance party had

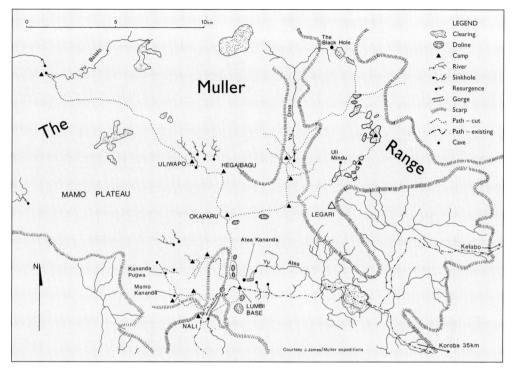

Fig. 9) The Muller Range

blazed a trail ahead to prepare a base of operations for the 23-member team. They would remain in the field two months.

With the benefit of aerial photographs, the coordinators noted that the Yu Atea ended at a prominent sinkhole just north of the large doline found on the reconnaissance. They opted to follow a valley northward, keeping this feature to their right. Despite the proximity and awesome potential of the Atea sinkhole – which can be heard from several kilometres distant – this was unfortunately not visited until the expedition was vacating the area in its final days.

After one and a half kilometres of prospecting, the explorers found themselves in incredibly broken terrain with vegetation so tenacious (including a variety of climbing bamboo) that it took them a week to cover the six kilometres to the first staging post at Hegaibagu (Camp Horatio). They considered it a good day if they covered two kilometres! As dusk fell on the 29th, they made camp again on an unnamed ridge in the cloud forest and named it Faultline Base (see fig. 9).

They were still cutting track two days later when at noon Kevan thought he heard a plane. Although they could not see it through the tree canopy, there was no mistaking the drone of a Cessna circling the area. At first they wondered why a plane would be in the area, but upon checking the log realised they had been out of radio contact for eight days! It was a search party!

Machetes rang out all afternoon as the Duna worked through difficult terrain, enthusiastically hewing a way through the dripping undergrowth. Suddenly, from somewhere down the trail a cry went up.

"Aiyee! Aiyee!"

They had finally found the clearing; Uliwapo at last. That very moment, the heavens opened and a myriad glossy leaves channelled cool rivulets of water onto the hapless band. The trail had

People of Telfol during an Independence Day celebration (Sept. 16, 1975).

been 13 days in the making and by this time enthusiasm was ebbing, along with the last glimmer of daylight. A camp was hurriedly cobbled together as the insect life tuned up for the approach of night.

Morale lifted when the next day dawned bright. The rain had stopped, and with the golden orb blazing down upon them, the clearing seemed almost idyllic. A kilometre in length and a few hundred metres across, it would make an excellent drop zone. Van returned to meet the main team in Tari, while Kevan and John remained at the new camp to make ready for the arrival of vital supplies. An air drop was scheduled for Wednesday, August 8. Isolated trees were removed from the clearing and a beacon fire built in readiness.

First investigations of the holes immediately around the camp proved disappointing. A few days later, however, John returned from a brief sortie into "the cheese" with more encouraging news. They cheered up a little, yet there were more immediate matters of concern: the air drop was several days away and Kevan was almost out of cigars!

On August 2, anxious eyes peered skywards as clouds scudded across their little oasis, blotting out the sun. A wretched mist crept in wraith-like amid the mossy trees and everything was soon wet with a clinging damp. Morale sank as food supplies ran dangerously low, and the weather continued over the next few days with little change. The campfire was soon a focal point in a dripping world of muted greys and greens. Another week passed.

They awoke on August 8 to clearing skies and their last tin of bully beef. Radio contact with Koroba confirmed that the drop was on, and amid mounting anticipation they placed a large square of yellow polythene in the centre of the drop zone, then repeatedly tried to light the fire. Soon the sound of a Cessna 185 could be heard approaching and still the fire would not ignite, despite encouragement from a litre of petrol. Panic gripped them, as they feared the pilot would fail to locate their camp. Their anxieties were allayed when he flew past on a trial run, dropping a bag of sugar as a rangefinder. Circling around, he lined up for the first of four runs.

Bernie Flanagan was a good pilot, one of the old school who enjoyed stick and rudder flying. To him, carrying out those little errands of mercy was just part of the rich tapestry of life in the tropics. It was full of cherished memories; beautiful mornings and mountain mists, Cessnas with the door off, Mendi Valley Club, beer, girls, and lost weekends at the Smugglers Inn.

The clearing was at an altitude of around 3,000 metres, and as a result the power output of the plane was reduced by 35 percent. Using full flaps as dive brakes, Bernie banked his tiny craft and came in steep, keeping his air speed as low as possible. Reducing flaps to 20 degrees at the last possible moment, he levelled off at 70 knots as his drop master kicked out the supplies. The engine strained to pull the plane up just as the treetops at the end of the clearing rushed forward to meet them.

The run was successful and the weather held long enough for more drops the next day. Precious cargo rained from the sky, and it was a welcome sight. Amongst the supplies was a 33 kilo plastic drum of calcium carbide, fuel for the cavers' lamps. It was marked "Papua New Guinea's answer to the French Test: Underground Nuclear Testing Device." Few casualties were sustained. Three bags disappeared into the bush never to be found, a further three containers of tomato sauce were totally destroyed, and the yellow bothy roof suffered a direct hit from a box of cabin bread. The latter was reduced to cabin bread crumbs and the plastic roof leaked from that day forward! They found a note from Bernie on a "Beaut Biscuit Bonanza Bomb." It read simply, "Air too thin to gain power. What a prick of a drop site."

Meanwhile, the main team was mustered at Kelabo for the long inward trek to Uliwapo. Amongst them was the elite of vertical cavers from Australia and New Zealand. They had all trained hard for this moment, yet the chain of events leading to the occupation of Uliwapo Base was to be severely strained by the atrocious conditions. When the last of the party had dragged their feet into camp, some of them well after dark, many of the vital links were close to breaking. For some the walk had been a nightmare due to the slippery log bridges, heavy rain, the fearful bamboo forest, and most of all, the jungle mud. At each stage of the trek they had problems with altitude sickness, campfires that refused to light, and a lack of food; one person had slipped and received a bamboo spear in his thigh.

Time heals however, and for most the memories of the inward trudge soon faded into a diurnal round of exploration and camp chores. Three areas were given priority for investigation: Uliwapo, the "cheese" immediately south of Uliwapo, and the ridge in the vicinity of a faulted glade, some two and half hours walk east. On Monday the 13th, one team left for the ridge region while Kevan led a group southward, seeking holes in the "cheese" area. His team penetrated the doline country, examining holes as they found them. It was slow going.

In one promising doline, they could not see the bottom for thick vegetation, but they could hear falling water somewhere below. When finally they found a way down to the stream, it merely vanished into a soak. It was a similar story in the next depression, which they descended for 180 metres to an eight-metre square cave taking a large stream. This was passable only for a few body lengths to a rock fall that barred further progress. They had the same luck everywhere. What appeared to be promising holes on the air photographs quickly became non-starters.

Disheartened, they sat around the campfire one night, reflecting upon the unknown caverns that must surely exist beneath them. Suddenly everything around camp began to gyrate vigorously. "Oh, yes, I forgot to tell you," ventured Kevan. "New Guinea is in an earthquake zone."

Further east, the shock waves – estimated at magnitude four on the Richter scale – passed through the camp on the ridge. Those in residence decided that the first hole of significant depth would be called Earthquake Hole (Uli Guria in Duna tongue).

They spent their first day out on the ridge bobbing up and down a handful of small shafts and dolines alongside the track from Camp Horatio (Hegaibagu) to Faultline Base. Some suspected a geological fracture line and hopes were high of discovering vertical caves developed along it. The first hole led to a few metres of small passage and the next descended 30 metres in four short drops; others simply choked or closed in, but not one produced the anticipated breakthrough.

Meanwhile, Phil Robinson was scuttling about among depressions when he stumbled upon a steep sided doline with an interesting look about it. Rigging a hand line through a "salad" in the southeast corner, he landed 15 metres below on a mobile mud slope leading to an enticing black space. After a 50-metre abseil, Phil returned to the surface, unable to contain his optimism.

After lunch Neil Montgomery, Mike Bourke and Jerry Atkinson descended with Phil and more rope. Dropping the entrance pitch they found themselves in a roomy shaft with walls covered in flakes that peeled off at the slightest touch. Two small holes led off from the rock-strewn bottom, one to a small chamber after a short way, the other leading to a 14-metre pitch in a narrow cleft. The landing consisted of an unstable rubble slope containing a small gap. Neil spent some time enlarging this and, after the crashing and distant rumbling died down, they decided it was a long drop. They placed an anchor and Phil squeezed through. Passing a ledge at 58 metres, he ran out of rope in a widening shaft, but could see no sign of the bottom between his swinging legs.

Back at the surface, they fought back the urge to return to Uliwapo to break the news; they decided to assess the area more fully before putting all expedition eggs in one basket. Since supplies were running low, Julia and Jane Dyson were despatched to Uliwapo the next day. Everyone there was by then questioning the decision to come to the Mullers when the bearers of glad tidings arrived, requesting more food and the 300-metre rope. In the interim, those at Faultline Base moved up to Camp Horatio, where they began improving the facilities in readiness for new arrivals. There was little food left and the only water supply was a dubious soak the colour of tea some way into the bush. After a meagre lunch, shaft dropping recommenced and the entrance pitch to Uli Mulmulum was soon discovered.

Mike Bourke descended first, but ran out of tackle at a depth of 35 metres, so Phil joined him with a longer rope. The pitch proved to be 73 metres. After passing a few small drops, they positioned a bolt to keep the rope clear of loose rock at the head of a second pitch, but unfortunately, the way down choked after only six metres. Luck was with them though: three metres down, they found a nine-metre drop that fell away into a narrow canyon in sharp limestone. They gave up for the day after exploring 40 metres of filthy passage.

Back at camp, John Cater had arrived with more food and that night they discussed plans for Uli Guria. A similar moot was held back at Uliwapo. While awaiting the return of Kevan's team, Julia and Van weighed up the various options open to them. Just after midday, following nearly a week of bush bashing, the "cheese" party returned torn, bedraggled and demoralised. They had cut four kilometres of track, explored five holes and between them spent less than ten hours underground.

The three co-leaders held a hurried conference. It seemed there was little hope of major discoveries in the honeycomb karst of the cheese: caves were surely there, but the problem was finding them in the hellish terrain. Uliwapo was also disappointing. At Camp Horatio there was at least a going hole, and others nearby gave promise of some depth. The decision to abandon

Uliwapo was unanimous. While camp was struck, those on the ridge impatiently awaited the long rope.

Friday dawned a gloriously sunny day, but there was no room for idleness. With the end of the expedition rapidly approaching, Neil returned to Uli Mulmulum and with Jerry Atkinson pushed beyond the previous limit. Forcing themselves along a grotty crawl that stank of decaying vegetation, they found a final filthy slither that led to a short drop. This was so muddy that it took them 30 minutes to rig it. Neil went down to have a look, quickly returning to report an even narrower continuation. With thoughts of greater depth and roomy shafts elsewhere, Uli Mulmulum was forsaken at a depth of 130 metres. Back at camp, Julia and Van arrived at dusk with porters, more supplies, and at long last, the eagerly awaited big rope.

By early morning, the entrance of Uli Mulmulum had been derigged in readiness for the big push down Uli Guria. Neil Montgomery and Phil Robinson formed a front-line team with the intention of exploring beyond the big pitch. Neil abseiled to the roomy ledge at 58 metres and "Below!" A rock inadvertently dislodged from the takeoff point plummeted towards Neil with a resounding crash that froze Phil's heart. Luckily for Neil, the missile bounced safely to one side and continued on its way to the bottom. After the dust and curses had settled, Phil joined him at the ledge. The rope was rebelayed here as an additional safeguard for the continuing descent. The shaft then dropped a further 65 metres to a blind rubble floor, but Neil spotted a ledge up the wall. After swinging in a pendulum over to this, he entered a continuation. They were both relieved to find the safety of a small passage, away from the main pitch.

They could hear a spattering of water ahead, and soon came to a pitch that swallowed a small stream entering from an aven. Neil descended the 33 metres while Phil provided backup. Twenty minutes later he returned after being stopped by yet another drop. Having used all their rope they had little choice but to head out. By this time the move from Uliwapo was complete and, for some of the team, the expedition was at an end. They had departed the area, leaving a dozen cavers at Faultline Base and the remainder in residence at Camp Horatio.

As they awaited news from the depths, those on the surface had continued to probe the surrounding dolines. Jane Dyson, Jerry Atkinson and Mike Bourke returned to Uli Ui, a pothole found and explored to 80 metres a day or two earlier. But due to the shortage of tackle, they could only add one more. At a depth of 90 metres, they landed in a chamber with a waterfall crashing in at the far side. The way on was to the left of their rope, into a low meandering stream passage, which narrowed to a slot taking the water. It was too thin at stream level, but by negotiating a wider part just above, they squirmed along a confined muddy canyon. After about five metres, this dropped into another chamber. The continuation emitted a resounding echo.

Later that same day the explorers returned from Uli Guria, having reached a depth of 220 metres with not even a bootlace of tackle to spare. And still the cave continued. How soon would it be before they could expect a large underground river? If they found one could they cope? Each was wrapped in private thoughts, his or her growing anticipation bordering on apprehension. On Sunday, Julia had to leave, with Uli Guria still a going proposition.

Van, Ashley Cody and Paul Caffyn now picked up the gauntlet, quickly reaching the short pitch that had stopped Neil. Meanwhile, the team at Faultline Base investigated an interesting doline that Van had seen in July, where he had followed a stream to a muddy sinkhole at the base of a bluff. A line of collapse features continued from this point. One of these had rock walls all around pierced by a number of enticing entrances. Once in the bottom, the team entered a largish chamber via one of the holes. This intruded into an adjacent doline, but just before this a high but muddy canyon passage continued to the right, leading quickly to a pitch with an enticing echo. Two more short drops in quick succession led to a small chamber with yet another

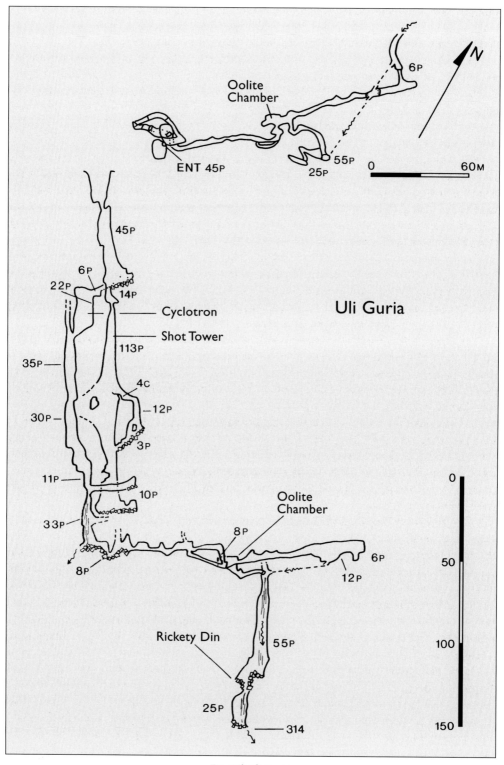

Oolite
Chamber

ENT 45P

6P

55P
25P

N

0   60M

45P

6P
22P
14P

Cyclotron

Shot Tower

113P

35P

4C

12P

30P

3P

11P

10P

33P

8P

8P

Oolite
Chamber

6P

12P

Uli Guria

Rickety Din

55P

25P

314

0

50

100

150

Fig. 10) Uli Guria

drop. By now everyone and everything was plastered in clinging mud. Keith Dekkers threw the last rope into the void and slid down, shortly returning from the end of the rope but not from the bottom of the pitch. They walked back to camp, thwarted but hopeful.

Meanwhile somewhere in the deeps of Earthquake Hole, Van, Paul and Ashley had reached the limit of the previous day and pushed their way along a disgusting crawl to a small widening that hardly warranted the title of chamber. But water could be heard ahead! Crawling along a low passage – the Toothpaste Tube – they popped out unexpectedly in an airy shaft. Water was falling from somewhere high above, hissing as it went by and disappearing into a growling darkness.

Paul was first down, but found the rope too short. With the bit between his teeth and undeterred by the moist conditions, he tied his jumar slings to the end of the rope and completed a wet 55-metre descent to the floor. This was comprised of unstable boulders pockmarked and dappled by the falling stream. A devious route through Rickety Din, led via some squeezes to a wet 25-metre pitch (see fig. 10). Below this, all hopes of greater depth disappeared with the stream into an impenetrable rock fall at a final depth of 314 metres.

The explorers surveyed out as they climbed to the surface, which proved a long and exhausting task. It was particularly harrowing on the big pitch due to rocks that fell out of the darkness without warning. These made such an impression on the party that the name Shot Tower came in an instant. Once the tackle was removed from Uli Guria, they once again focused their attention on the new going hole near Faultline Base.

Kevan, Keith, Phil Glasby, Peter Shaw and Millie Holl returned to the unexplored pitch. This turned into a 47-metre abseil landing in a chamber the size of a tennis court. This had an inclined mud floor along which a stream had carved a deep trench. A waterfall crashed in from the south side and chuckled off downstream to vanish mockingly into a muddy choke at the far end of the chamber.

Just beyond the choke a black void beckoned through a small orifice. Sounding this by hurling a rock over the edge, Keith pronounced it to be 20 metres. Climbing down on their shortest rope to a ledge, he was pleasantly surprised to find the drop still continuing. With more rope, Rift Shaft bottomed out just under 50 metres. Everyone hurried off, following a steeply descending vertical rift that turned back on itself beneath the large chamber. Ghostly stalactites loomed out of the gloom.

Two more short drops followed and the cave resumed a southwesterly trend in dry passage with a high triangular section where an occasional pool occupied the floor. Two of these filled the whole passage, and Keith helped the team past them by devising and leading two entertaining tension traverses. After this exciting interlude, they used their last rope where the floor fell away for six metres. Turning west, the cave continued more or less straight for a half kilometre, broken only by the occasional free-climb. A narrowing was reached where a stream, gathered from several minor sources, made its escape down an impenetrable slot. Forcing a muddy crawl nearby soon led to more walking passage, and after half an hour they could hear falling water ahead.

They reached the sound in a largish chamber where a stream fell from high up one wall. Gripped by deep cave fever, the explorers literally ran off into the distance, splashing through the water as it fanned out gracefully down a series of pristine calcite flows. The cave confounded them, however, for in utter despair they watched the stream gurgle into a boulder pile. Where was the way on? Mud floors rose on either side to form high banks and several blind avens pierced the roof of the chamber. In sheer frustration they tried every orifice. Then someone noticed an obscure hole to one side. They pushed forward into the uninviting passage, going

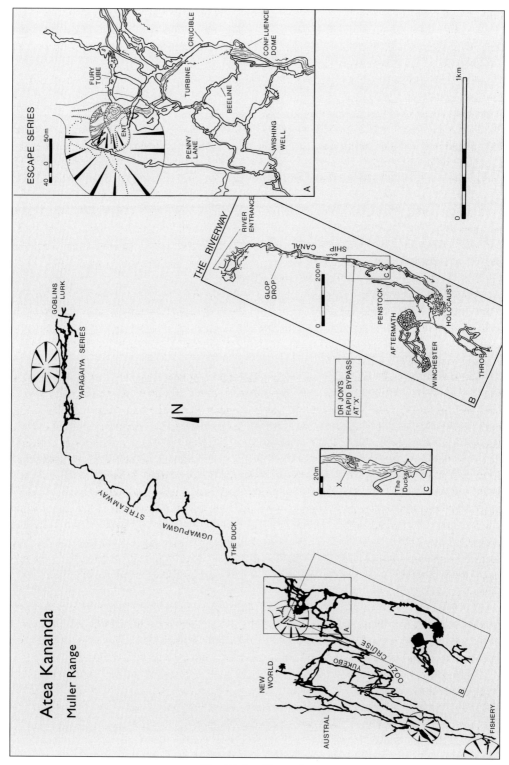

Fig. 11) Atea Kananda

through a tight squeeze that led to a sump after 28 metres. This they bypassed, but only to be stopped by another sump pool. This time there was definitely no way around. These final sections were oppressive, and everywhere there was stark evidence that the stream backed up considerably under severe flow conditions.

After recovering the surveying gear from some way up the passage, they retraced their steps as they mapped and detackled their way back to the entrance. After recording 1,500 metres of passageway, they eventually stumbled out into the jungle dawn at 7:00 a.m.; they had spent 20 entertaining hours below ground. Anxiety had been growing amongst those on the surface, and indeed they were preparing to mount a search party; Andy Pybus had even carried over the stretcher and medical kit! That night, no one could sleep until the survey data had been plotted, and threats to chain Phil Glasby to the drafting board were very nearly carried out. When drawn up, Kanada Heiowa Heia (Sunrise Cave) proved to be no deeper than Uli Guria.

It was almost departure time, but a number of loose ends remained. Neil, Van and John Cater returned to Uli Ui, inspired by tales of echoing voids. Negotiating the narrow slot at the previous limit of exploration, they alighted in an elongated chamber with a floor canyon a mere 20 centimetres wide. This quickly opened up, however, as the floor merged with a larger void. When plied with rocks, an enticing rumble answered back.

Three ropes were quickly knotted together to rig Pendulum Shaft giving them a free hang in a fine elliptical shaft. First down was Neil. Initially the pitch was dry but the stream entered again at the 50 metres level. He ran out of rope but with applied gymnastics reached a ledge from where, with care, it was possible to reach the floor. The stream disappeared into the gravel floor at a new depth of 175 metres.

On the surface jungle bashing continued and a number of new shafts were discovered. While some of the team began pulling back to the Okaparu camp on Friday, August 24, others went back into Sunrise Cave to photograph the large chamber. Within half an hour of their descent, heavy rain began to fall. Foliage dripped and the elongated fronds of pandanus ran like storm gutters. Caving boots left lying about camp were soon brimming over. Trickles formed streams that soon became a turgid flood, carrying with it a flotsam of jungle detritus into every sinkhole.

Below ground, some of the party returned from the 47-metre pitch, leaving Kevan, Keith and Millie to record the subterranean landscape, unaware of the deteriorating weather. They had set up two photographs when the stream seemed to increase in volume. Within five minutes the whole chamber changed out of all character, as a muddy stream thundered down what had previously been a dry pitch. They hurriedly packed their gear. Another stream burst from a hole in the roof and soon the air was filled with flying spray. Above the roar, communication was only possible by shouting fit to burst. They looked at one another and expressions said it all: it was time to get out.

The floor was by then awash as they set off up the 47-metre pitch, the increasing water making it an effort to climb. As they reached the top of each rope the danger lessened, until eventually the party surfaced, drenched but otherwise unscathed by their ordeal. What had been intended as a short photographic trip had unexpectedly turned into an eight hour epic.

The next morning, the teams abandoned the ridge camps and set off for Lumbi on the first stage of the long walk back to civilisation. Thoughts turned to the sinkhole of the Atea River. Three of the team had returned to Lumbi the day before and had already cut a route down into the huge doline. Their reports were exciting yet unnerving.

The Atea was the most impressive sight anyone had ever seen, a vast cauldron hemmed in to one side by 100-metre high bluffs (see fig. 11). The river, which had sunk in a canyon some way upstream, emerged from horizontal fissures in these cliffs before cascading over a wide front to form a graceful series of waterfalls. Some 50 metres below these a "boiling" plunge pool distributed an estimated 12 cumecs (cubic metres per second) of water into a yawning cave mouth. Rainbows completed the awesome tableau.

Could this cave be safely explored? Mike Bourke's experience just a few months earlier had already highlighted the problems with river caves, yet there were those who fancied their chances. Fortunately, the sloping northwest side provided an easy route into the doline. This supported a stunted community of strangler figs and broad-leafed hardwoods, giving way lower down to shrubs and herbaceous plants such as begonias and balsam. It was home to tree-creepers, flycatchers and rufus-crowned wrens. The noise of falling water was tremendous and vegetation danced this way and that, lashed by spray driven outwards from the turbulent pool.

By entering a smaller flood overflow conduit to the right of the main river entrance, the explorers gained a broad shelf and tentatively followed it above water level. Only 70 metres further, this narrowed to a ledge that quickly petered out, leaving the cavers gazing at the river hurrying along in a canyon below.

They visited the cave several times over the next few days, but could make no progress without resorting to aid climbing techniques to progress along the wall. It was frustrating to leave the Atea with its huge virgin passage disappearing off into the unknown, but personal commitments called and the question of what lay beyond was left to the future. Before the curtain came down on 1973, cavers in Australasia were already considering the implications of the Atea River. The resurgence was uncertain, though likely to be the Nali. It was an exciting prospect, but some questioned whether or not it could be safely explored, and some believed it was out of the question. Impossible is an alluring word...

While Van and Kevan were at grips with the tenacious vegetation on the Muller reconnaissance, a meeting was taking place in the Northern Hemisphere. In a room above the Craven Heifer, a popular cavers' inn on the edge of the Yorkshire Dales, some of Britain's most accomplished speleologists had gathered. An observer might have deduced from the enthusiastic throng that free ale was on offer that day, but it was the recent developments in New Guinea that had generated more interest and promised greater rewards than any amber nectar could ever offer.

It transpired that more than one group had been planning ventures to this wild land. In 1970 a second attempt to organise support for a trip had drifted into obscurity, never to be heard of again. Yet in the wake of the British Venezuela and Ghar Parau expeditions of 1972 and 1973 and the Pierre de la St. Martin explorations that same year, a few leading cavers were giving serious thought to distant frontiers. Additional inspiration came from an article that appeared in the first issue of *Niugini Caver* in January of 1973 in which the author, Malcolm Robb, painted a glowing picture of the limestone terrain in the extreme northwestern corner of the Western Province of Papua New Guinea. The article drew attention to one formidable feature, the Hindenburg Wall. This ran for tens of kilometres east to west, practically without a break into the foothills of the Star Mountains.

Robb described the wall as "dropping 8,000 feet to the plains of Papua," and wrote that "we were amazed by the huge rivers that poured out of the wall, often exiting half way up and cascading thousands of feet into the jungle below."

It was obvious from the meeting that each group alone lacked the resources and manpower to tackle the immense logistical difficulties of fielding an expedition to such a remote destination. The several groups thus decided to pool their resources. Ideas were exchanged and a basic plan thrashed out to start the ball rolling.

In early 1974, Howard Beck and Roy Blackham, two members of the Craven Pothole Club, secured employment in the New Guinea Highlands. They joined up with Kevan Wilde and

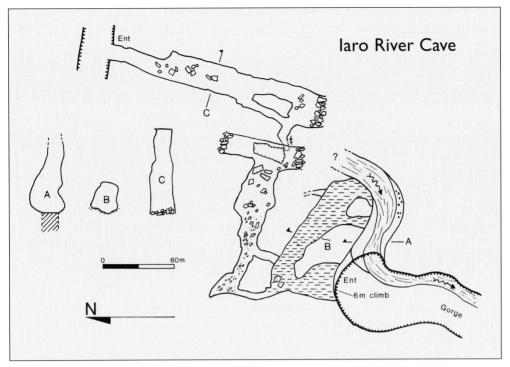

Fig. 12) Iaro River Cave

between them set about the task of organising from a base in Mount Hagen. Eager to begin caving, Howard and Roy prospected the limestone of the Waghi Valley, exploring a few small caves around town and in the Chimbu. When they met with Neil Ryan, who was working for the third-level airline operator TAL, he mentioned the spectacular Iaro River Cave. It was akin to holding a red rag to a bull, and they eventually managed a brief visit that September.

The wet season promised them an eventful journey when they returned the first weekend of October. Indeed, it took some eight hours to cover 130 kilometres of back roads to Pulupare, the nearest settlement.

The cave was everything they expected and more. They estimated the flow at upwards of 85 cumecs, making the Iaro one of the greatest known underground rivers in the world. Exploration of the riverway was clearly out of the question, but to the left an easy free climb opened onto about 300 metres of well-decorated fossil galleries (see fig. 12). They traced a strong draught down through boulders meeting many commuting bats along the way. They came to a musty series of rift passages and eventually debauched into a narrow, thickly vegetated canyon. By following this "downstream" they regained the river exit at the base of the climb. They noted several other caves on the way, but only one was partially explored for a few metres, and this included a fearful looking spider covered in orange fur!

Back in England, research continued for many months, but the question of which region to target was largely decided for them. The Mullers had the necessary relief, but it was the primary arena of activity for Australian speleologists, who were already holding meetings in Sydney to discuss a plan of action for the mighty Atea. Chuave could easily be reached but lacked depth potential, while of the outlying islands, only New Britain displayed massively bedded karsts.

Some thought that relief was insufficient here, a notion which the French later proved to be unfounded. This left only the remote country between the headwaters of the Fly and Sepik rivers, where the Territory spilled over the border into Irian Jaya.

The British procured aerial photographs and even satellite coverage. Geologists who had worked in the area were tracked down and their brains were picked for any information that could be gleaned. They processed all available data to provide better focus for a reconnaissance by the New Guinea contingent. The Hindenburg Range was an obvious choice, more than making up in relief what it lacked in accessibility.

Momentum was gathering, despite the lack of support from a Britain plagued by economic gloom. The expedition received generous grant aid and the Royal Geographical Society gave their approval to the venture. Patronage then materialised in the form of Eric Shipton and the Duchess of Kent, and industry was soon pledging support. The British Sports Council had promised grant aid to any expedition that would increase the standing of British caving. Now, a team of 24 scientists and cavers planned to spend up to six months in remote and unexplored mountains at the very heart of New Guinea's interior. The leader was the well-known Dave Brook, a caver with many new discoveries to his credit. They were evidently impressed by the aspirations of the ambitious undertaking.

Meanwhile in New Guinea, Howard and Roy were actively training for the expedition. In early March, they enjoyed an additional bonus when, with Kevan Wilde and Dick Knight of Goroka, they completed the second only descent of Bibima Cave. This they achieved during the wet season, taking a little over five hours to reach the bottom.

TO THE HINDENBURGS

At the end of March, Kevan arrived in Mt. Hagen to prepare for the start of the reconnaissance and spent the next couple of days with Howard procuring essential supplies. Over the phone some days before, Kevan had vehemently extolled the virtues of travelling light, then astounded Howard and Roy by turning up with one backpack devoted entirely to cigars and tobacco!

Roy was to remain in Mt. Hagen until a later date, while on April 4, Howard and Kevan flew into Telefomin as news reached them that the British Sports Council had proffered a substantial financial contribution to the expenses of the venture. They were about to begin a two-month investigation of the caving potential in one of the wildest regions of the country. This vast tract of virgin limestone between the Star Mountains and the Strickland River Gorge was selected as the new frontier of speleology for 1975 (see fig. 3).

At the outset, it was planned that an aerial fly-past should precede two ground patrols of four and two weeks each; however, the pieces of reality were not to fit the jigsaw of expectation without a little force. After off-loading supplies in Telefomin, they took to the air again with two local kiaps, Mark and Keith, and flew south over the Nong River towards Olsobip. This flight path was to take them over a honeycomb karst region bisected by a fault-influenced valley midway between Feramin and Bolivip. The plane proved a little too speedy and they had crossed the valley before they realised it. They were soon banking west around a corner of the Hindenburg Wall. Clouds prevented a look at features on the plateau above, so they flew west as far as the majestic Tere Falls and turned back toward base. Although the wall had obviously suffered from exaggeration, they saw several voluminous resurgences at its base. There could be little doubt that the plateau above held tremendous possibilities.

Part of the Hindenburg scarp showing numerous streams emerging as waterfalls.

Three days later they departed into the west again, this time on foot with four Eliptamin porters and rations for two weeks. They were heading for the Tifalmin Valley, home by reputation to a tribe of sorcerers. They reached Bufulmin village after two days trekking beneath 30-kilo packs bulging with survival gear, caving tackle, a shotgun, and of course Kevan's cigars. The weight proved too much, so that evening in the kiap hut they made a decision to leave behind the caving gear for the duration of the reconnaissance.

Shortly after dusk a disturbance was heard in the village. Yaiyok, the head porter, was despatched with obvious trepidation to investigate. It wasn't long before he returned to report that a man had died and *sanguma* was suspected. Yaiyok related how a *bom-bom* had been placed in the dead man's hand so that his spirit could rise and carry it to the house of the culprit responsible for his demise. Looking out into the inky night, they could indeed see a light bobbing its ghostly way across the valley. All four carriers were visibly shaken and refused to leave the hut until daybreak.

Soon after first light, the patrol set off up the valley and perspired over the following three days through the hot grasslands of the upper Tifalimin valley, before completing the first documented ascent of Mt. Aiyang (3,150 m). According to locals, the mountain was the abode of bad spirits. Indeed, during the course of the climb one of the porters gashed his leg with an axe, an incident which in the villagers' eyes merely lent credence to their point. But speleologically, the mountain proved of little interest.

Upon returning to Bufulmin, Kevan considered an area that had been recommended by Assistant District Commissioner Keith Winchcombe in Telefomin. This area was located 15 kilometres to the southwest, beyond a range of mountains terminated by Mt. Aiyang. The air photographs clearly showed large sinkholes and a clearing that looked ideal for use as an advance base. The local people called it Finim Tel and told of a trade route south to Tabubil that passed through it.

On April 16, they crossed the high Bahrman Mountains with supplies to last ten days. With the ranges behind them, they were soon trekking across a "plateau" that was anything but level. Feted swamps amid bamboo thickets punctuated undulating country. After nine hours of confinement to the forest, a long clearing stretched out before them like a welcome mat rolled out between the trees. This was to be their home for several days while they assessed the speleological potential.

Southwest of camp, the vegetated shaft of La Buum Tem appeared to be at least 60 metres deep with a large cave leading from the base (see fig. 5). Kevan and Howard were surprised to learn that the Wokkamins from below the wall hunted flying fox here by climbing down bush vines. They cringed at the thought. Over the next two days some determined machete work helped them reach two very large dolines south of their camp that were visible on the photographs. The skilled use of the compass and photographs to find these holes was a source of wonder to the porters. Several shafts and caves were also noted en route, yet the huge rock-walled pits – each estimated to be around 150 metres deep – dwarfed all. The area certainly appeared promising enough, so work began on an advanced base camp capable of housing the whole team.

One evening, light relief came in more ways than one while Kevan was answering a call of nature. Howard was relaxing with the porters by the campfire when he was startled by a yell that suddenly rent the still night air. Kevan had been crouched down just beyond the halo of light cast by the flames. Thinking the pallid apparition was a bush spirit, one of the porters had deftly hurled a handy log into the shadows, planting it square on Kevan's head. The incident certainly raised Howard's spirits and doubtless frightened away any genuine ones!

The base was well advanced when a return across the range became necessary, as other interesting areas awaited and supplies were running short. To the south of Urapmin a group of eight dolines were so huge that they had been marked on the geological maps. A meeting with local villagers established that the area was for the time being *itambu*, so they decided to return to Telefomin and rearrange plans for the remainder of the reconnaissance. While Howard and Kevan discussed their next move with Keith Winchcombe, a drama was unfolding elsewhere...

TRIAL BY AIR

All was peaceful in the forest. A gentle hum just at the limit of hearing filled the muggy air. A soft rustling betrayed some creature, a python perhaps, slithering surreptitiously through the undergrowth. At another place an isolated shaft of sunlight, penetrating the green defences, shone pallid on the leaf litter. Passing through this spotlight, a line of worker ants was strung out on some urgent errand of survival. Now and then a vague breeze, barely noticeable on the forest floor, sent shivers through the tree canopy. A cloud of vibrantly coloured parakeets took to their wings with an excited clamour. Something had violated their airspace...

Jim Farnworth and Mike Bourke gazed out of the windows of the Piper Cherokee, trying to imagine what lay hidden beneath the thick forest. A shadow of the plane wavered over the all-embracing green as below them flocks of birds wheeled about at their approach. It was Saturday, April 26, 1975. They had taken off that morning in a specially chartered plane from Rabaul Aero

The author backpacking through the high-altitude moss forest over the Bahrman Range
en route to the Finim Tel base camp.
Right: Hunters with tree kangaroo, the largest indigenous mammal of New Guinea.

Club and crossed St. George's Channel, a 50-kilometre stretch of water separating New Britain from New Ireland. The Lelet Plateau rolled by. Mike sat in the co-pilot's seat and Jim was in the back with another caver, Tim Sprod, as each attempted to make some sense of what they saw below.

A caving expedition was being planned for later in the year. In January Jim had spent a few wet days on the karst plateau with Kev Wilde examining the caving potential, searching for suitable air drop sites and making contact with villagers among whom they hoped to recruit carriers. This reconnaissance followed one the previous April when Mike Bourke and Allan Keller carried out a ten day patrol to the same area.

New Ireland is a narrow but steep land just off the northeast tip of New Britain and is the third largest of the lesser islands in the group. The intended theatre of activity was a 400 square kilometres tract of rough limestone country forming part of the Lelet where this straddled the island at its narrowest. The elevation was between 800 and 1,400 metres, while depth potential appeared to be at least 1,200 metres. No other area in New Guinea shared this combination of relief and accessibility. The main plateau, for instance, could be reached from the coast in six hours. It was for this very reason the Lelet had become the focus of Australian cavers hopeful of breaking world records.

With such thick limestones, Mike's principal aim was to establish that the plateau had depth potential. In five caving days they turned up 30 caves, five of them over 30 metres deep and four that they were unable to bottom because of a lack of gear. Mike felt that his true objective had eluded him. Though hampered by heavy rain and dense bush during the second visit, they located 15 caves, gathered useful facts, and come away with the impression that the area was worthy of further investigation.

Now, with the aerial photos on his knee, Mike peered alternately at these and at the bush below, trying to pinpoint something he could recognise. They were about an hour into the flight and all was going well. A large doline was tied into the photographs and they had located what seemed like an ideal drop site. Jim also spotted a remote bush hut where he thought he and Kevan had stayed back in January. Having just completed one last pass over the plateau at Mike's request, they were about to head off over the open sea for Rabaul. The pilot, Les Mitchell, remarked that the engine tone was peculiar and he thought it best to make for Namatanai, about 50 kilometres down the east coast, so it could be checked. His passengers commented that it sounded fine to them, but no sooner had they spoken than the cabin filled with smoke and the engine began to sound somewhat unhealthy.

As he turned his plane about, there was a sudden loss of power and the plane began shaking violently. They rapidly lost altitude, and Namatanai was now obviously out of the question. Les requested his passengers help look out for the airstrip at Lamerika Plantation. His voice cracked a little and Tim thought that if ever there was a time to convert to Christianity, this was probably it.

Coughing from the fumes, everyone cast worried glances at the approaching treetops, as isolated giants standing taller than the rest seemed intent on plucking them from the sky. Fortunately Les had 20 years experience of flying gliders. This he skilfully demonstrated as he managed to clear the forested mountains. The altimeter was by then reading only 500 metres. The prop was turning but no longer delivering any power. They searched frantically for the landing ground but no one was sure quite where it was. Then the engine packed in altogether.

Les announced that he was going to put down in the sea, after which everything happened quickly. Just before ditching, the pilot was still trying in vain to contact Rabaul before at last patching a mayday through to Port Moresby. About twenty metres off the sea, he yelled for everyone to tighten their seat belts. Tim and Jim in the back misunderstood and undid their harnesses, thinking this was to aid a quick exit. They overshot a sandbar and with a loud bang struck the water about 150 metres from the shoreline. In the next moment the plane flipped over and settled into the sea. Kicking out the perspex windows Tim and Jim were soon out and bobbing at the surface, but the pilot and Mike were struggling, still strapped in their seats underwater.

There were some anxious moments before they too managed to escape. In the confusion that followed a voice rang out. "Someone's still inside!" All four began diving to help, not realising each was out but had surfaced on opposite sides of the fuselage. Only then did they realise the water was only chest deep.

After swimming and wading ashore, they were taken to the nearby plantation where they were given a few stiff drinks and made contact with Rabaul. Apart from a few bruises and cuts sustained when the windows were broken, all escaped remarkably unharmed, which was more than they could have hoped for if they had come down on the plateau. The reconnaissance was subsequently deemed a success, despite its unexpected climax, and during the following month several meetings took place in Queensland to work out in detail the final stages of the expedition.

Unaware of events over New Ireland, Howard and Kevan left Telefomin to complete the second patrol of their reconnaissance. Departing on May 6, they crossed the Sepik River on a vine bridge to a trail south over the exposed grassy flanks of the Victor Emanuel Range. They then descended into the cool respite of the lush Nong Valley, and set up a rough camp for the night beside a clear running creek.

Climbing again the next day, they came to a clearing pierced on its east side by a deep sonorous shaft. They estimated it to be at least 120 metres deep, but for the moment it had to await the arrival of gear and the main team. At the top of the range, they reached a native shelter at Mogondabip, on the trade route south to Olsobip. Extending on either side of the track was the fault-controlled valley seen so briefly from the air.

Setting off east, they cut a track for six days, inspecting holes as they found them. Although the valley floor rose gradually, rugged tower karst prevailed where stunted trees clung tenaciously to what *terra firma* could be found. Nearly everything was draped in vine bamboo and lagged with liverworts and mosses which covered ridges, dolines and fallen trees alike. Daily rains and clammy mists permeated all and everything in a most depressing landscape. But the valley had its compensations.

The reconnaissance team found around 30 sinks and good looking holes adjacent to the track, lending weight to their belief that here was indeed the potential for the world-class depth they sought. Unfortunately the patrol came to a premature end on the morning of May 12, when Howard was badly hurt while bashing down into the bottom of one of the many forested dolines.

The day had started off well enough, too well perhaps. The sun was shining for a change and everyone was warming to the task in hand. Enthusiastically hewing tree ferns, Howard was clearing a route to the hint of a cave entrance they had spotted in a depression, when he chopped himself just above the left knee with a machete freshly honed that very morning. The blade bit deep and required a pressure bandage to stem the copious flow of blood.

Given their position there was nothing to do but abandon the patrol. Medical assistance was three days away at the nearest Baptist mission and there was a very real risk of infection. Tetracycline was administered before they embarked upon a gruelling trek over two ranges that was to put Howard out of action until the arrival of the main team.

While Howard recovered in Telefomin, Kevan took a helicopter flight over the impressive limestone terrain of Mt. Wamtakin, east of the station. Here he noted some impressive karst features. This served as a prelude to the final patrol of the reconnaissance in search of the "big holes" south of Urapmin. Two days after leaving Telefomin, Kevan had established camp close to the entrance of Agim Tem, a large cave mouth descending down dip. This dropped into what sounded like a large chamber. Leaving Agim Tem for a later day, Kevan traced the riverbed for five kilometres upstream of the active sink. Keith Winchcombe had told of an old patrol camp by a major bend in the stream. Kevan hoped to eventually reach the huge dolines east of this.

Continuing south on May 23, Kevan located the camp by late afternoon. Using what daylight remained, he immediately started cutting east with two porters while the others repaired the hut. Back in camp, further scrutiny of the air photographs confirmed Kevan's suspicions: either the holes had moved or the bend in the creek was incorrectly marked on the maps. But the aerial photographs appeared to show a major stream sinking some two kilometres southeast of the camp. It took them two days to reach the Ok Ruun, which they found to sink into a promising double shaft formed in clean, fossil bearing rock. Tramping through torrential rain, the patrol backtracked to the Ok Agim, reaching camp five days after setting out.

Disappointed at not reaching his goal, Kevan decided to have one last attempt at finding the elusive holes. He subsequently spent five days more cutting through confusing and waterless

Rudimentary camp utilised by Howard Beck and Kevan Wilde during their reconnaissance on the Finim Tel Plateau.

terrain, but again the patrol was abortive. The creature comforts of Telefomin began to prey on his mind so Kevan ended the patrol and headed for the valley: the carriers returned to Finim Tel to continue work on the bothy in preparation for the main team.

Despite Howard's injury, attacks from the typhus-carrying tick known as the "bush mokka," and fungal infections to constantly wet feet, the patrol's findings were evaluated favourably in the light of continuing research back in Britain. The groundwork confirmed that the area offered the best possible chances of depth for the British expedition. A subsequent cable to Telefomin advised that the proposed May departure would be delayed by several weeks. Kevan left for home in Goroka to await news while Howard settled into a routine of idle isolation.

No such frustrations beset a small group of Australians as they departed New Britain: a new caving adventure was about to begin.

A LELET INTERLUDE

What finer way to begin an expedition than with a moonlit boat journey across a tropical sea? Visions of a similar voyage to New Ireland still sparkled in their minds as four cavers descended into the underworld of the Lelet Plateau. It was Thursday, July 31, the start of a four-week, eight-man venture, the second to be led by Mike Bourke.

Together with Henry Shannon, Leigh Gleeson and Malcolm Pound, Mike had arrived in a dry creek bed ending in a cave. Villagers believed this to be the den of the masalai pig, Kanameroborunda. Though the entrance was substantial, it was partially hidden by logs, the accumulated jetsam of previous floods. Just beyond the daylight zone, the explorers found they could walk upright through a small chamber, but shortly the passage lowered again at a bend. To the right, wallowing along a low crawl through several pools, they followed a phreatic half tube in the ceiling. Flood debris everywhere was a grim reminder that this was no place to be caught in the wet.

After 70 metres the passage turned sharply right and a cobblestone slope descended into a chamber pierced by several pressure tubes. The exit was downhill once more as the switchback passage – initially a crawl – developed into a narrow vertical rift. This opened out dramatically 30 metres beyond, at a spacious ten metres high chamber, the largest in the cave. At its far side, a passage formed along a prominent joint beckoned from beyond some boulders. Leigh traced this for 100 metres to where it degenerated into a flat-out crawl through an uninviting pool. A short way back from this, a narrow vertical slot allowed voice connection with another passage above, which could be reached from the large chamber.

While Mike and his team investigated the pig's den, Paul Wilson and Jim Farnworth returned to a pothole called Lenbinbin, which had been partially explored the first day on the plateau. With them were two cavers who had been on the Ora Expedition, Lex Brown and John Webb. From the foot of the 20-metre entrance shaft, an unstable boulder slope funnelled into the next pitch, a drop of perhaps 13 metres. They descended – along with several rocks – into a beautiful, steeply inclined chamber with a floor of mud and boulders. This terminated at an impassable slot 50 metres below the entrance.

During the following three weeks, the group systematically investigated several caves and shafts in the lower regions of the Lelet Plateau, the village area. One of the most noteworthy was a pit in which a stone fell for nearly five seconds. Lambelubung, as it was subsequently called, provided a fine 81-metre free-hanging abseil that landed on a blind rubble floor.

They explored another cave linked with local superstition just north of the village of Liit. According to legend it was haunted by the banshee dog Ninggalau. Its bark, it was said, always heralded a death in the nearby hamlet of Bungaring. They had examined the cave during the first week, but as heavy rain was falling at the time, it was left to dry out. Upon their return, the cavers found a muddy chute from a surface gully that gave access to the entrance passage of Ninggalau. At first, this was walking height with many pools and an abundance of mud and flood detritus that imparted an acrid aroma to the cave that made the nostrils twitch. A lowering of the roof soon forced the cavers into a crawl leading directly onto a short but awkward drop overcome with a hand line. Increasing passage size then allowed easy progress to a canal. This became almost a duck where the roof lowered, but beyond this a joint-controlled rift cut through viciously sharp rock. It terminated at a narrowing with a noticeable draught; an encouraging echo emerged from beyond the restriction.

Chipping at the calcite eventually produced a way through to an easy 22-metre pitch. This was more of a series of calcite flows descending like a spiral staircase. On the bottom "step" the passage narrowed with an embryo trench incised in the floor. Pools prevailed and a number of short drops followed to an attractive column formation. As Jim crawled in to the continuation, the wind whipped through a low wet hole, chilling him as he pushed onwards for another unpleasant 50 metres. Although the draught indicated something large beyond, he could find no way around a fallen block that barred entry to whatever caverns lay ahead. In some 330 metres of cave, they had reached a final depth of 66 metres. Fortunately the canine occupant of the cave had not been in residence during their explorations and the villagers were able to recount the tale of the whitemen who entered the den of the devil dog and lived to tell about it!

Skull box on the outskirts of a village in the Mendi area of the Southern Highlands.

The final week of the first Lelet expedition was spent exploring the higher regions of the plateau to the northeast of the inhabited areas. This was the region with the greatest prospects for deep caves. Although a further 18 holes were located none exceeded the depth of Lowatkus-meri. After four pitches of 20, 33, 18 and 7 metres, this cave was lost in a rock fall at a final depth of 102 metres. The expedition was by then almost at an end.

Within two days everyone had pulled back to the idyllic palm-fringed strands of the New Ireland coastline. In spite of the lack of major finds above, the Dalum River efflux offered the possibility of tracing a major system upstream. At the time of this expedition around ten cumecs of very cold water were emerging from it, but lack of time prevented all but a brief look at just one of many resurgences. In a canyon passage a metre wide and three times as high, a sluggish canal was still going when the explorers abandoned it after around 50 metres.

The expedition came to an end in another coastal cave that was said to be used by a local sorcerer for the making of rain. Its large entrance was located on a hillside overlooking the village of Konogusgus and had previously been noted by Kevan Wilde. It was only 60 metres long, forming a single passage with two chambers. In the first of these, daylight penetrated down an aven, beyond which was the rainmaker's enclosure fashioned of timber and palm fronds. A coffin shaped receptacle built from stone contained a human skull, while nearby lay a clamshell holding a nest of human leg bones. A fireplace, wooden seats and hand stencils on the walls completed the subterranean cult site.

At the far end of the chamber a short crawl linked through to a second and larger cavern. Here the cavers stood around as shafts of light beamed in through yet another skylight, strangely reminiscent of the transporter room of the Starship Enterprise. The scene was somehow symbolic of a new and exciting era of discovery that was about to dawn in Papua New Guinea. Cavers would boldly go where none had gone before.

View across the Asaro Valley toward Mt. Michael, Eastern Highlands.

Haus Tamburan (spirit house) and its keepers in the upper Tifalmin Valley. It was through this remote valley that British cavers trekked in 1975 on route for the Finim Tel and beyond.

Urs Widmer

Urs Widmer

Sing Sing near Mt. Hagen.

Howard Beck

Before and after: Eliptomin porters building the advance camp on the Finim Tel Plateau in readiness for the 1975 British expedition, the first expedition to benefit from the luxury of a purpose-built camp.

NG '75

Urs Widmer

76

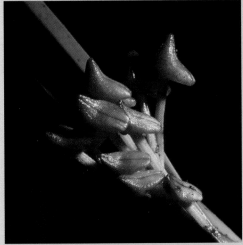

Above: Winged-like orchid, one of over 3,000 species endemic to Papua New Guinea.

Page 76 and 77: Exotic and diverse flowers lie hidden in the Papuan forests.

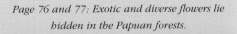

Jungle moss illuminated by a beam of sunlight.

*Marsupial possum (cus-cus in Pidgin) are com-
monplace nocturnal residents of the cloud forests.*

*Wreathed hornbill common to Papua New Guinea
and parts of Indonesia.*

Cave dwelling swift, Mt. Kaijende region.

Moth stuck to wet paint in Porgera. Wingspan 20 cm.

Dave Bunnell

A Cassowary Bird.

Chapter Three

CAVERNS OF THE CASSOWARY GODDESS

The British New Guinea expedition of 1975 was billed with typical British flair as the "Greatest Caving Adventure of All Time," the largest to leave England, or indeed anywhere else for that matter. It was to be the forerunner of a whole series of ambitious, large-scale expeditions to Papua New Guinea. The theatre of activity was an area comprising some 2,500 square kilometres of virtually trackless mountain forest. In the chosen region, limestone ranged in altitude from 600 to almost 4,000 metres above sea level. Deluged by a mean annual rainfall of up to 10,000 mm, water was expected to be problematic in the extensive caves the expedition hoped to find.

Two years of preparation and dreams became reality on Thursday, July 24, when charter flight P2-MAT was airborne, carrying the British team from the Highlands town of Mount Hagen. This was the final leg of the long journey from Britain to Telefomin, administrative centre of the West Sepik Province. After a breathtaking flight lasting one hour, the pilot began circling. Spotting something he alone recognised, and to the astonishment of all aboard the ageing Dakota, he began a white-knuckle descent, sending his craft into a spiralling dive through a hole in the near hundred percent cloud cover.

The craft levelled out above a vast grassy plain dotted with tiny villages amid patchwork-like gardens. Telefomin soon appeared beneath their wingtips; a very small landing strip surrounded by a cluster of tin-roofed houses glistened in the morning sun like a scattered herd of shiny armadillos. Touching down in a cloud of dust, they taxied to a halt opposite the District Office. There to meet them was an overjoyed Howard Beck, Keith Winchcombe, a gaggle of agitated locals, some dogs and the odd pig.

It was a welcome surprise to learn that the administration had provided a house for use as a base, together with an additional building that doubled as a store/photographic lab. Over the next few days, 14 tonnes of freight came in via the DC3 charter, whenever weather conditions allowed. It was the start of a frenetic week of resorting supplies into carrier loads and identifying objectives for the first month in the field.

Whilst logistics were attended to, some people took time off to explore the immediate vicinity. The station sat upon deep alluvial deposits that apparently were the bed of a former lake. This having drained away, the aggressive headwaters of the Sepik River had since carved a route down through the deposits. The result, 12 kilometres west of Telefomin, was a spectacular 300-metre deep gorge separating the Telefomin terrace from the "hanging" valley of the Ilam River.

Within a half-hour walk north from the airstrip a small group of caves sat at the headwaters of the Falfal Creek. The largest of these was Bem Tem, a fossil system recorded in 1965 as Great Cave. Although it contained only 150 metres of largish passage, it linked three entrances and possessed some handsome stalagmites; more important, it was home to some quite unexpected residents.

A view of the Tifalmin Valley towards Mt. Aiyang (peak), with the Bahrman Range to the left.
The route to the Finim Tel advance camp was over this range.

Petar Beron, a Bulgarian attached to the University of Sophia, had joined the British team as a biologist. He soon amazed everyone with his ability to identify at a glance many of the creatures he and another biologist, Phil Chapman, collected. In Bem Tem, the two spent many hours poring over the stinking guano floors. While engaged in this noisome task, they made the first of many startling discoveries. In the microcosm created by small drip pools, they spotted a tiny wormlike creature. This was identified as a polychaete, a marine relic whose nearest surviving surface relatives were recorded at only three other sites, two of them in Europe. They were to make this and many other discoveries over the coming months that pointed to drastic physiological changes in the recent past.

Petar was an avid collector, but his enthusiasm often overshadowed any sense of time or respect for self-preservation. Thoroughly engrossed with the world in miniature, he was sometimes caught out by dusk and forced to spend unprotected nights alone in the bush. A potentially serious incident involving Petar occurred in Ok Kitkil Cave, where he was flushed out by a flood pulse while enjoying an evening bug hunting trip. This close encounter served as a graphic warning of the speed with which caves respond to heavy tropical rainfall.

After much discussion, it was decided to field the entire team at the Finim Tel advance base begun by Kevan and Howard (see fig. 4). This would allow the team time to acclimate while improving its bushcraft skills. Later dividing into smaller groups, they could investigate more isolated regions where conditions were anticipated to be more demanding. A mission airstrip had recently been completed at Bufulmin, two days walk west of Telefomin, and they hoped to fly in supplies there and have them ferried by carrier line south across the Bahrman Range to camp.

An advance party prepared to move out to put the finishing touches to the base huts. Following a supply drop and once communications were established, the transfer of the whole team could then take place. One person was to remain in Telefomin on a rota basis to man the base radio and co-ordinate forward loading of essential supplies. Sid Perou, assisted by Frank Binney from Texas, intended to produce a film for British Television.

Kevan Wilde had been working with Carpentaria Exploration (CEC) at their Frieda River base and they readily loaned three AWA single-side-band radio sets. They had also agreed to have a morning standby on their daily schedules so in the event of an emergency, helicopter assistance could be summoned. The administration also loaned two TRA906 Squadcall sets. Hand held walkie-talkies were expected to be sufficient for line of sight communication and down deep shafts.

Kevan Wilde was an obvious first choice for the van since he personally knew many of the Eliptamin porters and was fluent in pidgin English. Moreover, he was the expedition's only caver with much New Guinea experience. Jack Sheldon and Mike Farnworth had worked well together during a venture to Venezuela two years before, so they completed the threesome.

Mike was a quiet type from England's Red Rose County and had an infectious sense of humour, almost the antithesis of Kevan, an ex-riot cop turned pacifist. Jack on the other hand was a Sandhurst man whose military background and sound approach to cave exploration made for a very competent team member in a tight spot, a fact he was to demonstrate on at least one occasion. He had a limited amount of leave from his unit, so he was anxious to be out at the sharp end.

As far as Tifalmin, the three-day trek followed in the footsteps of the Australian expedition ten years before. Darkness descends here with a suddenness unknown outside equatorial latitudes, and by 6:00 p.m. they were desperately trying to coax an acetylene lamp into life to cook a meal. It had been someone's bright idea to store his potato powder in the water bottles so it would remain dry. It was some time before it dawned on the group why the lamp would not light, and a further irate hour before the potato could be cleared from the lamp's water reservoir!

They were away early next day, wilting through the rolling grasslands of the upper valley. Swinging due south into the forest, they began the slow trek up and over the Bahrman Range. They ate lunch on a grassy knoll just below the summit, and by early afternoon they had crossed the head of the 3,000-metre pass and started down towards the plateau heading the Hindenburg Wall. Rain began falling with a vengeance and within minutes the trail was transformed into New Guinea's answer to the Cresta Run. Dignity was cast aside as they careered down through the steep forest.

After 300 metres, the trail levelled out through dense bamboo thickets where the cavers sank to above their knees in a fetid ooze. Despite their Venezuelan experiences, both Jack and Mike found the going tough; Mike, however, was suffering the consequences of three idle months escorting expedition supplies by sea. By late afternoon Kevan and Jack were out in front, the porters bringing up the rear beneath 38-kilo loads. At last they broke clear of the cheerless swamp glades and in the gathering shadows of dusk picked their way across the clearing through tussock grass and pitcher plants to the bothy. They were instantly set upon by clouds of beesties with a voracious appetite. Jack's heart sank as he made an entry in his diary. "What have I let myself in for?" he wondered. With nightfall upon them they bivouacked in the unfinished huts, thankful for simple mercies, a meal, and the trail's end.

Morning dawned bright and warm for the altitude; some four kilometres to the north, clouds were already clinging to the lofty summit of Mt. Aiyang. The clearing they were in sloped down to the west and was about the size of a football field, with isolated trees towering above the marshy scrub. The porters were instructed to fell these to provide a clear, low-level run for the expected air drop. A roof in durable yellow polythene and a kitchen area completed the base for occupation. The provision of an advance base complete with showers was an unexpected luxury. This was a buffer between the imagined horrors of bush life and memories of civilisation, and offered a welcome escape from the ubiquitous New Guinea mud. Unlike the Australians in the Mullers two years earlier, the British had the benefit of a "five star" accommodation.

Early next day, Mike awoke to the sound of heavy rain beating a tattoo on the roof of the dormitory. It was clear the plane would not be arriving, but when it failed to show up the next day as well, an air of despondency came over everyone. Within a few days, more of the team started to arrive and rations became a matter for growing concern. The air drop was cancelled indefinitely, but thankfully supplies started filtering through by carrier line.

Despite the attractions of a salubrious camp life, people were impatient to start exploring the caves they had travelled half way around the world to discover. With the base rapidly becoming crowded Kevan and Jack considered the possibility of investigating Mt. Fugulil, the huge plinth of limestone that towered some 750 metres above the base. Finding a route to the summit would be no easy matter due to its steepness and the density of the vegetation. Nevertheless, the lure of finding a cave system with a potential depth of over 2,000 metres to the base of the Hindenburg Wall was far too great simply to ignore on account of difficult terrain. And obvious karst features were visible on the air photographs.

They expected that once clear of the forest, progress would become easier. However, as they climbed higher, the ground ahead simply grew worse as the cloud forest gave way to an unyielding sub-alpine like shrubbery whose tenacity defied even the keenest of blades. After three days of relentless thrashing, one route eventually succumbed after finesse gave way to combined tactics. It was rather amusing to see Captain Jack, complete with immaculately waxed moustache, striving to maintain balance upon Mike's shoulders while, with one arm hooked around a branch, he hacked desperately with his bush knife at a veritable cornice of matted vegetation.

Seen from the summit, the Finim base shrunk to two insignificant yellow dots more or less at the centre of a vast saucer-like depression 80 square kilometres in extent. This was bound to the north by the Bahrman Range, terminating in the 3,000-metre summit of Mt. Aiyang, while the Hindenburg Wall represented the southern cutoff point, the first of many tiers of broken limestone ranges extending down into the Papuan lowlands.

Provisioning the Fugulil camp was difficult enough, but drinking water also became critical after a dry period. It was somehow ironic having to resort to wringing water out of the moss in one of the wettest places on earth. Porters were even called upon to backpack precious supplies in 50 litre plastic barrels from the Ok Tumak, almost 1,000 metres below! Despite these obvious drawbacks and nightly temperatures down to seven degrees Celsius, Kevan, Mike, Jack and Dick Willis endured a week-long camp. Significant cave development remained beyond their grasp and compensations were few. Each evening the western peaks were set ablaze by a crimson and golden spectacle, as the dying embers of a Capricorn day were slowly quenched by gathering dusk.

While the Fugulil group battled against the odds at 3,000 metres, those down below fared little better as they systematically checked out the features noted on the reconnaissance. The first site chosen for investigation was the deep shaft of La Buum Tem (see fig. 5). Tailok, one of the Tifalmin carriers, gave a nail biting demonstration of how, when he was a child, the village elders hunted flying fox by descending the hole using vines. While he flirted with his gods, the cavers used their preferred technology to descend the pit 72 metres to a sloping floor. But for the constant barrage of mud that assailed those below, the descent held no surprises. Vegetated boulders cascaded down into a chamber at a depth of 120 metres where daylight filtered down from a skylight. A small stream spattered from somewhere above, but this simply frittered away into a choke.

Back at camp, others turned their attention to the switchback trail originally cut due south from the base. This crossed the grain of the land and several creeks draining the western flank of Fugulil. They were believed to feed the Ok Finim, which flowed along the western edge of the camp clearing. Howard and Kevan had looked at the obvious feature of Kumun Tem. Here a river – erroneously thought once again to be the Ok Finim – emerged from a large sump, swirled across the base of the doline and disappeared among muddy boulders overhung by a beetling wall. The latter continued to a flood sink where a tide mark 20 metres overhead reflected the severe and total flooding to which any cave would be subjected.

To one side of the main sink, a draught emerged from a tube blocked by logs. Andy Eavis and Dave "Pooh" Yeandle dug here to enter a maze of rifts from which rose an ominous rumbling. Halted by a lack of tackle, they vacated the cave, confident that a major river system waited below. Returning later with tackle and accompanied by Mike, they descended several pitches, but these simply merged into a shattered chamber with a scummy sump.

They then targeted the twin dolines. From altitude, these appeared like deep fang marks piercing the forest canopy almost two kilometres short of the Hindenburg Wall. From a simple bush camp erected nearby, Andy and Pooh descended the most northerly of the two. Girtoil was an inspiring, near circular hole 66 metres across with exposed limestone on all except the northern side. A fault appeared to intersect the hole on a 330 degree bearing.

Once on the rope it was impossible to see the bottom due to the lush growths that included trees up to 30 metres high. The descent was initially confined to a gully down the northwest side and hung just clear of the wall for 75 metres. At this depth the explorers found their rope continuing down an ovoid shaft and a pendulum manoeuvre was necessary to reach and explore the half hectare comprising the doline floor. The secondary shaft began as a four metre wide pitch, increasing to 12 metres as it descended to a boulder pile below. A cool breeze whistled tantalisingly from between blocks against the wall. Though this suggested the presence of a large cave, they could not locate a way down.

The second doline was nearby and similar in size to Girtoil, with mostly overhanging walls that produced a marvellous echo. A stout tree again served as a belay point. John "Donny" Donovan let himself over the edge and began the 120 metre descent, cautiously wielding a machete to ease his passage through the tangled vegetation of the first few metres. An exhilarating abseil then hung a long way from the wall. Allan Goulbourne joined him on a high tallus cone beneath an overhang.

While exploring this subterranean botanic garden, they found to their discomfort that the vegetation included a variety of stinging tree. A brush with this or the equally potent selat plant provoked reactions varying from swollen lymph glands to acute nausea and stiffness of the muscles. Scrambling over the rubble slope separating the main doline of The Sting from the south wall, the cavers descended a gully. Once again the draughting gaps below were much too narrow to allow access to the cave they believed must exist beneath. The explorers returned to camp impressed yet disappointed.

During the following week they meticulously surveyed several other small caves and shafts in the vicinity. Unfortunately, everything either closed down or choked prematurely with little or no horizontal development. After only two weeks in the field, some were already voicing doubts about the potential of the area; apart from the rock-walled pits, they argued that larger caves existed back in Britain.

Despite the lack of discoveries, they appreciated the primordial beauty of their surroundings. At that altitude, the forest canopy was reduced to less than 30 metres with trees of small to medium girth. These included evergreen hardwoods and several species of cycads, or tree ferns, a sort of living fossil from the Carboniferous Era. Stilt-rooted pandans strode many-legged among giant gingers and a frustrating preponderance of climbing bamboo, lianas and vines.

Due to the lack of progress aggravated by illness, the morale of the expedition was failing fast. More people were developing tropical ulcers and other debilitating complaints. Jon Buchan, the doctor, found his mornings punctuated by ever-growing queues for treatment. This often included a liberal application of Dr. Jon's good sense of humour: it was imperative that inertia be maintained, so those that were fit enough could continue track cutting in search of the major caves that the team was still optimistic about finding.

Dawn invariably arrived with the bush steaming beneath the gathering heat of day. This was the result of an interface mist formed when the cold night air, trapped in the basin-like region of the plateau, mixed with the warmer air rising and spilling over the Hindenburg Wall from the Papuan lowlands. Pitcher plants competed with spiders for the day's meals on wings. Across the clearing, webs glistening with dewdrops shone like strings of tiny pearls in a fairy tale jewellery shop. One morning after surgery, Jon decided to trace the Ok Finim to its sink, but after a whole day thrashing through the forest undergrowth, he gave up. Even where the scrub was sparse, movement was impaired by the terrain and cave development proved evasive. The area was riddled with dolines, deep grykes and a fearfully difficult tower karst liberally endowed with the dreadful bamboo. Holes only came to light when virtually stumbled into.

By August 16, there had been little improvement. Dave and Pooh returned to Ok Kumun Tem to push a few grotty leads with Tony White, while Jon remained in camp to treat the sick and wounded. He suggested one group of "invalids" accompany him for a convalescent stroll. In conversation with a Wokkamin hunter the day before, Howard had learnt of a cave three kilometres to the southwest. Jon suggested they have a look.

For three hours Numeia guided Allan Goulbourne, Steve "Crabby" Crabtree and Dr. Jon along barely visible hunting pads, halting eventually on the rim of an enormous basin 500 metres long, half as wide, and at least 100 metres deep. A soaring wall of limestone formed the far side in

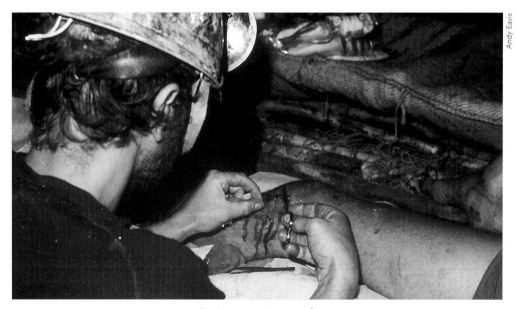

Dr. Jon sews up a wound.

In Selminum Tem an invalid team comprising Steve Crabtree, Jon Buchan and Alan Goulbourne were lured on by the black void of Warp Drive.

which a large cave mouth could be glimpsed through the trees. Picking their way slowly down the east side, they wandered through an enchanted world of giant arum lilies and stinging nettles, their footfalls deadened by the deep leaf mould of the doline floor.

They took lunch in the green twilight at the foot of the cliff. The hunter indicated a ledge above them leading to Selminum Tem, the flying fox cave. It was peaceful sitting there almost a week removed from civilisation. The air was humid and limp, only disturbed by some birdcall or the plaintive peep, peeping of secretive skinks. Or was it? Crabby noticed the shrubs and plants nearby were gyrating mysteriously. Examining the base of the wall, a wide opening beckoned from the depths and a chill wind blowing from within fanned their faces in a most alluring manner.

With aches and pains forgotten, their thoughts quickly turned to exploration. Numeia implored them to ignore the blowing hole in favour of "his" cave. With mounting impatience, they climbed up a gully a short way to reach the ledge, here dominated by a solitary stinging tree. Behind this a 50-metre wide passage floored with dried mud and boulders ran back into the cliff. Within a short distance it terminated at a boulder choke; however, not far from the entrance and again near the end, they found two curious man-made holes in the floor resembling primitive storage pits. When questioned their guide claimed no knowledge of their origin or purpose.

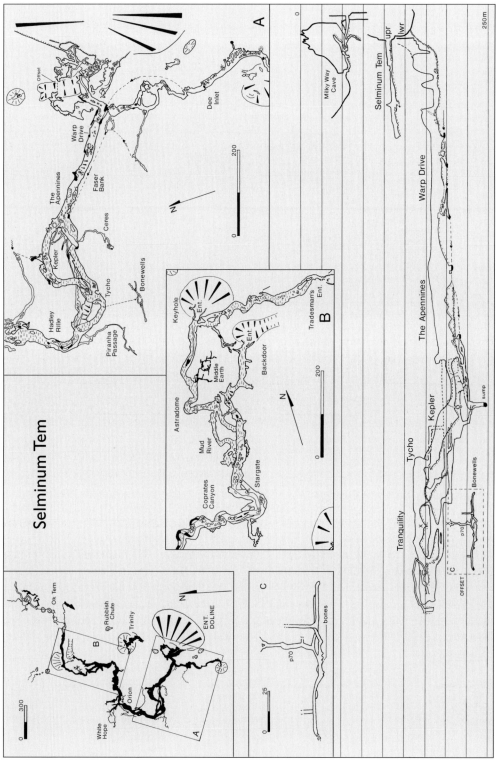

Fig. 13) Selminum Tem

With the upper cave concluded, the cavers virtually fell over themselves scrambling back down to the inviting entrance below. Numeia's protests faded behind as they ducked under the wall and found themselves trundling down a steep boulder slope. The roof shot out of sight and walls drifted apart whilst they picked a route between dusty boulders the size of houses. The way forward then levelled out along a dried mud floor to a sweeping bend with a major inlet cascading in from the left. It was a caver's dream come true. Ahead of them, Warp Drive bored into the mountain as a 50-metre diameter tunnel (see fig. 13).

This they traced without deviation for half a kilometre, while down to the right the stream played cat and mouse among boulders by the wall. The cave was still increasing in size as they tramped over the undulating sand dunes of The Appennines. With base at least three hours away, and given their "invalid" status, the perspiring explorers called it a day. With the huge passage disappearing into a guess, they returned to Finim Tel to convey the good tidings.

Having found little reward at Ok Kumun Tem, Dave, Pooh and Tony returned later in the day to find a base camp alive with a carnival atmosphere. The reason for the sudden transformation soon became clear when the jubilant threesome recounted yet again their extraordinary adventures.

The following day Allan and Steve had made a remarkable recovery and together with Andy, Tony, Pooh and Donny, they returned to Selminum Tem. The sandy wastes of The Appennines receded into dim shadows as the explorers wandered in awe along a spacious fossil gallery for a further 800 metres. At one place a shower bath lived up to its name as they negotiated a climb. An astronomy and space theme held favour, so the new caverns were christened Tycho, Hadley Rille, Newton and Orion. The latter ended abruptly where Coprates Canyon cut across the trunk route as an uncommonly deep vadose trench. It was impossible to climb into this without a rope, so after an amazing four hour trip they were forced yet again to return to the surface.

Since Jon felt he lacked the experience to join in the push at Selminum Tem, he accompanied Dave Brook in the continuing quest for the elusive Ok Finim sink. After bush whacking for almost two kilometres along its banks, they at last found the Finim vanishing into a sinkhole clogged with mud and logs. An overflow channel continued beyond and to the left of the active sink, where flood debris obscured a wide but low opening beneath a crumbling cliff. They removed tree trunks to allow progress as far as a short drop. Beyond this a joint-controlled maze coalesced into an obvious downstream rift with walls stained brown by vegetated floodwaters. Exploration ended for the day at a climb-down to a deep pool.

The next morning Dave and Jon explored Finim Tem with Chas Yonge and Chris Pugsley, surveying nearly a kilometre of flood prone cave in one trip. From the pool that had stopped them the previous day, a rift led through a breakdown area to an overhanging drop into deep water. This proved especially entertaining on the return. The downstream lowered to a crawl where minimal airspace forced the caver into a more intimate involvement with the water. Wallowing on, they soon arrived at another duck via a gently dipping canyon and pools. Ahead, the passage divided at an inlet entering from the west, while downstream continued to the final miserable sump.

Back at Selminum Tem, explorations continued apace, with trips of 12 and 14 hours becoming the rule. Progressing two kilometres into the cave Tony, Crabby and Pooh saw a boulder slope rising ahead of them. Filtered by a mantle of jungle, a shaft of soft green light angled downward from the Keyhole exit into the boulder floored chamber in which they stood. Completing that unreal tableau, cave swiftlets wheeled about, emitting staccato clicking sounds that somehow allowed them to navigate the perpetual night of the cave.

Peter Gray gazes down the magnificent phreatic borehole of Warp Drive.

The complexity of the system elsewhere revealed itself in the Rille Series and the Great Nebula Series, two confusing three-dimensional labyrinths beneath the main tunnel that were well watered by a medley of misfit streams. Many of these intricate passages were lavishly endowed with calcite concretions such as the White Dwarves, or dived down deep shafts to converge on the Sump Series.

After the eventful activities of the first few days, it was clear that a cave of major significance had been entered and that more manpower would be needed to realise its full potential. The Fugulil and Girtoil groups were recalled and a temporary camp established on a ledge outside the entrance to the upper cave. This formed an ideal site with plenty of sleeping space, protected from the evening rains by a convenient overhang.

As the cave continued to grow, more entrances were discovered. The party that first reached The Keyhole had left one of many side passages unexplored, so on August 23, Dick, Mike and Howard descended to investigate. After four hours picking their way through the trunk route, they were at last at the start of the lead, the great unknown lay before them. It was strange in a way, following that long silenced adit, like treading a spellbound path into another time, another dimension. Unusual calcite formations loomed phantomlike out of the gloom. Here and there a sickly green hue streamed down small avens, while lianas hung from fissures, forming a flimsy link between two worlds apart. The whole effect had a Tolkein fantasy atmosphere about it.

A caver pauses to replenish the water in his acetylene lamp during a lengthy trip in Selminum Tem.

All too soon, their helmets scraping on a lowering roof broke the charm and shortly they were blinking in a jungle-filled depression at the Tradesman's Entrance. Other holes nearby dived back into the netherworld. The natural reaction was to shout in case someone was within earshot, but like Frodo in the Old Forest their cries were strangled to a mere whisper. They had no option but to return whence they came.

THE WRATH OF AFEK

As the month end approached, the length of Selminum Tem increased to eight kilometres. The imbricate maze beneath the trunk route continued to confound with repeated multi-junctions where many streams had, under the influence of gravity, charted their devious courses beneath the plateau. Most plummeted into flooded shafts still a long way above the level of the resurgence below the Hindenburg Wall. In some places, the trunk route divided into two distinct levels. From The Appennines a large dusty oxbow named the Space Walk, crossed over Ceres and the Sump Series, and led, via Tycho and Tranquillity, back to the main trunk route at Hadley Rille.

Andy Eavis

After a fall that left expedition geologist Steve Crabtree with a suspected skull fracture, a seven-hour stretcher haul saw him successfully evacuated to the cave entrance.

Andy Eavis

Tony White

Jack Sheldon tends to Steve Crabtree on a ledge outside the cave.
Right: The magnificent vadose stream canyon of Ok Tem was discovered by the British team in 1975. These flood-prone passages led them past frequent log jams to a sump beneath the Finim Plateau.

Where Tranquillity turned north at a wide bend, an obscure pit in the floor tempted Paul Everett and Mike into new mysterious depths. The Black Hole was 21 metres deep and entered an intricate series of phreatic tubes. Like all outlets from the main cave, this too ended in a perched sump, but while mapping Paul crawled through into a narrow connecting passage and noticed something strange.

He called out for Mike to follow and indicated an alcove where a number of vertebrae and other bones protruded from the walls and roof. A rib was carefully removed and taken out for study. Back at camp, Jon carried out a "post-mortem" and the Geological Survey of PNG was advised that the fossil of a marine mammal had been unearthed.

Wednesday dawned with the promise of further revelations. Several groups entered the cave, some to survey, others continuing with exploration. There was still hope that something, somewhere beneath the main passage, would eventually penetrate the flooded zone and go deep. With these thoughts Jack and Steve headed for some undescended pitches beneath the floor of the Newton cavern. Steve was leading as they neared their objective. In some places the main passage was a devious traverse over, through or around a chaos of fallen blocks. He was chatting away when suddenly his foot slipped. The next Jack knew, Steve had disappeared from view, carried off balance by his backpack. For a moment time seemed to stand still, then there was a sickening thud and...an ominous silence.

Removing his pack, Jack made his way gingerly down to where Steve lay six metres below. He had landed face down and was wedged at an awkward angle in a crevice with a broken rock flake on top of him. At first Jack thought the worst, then to his relief Steve let out the feeblest groan. Exploring carefully in case of spinal damage, he first examined his companion's back before turning him over and checking his breathing passages.

His face was a mask of blood from a livid gash to his left forehead. His lamp was crushed and it was clear that Steve's helmet had saved his life. Miraculously, there appeared to be no other injuries, but Jack knew he must act fast. A survey team was in the cave, and not too far away, he hoped. Pulling the wound together, he bound Steve's head and left him in the coma position before going to raise the alarm. Within minutes he bumped into Tony, Pete and Chas. Tony made off in haste to locate Jon while the others returned to do what they could to make Steve comfortable. Jack then carried word of the accident out to Kevan on the surface, who immediately despatched a carrier back to Finim base to fetch the Paraguard stretcher.

Paul Everett, Dave Brook and Dr. Jon Buchan were surveying in the vicinity of the Backdoor entrance a further kilometre into the system. They had just enjoyed a late lunch, when about 3:30 p.m. the wiry Welshman arrived out of breath with a worried expression. Between gasps he managed to relay what had happened. The survey was abandoned and they left immediately for the accident site.

When Jon arrived the patient was rousable but lapsed periodically into unconsciousness. The stretcher was retrieved in record time and after an efficient seven-hour carry, Steve was being hospitalised on the ledge outside the cave. A ring of carbide lamps held by anxious team mates served as theatre lights under which Jon cleaned, sutured, and dressed the wound.

A brief entry for the day in the radio log at Telefomin read simply, "Crabby's hurt his head." At that stage those back at base were unaware just how serious a fall Steve had taken. They suspected his skull of being fractured and for five days he remained in a semiconscious state. Over this period his condition was monitored continuously. It was a time to act. In the event that Steve's condition might deteriorate a helipad was cut from the forest close to the rim of the doline. Over the radio, CEC were alerted and put on standby in case a helicopter evacuation became necessary.

After the fall the carriers were visibly nervous and withdrawn. When asked what was troubling them they replied that the fury of the *masalai* had been incurred. They were in no doubt that the accident was the result of violating the sanctity of the lower cave. Moreover, the ground on which they had been told to construct the helipad was also sacred. With hunted expressions they explained that one of them was certain to be next. They wanted to leave.

When questioned about the importance of the cave they refused at first to discuss the matter. It was only two days later when another man came forward – the keeper of a *haus tamburan* (spirit house) in the Wokkamin territory below the Wall – that the cultural significance of Selminum Tem came to light. He related how his tribe shared a common genesis with all the Min people of the surrounding mountains. Central to this creation myth was Afek, a mother goddess figure who, when wished to be seen, manifested as a cassowary.

According to the legend, when the lake where Telefomin stands today drained away down the Sepik Gorge it left behind a scene of utter desolation. Afek, they say, settled in the valley after coming from the east with her brother, whom she later killed with sorcery. Taking an underground route he departed for Bagelam, the land of the dead. Afek set off in pursuit, creating features of the landscape, tribes and spirit houses as she went. After crossing the mountains from Tifalmin she struck the ground, opening up the Selminum doline; she slept the night in the upper cave and designated it for the use of hunters. The next morning, she made the lower cave and, reserving it for her own use, continued her subterranean journey. Upon emerging from the base of the Hindenburg Wall, she closed the exit. The Nearby Kaakil resurgence was thus declared *tambu*, but a cave above was set apart for hunting flying fox.

During the remaining months of the expedition the amazing story of Afek became a constantly recurring theme, given to explain the existence of other cave systems, resurgences and major topographical features throughout the Hindenburg and Victor Emanuel Mountains.

At the outset Crabby's accident had resulted in a loss of inertia, but this soon passed. Many of the carriers came from outside the immediate area and, so cave exploration could resume without further disruption. The spiritual gravity of Selminum Tem became even more intriguing during a photographic expedition with the discovery, some 200 metres into the system, of the remains of *bom-boms* as well as a crude engraving of a bird, perhaps a cassowary.

Though the geology of the Finim Tel precluded any chances of great depth, the surveyed length of Selminum Tem, at 14 kilometres, was fast approaching that of Exit Cave in Tasmania, at the time the longest system in the southern hemisphere. With a record to be broken, everyone sought the extra metres with renewed impetus.

While prospecting west along an old *kiap* trail, John Donovan and Aiyangim chanced upon the sink of the Kaakil River. John returned with Allan Goulbourne and they explored Union Cave and an intriguing lateral complex that eventually converged upon a superb 33-metre deep river canyon. Ok Tem consisted of a smooth waterworn streamway sporting cascades and plunge pools leading after 450 metres to a sump the size of a municipal swimming pool. Huge tree trunks jammed at some of the bends provided the explorers with another reminder of the awesome power of the river when in spate.

Efforts to link all the entrances of Selminum Tem by surface traverse resulted in the discovery of a trio of minor caves and numerous open shafts. Armed with a 100-metre rope, Jack returned to the shafts with Dick and Allan. The pits mostly proved short; however, when Jack's turn came "his" hole appeared a little out of the ordinary. Jack recounted how they cast an exploratory rock into the pothole: "No sooner had the echoes faded away than Dick and Allan accused me of saving the best one for myself." Jack kitted up while Allan fastened the rope to a handy tree. The line was cast over the brink and greedily swallowed by the depths. Jack eased himself cautiously over the edge, fearful of the tangle no doubt waiting below. After 30 metres he halted and as his eyes grew accustomed to the dark, the shaft revealed its huge dimensions. "Surely this has to go," he thought as he strove to release the rope from a puzzle of rocks and branches.

He was suddenly aware that his stance was precarious, on a shifting "staircase" of rocks, mud and debris that had fallen from above. Even worse, as he despatched rubble into the void it became clear that the pitch was not vertical. The line of descent followed a chute, down which anything dislodged would be channelled with dire consequences.

Twenty minutes later he was still sending boulders the size of dining tables crashing into the unknown. When at last he was satisfied that his surroundings were reasonably stable he continued, stopping now and then only to clear loose flakes. Morbid thoughts flashed by of falling rocks, severed ropes and speed records for descents. Then he began to enjoy himself. He had been down the Rubbish Chute almost two hours when he reached minus 55 metres. Time for a smoke. There he was, oblivious to the others waiting above with growing impatience. Swinging comfortably in his harness with the odd rock hurtling by into the blackness below, he pulled out a battered briar and lit up! Drawing long and slowly on his pipe-weed, he peered through the gathering fug, contemplating the next section in anticipation. It looked nasty.

With pipe tucked safely away in his pocket he was on his way, the approaching floor vaguely visible in the dimming light. More stops for loose rocks. Then at almost 90 metres, he alighted beside a colossal boulder bearing the scars of his housekeeping. He was aghast. The block completely plugged the shaft like a pea in a pod: There was no way through. He tried several squeezes around the walls but the shaft repelled all his efforts. He felt about as choked as the scene before him.

Feeling somewhat cheated, he clipped his ascenders into the rope and, with a last futile glance about, as if expecting a way on to miraculously show itself, he set off towards the distant patch of daylight.

"How'd it go, Jack?"

"Ah, bloody thing choked."

While a small group remained at Selminum Tem to pursue length records, lightweight patrols to more remote regions became vogue. Paul Everett and Andy Eavis left on September 1st for a two-week trek to locate the sink of the Ok Migal and other rivers south of Mt. Fugulil. Soon afterwards Chas, Kevan and Chris Pugsley departed for the Ok Agim region. Both groups took porter support; Andy and Paul took the squad call radio. Paul and Andy had an epic patrol, during which a log bridge they were crossing fell on Andy, injuring his leg and resulting in a forced period of idleness lasting a week.

Having waited over three months for the chance to explore the inviting cave, at last Kevan found himself by the entrance to Agim Tem, balancing upon a slope made treacherous by a liberal coating of guano. The voices of flying foxes drifted riotously from the unknown depths. He rigged a first drop of 15 metres with a single length of rope. One after another, they each landed in a filthy pool, where the air was alive with flies and the stench of guano was almost unbearable.

The chamber resounded to the lazy *slap, slap, slap* of wings as the huge bats took to flight, disturbed by the intrusion of the cavers. According to local villagers these winged mammals represented the souls of the dead. Legend also related how a hunting party perished down the cave when an evil female spirit wearing a dog teeth necklace cut the vine down which they had

*Paul Everett looks on while Dave Yeandle attempts to free-dive a sump
in the Selminum Tem system.*

climbed to gain entry. Strangely enough, the cavers had noticed how carriers would never remain alone by the entrance.

Back in the depths, repulsive pink leeches waved at them expectantly, galvanised into motion by the heat from the cavers' bodies. Not wishing to loiter, all three shrank back from the walls, quickly rigging and descending a nine-metre drop into a well decorated chamber. A pleasant six-metre pitch then followed, dropping them into a deep green pool…*sploosh*, unclip, wade to the edge. They contemplated the cave ahead of them.

Dipping at 30 degrees, the passage continued with a rarely visible roof, and three further pitches following in rapid succession. Peering down the last of these, a seven metres drop, their lights were mirrored by the rippling surface of an ebony lake that swallowed their last rope. Having kept dry up to then, Chas cast aside his clothes and gallantly descended into the water to reconnoitre below. After a brisk 25-metre swim he gained the far shore at a boulder decorated with a formation resembling a poached egg. Hauling himself from the water and continuing, he came to the inevitable after a further 75 metres. Continuing its 30-degree plunge, the cave roof disappeared into a sump pool at a total depth of 167 metres, a gloomy terminus to a fine passage.

September 16 marked Independence Day for Papua New Guinea and corresponded roughly with the half way point of the British venture. With few exceptions everyone was gathered in Telefomin for the celebrations. While the Australian colours were struck and the PNG flag raised in its place, back at Finim base Dave, Pooh and Phil hoisted a tree trunk in symbolic parody.

An enticing hole in the Wall of Tranquillity had caught their eye. Phil and Pooh clambered up the makeshift maypole and entered Lumberjack Oxbow to explore the aggressive fissures of Piranha Passage.

Not wishing to appear idle, Dave wandered off west and discovered the Bitip River Cave, also entering a spectacular roof level above the Ok Tem canyon. He reached a continuation of this truncated tube by daringly crossing the river canyon on a tree trunk.

Meanwhile in Telefomin a crisis reared its ugly head. Frank Binney had dropped a bombshell by resigning as assistant cameraman. Even worse, Sid was desperately short on film sequences that featured the earlier stages of the expedition. Noel Plumley fortunately stepped in to fill the gap left by the capricious Texan. Following the welcome break for independence, Sid appealed for a return to Finim Tel for an "action replay." With much grumbling, most agreed to make the 40-kilometre return trek.

To prepare for the imminent influx of people an air drop of extra rations was arranged. The first of these went ahead without mishap. During the second air drop on September 28, Pooh gave a blow by literal blow account over the radio to those listening in Telefomin: the pilot, Peter Booth, and acting "bombardier" Tony White, were using the camp huts as targets. To the amusement of the listening audience, Pooh's "over and out" had an air of urgency about it as he dropped the microphone and made a frenzied bid for cover. It was a question of which way to run as several bundles rained about the camp and surrounding bush – some never to be seen again. This provided Sid with some dramatic footage.

Filming action then focused upon Ok Tem where the riverway provided some superb takes. Despite its magnificence, the cave demanded their respect since floods were an ever-present threat. Moreover, the rushing waters of the Kaakil had in some places honed rock flakes into many vicious fangs. In a moment of inattention one of these took a bite at Mike's left leg, resulting in further advanced needlework classes. After almost a week of filming, the long days were obviously taking their toll: in another incident, Dave Brook narrowly missed a fatal plunge into the chasm.

A break from acting allowed some diversions. Jon and Mike took the opportunity to blaze a trail into the area due south of Selminum Tem doline where they discovered the Milky Way Cave. This was a roomy fossilised remnant of an ancient cave, richly decorated with soft white amorphous calcite, sometimes referred to as "moonmilk." Though the passages were not extensive, one branch led them to a spectacular exit high in the cliff overlooking the Selminum doline.

Sid and his camera crew then moved to other locations on the plateau as Kevan, Peter Gray and Howard departed for Telefomin. They stayed a few days in the Tifalmin Valley en route. Whilst a number of deep shafts and relic tunnels were known to exist in the forested heights on either side of the Ilam River, it was the cultural aspect of those nearer the settlements that interested Kevan most. To the south of Bufulmin village, limestone cliffs stood out like hoary tombstones from the grassy spurs and foothills. These were riddled with rock art sites and the portals of burial caves watched over the villages like long dimmed eyes. At one site, a rift cave six metres up a north facing scarp, no less than six mummified bodies were found stacked on bamboo litters. The remains were perfectly preserved like human pincushions, bristling with arrows from some tribal conflict many years before.

For the remaining two months in the field, the aspiring British vertical cavers looked for their thrills to the east and south of Telefomin, in the Mt. Wamtakin massif and the fault-controlled valley respectively. The former was of unknown extent in so far as it had only been glimpsed briefly from a helicopter, whereas the fault feature at least had been partly explored by Kevan and Howard. Both held the promise of deep caves.

Chapter Four

EAST BY MOGONDABIP

At the start of October, Allan Goulbourne formed an advance party and with two native guides left for the Nong Valley, a day's walk to the south of Telefomin. A staging camp was to be established here on the supply route up over the range to the fault-controlled valley. Although the reconnaissance here had been cut short by Howard's injury, enough had been seen to suggest the region held great deep caving potential. This of course was the lure that brought the British here in the first place. The valley had to be a high priority.

When Allan arrived in the Nong he fell immediately under its spell, compelled to feel a part of the timeless, primordial surroundings. A fly was erected within a sluggish meander loop of the Ok Anaram, here flowing between high clay banks fringed with rain forest, regrowth and bamboo thickets. It was the epitome of the clear running tropical creek. Following it was easier than moving through the jungle and obviated the need to cut trails or forever consult the compass.

Wading downstream was occasionally impeded by fallen trees, barbed plants or log dams, but remained mostly a magical experience. Sunlight bouncing off the water surface shone like silver filigree on the underside of the overhanging foliage. Occasionally by some quirk of nature, the crystal waters would scatter a sunbeam into myriad prisms, only to be outshone by variegated butterflies – green, blue, yellow – that fluttered erratically by on "metallic" wings.

After almost a kilometre Allan's ephemeral state of mind was rudely jarred back to reality when the delightful brook took an impetuous leap into darkness. When he came upon Karibu Tem, he was already clad in his wetsuit and so it seemed only natural that he follow the watercourse underground. The chill air and gloom of the cave contrasted pleasantly with the world outside. Dropping with ease down two short cascades, Allan floated through a lake chamber of unknown depth.

As a moth drawn to a flame, he was lured towards a glimmering of daylight seen beneath a lowering roof at the far side. Drifting on the current, he emerged after 30 metres at the base of a rock-rimmed amphitheatre. He then followed rapids along the undercut northeast wall into a downstream portal, and within a few minutes returned once again to daylight at the narrow but lofty fissure of Nong Tem. On his left the water vanished into a log choke, but in front, just above stream level, an orifice invited the explorer to enter.

He rejoined the stream not far inside, and a deep rumbling ahead announced the presence of a pitch. A waterfall appeared at his feet, promising an exposed, spray-lashed descent. Allan balanced his experience against the risks of continuing alone, but there was no competition – exploration fever urged him forward. In the ceaseless agitation of a plunge pool, the stream dissipated in strength, its mighty voice swallowed in a high, vaulted cavern that absorbed the light from the explorer's cap lamp. Somehow missing the main way on, Allan squirmed down a log-obstructed outlet into the "Depths of Despair," and here was nearly entombed by a light failure. Luck was on his side, for after a desperate, barehanded dig through flood debris, he finally made his escape back to the light of day.

That night around the campfire, he scanned the aerial photographs, puzzling over a white mark one kilometre to the southeast. What might possibly account for such a feature he could only hazard a guess. It resembled a developing fault, perhaps bleach spilt on the print, but a nearby river seemed to appear from nowhere. The photograph run had been taken from an altitude of 10,000 metres, so whatever was responsible for the six millimetre wide mark, it had to be worth a look.

The next day the mystery resolved itself when five plumes of water sprang from the flanks of a small knoll. In flood, an estimated 23 cumecs of water emerged from Wek Ket as an amazing pressure dome one and a half metres high, the principal source of the Nong River. A dry streambed behind the efflux led uphill to a cave emitting a cool breeze. With his earlier solo experiences still fresh in Allan's mind, prudence this time proved the better part of valour and Ok Miben Tem was left until more of the team had arrived.

It wasn't long before Allan was transmitting glowing reports of river caves and huge resurgences back to base. Those in Telefomin listened in to the radio each evening as the next gripping instalment crackled through the static..."L. rge riv. r.. ve, i.. redible. Still going. Repeat s. ill g.. ng. Do y.. copy? Uniform Mike mobile over a. d o. t."

A week later Allan's Robinson Crusoe lifestyle was rudely interrupted by discordant shouts in the distance. Thin blue wisps of smoke from the campfire curled out from beneath the flysheet and diffused into the muggy air as Pete and Howard slithered the last downhill stretch and pulled into camp. Over a cool drink an animated discussion took place on the merits – or otherwise – of the caves so far found. That night they drew their plans.

The next morning all three returned to Karibu Tem but were astonished to find the downstream outlet barred by a sump, despite the lack of rain in the valley. Climbing into a dry continuation of the creek bed, they traced a vertical walled canyon forward to an inviting cave mouth. This led via a walking rift passage to the doline into which Allan had floated on a tide of euphoria a few days earlier. Perched together on the edge of a huge block of fretted limestone, they gasped in horror as two rivers surged from between boulders. A white-flecked river thundered into the downstream outlet. In so doing, the swollen tributary held back the Ok Anaram, sumping Karibu Tem. It could only be assumed that storms high up on the ranges, perhaps in the Fault Valley itself, were being drained to the Nong.

Returning to the unexplored cave behind the Wek Ket outflow, they explored an ascending passage along flowstone deposits to a slot opening to daylight. They passed a ledge above them where a human skeleton was calcited in situ. According to a local informant, these bones were the remains of a woman, a member of the Alkelmin clan killed by *sanguma*. The whole Nong region was mysteriously devoid of habitation, although extensive regrowth areas suggested this had not always been the case. Guarded tales hinted at a campaign of genocide by sorcerers in the recent past. If only walls could talk.

Leaving the ledge to its ghost, the cavers followed a boulder slope down to the left into a sandy-floored passage. The latter gradually widened past tiers of splendid gour pools and after 180 metres a small inlet entered the passage. This tinkled in from an immature fissure on the left, but something else caught the ear: the muffled but unmistakable sound of a large river, and not too far ahead. Adrenaline coursed through their veins, as with each compelling step the grumble became a growl.

They were practically running when they rounded the last corner and like children on a seaside outing, kicked bucket steps down a sand dune. In front of them, a river swirled along a

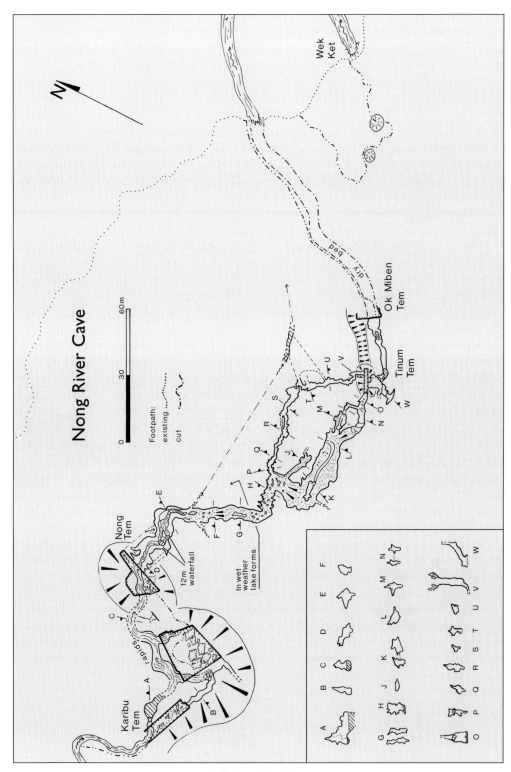

Nong River Cave

Footpath:
existing ....
cut —··—··—

0   30   60m

Wek
Ket

Ok Miben
Tem

dry bed

Tinum
Tem

Nong
Tem

12m
waterfall

In wet
weather
lake forms

Karibu
Tem

rapids

14) Nong River Cave

wide passage to disappear with an angry roar down a slot in the floor. Clinging to one wall, they traversed forward hopefully, but were brought to a halt on the shoreline of a lake occupying the continuing tunnel (see fig. 14). Further progress was out of the question. That evening on the 6:00 p.m. radio schedule, Telefomin received a request for a dinghy and life jackets.

When Kevan arrived with the inflatable a day or two later, they were beside themselves with anticipation. Ears were still being bent with tales of lakes and wild water, as four wet-suited cavers in bouyancy vests negotiated Miben Tem. The skull on the ledge grinned mockingly at them as they hauled the fully inflated boat through passages as silent as the grave. Silent? Kevan flashed doubting glances at the others. They strolled up a passage that earlier had been awash with whitewater; all that remained was a few languid pools. Everyone stared with disbelief at the lake – or rather they considered a silt slope where it had once been. What could possibly account for a vanishing lake?

They could now hear falling water ahead and somewhere below. Sinking ankle deep in the mud, everyone loped off down to the bottom of the lake, perhaps 30 metres, to be confronted by a high waterfall. Pete and Allan scaled this, then by leaping rashly from rock to rock they traced the riverway upstream to within a few metres of daylight. The current, however, prevented them making an exit. Had they been able to do so the true nature of the system would have been revealed. They were not aware until the cave was later surveyed that this and the hole that had very nearly entombed Allan were in fact one and the same, changed out of all recognition by dramatically fluctuating water levels.

Somewhere several kilometres east, Chas Yonge and Chris Pugsley were grappling with a mystery of their own. They had departed four days after Allan for a mountain called Wamtakin (3,658 m) 25 kilometres east of Telefomin station. After repeatedly crossing rivers and ridges washed by tropical cloudbursts they found themselves in confusing country, at the headwaters of the Ok Um to the northeast of the isolated village of Feramin. The weather was atrocious, such that when a vantage point was reached, visibility was nil due to the clammy clouds that swirled through the trees. Nothing seemed to match the aerial photographs and they had little hope of fixing their position. The few karst features they located merely produced minor, choked caves with little depth potential; it was all rather demoralising. When Andy caught them up several days later, they learnt that their guides had taken them to a mountain they knew as Wam Tigiin. This misunderstanding of pronunciation meant they were in effect 16 kilometres off course!

Supplies were by then low, so Chas and Chris retreated to Telefomin for provisions and caving tackle. Meanwhile Andy sorted out the *malentendu*. With one porter he continued the quest for lost mountains and deep caves. Struggling on with large loads, he and Tikiok eventually reached the real Wamtakin after several days back tracking.

When Chas and Chris rejoined Andy a week later cave exploration could at last begin. The eastern side of the Wamtakin massif formed a plateau at an altitude of 3,000 metres. Depth potential was considerable and believed to be in the region of 1,500 metres. They crossed the plateau by the main Feramin to Oksapmin trade route, and adjacent to this, explored a few interesting potholes to conclusion. These included the two stream caves, Ariyorba Tem (120 m) and Fungi Tem (140 m), the latter sporting a superb 67 metre entrance shaft.

Perhaps the most rewarding discovery was Owillfore Tem (see fig. 15). While Chas and Chris had been restocking back at base Andy was shown a stream where it plummeted into an impressive 30-metre wide pit. At the time, he could only gaze longingly at the plumes of spray billowing out from below. By consensus the patrol divided; Chas and Chris were to continue east into the Oksapmin polje while Andy returned to the unexplored shaft.

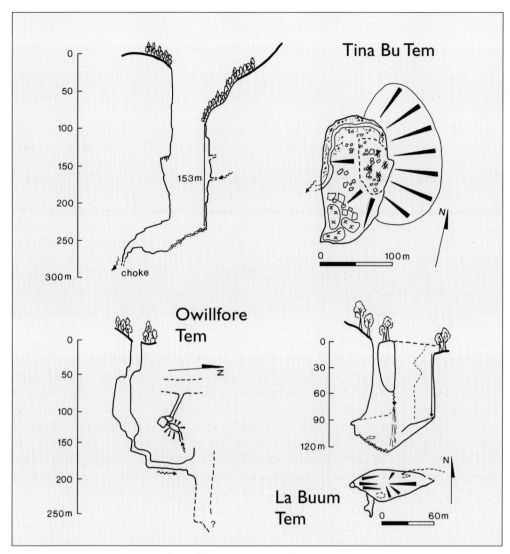

Fig. 15) Owillfore Tem, Tina Bu Tem, La Buum Tem

Andy rigged Owillfore Tem, which gave an atmospheric 45-metre free hang onto a boulder floor lashed by the stream. The main water lost itself among rocks here, leaving a trickle cascading down a series of steps. These formed the prelude to another fine shaft of almost 70 metres. Near the foot of this the pitch formed a gulley which the lone explorer shared with an uncomfortable volume of water. The cave then swung north with more flumes leading onto a boulder-strewn ledge. Two drops followed, 15 and 12 metres each, the last intruding into a high but narrowing rift. Expecting a sump at any moment, Andy was shocked to find himself teetering shortly on the edge of a resounding void. The stones he dropped into this fell free for three seconds before clattering off to greater depths. He could barely glimpse a waterfall at the far side; however, with tackle exhausted he had to leave the cave, still going and at a depth of more than 200 metres.

INTO THE DEN OF THE BLAK BOKIS

Back in the Nong, attention was diverted to the huge elongated slot located beside the track up to the Fault Valley. Earlier in the year Howard and Kevan had pondered this fearful void with mixed feelings. The Uun Tem Tigiin clearing angled steeply downwards into what was evidently a hole of considerable depth. When asked if it had a name, the Faiwolmin porters replied in their tribal tongue, *"Tina Bu Tem"*.

"Callim wanem?" asked Kevan again.

"Tee-nah-Buu-Tem," then in pidgin with much arm waving: *"Man inap long lukim tasol! I nogat kissim em."*

Roughly this translated to mean a hole to look at but not to go down, and it was easy to understand why (see fig. 15). Hunters in pursuit of their favourite delicacy, the *blak bokis* (flying fox), had by all accounts been repulsed in their attempts to climb down on lianas, for the hole, they said, was bottomless or even deeper. When the cavers announced that they were not content just to look but intended to go down, they were surveyed first with an air of disbelief. Then, smirking wryly, the porters announced that it was fine, so long as some *blak bokis* were brought out.

The four cavers were shadowed by a group of villagers all the way from the Nong camp to the great shaft. By the time the impressive entrance was reached the crowd had swelled to include women and children, several mangy hounds, uncle Tom Cobley and a cloud of over friendly sweat bees. Gear was checked and re-checked, and the rope secured to two stout boles. From the undergrowth many faces peered wide-eyed.

When it became clear that the cavers were serious about descending the shaft the expressions of muted awe quickly turned to those of visible distress. One of the Telefomin carriers, the fatherly Bimansep, assured them that the cavers were quite capable of going down the hole, rope in one hand while eating *kai-kai* (food) with the other. They hoped he was right. Pete had already vanished over the edge, a tackle bag containing 200 metres of 10-millimetre rope slung from his harness. Shafts were often heavily vegetated for the first few metres, and they had leant early on that it was preferable to abseil while paying out the line as required. This avoided hopeless tangles and improved the line of descent through the scrub. Pete was not gone many minutes when a shout came up that the bottom could not be seen for vapour clouds!

Continuing down the rope he could be heard exercising his vocal chords in his usual inimitable style. After about 15 minutes, a dull roaring suddenly overwhelmed a distorted rendition of Fiddler's Green drifting up from below. The sound grew from the threshold of perception until it resembled an express train arriving somewhere below. The cavers exchanged puzzled glances as the onlookers wailed even louder.

The source of the noise soon became apparent as the sky turned black with huge fruit bats winging out of the hole. Howard recalled his turn to descend: "I was the last down and couldn't help feeling vulnerable, glancing first at the slender rope, my lifeline back into the world I loved, then at the motley band of villagers. Everyone in New Guinea seemed to be armed with axes and knives; even the youngest children carry machetes around with them." He issued instructions to leave the rope well alone. *"Yupela! Dispela rop itambu tru. Yu nogat kissim em o mekim baut na baut samting. Yu savi?"* Thirty heads nodded in unison.

Threading the rope through his descender, he lowered himself nervously over the brink of the chasm with a final anxious glance first at the tether then at the many blades gleaming in the undergrowth. A shotgun was slung over one shoulder, on his back a rucksack contained camera, food and ammunition. After 60 metres or so he peered skywards. Bats were wheeling about like creatures from another age, daylight shining through their translucent wings to give "x-ray" pictures of their frail limbs. A thought suddenly occurred to him: if Sir Arthur Conan Doyle had been a member of the expedition, surely he would have found inspiration in the depths of New Guinea's underworld.

As he arrived at the only usable ledge after 100 metres, a number of freshwater crabs scuttled out of the way of his boots. The bottom was still a long way off, but between his legs he could see the others moving about like ants in what was clearly a large cavern. Leaving the crustaceans to their high rise home, he continued. The end of the rope slowly approached and at length he reached a floor of boulders and guano banks. A few splintered trees littered the bottom, having met their nemesis at the brink of Avernus. The floor heaved and pulsed with cockroaches and other creatures that thrived on the stinking guano.

The chamber was high and wide, with an inclined roof scooped with alcoves and pitted by pressure tubes. On its western side the roof angled downwards to meet the floor at the cave's lowest point, a miserable choked slot at a final depth of 275 metres. It was captivating to see water emerging from fissures around the sides of the great shaft, and in majestic streamers falling 75 metres to the floor. While Pete returned up the rope, Kevan downed some of the flying fox to present to the Faiwolmin host waiting above. The shot reverberated around the shaft with a noise like Vulcan forging thunderbolts for Jove.

With an ear-piercing screech, countless airborne flying foxes summoned their brethren still couched in their airy roosts; everywhere suddenly was a mass of flapping, gyrating, leathery wings. The air was so thick with the creatures that one cartridge brought about a dozen falling to the floor. They were hideous to look at, about the size of a rabbit but with a head resembling that of an Alsatian dog shrunk until its eyes bulged to the point of popping. With a wingspan of one and a half metres, these are the largest bats known to man. Those not killed outright flapped pathetically among the stones, snapping at the cavers' boots as they walked uncertainly among them.

It was Howard's turn to go up. After prussiking 80 metres he had further thoughts. "What if the bats seek revenge by attacking the rope?" He rebuked himself for being such an ass. "Watched too many Hitchcock movies" he hissed between laboured breaths, and with increased resolve he continued the climb...legs bend, stand up and reach. There was a loud click as he passed the ledge and his heart skipped a beat. It was just a krab – carabiner that is – repositioning itself where it clipped into his chest jammer... Sit, legs bend and stand...

Soon the vegetated top appeared and a few more metres later he dragged himself over the lip, satisfied and immensely thankful to be out. Kevan followed but at a bulge just below the crab ledge, he found the rope had abraded quite badly due to a slipped protector. He pulled up the line, knotted it, and continued to the surface. After some delay an irate exchange of colourful adjectives established that Allan could no longer reach the rope. Pete abseiled back down to a psychological ledge to have a look. Another rope was joined on, but in the process Pete dislodged a flake that struck Allan a glancing blow.

After the eventful descent of Tina Bu Tem, Kevan and Allan left for Mogondabip, the proposed springboard for exploration of the Fault Valley. Pete and Howard meanwhile returned to the Ok Anaram camp. Over the space of the next few days they languished in idyllic splendour while overseeing supply porters as they passed through. They had mapped just less than a kilometre of the Nong River Caves before joining the remainder of the team up the mountain.

By then, exploration along the eastern branch of the valley had progressed nearly two kilometres from Mogondabip. Eleven holes had been explored but these either choked off or became too tight. The second camp was built in an area known to the Faiwolmin hunters as Anawoltuman (see fig. 3). During efforts to force an easier bypass to the track blazed months before, Howard partly explored a nice looking hole. At a depth of 32 metres a ledge formed a polished chute that side stepped into a larger continuation of the shaft. Sid decided to shoot some "wild track" in Anawol Tem featuring the discoverer making the "first" descent.

The next day dawn crept in like cold, bony fingers leafing through precious enclaves of camp comfort. Howard awoke with an inexplicable sense of foreboding. After mooching slow and tacitly over breakfast, he simply refused to go back down the new shaft, so Pete Gray volunteered. He rigged the first pitch while Sid and Noel made ready for filming from an electron ladder in a corner. Pete was on the rope drilling an anchor for the second drop; he felt great and the hole looked good. The ringing sound of the hammer was somehow reassuring that at least solid rock was being dealt with for a change.

There was little warning as the boulders beside Noel shifted imperceptibly. Then there was a sudden *whoosh* coinciding with a yell from Sid.

"Below!!"

Pandemonium broke loose as several tons of rubble descended toward the ledge with an almighty roar. Those above remained powerless to do anything but watch with horror. After the noise and dust had settled, only an empty rope remained, snaking ominously into the sepulchral darkness below. Sid called out.

"Pete!? Peter!?" A pregnant silence welled up from the depths. He called once more, then again, not wishing to believe that fate had perhaps dealt the final hand. But this time, the "victim" swung into view from around a corner, still spitting limestone dust. Miraculously, he had cheated death by virtue of his spontaneous reflexes and a stroke of good fortune. As soon as he heard Sid's shout Pete had kicked off the wall and swung out over the unknown drop. It was pure luck really. Finding a crack, he jammed in his fist and there he hung protected by an overhang while the avalanche swept by. He was indeed fortunate that the rope had not been cut.

Only when it was established that Pete was unscathed did Sid discover that the rock fall had taken with it a pack containing his main tape recorder and boom microphone that had been secured to the ladder they themselves stood on. After everyone's nerves had calmed, Allan made a solo descent to a choke at 76 metres. Here he found the sorry remains of Sid's sound gear, suffering from severe distortion. So much for the "wild track."

Pete was not the only one left shaken. Others too were already suffering from attacks of lassitude, now exacerbated by SRT phobia. Howard was convinced he had been spared by a premonition. Feeling beneath the weather since the descent of Tina Bu Tem, he was under no illusion that if he, and not Pete, had been on the chute, his reactions would not have been nearly so sharp, and the outcome could well have been very different.

After this near fatality, track cutting continued with subdued fervour, some perhaps wondering if Afek was seeking retribution yet for the violation of Selminum Tem. The terrain was predominantly undulating tower karst, the worst yet encountered during the expedition. The forest "floor" was mostly a tangled nightmare of roots, fallen logs and moss, perhaps half a metre deep. Most trails provided a precarious footing on vegetation suspended over deep grykes, pits and tottering limestone towers. It was not so much a case of finding caves as the caves finding the cavers; one careless step held the prospect of a broken leg or worse, a plunge to oblivion in some hidden crevice.

When exploration of the valley had proceeded a further three kilometres east of Anawoltuman, it became necessary to shift camp once again. Like the others before it, this was rudimentary, a simple fly erected in an area cleared of undergrowth, the only concession to comfort being the provision of sapling beds raised from the ground. This was perhaps just as well, for with the onset of the seasonal monsoon living quarters were frequently inundated.

Caving cameraman Sid Perou with the remains of his sound equipment following a rockfall in Anawol Tem.

The contrast with Finim Tel could not have been more damning. Almost everyone was afflicted with diarrhoea, and a shortage of healthy cavers meant that exploration was slowly grinding to a standstill. This was offset by the timely arrival of Roy Blackham and Jim Farnworth. Donny arrived too, after having spent three weeks with Dick Willis on yet another fruitless quest for the fabled "big holes" south of Urapmin. Jim was still a little nervous of exposure after the air crash off New Ireland, but Roy and Donny quickly injected some impetus into the flagging group, enthusiastically exploring new holes further to the east.

A day or two after arrival, Lang Lang Tem was discovered. The entrance was in the southern-most of three prominent dolines. It led into a well-developed rift and down a couple of short drops before it opened via an exposed traverse onto a shaft of 50 metres. With difficulty, they rigged to a natural funnel containing rocks stacked treacherously at the angle of rest. These formed a rather doubtful takeoff for a further drop estimated at 35 metres. Here they called it a day, returning to camp after an entertaining six-hour trip.

With a going hole at last the mood changed, though sickness was still rife. Donny returned to the previous limit, this time accompanied by Kevan Wilde. The new pitch bottomed out at 44 metres, and from here a series of cascades led downstream to a restricted crawlway. Donny tried pushing this with little success so they halted for lunch prior to setting out. Before long they noticed the water was discoloured and rapidly rising.

Without delay they started up the two short drops and Kevan took the lead on the first big pitch, the stream visibly increasing in strength. At the top of the climb an overhang rounded into the "funnel," where Kevan clipped into the next rope for security to await his companion. Then, disaster struck unannounced.

A large rock, dislodged from above by the rising water, slammed into Kevan, hitting him across both knees and swinging him out over the shaft into the far wall. As he pendulummed back to the stance the rock continued down the pit, striking Donny a glancing blow as he followed up the rope. Kevan was in great pain if he tried bending his legs. To make matters worse, the stream was buffeting him and visibility was hampered by heavy spray filling the shaft.

Donny joined him. Their situation was growing desperate. The ledge was rapidly becoming untenable and the rising water increased the ever present threat of further rock falls the longer they delayed their exit.

"Out! Out!" Donny yelled. "Get up the bloody rope!"

They were in trouble, for the stream was by then repeatedly extinguishing both their lights. Trying to remain calm and with hands numbed by the waterfall, Kevan eventually managed to get his emergency electric lamp working. Ascending in tandem, Kevan moved off, slowly, with Donny following without a light. When at last they reached the traverse Kevan was able to move no further. By then, mercifully, they were above the flood and out of immediate danger. Donny climbed past his companion and headed out for help, leaving Kevan in darkness, secured to a bolt.

Everyone was hard asleep when he staggered into camp to raise the alarm. At just gone midnight, Kevan was greeted by three wise men bearing gifts in the shape of hot coffee, a cigar and reassurance. Jon directed the rescue, and with the provision of splints fashioned from the jungle, Kevan was slung along the traverse in an upright attitude and frogmarched back to camp. Allan ventured, "Look Dr. Frankenstein, it verks, it verks!" and the tension of the moment was released. Kevan's suspected broken legs turned out upon examination to be nothing worse than severe bruising; even so, it was to be a couple of weeks or more before his full mobility returned.

There was an understandable reluctance to be the next sacrificial offering to Lang Lang Tem. Despite the hazards, Jon Buchan got his act together and in a display of great fortitude, forced himself along the tight rift that had halted Donny. He reached a point where he could peer down an 18-metre shaft. There were grave doubts as to whether this new drop could be tackled. Moreover, the threat of floods and their accompanying dangers was increasing cause for concern. After discussion, the team decided it was too great a risk to continue and the hole was abandoned in favour of another promising new pothole.

Together with Pete, Howard had made a preliminary investigation of Terbil Tem. Here a trio of 13-metre shafts pierced the jungle, one carrying a sizeable stream, and all of them uniting upon a boulder slope littered with decaying trees. This descended to a clean washed streamway and two free climbs. The water then cascaded over the lip of what appeared to be a very moist shaft. By traversing out over this, the rope could be hung free for 70 metres to avoid the water and rope abrasion. The way on then divided with the stream cascading ten metres into a plunge pool. Almost immediately, a further pitch landed the explorers in a spray-lashed chamber in beautiful dappled limestone the colour of toffee. With no more rope they vacated the cave.

Back at camp everyone was filled with renewed optimism, but the adverse conditions and tensions of the moment were causing personality clashes. Pete and Howard returned to pursue greater depth, but at the second pitch a difference of opinion on self-sufficiency versus team-work resulted in Pete being left to continue alone. Following a dry bypass, he rigged a pitch of 54 metres from an exposed traverse and regained the stream below in a narrow vadose canyon. A climb then preceded shafts of 33 and 20 metres, both requiring careful rigging to avoid vicious rock flakes.

At this point Pete's acetylene lamp faded; efforts to relight it merely resulted in a hopelessly blocked jet. He made his exit by braille, crawling from the head of each pitch to locate the next rope. Many hours later he arrived in camp, looking drawn but now possessing an intimate tactile knowledge of the cave floor.

Terbil Tem was formed in sound, light-coloured limestone but with a dearth of natural belays. As a result, it proved a technically difficult system to explore, with mostly narrow pitches that required bolt belays from long, exposed traverses. Over the space of two or three days, Pete succeeded in reaching a depth of 230 metres. Allan and Roy then joined him in pushing on down the steeply descending cave. Together they negotiated a further pitch of 33 metres. This was followed almost at once by a scramble and another vertical where tackle ran out yet again. The cave was looking good but motivation was waning as the days went by.

Donny joined Allan at the limit of the previous trip and together they tackled five new pitches in a trip lasting 16 hours. Unfortunately the cave then closed right down at a crack only 10 centimetres wide. Though the end was a disappointment, it was perhaps with some relief that the exhausted duo returned to camp knowing the cave had finally finished. The repeated stumbling through the tower karst after dark and the technically demanding rigging was beginning to jade.

By the end of October it was clear from the reports reaching Telefomin that exploration in the Fault Valley was at its lowest ebb as morale plunged in sympathy with the barometer. Conditions were appalling. It was cold with heavy rain every day, turning camp into a running quagmire; the latrines had flooded, threatening camp hygiene. Where were the expected reinforcements?

Andy and Mike had departed on November 1st for a three-week (and highly contentious) patrol into the eastern Star Mountains, and there had been no radio contact with the Finim Tel "caretakers" for over two weeks. Meanwhile, Chas and Chris were taking a well-earned rest at Telefomin, after nearly three weeks of continuous walking. Having trekked 45 kilometres to the east of Wamtakin, they had located choked sinks above the Strickland Gorge with an apparent depth potential of up to 1,500 metres. With dwindling rations, they had then set off back for base via Tekin and Bimin, west along the foot of the Hindenburg Wall, then re-crossed the range slightly east of Mt. Burimsakin to reach the headwaters of the Lutap, a feeder of the Sepik.

After returning to base, Chas and Chris heard on the radio that Terbil Tem had finished at a depth of 354 metres. In all, 20 verticals had been rigged in trips lasting as many hours. However, another interesting pothole had been found a short distance further up the valley. The message was clear: there were going holes, but with the end of the expedition almost upon them, a desperate shortage of healthy cavers threatened their last chance of breaking any depth records.

TWO CLOSE ESCAPES

Meanwhile on the Finim Tel, the reason for radio silence was nothing more sinister than flat batteries and no generator to recharge them. With adequate supplies the explorers – Dave Brook, Dave Yeandle, Tony White and Phil Chapman – were in fact revelling in their splendid isolation. The small team remaining there simply carried on with routine exploration, survey and special studies. It was a time for culinary experimentation: While those in the Fault Valley were struck by diarrhoea and unable to face food, on the Finim, they were enjoying exquisite curries, fruit crumbles, trifles and chocolate sponge cakes!

Virtually at the eleventh hour, news came through that Rod Wells, a palaeontologist from Flinders University in Adelaide, was arriving to join the British expedition. With a brief from the Geological Survey of Papua New Guinea he was to examine in situ, then remove the mammal fossil discovered down the Black Hole in Selminum Tem.

On the morning of November 4, Tony White, Phil Chapman, and Dave Yeandle set off from the Finim camp for the base of the Hindenburg Wall, intending to examine the main efflux of the Kaakil River, the postulated resurgence for Selminum Tem. Dense vegetation had thwarted two earlier attempts to reach this. With the aid of local guides, they at last pinpointed the exact point at which the Kaakil emerged from the scarp face. The Wall was impressive from so close, a sheer to overhanging cliff with its top usually obscured by the weather blowing in from the lowlands. To their chagrin, the main water surged up from impenetrable fissures and a jumble of boulders; however, from the campsite on a nearby ridge they could see a number of caves in the cliff above.

The first effort to reach one of these was abandoned after a close encounter with a rock fall that came clattering unannounced from out of the clouds. Aiyangim then demonstrated his potential as a scaffold rigger by lashing together an amazing sapling ladder up to the entrance. Negotiating this was a spiritual experience.

Beyond the entrance, they discovered a complex, paraphreatic network of pressure tubes, shafts and galleries, beneath which they heard the river rumbling in some hidden conduit (see fig. 16). Several pits pierced the floor of the main passage, but only one allowed access to the water. Unfortunately the river sumped both up and downstream. The explorers had the impression that the cave received a regular flushing throughout, and there was precious little desire to dwell.

During three nervous days, they charted almost 300 metres of extremely flood prone cave before vacating the Kaakil system. The following morning their fears were vindicated when they awoke to the noise of the river in full spate. A turgid waterfall was pouring out of the upper entrance just a few hours after they had left it. After contemplating the power of nature, Tony departed for the Ok Tedi mining base and the others returned to the Finim Tel camp.

When the little twin engine Partannavia touched down at Tabubil amid gathering rain squalls, Tony White was on the apron to greet Rod Wells. The pilot was anxious to have his passenger and the mail out and be on his way before the weather closed in. This was achieved with some urgency and the plane roared into the air, trailing a slight hint of black smoke from an ailing starboard engine. Tony offered to act as navigator for the helicopter pilot, Roger Dundas, who would shuttle Rod the 17 kilometres to the cavers' base camp.

The three of them lifted off the next day in a five-seater Hughes 500C, work horse of the Ok Tedi Mining operation. While at the Kaakil, Tony had spotted an impressive cave opening about

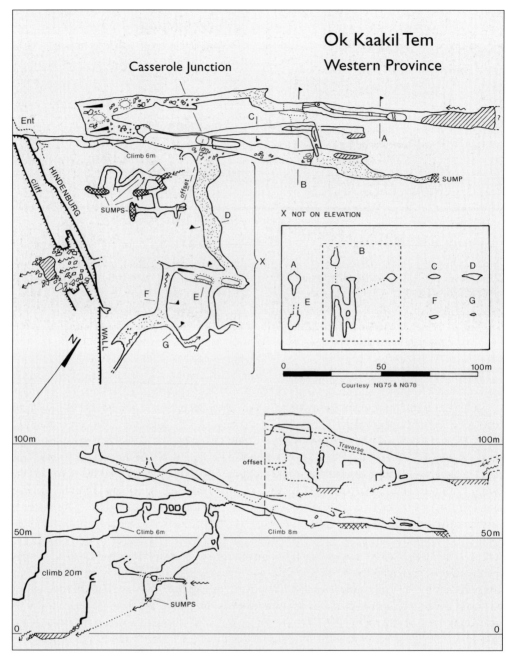

Fig. 16) Ok Kaakil Tem

halfway up the Hindenburg Wall to the west of the resurgence. He talked the pilot into flying as close as was possible to obtain a better look. This of course was small beer to a Vietnam chopper veteran like Roger, but unnerving for Rod as they hovered with the sweep of the rotor blades dangerously close the rock face. The wash from these fanned the vegetation as Tony stared with wonder into a gaping hole receding into a fathomless darkness.

The Hole in the Wall (Era Tem). Right: In Terbil Tem and other systems in the Fault
Valley, the technical and confined takeoff to many pitches was to extract a toll on morale.

In his mind Rod found himself trying to "push" the helicopter away from the Wall with his feet! To his relief they pulled away, and none too soon gained height to clear the top of the huge scarp. There dead ahead of them was the Finim Tel camp, easily spotted on account of the bright yellow bothy roof. Within minutes, Roger settled his machine down on the nearby helipad and his two passengers leapt out into the swampy clearing. With an increased whine of the Allison turbine and the familiar slapping noise of the rotors, P2-PHM was up and gone. Peace returned to the forest.

Later that same day Mike and Andy arrived at the Mt. Fubilan copper prospect in the southern foothills of the Star Mountains. They had trekked a more or less circuitous route, following in reverse the footsteps of the venture led by Shepherd ten years before. They had been on the trail for two weeks searching for evidence of deep caves. After the solitude of the high peaks, the Longyear drilling rigs and shiny helmeted crews were a harsh but welcome contrast. Fubilan was a curious place, perhaps more so because of its treeless summit, resembling an island oasis in an undulating "sea" of chlorophyll. This barren state was due perhaps to the inhibiting nature of the extensive mineralisation, composed largely of copper and gold ore. To the locals, Fubilan was the abode of evil spirits and demanded silence as a mark of respect. When on its blistering wastes, itinerant natives would keep their children quiet, even gag the village hounds while crossing the mountain.

Weather permitting, helicopters shuttled back and forth perhaps 30 times daily between Tabubil and Fubilan, supplying basic necessities for drilling and the copious quantities of grog on which the gangs seemed to thrive. Andy and Mike hitched a lift on one such chopper returning on the down flight, a five-minute hop that saved them several days walking. They arrived on November 13, having just missed Tony and Rod, who had departed Tabubil a few hours earlier.

Beneath the main phreatic trunk route of Selminum Tem lies a maze of interconnected percolation inlets that respond rapidly to the onset of rainfall.

Paul Everett passing through a streamway beneath the main trunk route of Selminum Tem.
Right: Delicate straw stalactites in the Great Nebula Series of Selminum Tem.

The Great Nebula Series forms a well-watered labyrinth of smaller passageways beneath
the main trunk route of Selminum Tem at Orion.

Streamway above the Atea entrance.

The Cobble-strewn streamway of Union Cave. A pleasant contrast to the huge, dusty tunnels of Selminum Tem.

Howard Beck

Warriors of the Yamuga clan during a tribal conflict in the Waghi Valley.

Howard Beck

Tribesman at village pig-killing ceromony. Each male wears a "skirt" of platted pigtails.

BENEATH THE CLOUD FORESTS

Warrior from the Waghi Valley wearing a human hair wig beats a Kundu drum at a village sing-sing.

117

Lavishly dressed wife of a tribal "bigman," Waghi Valley sing-sing.

Old man from the Telefomin region wearing cassowary quills through pierced nostrils.

Young child with an infant tree kangaroo.

As the operation at Finim Tel was winding down, Rod set off for Selminum Tem with Tony, Phil, and two New Guinea geography students whose arrival had coincided with that of Rod. It was raining heavily by 2:30 p.m. when they finally went underground. After assisting in the descent of the pitch into the Bone Wells, Phil departed with the two students to explore elsewhere in the cave.

At the foot of the shaft, Rod was alarmed by signs of recent and total flooding in the narrow passageways. Tony assured him there was nothing to worry about and they made their way through a dry sump to where the fossil was located, in an alcove some 30 metres from the rope pitch. The passage was less than a metre in diameter and working conditions were cramped to say the least. Rod could distinctly hear water running somewhere beneath. He felt uneasy and could not take his mind off the froth on the walls.

He spent an hour extracting bones and encapsulating them in protective foam. It was clearly the remains of a sirenian or sea cow that had grazed the "fields" of kelp some 25 million years ago. It was a unique find. But suddenly the tone of the stream changed.

Both noticed it but only Rod voiced any concern. Tony was once more reassuring and declared that it was time to eat. While he filled his lamp with a fresh charge of calcium carbide, they heard a louder rumbling. Not waiting for further explanations, Rod grabbed the bag of fossils and scrambled out of the alcove. He crawled until he could stand, then ran full tilt back to the rope, with Tony behind him carrying the camera. The noise was deafening and a gale suddenly started blowing through the narrow tunnel, pumped along by the approaching wave of floodwater.

The stream began welling up through holes in the floor and Rod, gripped by mild panic, fumbled to rig his prussik gear on the rope. Tony shot off hand over hand up the line in order to assist from above if necessary. "Keep cool and sort out the mess" Rod told himself as the flame from his lamp danced wildly in the draught. The water was rising rapidly around his thighs.

When at last everything was ready, he began moving up the rope, showered by mud, his pulse beating like a condemned man's drum-roll. After what seemed an eternity he flopped, breathless, over the lip of the dismal pit. The main cave reverberated to the united voice of many swollen inlets. The heavy rain was clearly getting through.

Making their way back the way they came proved equally fraught, as all the streams they had forded coming in had swelled to many times their normal size. These could only be safely crossed by linking arms as security against a slip in the fierce current. None too soon daylight could be seen filtering down the entrance slope. Rod could not have been more thankful to arrive in the rain-soaked doline.

Rod refused to go underground again the following day when it dawned to light rain. In what was to be the last caving trip on the plateau, Tony and Phil volunteered to go back in to see if the Bone Wells was passable. They were successful in recovering all the abandoned equipment and some of the bones, but all the passages below the shaft had indeed been completely filled with floodwaters.

Chas and Chris were unable to delay their departure from Telefomin any longer and on November 10, they trekked south over the Victor Emanuels to join the Fault Valley team. En route they met Pete and Howard at the Nong, returning in the van of those who had had a stomachful of conditions up the mountain. Upon their arrival late the next day, Chas and Chris learned that an enticing tube had been seen part way down a 30-metre shaft, at a depth of 261 metres, in Terbil Tem. Though no one had tried to reach this, it presented the possibility of a bypass to the terminal rift. They eagerly descended the cave and traversed into the unexplored passage. Unfortunately, they found that the rift merely rejoined the known cave further down.

Attention then focused on the latest discovery, Camp III Hole, which was so new it had not yet been given a name. It began as a fine 39-metre entrance shaft first descended by Allan and Chas to where a stream from a nearby sink entered through boulders at floor level.

Saturday, November 15 dawned bright after a night of continual heavy rain. In fact, it was the first fine weather in four weeks. Taking advantage of this, Kevan and Noel descended Camp III Hole, while the others returned to Terbil Tem in an epic trip combining Sid's filmmaking with detackling.

In Camp III Hole, Kev and Noel rigged beyond the 39-metre shaft. With mounting optimism they descended a series of short easy pitches that terminated in a booming shaft. They turned to exit for lack of rope, but this time they thought they had a chance of hitting the big time. As exploration had progressed further up the valley and deeper into the Darai Limestone, the holes seemed to be better developed. They hoped that this hole would be The One.

Most people had by then had enough of the dreadful karst and deteriorating conditions of the valley. At the end of filming only Donny, Chas, Allan and Jim remained. Everyone else had pulled back to the Ok Nong with the filming crew, or returned to unwind at Telefomin in readiness for the exodus. Despite the promise of the going cave, it was another four days before those remaining could psyche themselves up to go underground. All except Jim descended to the head of the new pitch. From a windy ledge, Chas traversed out over the void and placed an anchor bolt in an effort to provide a dry hang. He had limited success, however, when not far below a small ledge deflected the water, filling the shaft with heavy spray.

With dampened spirits Chas continued downwards, his rope passing dangerously close to a huge flake jutting out into the shaft like an executioner's halberd. He could do little to protect the rope and, flayed by the waterfall, hoped for the best and continued to the bottom, nearly 50 metres below. Perhaps Afek had now forgiven them their sins, for the rope remained intact. Allan and John Donovan joined him on a boulder slope supporting a block the size of a hearse. In the rift above dangled a precarious assemblage of its coffin-sized cousins. White scratch marks everywhere bore witness to the instability of the chamber. With a hush they fixed a hand line and briskly lowered themselves into the continuation, a restricted canyon winding out of sight.

The small stream chuckled off down a miscellany of short cascades and climbs before flowing into a strenuous, meandering section that reminded them of the caves back home in England's Yorkshire Dales. The passage was trending north, down the dip towards the Nong and the Wek Ket outflow. There was an air of anticipation for it was the only system explored in the valley with significant lateral development. Perhaps the change in character was significant. Would this cave prove to be the jackpot? Time was running out.

Turning completely back upon itself, the streamway became an obstacle course of rockmills, false floors and cherty nodules forming wetsuit shredding walls. The cave seemed to be opening up when, at a depth of 292 metres, they entered a depressing chamber floored with a knobbly chert bed resembling a cobbled street on a wet night. The only way forward was a muddy crawl that Allan contemplated with disgust. Reluctantly he forced himself into the tube and shortly reappeared with a filthy grin to announce he had reached the head of another drop. He then changed places with Chas, who went back in with a rope.

The takeoff was via a "window" in a chert bed and was awkward in the extreme. An eyehole at roof level provided a fortuitous thread belay through which the rope was secured and lowered into the gloomy depths. Chas descended cautiously while his companions provided backup in the chamber above.

It proved a magnificent abseil, the line snaking down the centre of a perfectly circular shaft. Part way down the stream entered to provide a liberal amount of spray. Despite a feeling the cave was going places the end came in a shattered chamber 21 metres below. The stream simply percolated through the boulder floor, taking with it any hopes of further depth. Chas returned to his companions and they set off out, reaching camp after 14 hours below ground. A further trip was necessary to survey and detackle the find.

With the conclusion of Camp III Hole, the British expedition was all over but for the shouting. Although marred by accidents and close calls, it was a manifest success. Over two hundred caves had been explored and 37 kilometres of passageways surveyed. The length of Selminum Tem had exceeded by several kilometres that of Exit Cave in Tasmania, establishing a new length record for the Southern Hemisphere. In a two-month study of the Fault Valley, six kilometres of track had been cut and 36 holes explored. Both Terbil Tem and Camp III Hole had bottomed out at 354 and 330 metres respectively. Despite the failure to find anything deeper than Bibima, these discoveries brought to four the number of New Guinea caves 300 metres deep or more.

Though the exploration of the Fault Valley had presented many difficulties both in the forests and below ground, it was generally believed that even further east – towards the remote cirque overshadowed by Mt. Burimsakin – the prospects for discovering caves of world-class depth must surely improve. Time had run out for the British, perhaps just when the caves were beginning to develop. What lay beneath the remote karsts further east would have to await a future generation of explorers.

A CHIMBU CHRISTMAS

Following the British exodus, most returned whence they came, while others sought further thrills. An exciting raft journey took Tony, Chas, Noel and Chris down the August River. Afterwards Chris, Mike Bourke, Tim Sprod and Alan Olden joined Kevan Wilde for Christmas in the Eastern Highlands. That social scene formed the prelude to a productive week of caving in the nearby Kainantu districts and Chimbu Province.

A small extension was made to the well-known Hell's Gates system at Henganofi, before Alan had to return to Rabaul. The group was then augmented by the arrival of Tony White and Chas Yonge, and they headed for the Chimbu. Mike Bourke had hoped that at least one of a number of unfinished caves in the area might be explored to a conclusion. Following a sightseeing visit to Irukunguai Cave on December 27, they examined the nearby Mebikombogo Cave, one of the many holes first entered by Fred Parker.

Chas, Mike, Tony and Tim returned the next day and surveyed the cave, entering a lower streamway that Kevan Wilde had suspected on a previous trip. The cave terminated in a mud choke after being extended to 740 metres. In the lower stream passage, they had found that the water was running very discoloured. When they exited, the river Kwi was in high flood. With some trepidation they coaxed the Toyota Landcruiser along the narrow dirt (mud) road back down the Chimbu Gorge.

Darua Muru had been one of Chimbu's most promising "loose ends" of 1973, when Van Watson and Kevan Wilde had turned around at a depth of 170 metres. The cave had a potential depth of around 300 metres. Tony, Chas and Mike descended the cave on the last day of the year and pushed quickly on to the previous limit, a five-metre drop. The passage narrowed here, and part way up the walls a mud tide mark gave fears that a sump lay just ahead. However, after

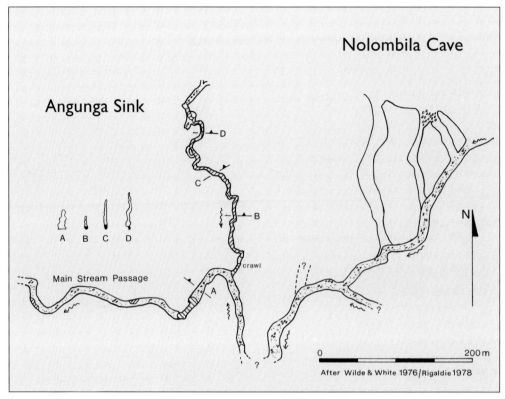

Fig. 17) Angunga and Nolombila Sinks

about 80 metres they were stopped by another cascade estimated to be seven metres deep. They regained the surface after almost 12 hours underground. The resurvey of Darua Muru showed the cave had reached a depth of 197 metres.

For the final two days of the meet, Kevan guided the group to the Angunga sinkhole, near Nola village in the Chuave district. He had previously noted this but had not descended it. He believed the shaft had every chance of connecting with the Kiowa river system. From Angunga and the nearby Nola sink it was five kilometres to the assumed outflow at Kirova Cave, 300 metres below.

Tim Sprod and Chas Yonge rigged the entrance, a free hanging 44-metre descent in a clean, well-watered shaft dropping into a spacious vadose rift. After 250 metres, an easy climb preceded a wet crawl that debauched suddenly into a magnificent river passage. A few minutes downstream they encountered a canal at what they believed to be a sump, while in the opposite direction a deep, fast-flowing stretch proved a little too fierce for cavers without buoyancy aids. They returned the next day to continue mapping.

Swimming into the "sump" they peered around a corner and were amazed to see the passage continuing to the right, larger than ever (see fig. 17). Dragging themselves out of the deep water, they romped along for an additional 200 metres, stopping only to admire a splendid calcite flow. At this point they became apprehensive about pursuing the system further without support; besides, time was running out. They vacated the cave with a length of 500 metres and a passage showing no sign of closing down.

LEMERIGAMUS DISCOVERED

Only six months elapsed before Tim Sprod and Mike Bourke were participating in yet another caving venture to New Ireland. Despite the lack of major finds there, most Australian speleologists still believed that deep caves were there to be discovered. Mike was one who subscribed to this view.

During the second week of the 1975 Lelet Expedition, a team had been cutting track along a scarp edge overlooking the northeast coast. They were stimulated by the sight of the Dalum resurgence some 1,200 metres below and five kilometres distant. With a favourable wind it was just possible to hear the surf rolling up onto the shore. Local tales related how it was possible to enter caves on the high plateau, and travel all the way underground to emerge on the coast. Although merely legends, these somehow enhanced the feeling that record-breaking caves were sequestered somewhere in those dense forests. On this basis the second Australian expeditionary group returned in 1976.

Under the leadership of Dave Gillieson, a geomorphologist from Queensland University, ten cavers spent July wallowing in the main outflow caves at Dalum and examining the seemingly countless dolines that gave the Lelet its rugged appearance. During four weeks in the field, over 150 cave entrances were discovered.

High on the plateau, shaft dropping progressed for several days but revealed frustratingly few going holes, which mostly ended in sumps or regions of instability. The major discovery came half way through the month. While Friday, July 16 was a rest day for most, Stewart Wilson was too active to fritter away the limited time available. He prowled about camp like a bandicoot with a thorn in its paw until the lethargic atmosphere threatened to cloud his mental well being. He shot out of camp into the all embracing bush.

After some time, his ferreting paid off when he stumbled upon a gully leading to the base of a vegetated cliff, where a small stream lured him with waxing anticipation into a restricted cave mouth. Once out of daylight, he followed Lemerigamus down a five metre-high rift passage that was tight but passable with a widening at floor level. The sound of falling water greeted him just ahead. Crawling for a few minutes, he was soon gazing down a drop of about seven metres into what appeared to be a larger passage leading off from the bottom. Not having any tackle, he made off back to camp.

Over the following four days the team shuffled along a passage that meandered in an easterly direction, gathering several tributaries and gradually increasing in size. The passage was particularly well decorated in parts and at first retained its vertical rift section. It was punctuated by four short drops, then changed character where an arched section developed over deep water. The passage quickly became a narrow rift once again, and after 200 metres a second arched canal section led almost immediately to a pitch. They estimated this to be 20 metres, but with no rope left, they had to surface. They were 650 metres from the entrance (see fig. 18).

The last day on the Lelet arrived. Although the team had only reached a depth of 100 metres, they were confident the cave would plunge deeper. Tim Sprod, Neil Hickson and Ralph Page were given the option of pushing on below the new drop, but this had to be abandoned when the bolting tool became inoperative. There were no available natural belay points, so the cave was reluctantly vacated. The second Lelet expedition thus came to a frustrating end, with the lower reaches of Lemerigamus remaining a mystery for three more years.

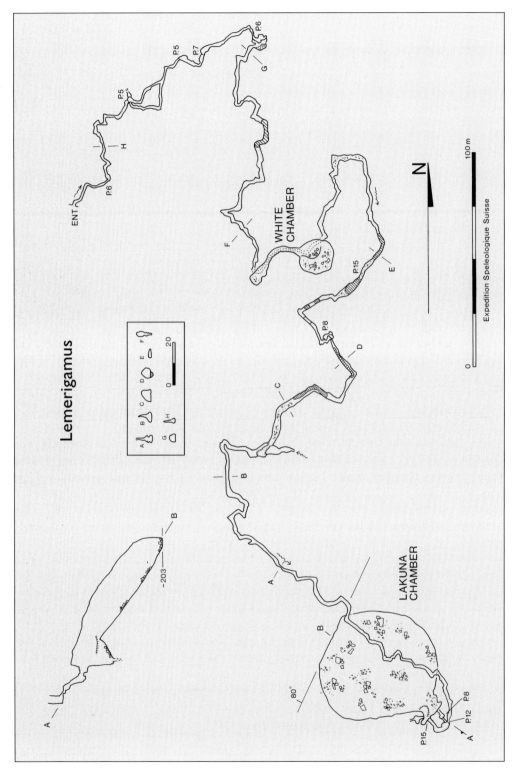

Lemerigamus

WHITE CHAMBER

LAKUNA CHAMBER

ENT

Expedition Speleologique Suisse

0   100 m

N

Fig. 18) Lemerigamus

Chapter Five

CHALLENGE OF THE YU ATEA

From time out of memory the Huli, Bogaiye and Duna tribes had been hunters and gatherers in the remote Muller Range. In this great wilderness at the frontier of their world the forests remained unchanged, as they had for millions of years since the first cycads unfurled their feathery limbs to the warming rays of the Pacific sun. At Himbiraga, an area traversed by the Koroba to Nomad trail, interlocking ridges could be traced between depressions, skirting slightly north of the "World's Largest Doline." From here native traders and hunters occasionally glimpsed plumes of vapour rising through the trees to the north, and from this direction came a muted roar. The source of this phenomenon was the Atea Kananda.

There are probably few more stunning sights in the natural world. An encounter with this huge cauldron is almost intimidating. The ground vibrates and trees shake like giant tuning forks resonating to nature's timpani. Over the brink of the abyss, picturesque waterfalls drum into a boiling plunge pool before conducting its own version of Handel's water music down a nearby cave mouth. Spray lashes at the vegetation and when sunbeams play among the countless watery prisms, nebulous rainbows add a transient beauty to an otherwise rugged tableau.

Duna tribesmen had always been aware of the Atea Kananda. Children quaked when they heard its mighty voice and saw the trees sway in its clammy breath. For generations the Duna had wondered at its insatiable thirst, greedily swallowing the Yu Atea. No one could navigate that starless river and expect to return to tell the tale. It commanded their respect. Word of this amazing sinkhole first reached the caving community in 1973 when members of the Australian Muller Expedition became the first white explorers to witness this awesome spectacle at close range. To the Duna the Atea Kananda was a window into a mysterious realm peopled by evil spirits; to Australian cavers it was the key, perhaps, to the deepest hole in the world, the goal sought by all vertical speleologists.

The 1973 Muller trip jointly led by Julia James, Van Watson and Kevan Wilde had consisted of the elite of Australasia's vertical cavers. They had been well versed in vertical caving techniques, but few had been psychologically prepared for the gruelling conditions they were to encounter both within and beneath the forests. Disenchantment with life under canvas had been such that, out of the 28 participants, only three eventually were to return in 1976 for a second round with the tropical jungles.

Safely exploring the underground course of the Atea River had been questionable in 1973, as highlighted by Paul Williams, professor of geography at Auckland University. Basing his opinion on expedition reports from the first tentative sortie, he believed it was remotely possible to follow the river canyon using aid-climbing techniques to proceed along the walls. Progress would be slow and under constant threat from flooding; on balance, he thought the risks far outweighed any possible gains.

Despite the obvious difficulties of finding and exploring new caves in the dense forests, the inherent discomforts of camping, and the terribly broken terrain, the rugged hinterland of New Guinea held a strange fascination for cavers. With the only guaranteed outcome being gross discomfort, damp sleeping bags and endless days of slogging through the jungle mud, Kevan, Neil and Julia succeeded in leading a team of ten to the Muller Range in 1976. They could of course draw upon the logistical experiences of both the British expedition of 1975 and their own trip three years before. The cavers overcame the discomfort of tents in 1975 by adopting open sided shelters built of bush materials and roofed over with plastic sheeting. Since it was much smaller, the 1976 expedition would be more manageable and could get along with fewer porters than was necessary in 1973. With hindsight however, they had perhaps set themselves a much too ambitious programme for such a small group, the majority of whom had precious little knowledge of what to expect.

Within the constraints imposed by only four weeks in the field, some progress was in fact made on all the major objectives that year. Yet if it had not been for a change in fortunes at the Atea, the venture could easily have returned in failure. As it was, forceful and determined effort on the part of two team members provided the essential ingredient for success. The breakthrough came on Wednesday, August 17th.

It took Dave Rothery and Richard Willson 20 minutes to descend into the Atea Doline. Several cave openings beckoned from high up the northeast side of the doline above the main cave entrance. How could they reach them? Fording the river was the crux of the matter. Three years earlier water levels had been consistently higher, precluding any hopes of reaching the enticing black holes. This time somewhat drier conditions made it possible – though perilous still – to wade the river where it entered the main cavern. Buffeted by the wind and soaked by flying spray, they succeeded in crossing the Atea and climbed into the highest hole nearest the waterfalls. They were surprised to find that the cave actually continued.

With only one suspect carbide lamp between the two of them they hurried off for a brief look into the gallery ahead. Within metres the darkness closed in behind them in a high, wide fossil passage – the Fury Tube – that lured them into the unknown. After about 300 metres and with lamp failure imminent, they retreated with the good news. Everyone was astounded that a dry way into the Atea Kananda existed and that the cave was wide open after all. They believed the chances of safely exploring the underground river to be greatly improved.

The following day the two original explorers, accompanied by Neil Montgomery and Randall King, returned to the cave just before noon. In the dry but windy passage, the tube seemed to act as a megaphone for the cataract that howled ferociously just outside the opening, making for a unique but unnerving experience.

At a major junction Randall and Dave turned left to follow an inlet as the remaining pair explored the Mill Series to a balcony overlooking an extraordinary underground landscape. The full force of the river swept around a corner and down a spillway, falling some ten metres in the process. Here the sound of the river was deafening as it literally was squeezed into The Turbine, a slot little wider than a phone box. This was an especially intimidating section of the cave; communication was possible only by shouting and the cave walls seemed to reverberate with the power of the river.

Meanwhile up the Ugwapugwa (Duna for snake) Passage, Dave and Randall had reached their agreed turnaround point. After an hour of continuous caving, mostly in walking passage, they were obliged to return after having covered an estimated one and a half kilometres. At the limit reached, a calcite flow restricted the streamway though the passage beyond showed every sign of continuing.

Cavers in the entrance to the Atea Kananda, with waterfalls in background.

News of these developments soon reached the two field teams exploring other parts of the plateau. Consequently they pulled back to Lumbi to help pursue the Atea. With only a few expedition days remaining, it was the scene of much frenzied activity as the cave was pushed for every metre of passage it would yield.

The Mill Series developed into a fine 35-metre-high canyon at Grindstone Alley (see fig. 11a). Here the walls were scoured clean by floodwaters that undoubtedly tore through at a terrific speed during the height of the wet season. A tree trunk wedged above them was further proof of the river's erstwhile power. Exploration terminated on the brink of a deep rock mill, The Crucible, six metres wide with a drop of nine metres into a dark pool. At the far side of this the continuing canyon echoed their frustrated cries, whilst the water surface below reflected the looks of anguish on their faces. In a superb piece of rock gymnastics Neil Montgomery overcame this impasse by abseiling to a point just above water level. By swinging over to a small ledge, he could just reach a rising flake. Placing a fortuitous nut, he managed to reach a ledge ascending to the left, and a couple of exposed moves later he stepped into the continuation of the passage leading to Confluence Dome. Here he encountered the Yu Atea surging from a large sump pool and flowing off into a high, wide trench. Through this, he cautiously negotiated a series of rapids to reach the start of the more languid Ship Canal, the end of exploration that day.

Six Molar pitch photographed by Lex Brown after he had descended into the Iguanodon just seconds in front of a flood pulse. Floods in the Mamo Kananda system resulted in a curfew being imposed to avoid afternoon rains.

While preparations for the walk out were underway Dave Rothery made another important discovery by descending into The Beeline at Drone Drop. From here he traced 200 metres of keyhole-shaped passage to where the meandering rift pitched into the riverway from the roof of Confluence Dome. A right branch just before this led after 70 metres to Glop Drop, providing an easy descent directly into the Ship Canal. The Beeline was to play a major role in a later episode of the Atea story.

In the closing days of the expedition Peter Ruxton and Neil Montgomery descended into the Nali Gorge to the southwest of the Atea. Though reputedly inhabited by venomous snakes and bad spirits, the area was a picture of beauty with many colourful orchids and pitcher plants. The source of the Nali River was located where the main resurgence emerged from between large boulders, a volume estimated to be three times that sinking at the Atea. In flood it was clearly much larger, as flood channels had carved stark corridors through the rain forest. These were strewn with silt banks and boulders the size of houses. Surveying back from the outflow, they determined the vertical separation between the two points to be 750 metres over a distance of two kilometres. At Lumbi, the Muller Range drops off as a steep scarp to the Nali, Burnett and other tributaries of the mighty Strickland River.

To reach its outflow the Atea was expected to follow a high gradient course. If the Ship Canal pitched, its exploration would test the prowess of Australian speleologists to the extreme, and Professor Williams might after all be proven correct. Only one cautious look was taken downstream from Glop Drop: in yet another unmitigated act of daring, Neil lowered himself into the dark waters of the riverway and, tied to a line, allowed himself to drift with the strong current. The Ship Canal started out four metres high but soon increased to around ten, with width enough to sail a small boat through. Neil was out of his depth throughout the section until, 110 metres from base, he grounded on a sandbar. The riverway appeared to continue unchanged for perhaps 30 metres. The atmosphere was oppressive and the air still. Since there was only an eerie silence, he could not be certain whether the passage ahead sumped.

In all, some four kilometres of passageways were mapped. More important for the future, these discoveries proved that high level galleries existed that could provide a bypass to sections of the riverway otherwise deemed impassable. Plans were set in motion for a return in 1978.

While cavers in Sydney pondered the nature of the Ship Canal beyond the explored limit, resident expatriate cavers remained active throughout New Guinea in 1976. On the mainland there were a number of visits to caves in the more accessible regions – the Chimbu, Chuave and Central Province, for instance – but only minor finds or brief extensions to known systems resulted.

Bougainville received attention from Hans Meier, who in June flew over the Keriaka Plateau and sighted many large dolines. Several cavers, including Hans, Malcolm Pound and Michael Kiap, visited karsts at the northern end of the island, the most notable exploration being the hitherto unrecorded river cave called Toroku Nantaut. This was later pushed to a depth of 100 metres over almost two kilometres of passageway.

An interesting event remotely connected with caving occurred that same year. At Tavurvur Volcano near Rabaul, the provincial capital of New Britain, a pseudo-cave appeared near the volcano base following a violent earthquake on July 19. The hole measured some five by four metres and dropped 12 metres into water. Tim Sprod investigated this with Mike Bourke, Vic Dent and Don Flanagan. The latter tried diving but found the water too hot for swimming.

Between 1976 and 1978 there was no expedition activity. Following their success in the Hindenburg Range, the British were moving on to bigger things in Sarawak and paving the way into China's vast limestone regions. For years cavers from the United States had been threatening to visit New Guinea but were unable to do so, though they had some brilliant successes in southern Mexico.

In August 1977, Mike Bourke attended the 7th International Speleological Congress held in Sheffield, England, where he was approached by various groups that expressed interest in the caving prospects of New Guinea. Included among these were cavers from Belgium, Switzerland, the organisers of a proposed French venture, and a Spanish group who even flew Mike to Barcelona, where they wined and dined him Mediterranean style. The Spanish wished to go to the Muller Range; however, Mike suggested that they chose the Lelet Plateau or the Chimbu. Lemerigamus was unbottomed and the latter area offered great potential for expeditions with a limited budget.

In late September 1977, the Geological Survey of PNG approached local cavers Malcolm Pound, Allan Goulbourne, Kevan Wilde, and Jim Farnworth for assistance in carrying out a survey of the Ok Menga Gorge. This formed part of a feasibility study to provide hydroelectric power for the Ok Tedi mining operation at Tabubil. On September 24, they flew out to the Western Province. In a week of fieldwork, the deep canyon provided some exciting whitewater exploration, but the group recorded no worthwhile caves.

The following December, the ubiquitous man of the wilds, Kevan, and Mal Pound were off again on the ceaseless quest for new caving horizons. Their objective this time was the Huon Peninsula to the northwest of the east coast port of Lae (see fig. 1). The mountains of the Huon form a steep divide parallel to the central cordillera of mainland New Guinea, from which it is isolated by the Markham-Ramu basin. The range continues east as a bathymetric ridge surfacing after 80 kilometres as the precipitous island of New Britain. Vertical cavers have long been fascinated by the prospect of these lofty mountains. At first sight they appear to offer tremendous scope for vertical development. The theoretical depth potential in the Saruwaget, Finisterre and Cromwell ranges, for instance, is a staggering 4,000 metres and more, over twice that of the world's deepest known cave. All the drainage is underground and large sea level resurgences are documented.

They spent six days at altitude engaged in a ground reconnaissance covering part of the Cromwell Range. This was followed by an all too brief fly-past. Despite its promise and in complete contrast to its eastern extension across the Dampier Strait, the range produced not one single caving prospect. In defence of the region, only a very small proportion of the 9,000 square kilometres of karst was examined. The massive limestone deposits alone seem sufficient justification for further and more thorough investigation.

BREAKTHROUGH AT PENNY LANE

From a caving standpoint 1978 was an especially good year for New Guinea, with no less than five international expeditions. These included a pair of French speleologists, a small and highly mobile group from Britain, and a large scale venture with a roll-call resembling a Who's Who of Australasian speleology. It was a fruitful year too, with over 89 kilometres of spectacular new cave being discovered and seven more systems being added to those exceeding 300 metres in depth. The Muller Range was the theatre of activity for the forerunner of these success stories.

The 1978 Australian Atea Expedition was organised by several Sydney cavers and involved members of the four principal clubs. It enjoyed a gestation period of two years and was born out of the inconclusive end to the cave reported by Neil Montgomery. Midwife to these nagging doubts was that inimitable lady of Australian caving, Julia James. The previous Christmas, she had reached a depth of almost 760 metres in Mexico's La Grieta system. She was ready to take on the Atea and secretly hoped that in the Muller Aussi cavers would surpass the magical kilometre. Everything hinged on the riverway.

If the impressive doline was the heart of the Atea Kananda, then the Ship Canal was doubt-less its principal artery, along which its lifestream, the Yu Atea, flowed at the rate of up to 12 cubic metres per second. It was this sheer volume that would present the single greatest obstacle to downstream exploration; upstream was another matter. Should the Ugwapugwa inlet continue its 1976 trend for any great distance, there was a clear chance it could link to potholes such as Uli Guria found five years before. With a depth of over 300 metres, this would give the Atea an overall vertical range of at least 1,500 metres.

The expedition was successful in obtaining some backing from Australian industry as well as from several New Guinea companies. It received recognition from a number of official bodies, principally the Institute of Papua New Guinea Studies and the University of Papua New Guinea. Various disciplines in the natural sciences were the subject of a scientific programme planned to co-exist alongside sporting exploration of the Atea and its environs. A technical committee was appointed to manage this programme and comprised Professor Joe Jennings of the Australian National University, Professor Paul Williams, and Drs. Guy Cox and Julia James, both of Sydney University.

The advance team comprising Peter (Rucko) Ruxton, Kevan Wilde, and Tim Daniel moved into the area during June to prepare the base campsite and clear overgrown trails. At the begin-ning of July six tonnes of food and equipment was air dropped into a clearing at Geroro, a five-hour trek east of the Atea. From here it was shuttled directly into the base camp by Bell helicop-ter. Initially, they had considered portering supplies in from the drop zone; however, to employ more than a dozen carriers could quickly turn an expedition into an industrial relations night-mare. The maximum load a Duna carrier could manage over rough terrain was 20 kilos. Simple mathematics showed that it would have taken ten porters three months to move the cargo into the field.

When the main group arrived on July 12, they were greeted with tales of gloom and despair. Kevan's team had been down the Ship Canal that same day rigging it with floating polypropylene rope beyond Neil's 1976 limit. The water varied from one and a half to five metres in depth in an ominously silent passage. Swimming down it was a sobering experience, the flickering light from the cavers' caplamps casting an eerie glow on the features ahead. Vertical walls slid by like the work-scarred sides of super tankers looming out of a foggy night. After a further 300 metres of oppressive tunnel the roof plunged straight down into the dark water at what they took to be a sump.

Necessity is the mother of invention as they say, so undeterred a party entered the cave the next morning, hopeful of discovering a bypass. Neil Montgomery, Al Warild and three pommie cavers – Steve Worthington, Rob Kay and Richard Bartrop – examined Beeline. They checked out several blind leads, and success came with ridiculous ease. Overcoming a ten-metre climb Richard entered Penny Lane, a fine walking size phreatic tube, and 15 minutes later peered down a muddy pitch. It was the "open sesame" to many kilometres of virgin cave.

The Wishing Well pitch was 15 metres deep and the precursor to a series of equally grotty climbs and drops leading down to the Ooze Cruise network. This was a major streamway, in places consisting of a few centimetres of water overlaying deep thixatropic mud. Ooze Cruise proved hellish to explore, especially for the British contingent whose favoured footwear was Wellington boots. Though these still hold a place in English caving heritage, they tended to be sucked from the wearer's feet in such muddy passages. Exploration here gave rise to HMCT (Horizontal Mud Caving Techniques), the usual method of progress being to lay flat-out in the water and bodily claw along the gooey surface like a mud skipper. The pitches were also a constant source of anxiety, as jammers began slipping on muddied ropes. Despite its difficulties, Ooze Cruise was to lead to some fine passageways extending the system southwards and, of course, closer to the Nali outflow.

While developments took place in Penny Lane the sump in the riverway was found to have 30 centimetres of airspace, a lot under any other circumstance but unnerving with a river the size of the Atea beneath it. The way forward was straight ahead but not all that obvious, so it was

Under normal flow conditions the Yu Atea forms several cascades into the Atea Doline.
In 1976, entry to an obscure high-level entrance into the wall to the right of the river entrance gave
safe access to a network of dry passages.

never clear whether the first team down had simply missed the way on. Moreover, it was too early to say how much rain it would take to close the ducks (very little was the general consensus), or indeed how long they might remain sealed after a flood subsided.

Rowan Emberson and Guy Cox surveyed through several low air spaces separated by large, dismal chambers that seemed to soak up the light from their lamps. Swimming, wading and floating eventually brought them to a landfall at Normandy Beaches where the roof reared up. Ahead of them brief swims were separated by rocky islands offering welcome respite from the water, and a final deep stretch appeared. Not far along this the current increased but with no rope left the party turned back. A roaring sound from down the passage fuelled speculation that the cave was at last beginning to go vertical.

The following day Guy Cox, Ian Hickson, Tony White, Peter Ruxton and Malcolm Handel went in to find a reduced airspace in the ducks; the weather was doubtful however. After waiting an hour to see what the river would do, the water began rising so they swam back up the Ship Canal, discovering two passages leading off the west bank.

After 18 millimetres of overnight rain, water levels in the riverway on the seventeenth were high, and remained that way for some time. This was frustrating for Julia and other vertical cavers whose sole purpose in being there was to explore deep cave. The Ship Canal was the *raison d'être* of the 1978 expedition (see fig. 11b); however, the ducks remained closed for several days, shutting out their aspirations and diverting attention elsewhere. But there was much to do.

A small group set off in search of fossil caves above the Nali resurgence, while filming progressed in the Atea under the capable direction of John Davis and Garry Steer, an officer with the New South Wales National Parks. "Atea '78: The Search for the World's Deepest Cave" was the grand title for the expedition documentary film. That day the camera team focused on the Ugwapugwa streamway.

It was a typical day in the mixed fortunes of the cave-bound moviemaker. At Monty Python's High Level Bypass (which of course was a duck-under) the pool was drained to allow the film crew through dry shod, but they filled this again afterwards to "improve" the action! Curses were muttered beneath gasps for breath. For the climax of that ten-hour day, Steve Worthington and Alan Warild had to climb three metres straight from a chest-deep pool – new exploration filmed as it happened. Imagine the scene: John stands motionless with the pool lapping his armpits, tape recorder slung around his neck, and arms outstretched holding the gun microphone above his head. Garry is beside him, camera touching water, with Chris Pugsley almost singeing the hair on the back of their necks as he wields 100 watt lamps in the confined chamber directly below the climb. A last minute check, then…"Cameras roll!" The clapper board snaps shut and…"Action!" In a bridging move, Steve promptly pours wellies-full of cold, muddy water onto the film crew beneath! Revenge is so sweet.

While the stars of the celluloid were up the Ugwapugwa without a paddle, Rudi Frank, Dave Martin and Rob Kay pushed on down Ooze Cruise intending to survey Strawberry Fields, an extensive network they had found earlier. On the way they discovered the delights of Yukebo, a 900 metre long, joint-controlled rift carrying a small stream and sporting some of the vilest caving imaginable. Even this would be surpassed by the lugubrious Imperial Mud Standard. Tony and others had planned to push on down the Ship Canal beyond the ducks, but with higher river levels prevailing Tony set off instead to help chart Strawberry Fields.

At a prominent landmark in Ooze Cruise he found a note scribbled by Dave saying they had gone out because of suspect weather. Tony however continued alone. After following Hidden Inlet up a number of entertaining climbs, he retraced his steps for Ooze Cruise. About 200 metres before the junction with this he noticed an inconspicuous side passage on the right. Crawling into the opening he was soon on his feet again and striding along a roomy fossil gallery with an undulating floor of mud and boulders.

The passage trended northwest with a number of small streams chattering in from obscure inlets. Ignoring these, he traced the steadily rising passage to a major junction after a further 200 metres. The left lead was hopelessly blocked with mud, but the two remaining leads united at the well-decorated Dvorak Hall. At this point, the passage assumed impressive proportions and was adorned with stalactites hanging two metres from the roof. Back in camp the Australians were at first alarmed to learn of Tony's solo exploits; when he surfaced at 9:00 p.m. they were astounded that he had single-handedly discovered and mapped a kilometre of new passages in the New World Series, including some of the finest sections in the cave.

The Atea was expanding on all fronts and it was clear that many more kilometres remained to be found. The Ugwapugwa Passage seemed to go on forever. Beyond the 1976 limit of exploration, several groups had added a further two kilometres to its length and reached the Dry Run. The latter marked the start of the Yaragaiya, a dusty series of galleries long forsaken by the aggressive waters, which had once carved them from the fabric of the earth. It proved to be an intriguing area of the cave, the main attraction being the possibility of a link between the Atea and the Dina River to the north. During the pre-trip patrols Kevan and Tim had flown over the area by chopper and spotted the main sink. A dry valley downstream from this point turned due west. Close to this prominent bend a large doline was believed to be more or less over the northernmost extremity of the system.

Because the remoteness of the Yaragaiya necessitated a 14-hour round trip, an overnight camp was established to facilitate further investigation. Donna Mroczkowski, Neil Montgomery, Ian Miller, Glen Campbell and Malcolm Handel spearheaded a push team. Reaching the bivouac site was slow going since the further reaches of the Ugwapugwa streamway were quite restricted in places, motion being possible only by shuffling along crab-like between walls sometimes as little as 24 centimetres apart. It was thus with some relief that this section was eventually left behind in favour of the more spacious dry passages beyond.

The Yaragaiya was a complex, three-dimensional phreatic maze centred upon an ancient trunk route, the Crystal Highway. In these timeless galleries silence had reigned supreme for millennia. Quite appropriately, a layer of dry silt covering the floor, sometimes to a considerable depth, deadened the explorers' footfalls. Around each new bend the explorers gasped as their lamps brought a brief dawn to the strange subterranean landscape before them. Amid pristine stalactites, stalagmites and columns they strolled, in a kaleidoscope of mineral enriched hues. The effect conjured up vivid mental images of a forest frozen in an unearthly parody of reality. Crystals glistened, while here and there gypsum flowers grew in petrified herbaceous borders.

All that glitters is not gold, however, and despite the intrinsic beauty of these time-enduring passages, hopes for a connection with the surface faded into mere speculation. The cavers could not hide their disappointment: High Hopes, Canyons End and False Promises reflected the frustration of each individual as lead after lead simply petered away to dead ends. They passed along The Shades with its macabre parade of bat skeletons; Dismal Inlet led them through an eerie passage vanishing into the equally oppressive Pikers Sump. The final ignominy of their failure was Goblins Lurk, a dark chamber with a deep brooding pool, which on a later trip threatened to swallow Richard Bartrop without trace. This was the remotest point from the entrance. After increasing the length of the cave by perhaps 1,500 metres the Yaragaiya camp was vacated and the explorers began the long journey out, reaching the surface after 36 hours underground.

THROUGH THE RAPID BYPASS

Robert Allen, a staff reporter with the Sydney Morning Herald, arrived in camp on Saturday, July 22, to cover the remainder of the expedition. He was soon immersed in the delights of caving "Atea style" with a cruise through the ooze, emerging afterwards plastered from head to foot, to announce it was his first ever caving trip and quite definitely his last. Notwithstanding his own trials and tribulations, he did not have long to wait for a drama to colour his despatches for the media back home.

The following Monday Jon Buchan, Bruce Unger[1], Tony White and Al Warild set off down the Ship Canal to rig float rope beyond the ducks and investigate the rumbling noise beyond. They found the previously rigged rope severed just before the last tie-off point at Usitanh Kananda, where the way forward was via a scramble up and over a pile of angular rocks. The latter formed a natural dam diverting the river to the right into a low oxbow, which at the time was believed to be sumped.

Jon Buchan joined Tony at the end of the rope and both noticed the current was quite strong. Before they could repair the break in the line Jon somehow lost his grip and to everyone's horror, the river took him. He was immediately swept towards the flooded overflow channel. He tried swimming back but could make no headway against the swiftly flowing river.

Tony saw Jon's head go underwater and his lamp go out. In fact, Jon was making a desperate attempt to return to safety by swimming crawl. But it was no use. Wearing Wellington boots and with saturated clothing, he was rapidly becoming exhausted. Tony recalls how he saw Jon scrabbling at the low passage roof in a frantic attempt to avoid being sucked irresistibly into the diminishing airspace (see fig. 11c). He was all in. "Relax and go with it," Jon told himself. He succumbed and saw the lights of his group quickly fade as the darkness enveloped him.

With frayed rope still in hand, the others watched their companion disappear from view…then there was silence. Everything had happened so quickly that they were still reeling in disbelief. Joining on a new length of line, they let it float down the passage, though everyone inwardly believed that it was the last anyone would see of Jon.

The oxbow was in fact not a sump, though airspace was indeed minimal. The harrowing traverse of "Dr. Jon's Rapid Bypass" ended abruptly as he was spat out at the far side in a series of rapids. The rest of the party crossed the river and negotiated the breakdown zone. After 30 metres, they were overjoyed to find their friend cowering in the darkness, ashen-faced and quite obviously shaken, but otherwise miraculously unhurt. He recounted how, at the last minute, holding his breath he was pulled into the sump. Expecting at any moment to start breathing water, he suddenly found himself in a roomier passage with airspace. He rolled and tumbled over and over in the powerful current as it carried him further downstream. In the pitch black the water ahead sounded very loud, and his worst nightmare was of being washed over a waterfall into oblivion.

As he tumbled in the water, his arms and legs struck bottom; it was then that he realised the river was not so deep. He managed to grab hold of a rock and, in total darkness, haul himself with some difficulty onto one of the few shingle banks along the riverway.

After Jon had recovered from his ordeal everyone pushed on, rigging ropes in the fast water sections beyond the ducks. They were oblivious to the fact that a thunderstorm had broken loose over the Muller. Fortunately, they decided to call it a day and turned back at more or less the same point that halted the previous party. On the surface, 17 millimetres of rain had fallen within an hour and everyone in camp was anxious for their safety.

---

[1] Shortly after the Atea trip, Bruce was tragically killed in a caving accident in the United States.

No sooner had the last person returned through the ducks when the flood pulse arrived. Even with the aid of pullback lines, it was only with a monumental effort that they were able to return against the increasing flow. They were extremely fortunate not to have been trapped behind the ducks, for these remained sealed for five days afterwards. The fact that they had run out of rope in this case proved their salvation. After these events, a 4:00 p.m. curfew was religiously followed, all parties returning to the near side of the low airspace sections before the onset of the afternoon rains.

By the end of July the length of the cave had increased with the discovery of the Austral Series. This section of the Atea was predominantly phreatic, mostly clean and well decorated, especially at the Rafting Ground where deep blue pools were covered with a form of rare calcite "ice." Towards the furthest extremity, a curious reversing air current at The Fishery gave vain hopes of a new entrance, since the passageway was almost directly beneath the Largest Doline in the World. Surface exploration in this area revealed a few blind shafts but no new way into the far reaches of the cave.

After three weeks of pushing lead after lead, the Austral grew to four kilometres. All the while rainfall was monitored and the level of the Ship Canal closely watched. When at last water levels had dropped sufficiently a team of five including Tim Daniel, Neil Montgomery and Guy Cox returned to seek a way on downstream of the ducks. The final swim carried them beneath a knobbly ceiling on a steadily increasing current to where more rapids all but filled the broad passage. The source of the noise heard on earlier trips was found to be the Impeller, where the river thundered into a restricted outlet similar to the Turbine further upstream. There was no hope of following the river in that direction, but to the left a colossal slope of corroded boulders intruded into the riverway.

The first breakthrough at the Holocaust came on Saturday, July 22. Ian Miller struck lucky when his ferreting about located a small hole among boulders close to where the river slid into the Impeller. Ahead was a pile of driftwood clogging a space between rocks. A few minutes' work removing this and manoeuvring boulders aside soon produced a way forward. Crawling on hands and knees, Ian was at length faced with a low, dark chamber. A dripping roof extended above an ominous pool; he could hear his own heart beating as the adrenaline started coursing through his veins. The booming of the river in the near distance reminded him of the fall of Gandalf at the Bridge of Khâzad-dum. He felt exposed.

Not being an especially confident swimmer, it took Ian a few days to summon the courage for the voyage down the Ship Canal, and then only when it had been fully rigged with float ropes. Forcing himself into the pool, a mercifully brief swim brought him to a welcome block forming an island. The sound of the river was by then quite deafening. Feeling a little insecure Ian sought the support of the others back in the choke. Guy Cox and Steve Worthington joined him in the new passage and they traced another dismal section of river passage around the eastern perimeter of the boulder pile.

Water showered from fissures in the roof while a stretch of rapids threatened to wash them off their feet; waves dashing against boulders flung water into the air. Swirling around a bend, the river plunged furiously into the Penstock. With high expectations, the team scrambled cautiously down into the wide rift chamber. The water thundered briefly along the left-hand wall before a spray-lashed sump swallowed it, less than 100 metres below the entrance. Time was advancing and although they could see a large passage continuing at the far side of the chamber, they had no desire to tempt providence. They made a hurried exit back to the upstream side of the ducks.

The next morning dawned in typical Muller fashion. The tree-clad hillsides leading down into the doline were lightly swathed in drifting cloud. Gradually this cleared to reveal patches of blue between the tall trees. Those planning exploration around the Atea doline, or who had surfaced late from a hard trip the day before, were still in bed, lined up in their sleeping bags like rows of bangers under a grill. The muffled sound of the Atea waterfalls filled the air – and the thoughts of those already awake. What would the new day bring?

Hoping the weather pattern would not radically alter, Richard Willson, Neil Montgomery, Steve Worthington, Guy Cox and Ian Hickson set off again into the cave. Their goal: the Penstock and whatever lay beyond. Once through the Holocaust they once again faced the violent sump chamber. A floor of silt-covered boulders led north into what proved merely to be a tributary. A diminishing passage provided 200 metres of unpleasant caving terminating in a scummy sump pool at Warimoo Oval.

Back amongst the boulders of the Holocaust there were no noticeable draughts, but the route taken by floodwaters could be divined in the piles of flood detritus and wisps of vegetation neatly wrapped around rocks. Following these "signposts," Neil spent some time negotiating an obscure route through the boulders, and, after perhaps 80 metres, he suddenly emerged upon a boulder slope angling down into a large open passage.

Duna Sands was dominated by rippled siltbanks deposited by the receding waters of previous floods. The others joined him and, inspired by visions of glory, they raced off together through another kilometre of passages. But for the occasional waist deep pool the cave was silent; nowhere did they meet the river again, yet it was clearly no place to be if the rains came.

At the right turn of a T-junction, a walking rift passage suddenly ended at a ten-metre high wall of clearly mobile boulders. Above this an enticing echo gave hint of a large void. The explorers climbed warily into the Aftermath, a colossal breakdown chamber, which at 100 metres in diameter was easily the largest cavern in the system. With a respectful hush they fruitlessly probed the walls and floor, looking for a way out of the cavern. Back at the foot of the climb a doubtful hole led off to the left, beyond which a joint-controlled rift grew wider and higher as it continued west. Ian was singing that ridiculous old Goons song, "Backwards to Christmas," as he waded through the occasional canal. Another junction offered a choice of crawls and tight rifts that doubled back to end beneath The Aftermath, whilst in the opposite direction, the passage ended in a pitch. Oh, for a rope!

Back at the junction with Duna Sands, Silent Thunder turned southwest in a fine six-metre diameter pressure tube. This eventually divided into the smaller Capillaries, each branch terminating in a rock fall. A muffled grumbling rising from somewhere beneath The Throb only deceived those who were hopeful of greater depth. On a later investigation, the noise was found to be caused by the acoustical combination of a minute stream in an equally small fissure and not the main river, as was at first thought.

The next day Rob Kay, Steve Worthington and Guy Cox returned through the Holocaust to tackle the undescended pitch. After rigging Acid Drop with a 30-metre rope, they descended a superb free-hanging abseil and landed on the boulder floor of Winchester, a 50-metre-high breakdown chamber. One or two holes going down between boulders were forced to silt chokes after 15 metres but these offered little promise of continuation. The surveyed depth of 143 metres proved to be the deepest point reached in the Atea.

OUTLYING AREAS INVESTIGATED

With new ground becoming increasingly elusive, emphasis inevitably shifted to outlying areas. Julia thrived on the logistics of co-ordinating this diversification of effort whilst pursuing her own understanding of the complex hydrological jigsaw and local water chemistry. During the 1976 expedition, Peter Ruxton and Randall King had traced an eastern trending valley some distance from Okaparu, but found it devoid of sinks. Aerial photographs indicated a major catchment; consequently, finding the main sink became a primary concern in 1978. On July 9, a helicopter reconnaissance northeast of the Atea traced the Okaparu Valley to a bend three kilometres east, then northwards located the sink of the Yu Dina.

Survey plotting revealed that the Yaragaiya Series was at most 50 metres below the floor of the Yu Dina valley (see fig. 9). The sink itself was six and a half kilometres from the Nali outflow, which a positive dye test had proved. Though the Dina did not appear to enter the known sections of the Atea, its proximity with the Yaragaiya Series suggested some connection in the past was likely.

After leaving the Atea base on July 21, Kathy Handel, Tim Daniel, Judith Bateman and Kevan Wilde spent a week investigating the rugged country in the vicinity of the Yu Dina. This patrol revealed much crevice karst but few caves. They returned to base and a day or two afterwards despatched two Duna carriers to search for the point where the Yu Dina went to ground. They returned 12 days later having found a large sinkhole.

By early August, explorations in the Atea had pushed its length to over 26 kilometres, firmly establishing it as the longest system in the Southern Hemisphere. Although a few minor open leads remained, impetus was by then flagging. The most likely places for further breakthroughs entailed trogging through the filthiest passages in the cave. Apart from some misguided souls or the dedicated few who upheld Julia's dream of depth in the Atea, this tended to put off would-be pioneers.

The Atea was many things to many people. To some, the lack of depth was a gross disappointment; others found the growing length and variety of the passages a challenge in itself. A few believed that the Atea was merely developing into a statistical exercise. All length records outside of Europe and America had been outstripped, yet they had failed to find any big wet shafts or the great depth that had been the principal stimulus for many team members. Within a couple of days' trek from the Atea lay some of the wildest tracts of virgin limestone country in the world. There was a sudden rush to snaffle supplies and equipment for patrols and satellite camps.

Bruce Unger, the vertical caver from Denver, was particularly disillusioned by overcrowded base camp life. He was interested in carrying out a solo reconnaissance to the Lavani, the famous "lost valley"of the 1950s. Rob Kay shared Bruce's sentiments and offered to go with him. On August 9, the pair of them departed with carriers as far as the junction of the Harage and Lavani trails near Geroro. Here they parted company with their guides and, shouldering their 30-kilo packs and rations for ten days, set off southeast towards Mt. Karoma.

By then Tony and Kevan had been in the Yu Dina valley a week and established a further field camp. From this base of operations, they spent several days cutting track east and to the north. Rudi Frank and Tim Daniel joined them. Tony and Kevan blazed a trail up a prominent ridge west of their new camp to examine an obvious feature visible on the aerial photographs. They descended the walled doline but found no worthwhile cave. Meanwhile to the south of camp, Tim was investigating numerous dolines when he lost his footing and stumbled into a deep gryke, gashing his leg.

While Tim laid up the following week, Kevan extended the trail up the western ridge but ran into appalling crevice karst and vine bamboo that made progress rather difficult; the route was therefore abandoned. Tim's condition grew steadily worse and Jon Buchan had already departed. Over the radio, a request for aerial evacuation provoked some heated arguments between Kevan and Mike Martyn, a final year medical student. Eventually Mike walked in from the Atea base with Geoff Francis but by then, Tim had lost mobility and Mike found that he had developed osteomyelitis. Helicopter assistance was finally summoned and two days later he was evacuated to Sydney.

In the absence of reliable topographical maps, the use of aerial photographs had become the accepted means of navigation through the New Guinea forests. They allowed large scale features to be located, but were of limited value in determining the difficulties that lay between, as graphically illustrated by Tim's accident. On the run of pictures covering the area, a group of clearings were quite visible on a mountain three kilometres east of the third Yu Dina camp. Local hunters referred to the region as Legari. These grassy oases were pitted by a number of promising dolines. The day of Tim's airlift Kevan, Tony, Rudi Frank and two very apprehensive Duna porters took to the air in the chopper, quickly reaching the largest of the clearings (Though the flight took just ten minutes, it would have been a five-day return journey on foot).

They established a camp and began a systematic investigation of the holes to the southwest. Two days and four kilometres later, a lucky diversion into the bush chanced upon the awe-inspiring gash of Uli Mindu. This shaft was fringed with tree ferns, and cobbles hurled into the depths returned a marvellous echo that growled back at them in a most impressive manner. They shifted camp the following day so that Rudi and Tony could have a crack at what was clearly a hole of respectable depth.

There were only two ropes available, of 55 and 35 metres. They set off with these, rigging to a ledge at -70 metres. The roomy shaft pinched in slightly at this point but continued to drop into velvety blackness. After a few deviations Tony came to the end of the rope without reaching a floor. Sounding stones fell free for three seconds before striking bottom. The explorer retreated to the surface suitably impressed, estimating the drop at 160 metres. With rations practically exhausted, they had no option but to backtrack to the Atea base, leaving Uli Mindu for the future.

In 1973 the Hegaibagu region had revealed significant vertical development with Uli Guria and Kananda Heiowa Heia, both exceeding 300 metres (see fig. 9). A strong belief persisted amongst some Sydney cavers that a connection between this area and the Atea was a possibility, albeit remote. Moreover, when Uli Guria was detackled by the original explorers five years before, a number of questions had remained unanswered.

On August 8, a team comprising Richard Bartrop, Donna Mroczkowski, Ian Hickson, Neil Montgomery and Ian Miller returned to the region. The old 1973 camp was overgrown and barely recognisable and Neil was amazed how thoroughly nature had reclaimed the tracks cut that year.

Discoveries in Uli Guria proved limited. At the base of the 45-metre entrance pitch, the 1973 route to the bottom led off on the west side. Opposite this the Cyclotron was explored down a new passage, a steeply descending narrow fissure parallel to the Shot Tower (see fig. 10). Five rope pitches and a number of climbs later, they eventually rejoined the main route at the base of the original big pitch. As in 1973, the latter proved just as fraught from falling missiles. Braving the dangers, the team traversed into Oolite Chamber and found a further 50 metres of unpleasant passage. The emergence of a very cold draught from the system suggested the cave linked in with bigger caverns somewhere below – perhaps a long way below – but unfortunately for them there was no improvement on total depth.

A BEAUTIFUL BUT HAZARDOUS FIND

The length of the Atea Kananda had reached almost 30 kilometres. By August 12, exploration was practically finished. It was to be a momentous week for the Australians, not because the cave by then ranked as the longest system outside Europe and the United States, but because a much sought-after breakthrough was about to occur on the nearby plateau.

The Mamo Plateau had been a priority objective on the two preceding Muller trips but each time the doline karst had proved so fierce that the intruders scarcely penetrated in from its edge. On its southwest fringe, close to the track down the Nali scarp to Nomad River, the aerial pictures appeared to show a number of sizeable sinking streams, though it was uncertain whether these flowed. Although they had attempted to reach these in 1976, Neil Hickson and Malcolm Handel had come up two kilometres short. It was Neil once again, with Alan Warild and Peter Ruxton, who forced a new route onto the Mamo via a dry creekbed intersected by the track leading down to the Nali.

Returning with Steve Worthington on August 14, they set up a fourth camp beneath the overhang of a large dry cave. After dropping a few uninspiring pits, they decided to examine their own "backyard," exploring 300 metres of walking passage to an aven. Not many metres from the campfire a small stream chattered down a restricted slot in the floor. By way of an evening diversion they decided to rig this for the sheer hell of it. However, they found it tight and a little too damp for comfortable caving. There was no detectable air current, but since it was handy they decided to persevere, descending again the next morning with ropes.

After four wet, confined pitches, the hole began opening up. The next drop was a fine shaft offering a free hang of 40 metres; at the bottom, Neil reported a miserable wet crawl with little scope. Across the top of the shaft though, his two companions entered a high level continuation. Neil joined them and together they strolled for 500 metres along Mainline, finding side passages entering with almost monotonous regularity (see fig. 19). They passed beneath a daylight aven that would later provide an easier way in.

With the return to Australia only a week away, a radio message soon brought an enthusiastic influx of cavers from the Atea base and elsewhere. Hadia Yaneabogairi was explored with mounting excitement over the next few days. In one amazing gallery, called the Sacking of Rome because of the unavoidable damage done by the first explorers, delicate spires of erratic stalactites adorned walls and roof in a crazy, twisted forest.

Al found and descended a new pitch, dropping into a passageway developed along a silt-stone bed. Later, he and Neil followed Siltstone Blues to a major junction, bearing right through, an oval pressure tube with the occasional deep pool that ended abruptly at a six-metre wet pitch, Six Molar. They could hardly believe their good fortune when an enormous echoing void opened before them. After eagerly rigging the short pitch they entered and marvelled at the cathedral-like grandeur of the Iguanodon, an immense breakdown cavern far bigger than anything previously found beneath the Mullers.

Sunday, August 22 would prove an unforgettable day for Neil Hickson, Julia James and Al Warild. The expedition pull out was practically underway when they discovered a way on at the eastern extremity of the Iguanodon, and pushed on to a depth of 175 metres in a lead they named Screaming Frog. At 5:00 p.m. torrential rain swept down across the Muller Range and within the hour, 87 millimetres had been recorded at the Atea base.

After five hours underground, the team was heading out through Rinse Cycle. At 6:00 p.m. Julia noticed the stream rising fast, so they made a dash for the entrance series. When they reached the top of a slope leading from Rinse Cycle to the drop back into Tetley Tarns the

*By overcoming The Crucible, Neil Montgomery became the first person to reach Confluence Dome
and the start of the awesome Ship Canal.*
Right: Steve Worthington in the Sacking of Rome, a well-decorated passage leading out of The Iguanodon.

passage ahead was brimming full of swirling water, ready at any moment to pour down upon
them. They were horrified to see a lake stretching ahead of them where previously there had
been only a knee-deep pool; a duck further upstream would certainly be sumped. Their only
hope of safety was back in the large chamber. They turned back.

In the couple of minutes it took to turn about the flood overtook them. A hurried retreat
downstream brought them to a sump which had closed just seconds before they arrived. Julia
was no newcomer to such conditions, having been surprised by floodwater two years before
while exploring the Quashies River Cave in Jamaica. But this time both Julia and Neil were
confused by the changes wrought by the rising water; there appeared to be no escape and Neil
was convinced they were about to die. Al retained his composure and found a high level bypass,
not a moment too soon. It had 15 centimetres airspace and was closing fast. No sooner had they
scrambled through this than it promptly sealed behind them. Their position was now grim.

Downstream the passage was one to two metres wide, but the water had risen an alarming
three metres in ten minutes and was still rising. In an attempt to seek refuge in the Iguanodon
they floundered downstream, roped together in deep, raging floodwaters. Al fastened himself
onto a rope and leapt in, allowing himself to be washed downstream while Neil acted as back-
stop. When the rope was run out, Julia slid down secured by a carabiner, and Neil following on

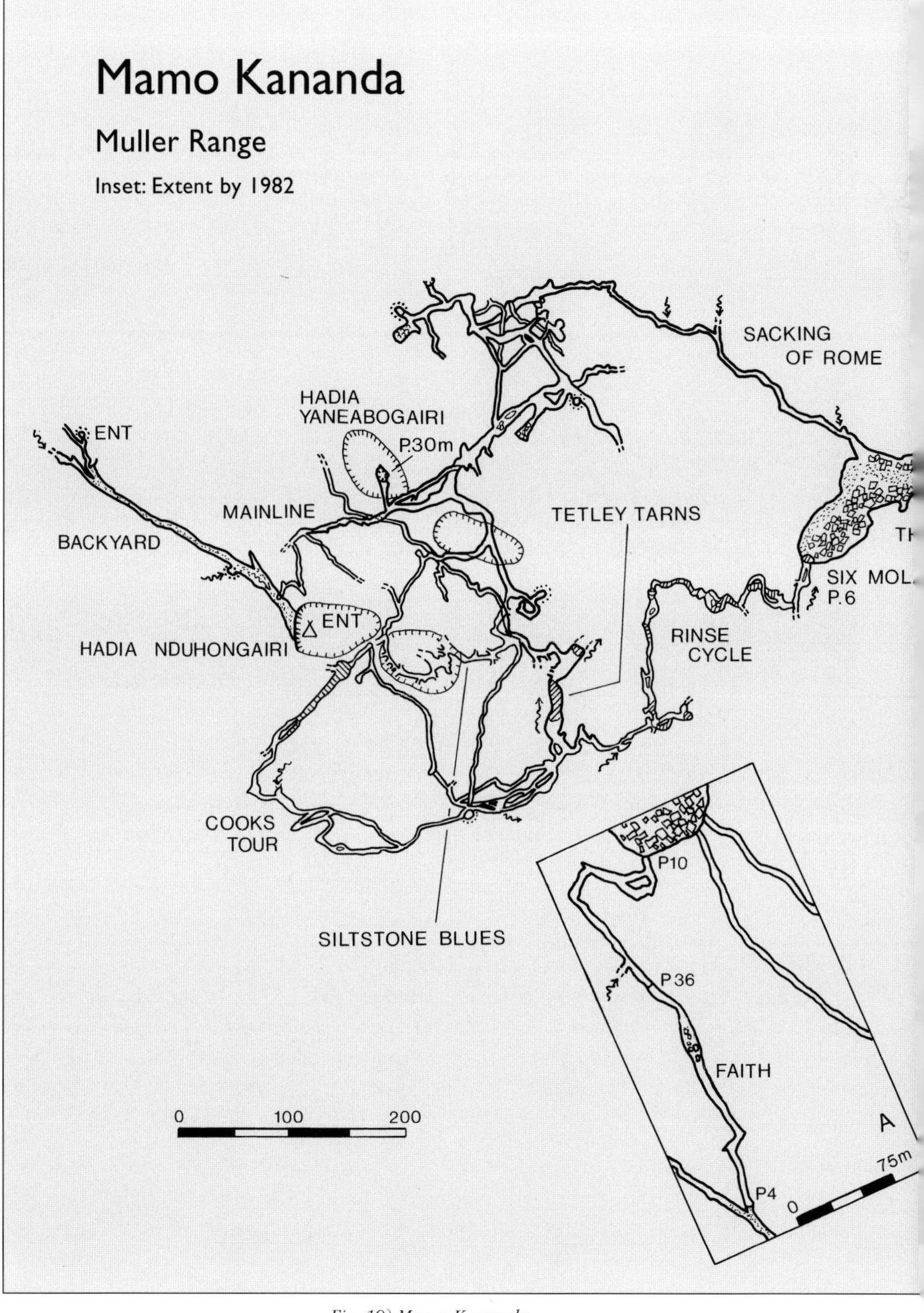

Mamo Kananda

Muller Range

Inset: Extent by 1982

SACKING
OF ROME

HADIA
YANEABOGAIRI
P.30m

ENT

MAINLINE

TETLEY TARNS

BACKYARD

TH

SIX MOL.
P.6

ENT

RINSE
CYCLE

HADIA NDUHONGAIRI

COOKS
TOUR

SILTSTONE BLUES

0   100   200

P10

P 36

FAITH

A

75m

P4 0

Fig. 19) Mamo Kananda

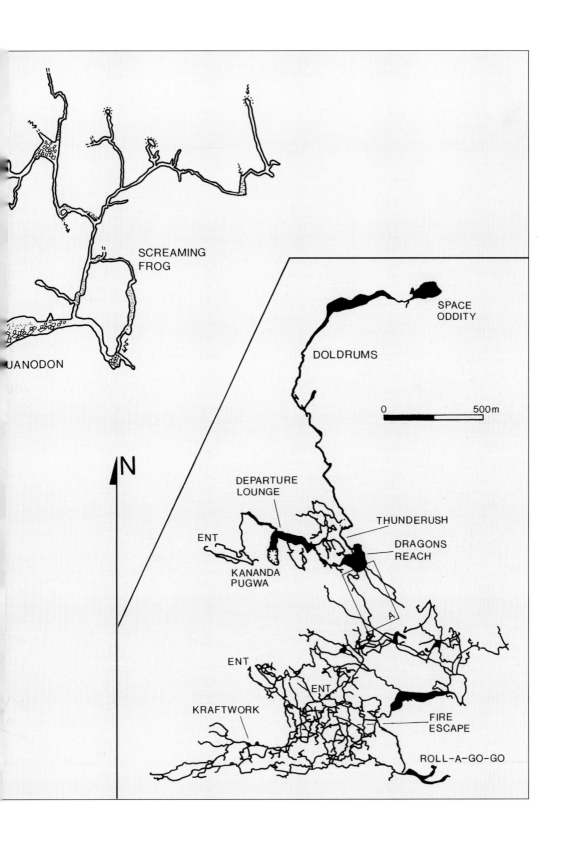

SCREAMING
FROG

UANODON

SPACE
ODDITY

DOLDRUMS

0   500m

N

DEPARTURE
LOUNGE

THUNDERUSH

ENT

DRAGONS
REACH

KANANDA
PUGWA

A

ENT

ENT

KRAFTWORK

FIRE
ESCAPE

ROLL-A-GO-GO

In 1978 and 1982, Al Warild, Neil Hickson and Julia James (from left to right) were to experience more than one close call in the flood-prone Mamo caves.

the rising tide. As he swept by, ricocheting from bend to bend and fighting to keep his head above water, they fielded him forward to repeat the process.

It was clear after doing this a couple of times that they would probably drown unless they could find safety from the still rising river. As luck would have it, they had a plentiful supply of climbing gear but in the panic to find the étriers in Al's pack, Neil cast into the flood anything that got in the way, including Al's camera.

An aid traverse at water level allowed Al to reach a stance after ten metres. Using a tyrolean the others joined him at a tiny ledge. This was barely a metre above the swirling stream, but a rising crack split the opposite wall. Using a tension move it was possible to lean across on a line and gain a footing. By then the water was lapping close to their armpits as Al forced a peg route to reach a dry oxbow five metres higher. Here they spent a draughty night in troubled slumber while the river roared by below them.

Back in camp it was not until 6:00 a.m. that anyone noticed the empty beds and realised that those below might be in danger. The flood had by then subsided sufficiently for the cavers to make a move. After breakfast the "rescue" team descended and met the "victims," who were starting out for the entrance, having just gathered the strewn contents of Al's pack from down the passageway. When asked about their experience, Neil responded, "It isn't every day you get to throw away an expensive camera!"

The flood caused problems elsewhere. In the Lavani and neighbouring valleys Rob Kay and Bruce Unger had found and partially explored 16 significant speleological features, including Gewane Kananda, which at over a kilometre was their largest find. As a climax to their venture the rains arrived, marooning Rob on the wrong bank of the Emama River where he was forced to spend an unprotected night out until the waters subsided. The storm also hit the Hegaibagu area.

In their final day of caving, Richard Bartrop, Ian Hickson and Ian Miller were pushing Uli Eta Riya, a promising pothole discovered two days before. After the imposing 60-metre entrance shaft, four pitches in rapid succession ended on the brink of a deep rift 150 metres below the entrance. It was here that their problems began. While Ian Miller remained at the head of the previous shaft the remaining two rigged the cave below. After several attempts to place a bolt in rotten rock they eventually settled for a shabby peg. The water soon increased to compound difficulties, pouring over the lip of the shaft in a concentrated spout.

A 60-metre rope was secured and Ian descended with more line and tackle. Twenty minutes had elapsed without any word from Ian when he came back up and Richard could see he was in a bad way from the cold. The stream had by then become a torrent. He was immediately sent up the next rope to where Ian Miller was waiting. Richard followed on detackling as he went.

After tying on the tackle bag, Richard began climbing to join his companions, but within a few metres the leg loops of his prussik rig broke. Retying these, he continued but the knots kept slipping, resulting in further halts in the cataract for running repairs. Richard was by then feeling the cold. After a slow ascent he at last joined the others. Ian Hickson was given some chocolate and told to keep moving towards the entrance.

Derigging was slow, but they eventually caught up with Ian on a windy ledge below the first pitch. He was subdued and appeared to be losing coordination, clear indications of the onset of hypothermia. The water had increased fourfold and was still rising. Ian was enveloped in the falling stream as he silently clipped his ascenders to the rope and started prussiking. After only a few body lengths he stopped under the full force of the waterfall. Fearing that a rescue situation was rapidly developing, Richard and Ian Miller bellowed words of encouragement above the noise. He slowly started moving again, and at length they saw him disappear over the head of the pitch. The others joined him there, and all three finally surfaced after seven chilly hours underground. Camp was three kilometres away along a switchback trail through rough bamboo country, and it was 7:00 p.m. before they finally staggered into the welcoming halo of light cast by the campfire.

And so the Atea expedition ended on a note of drama. Flooding below ground is something every caver has to come to terms with at some stage, though this usually involves nothing more serious than a trip cancellation. In Europe, and especially in the restricted stream caves of England's Yorkshire Dales, the threat of flooding is ever present. In the tropics it is even more life threatening.

Running more or less concurrently with the Atea expedition, a team of eight Spaniards spent three weeks caving in the New Guinea Highlands. The leader was Alfred Montserrat, a gemmologist working with the University of Barcelona. With limited resources they restricted their activities to a previously neglected region of the upper Chimbu Gorge close to Duglpagl village. Over a dozen caves were explored or extensions made to existing systems. Of special note was Kege Mur with its fine 168-metre entrance pitch, a new record for the deepest single drop in the country.

Maig Mur, otherwise referred to as Mebile Cave, was pushed to a depth of 132 metres. Some five kilometres southwest of there, a trip down Darua Muru increased the depth of this system to 230 metres, again without reaching a bottom. Exploration was curtailed by very wet conditions where a pitch once again halted further progress.

After concluding their investigations in the Chimbu Gorge, the Spanish team eventually moved west to Mount Hagen. A short stopover stay with Howard Beck preceded an equally brief visit to the Enga Province further west. The extent of the limestone here at Mt. Kaijende, despite excellent access from the Highlands Highway at Porgera, was beyond the scope and remaining time of the Spanish.

A view of Era Tem and the Hindenburg Wall.

148

Chapter Six

THE HOLE IN THE WALL GANG

Consider a cave entrance 40 metres wide that could be reached only after a week of treacherous climbing. Imagine teetering on the threshold of that mysterious portal, with your ears assaulted by the screeching of giant fruit bats flapping uncomfortably close to your primeval fears, while gazing down upon an ever-shifting ocean of cloud. Except to those expedition-bitten individuals who have experienced true wilderness, such a sense of isolation is hard to comprehend.

The Hindenburg Wall lies in the remote interior of New Guinea's Western Province, two full days hiking through undulating bush country to the northeast of Tabubil, operations base of the Ok Tedi Mining Corporation. At a point midway up this towering scarp Era Tem stares defiantly out across the Papuan lowlands (see fig. 20). It was first spotted from a passing helicopter by a member of the British team that discovered and explored Selminum Tem, the extensive cavern rambling beneath the plateau high above. It was the proximity of the "hole in the wall" to this labyrinth that had drawn a handful of British adventurers to this exciting backwater of the western pacific.

The venture was the brainchild of Noel Plumley, son of a Cambridge professor of Egyptology. In 1975, he had joined the British caving team as assistant cameraman to Sid Perou following Frank Binney's resignation. Since then, Noel had been haunted by an almost obsessive desire to return to the country and had considered several ambitious projects (a potentially suicidal canoe trip around the coastline being one that he dismissed).

Tony White knew all too well the meaning of frustration, for it was he who had gazed longingly into the beckoning gloom of Era Tem from a chopper hovering just a few nerve-jarring metres from the cliff. "What happened beyond the twilight zone?" he wondered. Secreted within those deep shadows was perhaps the key to extensive caverns developed between Selminum Tem and its outflow from Kaakil Tem at the foot of the Wall. Its unique position promised a divergent fauna developed in isolation from its nearest relatives in the primary forest below.

When the Atea expedition dispersed at the close of August 1978, Tony White, Steve Worthington and Richard Bartrop flew by chartered Baron from Koroba to Tabubil, 100 kilometres west. Noel and Norman Flux, a fellow Englishman from Yorkshire, were already in the area making contact with villagers and prospecting regions visited by few white people, and never before by speleologists. These included the area from the Ok Tedi to the foothills of the Star Mountains, the headwaters of the Wok Feneng (Fly River), and Sogolomik above the Hindenburg Wall. By the time the remainder of the team joined them, Noel and Norman had in two months visited or recorded over 40 cave sites and learned valuable lessons in lowland bush craft.

At the outset, Noel had been fortunate to find Aiyangim, a likeable Faiwolmin hunter who had proved invaluable on the expedition three years earlier. Once again he was to show his worth as guide, translator and odd-job man around camp. Already familiar with the aims

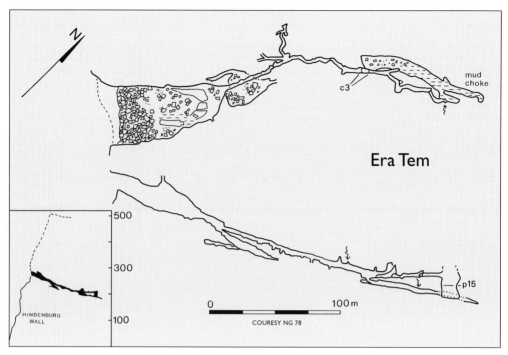

Fig. 20) Hindenburg Wall and Era Tem

of the cavers, he was able to convey these to the villagers they would meet in the forthcoming weeks.

Though Era Tem was the primary objective of the expedition, they could not be certain that reaching it would be possible. To reach it by climbing was a daunting prospect, made more so on account of a reported avalanche. There were political implications too: the frontier with Indonesian-held Irian Jaya had been a sensitive issue ever since Sukarno pulled the colonial rug out from beneath the Dutch. Since then Irianese, or free Papuan refugees, had been a continual source of embarrassment to the New Guinea administration. In 1978 they continued to pour over the border. Officials in Canberra watched border developments with increasing concern.

Most anxieties dissipated into the sticky atmosphere when on Monday, September 4 – their second day out from Tabubil – the five cavers and their retinue of porters stumbled the last few strides to the top of a ridge overlooking the Kam valley. With eyes screwed up against the sun, each man squinted across the treetops into the distance. Drinking in such a scene, it was hard to understand how bombing raids by Indonesian Strikemaster jets could have taken place within the territory, reportedly razing villages. With hostilities barely 25 kilometres west of Tabubil, the expedition could have floundered at the outset.

Steve and Richard now had their first glimpse of the Hindenburg Wall. Although still at least five kilometres away, it was an awesome feature, rising out of the jungle ahead of them like the improbable, weather-scarred headstone of some giant tribal chieftain. They stared at the white scar where the landslide had occurred. Wrapped in private thoughts, each strained to pick out his *raison d'être*, willing the imagination to picture the forces that in January the previous year tore away an estimated 15 million tonnes of the Hindenburg Wall, turning a vast tract of forest into so much matchwood.

The hole was clearly visible, located safely to the east of the devastation. Further east still, the cliff merged into a barely perceptible suggestion of indigo extending beyond sight. To the west this vision gave birth to the Benstead, Benkwim and Ross Bluffs, which formed the southern bastion of the Star Mountains. In all, some 25 kilometres of almost unbroken scarp formed an obvious barrier to northwards travel.

How best to reach the cave at this stage confounded them. Abseiling from the top was one option, but the overhanging face made it unlikely. In 1975, Tony had been to the very brink of the Hindenburg Wall and vividly recalled how he and his companions had fought their way through vicious tower karst and bamboo forest, where a good days' progress, with luck, was 200 metres.

Three days later they had set up their flies within a stone's throw of the Wall, on a narrow switchback of a ridge overlooking the Kaakil River a kilometre due south of their objective. While finishing touches were added to the base camp Tony and Steve set off to assess climbing prospects. A shallow gully could be seen more or less extending up to the vicinity of Era Tem. It had possibilities but the rock was heavily vegetated and appeared quite rotten – unlike the wall above the Kaakil outflow further east. This soared impressively up into the swirling clouds, an especially blank face that might have taken weeks to ascend. Although equipped for prolonged aid climbing, Steve considered the alternatives.

The lower section of the gully was formed in vertical tufa, a reef-like deposit built up over a period of time by calcium-rich water. Beginning 50 metres to the right of this, Steve led off up a vague crack that continued with easy scrambling through near vertical jungle. Two sparse sections dictated moderate aid climbing. At the end of the first day, they had gained the top of the tufa bank. Though they had climbed 175 metres, they were only 60 metres off the ground. Excitement came unexpectedly when Steve hauled himself wide-eyed onto a ledge and came face to face with a snake. Perhaps the sight of a hairy caver was more frightening to the serpent, for the latter beat a hurried retreat into the undergrowth. Rigging the rope from a suitable belay, they abseiled down and returned to camp for the night.

By morning, the forest canopy was veiled in grey cloud and persistent rain sheeted across the rock face in an unappetising manner. This was to set the pattern for the following week. The day yielded 130 metres of easier but vegetated climb, and they soon reached a roomy ledge; they were about half-way to the cave. By mid-afternoon both climbers were soaked through, the cold having penetrating their fibre pile suits and Goretex shells. They called it a day and bailed out, rigging a 200-metre length of 10 millimetre rope as a fixed line. This was rebelayed at every opportunity to convenient shrubs to reduce the danger of abrasion.

On Saturday, the clear dawn was almost palpable, though it was hidden by the trees. But as the morning arrived, it clouded over almost before they had reached the base of the Wall. A 45-minute prussik saw Tony and Steve back at the ledge, surveying their next move. Below them a few forest giants poked their ragged heads through the mists, islands of chlorophyll in a hazy sea of shifting surf. The distinctive call of a riflebird echoed across the canopy and a tree exploded with biological shrapnel as a flock of fruit pidgeons scattered to the wind. Under any other circumstance the day would have been paradise on earth, but today there was work to be done...Being the most experienced climber in the team Steve once again grasped the gauntlet.

Elsewhere that day Richard, Norman and Noel found and cleared the old 1975 track to the Kaakil Tem. When threatening weather had forced a retreat at the end of the expedition that year, many questions were left unanswered; the flood prone nature of the cave had presented a major obstacle to safe exploration. This time there were hopes of entering a major river system.

As in 1975, access to the entrance was obtained with the help of a sapling ladder constructed by Aiyangim and other bushmen. Once in place, exploration proceeded, and the cavers soon discovered 400 metres of new passage leading off from the main parting of the ways, the complex Casserole Junction. Lack of tackle dictated that numerous pitches dropping to the lower river level had to be left for another day. Following one six-hour trip they had surfaced to torrential rain and a swollen Kaakil River. Enthusiasm was tempered by the fact that in the first seven days at the Wall, 444 millimetres of rain was recorded – almost as much as London receives in a whole year! It made for dangerous caving and miserable climbing.

Back on the Wall, the featureless face seemed to exude menace, but the climbers parried this with a delicate move left and out along an ascending ramp to a narrow ledge, 40 lip-biting metres away. This provided an exposed stance, relieved by an opportune break in the clouds and a glimpse of the impressive cliffs towards the Kaakil. They also enjoyed a first close up view of their goal at the top of the main gully. Almost as instantly as it arrived, the vision became a memory as the weather wrapped its dripping cloak about the climbers once again.

The air was clammy and chill, a swirling murk punctuated by the staccato clicking of unseen cave swifts echoed by a cave that was tantalisingly close. Their noses confirmed that they were near, wrinkling to the unique aroma of tropical caves, a blend of dank limestone, decomposing vegetation and the powerful odour of ammonia-rich guano beds accumulated over time. It was so close, yet the rock was shabby and progress painfully slow.

Steve lined Tony up on a doubtful three-peg belay, with no problems. But from there they gained precious little ground, a solitary 25-metre pitch before abseiling off as the advancing day turned out the lights.

That night the air was rent by violent electric storms that flashed and clattered on the plateau high above them. The occasional rock fall disturbed the small hours. The team passed the night in fitful slumber, haunted by fleeting visions of avalanches and gangly, multi-limbed creatures washed in an unearthly blue glow as brief flashes flickered through the trees surrounding camp. The lightning hissed and the air was heavy, almost suffocating. The night seemed endless.

Dawn arrived at last to an eerie calm and an atmospheric freshness typical of the forest after a persistent downpour. They ate breakfast listlessly, hearing the arrival of the now familiar rain squalls. The climbers declared a day of rest, while at the Kaakil the remainder of the team pursued tenuous rewards for investigating the outfall cave, always keeping one eye on the weather.

THE THRESHOLD OF ERA TEM

By now it was taking at least three hours to slither up the muddy trail to the wall and climb back to the previous high point. The corner above the triple peg belay seemed to offer the line of least resistance, but even so there were other worrying moments. Steve was reminded that pitons are not always the most reliable anchors when he took two falls: the first when one broke, the second when another pulled out while he put his weight on it. His heart skipped a beat and he wondered if back-up belays would hold fast.

More loose rock forced a bold move up a very green wall to the left. He peeled off twice more as the insecure scrub parted company with the limestone. As luck would have it, he found more solid rock beneath the mantle of vegetation, and he was able to place a few secure pegs. The wall above was dotted here and there with metre-high bushes. Sod it, he thought. Casting ethics to the wind, Steve lassoed these in turn, pulling up on them with a sharp intake of breath.

Somewhat unorthodox but nothing ventured…a rock came loose and whistled off below – fortunately falling clear of Tony – to crash with a distant thud in the jungle below.

Securing himself to as many of the most permanent-looking shrubs as possible, Steve lifelined his second on a tight rope. Together they scanned their airy perch. A well-rooted tree approximately 20 metres above appeared to offer a sound belay for the abseil down, so they wasted no time gaining this and descending to a well-earned dinner. A long, damp day and three more pitches had taken them only 70 metres nearer their objective.

Richard accompanied Steve on a 5:00 a.m. start to the fifth day of climbing. Just for a change, sound belays ensured rapid progress for the next 100 metres, and the pair arrived back in camp unexpectedly by mid-afternoon. After the nineteenth pitch, only 20 metres of steep climbing separated them from the cave mouth.

The following day was the moment they had all been waiting for and without exception, they were poised for action. Nevertheless, it took nine hours for the whole team to assemble at the limit of the previous day's climbing; enough food and equipment had been hauled up for a two-day bivvy. When Steve at last moved off, only two hours of daylight remained. Dusk descended upon them before they could negotiate the final pitch, 20 metres of loosely cemented boulders that gravity had eased from the cave roof and deposited in the gully below the entrance.

At length, the group was finally mustered on the threshold of what seemed the most isolated cave entrance known to man. As nightfall eclipsed the outside world, some flat slabs were chosen as a hasty bivvy site. While a brief sortie into the cave established that it quickly diminished in size, attempts to light a fire proved futile. Resigned to a meal of dried rations partially revitalised with cold water, they ate their dinner mechanically. Few hunters in the forests below would have noticed the five tiny pin points of light flickering in the cave high above them. Each went out one-by-one as the cavers bedded down for a night of wild dreams. The climax of three year's curiosity would have to wait until morning.

When they awoke, the first tentative rays of dawn were already searching the entrance chamber, a slope of moss-covered boulders heading down into the mountain. Before rushing off to explore, the group held a photographic session for the benefit of sponsors, knowing the weather would soon move in to obliterate the view across Papua. Donning caving suits, they eagerly explored over half a kilometre of fossil galleries, in places adopted by small misfit streams. A few short climbs converged all too soon upon a chamber as silent as an Egyptian tomb where an apparently solid mud choke barred further progress. The 90-metre-deep cave was surveyed and biological specimens collected before the team vacated the site.

Though the cave itself proved something of an anticlimax, its position and particularly the 20-pitch climb required to reach it represented the summit of their endeavour. One had to face the fact that not every caving expedition has to put up such a route to realise its ambition; it was a situation without parallel.

While Noel, Richard and Norman abseiled off with the gear, Tony and Steve had the unenviable task of bringing up the rear, derigging the climb as they went. It was a white-knuckle descent if ever there was one. After each pitch, with the rope successfully pulled through without snagging, both were able to breathe a sigh of relief. Time marched on however, and before they were halfway down, the brief equatorial twilight had been eclipsed by a night almost as black as the netherworld. It was raining with a determination that is peculiar to the tropics. The two experienced some difficulty in keeping carbide lamps alight while preventing the ever-increasing mass of rope from entangling itself in the vegetation.

At one point, Steve was standing on a ledge dripping when suddenly the rock beneath him gave way. He instantly dropped a metre or so, letting out a shriek that pierced the silence of the jungle night. While Steve dangled on what was probably the most dubious belay of the whole climb, Tony instinctively sprang to one side. There was a loud crash followed by the pungent smell of shattered rock as the projectile bounced off the ledge where he had stood a split second before. In the dark he could only imagine its size but when he later saw the crater made by the 50-kilo boulder at the foot of the rope, he realised just how close he had come to meeting his maker. By 9:00 p.m., the two bedraggled but relieved cavers stood at the base of the wall amidst a confused heap of rope, rocks and brushwood.

After the excitement of the climb to Era Tem Noel, Norman and Tony trekked back to Tabubil to replenish supplies while Richard and Steve stayed behind to carry on exploration in the Kaakil. Upon returning from Tabubil on Tuesday, September 19, they learned that trips into the cave had been postponed when heavy rains repeatedly washed away the bridge across the river. Steve had also been struck by a mystery illness during their absence.

Three days later everyone was awakened in the small hours by an almighty rumbling noise. The ground shivered and trees rattled as Tony sat up in his sleeping bag rubbing his eyes. His immediate thought was that an earthquake had hit. Shadowed streaks tore past the end of the flysheet as the porters vacated camp with a speed that would give them a place in the Guinness Book of Records. Richard was just pulling his pants on when the noise died away. Only then did the porters return, laughing, when it transpired that a landslip had taken place at the wall, the second within a week. It was sobering to find that their previous camp had been right in its path.

The following day Tony and Richard entered Kaakil Tem to tie up loose ends (see fig. 16). They descended one of the pitches in the passage floor to reach the main river flow; unfortunately this sumped both up and downstream. Part way down the climb however, a descending traverse along the left-hand wall gave an exposed route into a few metres of large streamway. Soon they were stopped again – this time by a lake – but a loud roar from somewhere beyond it suggested the presence of a waterfall.

Monday saw Norman embarking upon an unusual subterranean voyage. Naked and spread-eagled between two 25-litre plastic drums lashed to a pack frame, the "volunteer" performed a nervous sort of breast stroke-doggy paddle, propelling his makeshift craft along the River of Lethe. He was ever mindful of the approaching turmoil as the flame from his lamp danced wildly in the wind, generated by whatever lay ahead. Unfortunately the swift current prevented him ever reaching the base of the cataract. Steve made a further attempt but faired little better. At the point reached no easy route up the waterfall pitch could be seen. Worse still, froth deposited high up the walls indicated the stream had recently backed up to an incredible 75 metres above resurgence level!

Although there was every chance of entering an extensive river system beyond the lake, everyone was alarmed by the tide mark. Predicting flow levels was impossible and localised storms on the plateau above could at any moment send a flood pulse boring through the cave, with fatal consequences. With nerves on edge at the constant threat of drowning they decided to abandon exploration.

As the end of the month approached, everyone decided to return to Tabubil for a bit of rest and recuperation, Australian prospector style. Although two months of the expedition remained, they still had a great deal of ground to cover and many cave entrances to investigate. Wol Tem and Arem Tem were two of the more promising. Noel had discovered both, the former while returning from a patrol north of Mount Fubilan. Arem Tem, on the other hand, was located almost ten kilometres southeast of Tabubil midway between the Ok Tedi and the gorge of the Ok Menga.

Arem Tem, a flood-prone system over 300 metres deep discovered by a four-man British team in 1978.

FRAYED HOPES, SHATTERED NERVES

On September 29, the group split. Noel and Richard left to explore Wol Tem, while the remainder of the group headed for the Ok Arem. The latter was only a three-hour walk along the Migalsimbip track from the new Tabubil to Ningerum bush road. Upon arrival at the Arem it took Steve, Richard and Tony another hour to locate the main sink in spite of – or maybe because of – Noel's directions. Here they found the whole of the river being swallowed by a cave formed in steeply dipping creamy coloured limestone. The entrance was partially obstructed by washed-in logs. A ten-metre wide flood overflow channel continued 50 metres further west before leaving the surface down a short pitch that would be impassable in wet weather. Intuitively Steve peered behind this, locating a slightly higher cave that might promise a safer way down via another drop.

Norman descended for a solo investigation. From the entrance chamber a clean-washed passage led off in light scalloped rock that was a pleasure to explore – or would have been but for having to keep an ear cocked for the possibility of an approaching flood. A walking-sized rift plunged down several easy climbs to where the lone explorer was halted by a deep shaft and forced to retreat (see fig. 21).

On Saturday, September 30, he returned with Steve and Tony. At the new pitch Steve traversed across the void and, negotiating a climb, reached and tackled the 15-metre drop. Using a 10 millimetre line, Norman descended to a point below a ledge where he could see the rope hanging free with a further ledge dimly visible below. He decided against continuing until the

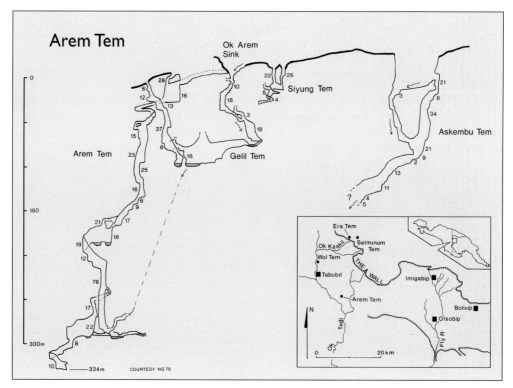

Fig. 21) Arem Tem

rope had been re-rigged – quite fortuitously, since Steve found the sheath of the rope severed at the first rub point. After repositioning the rope using protectors, they pushed the system to a depth of 140 metres, but ran out of tackle after eight technical pitches.

They surfaced at 6:00 p.m. At around midnight heavy rain descended on camp and continued without break well into the following morning. When the deluge finally abated they checked the river level to find discoloured floodwater thundering down the cave. A porter was despatched to Tabubil with a note requesting the others join them with more gear to continue what would clearly be hazardous exploration.

Noel and Richard arrived back at the mining camp earlier that same day after completing their investigation of Wol Tem. Where the Ok Tedi had carved itself a winding canyon some four kilometres north of Tabubil, five holes in the gaping riverbank invited entry into a labyrinth complete with active streamway. During the reconnaissance Norman had partially examined the cave, which was especially memorable for the profusion of bats and bloated pink leeches, often spaced out at 15-centimetre intervals on the passage walls. What the latter lived on when cavers were not on the menu beggered understanding.

Working from a makeshift camp within the cave, the two spent nine hours mapping nearly a kilometre of passageways. On the day of their departure they awoke to discover the Ok Tedi outside the entrance had risen alarmingly, making it impossible to return the way they had come, along the east bank of the river. Their only option was to go back through the cave, shouldering all their gear, and exit from one of the upper entrances. This they did, negotiating an exposed cliff above the river to effect their escape from the gorge.

On the fifth, Richard and Noel joined the team at the Arem camp, where the flow entering the flood entrance of Arem Tem had been improved by removing debris blocking the main sink. The cave was still not bottomed, principally due to the ominous weather. The entrance at the main stream sink remained unexplored and Gilel Tem had been followed as far as a lake at minus 80 metres, but had not been pushed. A fine moonlit night raised hopes of descending Arem Tem the next day.

Back at the cave the following morning, Tony and Steve observed tide marks that left enthusiasm wanting. Ropes left *in situ* had been shredded beyond redemption by the floodwaters, one line hanging by a mere two millimetres. They were aware of the hazards, having both been caught by rising water on separate occasions in the new going cave at Mamo. No one spoke of the risks but each was silently attuned to those first indicators of an approaching flood.

Taking a plentiful supply of rations and space blankets, they re-hung the damaged lines and with some urgency pushed silently on pitch by pitch. Chances were they would be on a rope if a cloudburst overtook them, and possible refuges were few and far apart. When they reached the head of the thirteenth vertical – a drop of over 100 metres – the loud rumbling was the last sound either of them wished to hear.

The adrenaline surge eased when they realised with relief that the sound was not the roll-call of their demise, but arose enticingly from below the rim of the shaft on which they teetered. After regaining composure, their fright merged seamlessly into optimism. At the foot of the pitch a heavy stream tumbled down a short climb to their right and foamed around a corner to languish in a spacious sump pool.

With disappointment tempered by relief, they set off out detackling. In the south wall of the final shaft a void caught their attention, and with hopes of a bypass they pendulummed eagerly into the hole and pursued a new descending rift. They continued rapidly onwards and down towards the growing murmur of a large stream. Shortly they were peering down another drop with the sound of water drifting up from below. It was likely the upstream section of the large

Manoeuvring tacklebags along a traverse above the first underground pitch in Arem Tem.

inlet at the bottom of the cave and not worth the risk of outstaying their welcome in this flood-prone system. While they continued to the surface, the rain began to fall.

At 8:00 a.m. Richard awoke with a start to rainfall beating a tattoo on the flysheet. Steve and Tony had not yet returned from Arem Tem and when the gauge was checked it was found to contain 21 millimetres of rain. Anticipating a rescue he roused Noel and Norman from their beds and together they hurriedly kitted up. Just as they were about to depart the overdue pair drifted into camp 18 hours after going underground. Luck had been with them.

The plotted survey showed Arem Tem to be 295 metres deep, but more important, it was clear that the rumbling heard below the undescended pitch could not be the inlet encountered at the bottom. A further trip down was necessary. In a final sortie Richard and Steve returned to the new pitch and at its base found the source of the noise. Here the stream from the old down-stream sump had its confluence with another river, equal in volume to the Ok Arem. The increased flow of water dropped eight metres then tumbled down a descending rift forming two short climbs. It was an atmospheric stretch of passage, the final drop of ten metres being overcome with combined tactics. With only one six-metre rope remaining, all available slings were knotted together and hung in the direct force of water, swallowed by a two-metre wide fissure. Clinging desperately to the walls to avoid a wetting, they landed in a spray-lashed chamber where the river sank under a boulder floor at a final depth of 334 metres.

After forcing both Gilel Tem and the main river sink to a depth of only 100 metres, the last remaining lead was a new hole discovered by Richard and Noel in a nearby parallel valley. Askembu Tem (Hurricane Cave) had an incredible gale blowing from it that created plumes of vapour as the cooler cave air met the humid atmosphere of the Papuan jungle. A sizeable stream entered the new cave, but they chose an alternative dry series, hopeful that this might provide a flood-free way into Arem Tem beyond the known limit.

Although water imparts life to a cave, its sheer volume may threaten life itself. Caves and water are virtually inseparable: one complements the other. It was perhaps inevitable that the waterways would eventually rejoin in Askembu Tem. The system followed a more or less identical pattern to Arem Tem, but because of the high water flow and lack of refuge from possible inundations, it quickly developed into a more serious proposition. It was a time-consuming task to rig each pitch for a dry hang. After rigging eight drops to a depth of 120 metres the explorers doubted that they could continue. Further wet descents offered no escape from floods, so with their remaining expedition time better spent elsewhere they abandoned Askembu Tem in favour of the move east.

SPIDERS AND SUPERSTITIONS

Leaving the steaks, booze and videos of Tabubil behind, the team flew east to Olsobip. The flight saved the expedition almost a week of arduous trekking and gave them a bird's eye preview of the terrain. South of Olsobip extensive limestone mountains running sub-parallel to the Hindenburg Wall formed the heavily dissected Il, Emuk, Kaban, Donaldson and Blucher ranges (see fig. 3). This was the so-called "broken bottle" country that between 1926 and 1928 presented such a fearful obstacle to Ivan Champion and Charles Karius in their trans-island crossing from the Fly River to the Sepik.

Immediately due south of Olsobip the Gum Gorge formed a deep gulf separating the Il from the Emuk Range. The infant Fly slipped through this "mountain gate" to enter the plains of

A backlit caver silhouetted while prussiking the third pitch of Askembu Tem.

Papua. When the cloud base was down, madcap pilots plying the route between Kiunga and Olsobip were known to follow the winding Fly on its pseudo-subterranean course. It was debatable which was the more hazardous, crossing the ranges among clouds with solid centres or dicing with death in the confines of the canyon.

As the cavers gazed through the tiny windows of the plane they were thankful not to be faced with such a choice. However, it was a view that attracted superlatives, a shifting scene that kept them guessing what must lie beneath the jungle-clad plateau flanking this serpentine chasm. It would keep for the time being. At least a week would be needed to reach the first of these broken ranges.

With so many promising leads to follow, they opted for a policy of divide and diversify. Noel and Norman hiked east to Bolivip in the territory of the Unkiamin people to investigate reports of resurgence caves there; the remaining three intended having a look on the Il Range. Each group carried walkie-talkie radios, but they were often out of range of each other, limiting their usefulness.

At 9:00 a.m. on October 29, Steve, Tony and Richard left Olsobip with four native porters and a guide. Striking south by the airstrip, they headed for and crossed a vine bridge over the Fly and headed into the mountains. It only took three days to become disenchanted with the Il Range, as the locals were either reticent to show caves or simply had no idea where they were. Of those they did see, only Bum Tem offered any sizeable development, a wide shaft dropping 45 metres to a boulder choke. The country was waterless and rugged in the extreme, crevice karst riddled with deep fissures. The few hunting tracks there were barely made inroads into the vicious karst, and those that did often spanned chasms on flimsy sapling bridges that creaked and sagged alarmingly.

Not very impressed with the first of the limestone ranges, they set off back for Olsobip, stopping to bathe in the Fly River despite reports that it had its resident three-metre crocodile. They were perhaps lucky that day, even if they say this ravenous creature never eats fresh meat!

Imigabip was said to have two significant outflow caves located at the foot of the Hindenburgs, Birak Tem and Ligin Tem. These were 15 kilometres north and 1,000 metres higher than Olsobip. When making further enquiries about these two caves, the cavers were told they were of a minor nature, but that there were some large holes worthy of investigation above the Hindenburg Wall. On November 2, the trio departed for the three day climb. At the end of the first days' walk they overnighted in a village set like a Tibetan monastery on a razorback ridge overlooking the most inspiring of panoramas. The men's house was put at their disposal. Nearby some boys had been shut up in the tamburan house, and after ten days living off the milk of coconuts they emerged that night as men to a *mu-mu'd* [1] pig, the climax of their initiation into manhood.

Resuming the ascent the following morning, they picked their way slowly up to the plateau high above the village. It was a hard day. The route required extremely steep scrambling, with vertical sections equipped with native ladders lashed to the rock. It was no place for anyone with a weak disposition. After lunch the last 20 metres was behind them and they stepped into the Elfin-like realms of the cloud forest, silent and shrouded in dripping moss and liverworts. They entered a valley, the western extension in fact of the same feature explored three years before by Dave Brook's team. With Imigabip four hours behind them, they came upon a small stream sink with an overhanging cliff nearby. Here they bedded down for the night.

In the morning their guide showed them Fok Tem, a 10-metre-deep shaft in shattered rock. Having been prepared for exploring resurgences they had brought a limited supply of rope. Richard made the initial descent. The hole was located in a deep shakehole that was the focal point for several small creeks. As a result the descent was expected to be a little damp.

After reaching a ledge he encountered heavy spray. A convenient chockstone formed a belay and he climbed a further 15 metres where, placing a peg, he was able to re-belay the line and reach a wedged tree trunk. This provided yet another deviation. Below this the cave levelled momentarily before developing into a steep ramp terminated by a drop. Stones cast into the hole landed with a muffled thud suggesting a floor of mud. Richard estimated the drop to be 60 metres. He carried out a grade three survey and joined his waiting companions after an hour underground.

[1] *A mu-mu is a pit oven in which food is wrapped in leaves and sandwiched between hot stones, and covered with earth.*

The Ship Canal, Atea Kananda. 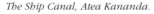 *Languid Lakes in the Ugwaguw, Atea Kananda.*

Before evening set in they cut some track along a shale-limestone boundary along the valley, hopeful of finding some caves. But enthusiasm quickly waned when they encountered rough terrain in dense bamboo. Over the next two days they located more sinkholes, then Steve returned to Fok Tem. He descended the entrance pitches in one single descent of 60 metres; those on the surface then lowered the rope to him on a vine. Armed with a survey tape, he set off into the unknown, returning two hours later after having reached a lake of unknown depth a further 30 metres down.

By November 8, everyone had returned to Olsobip. Noel and Norman had enjoyed little success at Bolivip, the most interesting feature having been Um Tem, a cave in which locals once hunted flying fox. It was reported to be large, and villagers related how one man had spent a whole day inside without realising he was in a cave! Despite the exaggeration factor, the cave was nonetheless impressive. The duo mapped about 500 metres of passage in cave that appeared to carry a considerable flow in times of flood.

Over the next day or two, the team at Olsobip cleaned and repaired caving gear and plotted surveys while they contemplated what their next move would be. With only a week or two remaining it looked as though the Emuk and Kaban ranges were their only chance of discovering something really deep. Some good-looking holes could be seen on the aerial photographs, but recruiting guides proved problematic. Villagers were mysteriously reticent when plied for information about caves in the Kaban. In one settlement, when pressured for information, everyone suddenly developed a mysterious sickness and had to depart for the *haus sick* (village medical centre).

A day or so later an army plane landed with supplies for a company of soldiers who were trekking through from Wewak on the north coast. Rebels from across the border had been terrorising kiaps well into New Guinea territory. The cavers learned from the pilot that while they had been at the Kaakil camp, guerrillas had been fighting over the next ridge a mere ten kilometres away.

On the 11th the cavers left Olsobip, and three days afterwards had departed from the hamlet of Duminak and gone their different ways. Noel and Tony headed off up onto the Emuk Range, while Steve, Tony and Richard took a hunting trail southeast through a col dividing the Emuk from the Kaban Range, their ultimate goal. Due to treacherous terrain and the porters' reluctance to carry, progress was slow. On the Emuk, Noel and Tony were constantly plagued with nasty red biting flies, but despite this and the vicious pinnacle karst, they succeeded in bottoming a number of deep shafts. These mostly ended in boulder chokes inhabited by some large and nasty looking spiders.

The story was much the same on the neighbouring Kaban Range. After an eight hour trek to the southeast, Duminak, Steve, Richard and Norman entered the shallow Delpinalu Basin where on the 15th they made the first descent of the impressive Gebemi Tem. Rigging the wide shaft from a suitable tree provided an impressive 84-metre free hang into a huge chamber estimated at one million cubic metres in volume. As is so often the case with large chambers, there was no way out from the bottom.

Further down the Delpinalu Valley a prominent meandering riverbed could be seen on the air photos. Richard departed with Suneng to investigate this, yet after walking for about an hour his guide suddenly stopped and announced it was as far as he was prepared to go. When pressed for reasons the guide related a tale of a river sink that would overflow and flood the valley to the treetops if anyone entered the cave that swallowed it. Similar stories were encountered by other groups of cavers elsewhere in New Guinea, notably in the Finim Tel and Ok Agim areas during the 1975 expedition.

Time was running out and, severely hampered in their efforts to break new ground, they had to return to Tabubil. Nevertheless, depth potential on the Kaban seemed to be in the order of 1,500 metres, even as much as 1,900 metres. It appeared to offer excellent prospects for discovering world-class cave systems. The main barrier to exploration here may well prove to be subjective rather than one merely of difficult terrain. The latter was clearly a deterrent to barefoot guides who, even in quest of the highly prized flying fox, never ventured into the vicious karst of the Kaban and Emuk. These factors apart, there was a distinct feeling that there were bad spirits on the Kaban. There was understandable disappointment in the team's failure to reach what seemed to be one of the most promising regions in the country. However, they could count themselves fortunate in having seen these virgin caves first-hand, in a most wild setting. Arem Tem was a significant pothole and the memory of Era Tem would remain with them to the end of their days.

The two years up to 1980 would witness some of the most dramatic developments in New Guinea caving. Forceful techniques by expedition-seasoned speleologists from Europe were used to explore caves previously regarded as impossible. Both national and Southern Hemisphere records would be broken, but at a cost.

A caver lands in Minye after a descent of over 300 metres.

Chapter Seven

THROUGH HELL
ON A WHITE HORSE

There may not be any more Darwins to inflame scepticism or Cooks to carry the colonial flag to distant shores, but national pride derives from the soul and is not easily extinguished. For the very first time since its inception the Fédération Française de Spéléologie (FFS) was planning an overseas expedition with just such a level of stateliness. With few exceptions amongst their counterparts around the world, the French cavers enjoyed recognition and respectability backed by state funding.

The New Guinea group of islands was exotic, remote and rugged and from a caving stand-point, largely untapped. In short, it presented every conceivable impediment to caving in a land where adventurers could expect to capture some of the glamour associated with exploration in the manner of the great pioneers from the turn of the 19th century and earlier. New Britain in particular offered a caving landscape in many ways unlike anything anywhere else, even on mainland New Guinea.

Like the central ranges there, the mountains forming New Britain and other islands in the Bismarck Archipelago appear to have been uplifted due to the slow, inexorable collision be-tween the Pacific and Australasian continental plates. As a result of this tectonic interaction the region remains in a continual state of flux.

In New Britain earth movements are commonplace and usually occur on its northern littoral fringes, here dominated by a belt of active volcanic vents. South of this zone, volcanic deposits gradually give way to the massively bedded Yalum Limestone, a geological sequence extending to the southern coastline. The plateaux here have been uplifted to form an undulating country of countless dolines, some of which, as we have seen, attain gigantic proportions (see fig. 5).

When he met the French organisers in England in 1977, Mike Bourke had recommended the Nakanai Mountains of New Britain on the assumption that the region would present major river caves for an experienced team willing to accept a unique challenge (see fig. 22). However, surface exploration would be difficult. High diurnal temperatures and humidity have a combined debilitating effect and overland travel is hindered by the excesses of rainfall, vegetation and difficult terrain.

By this time the British had seemingly relinquished any interest in deep caving in Papua New Guinea, instead moving into the realms of largest and longest with Sarawak and the Orient being their favoured theatre of activity. Cavers from the United States and later Australia had been seduced by the prospects of Mexico's limestone regions. The French, in their ceaseless quest for depth, continued to pry into the lapiaz karsts of their homeland where in the Pyrénées, for instance, deep caves were revealed almost with monotonous regularity. This was not enough however; it lacked the kudos attached to the antipodes.

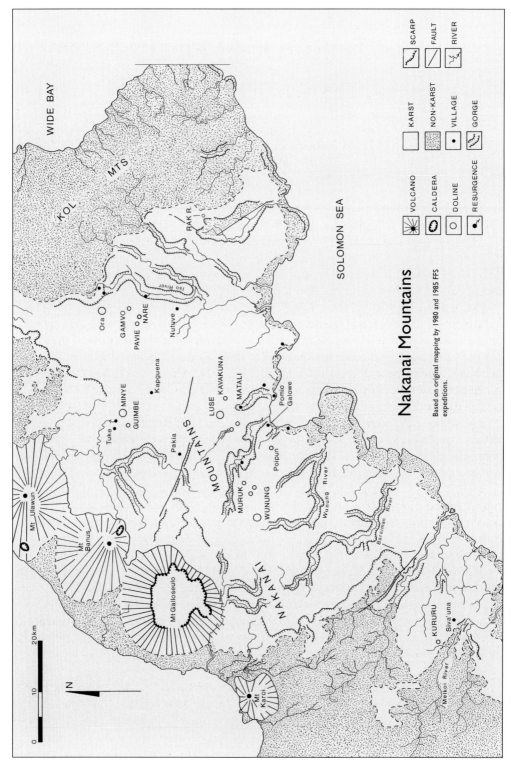

Fig. 22) Nakanai Mountains

MEGADOLINES CHALLENGE FRENCH CAVERS

Between November 2 and December 31, 1978, a six-man team including Richard Maire, Director of the Scientific Commission for the FFS, undertook a reconnaissance prior to sending in a larger group the following year. Mike Bourke joined them in Pomio. Having the benefit of local knowledge, he was to assist them during the first two weeks of their stay in the central Nakanai. They had designs on Nare, Minye, Ora and Kavakuna, four of the largest natural cavities in the world.

The remaining members of the group were Jean-Louis Fantoli, Daniel Martinez, Frédéric Poggia, Xavier Goyet and Gérard Savournin, their medical man. It was not the first visit to New Guinea by French speleologists; during the previous July, Patrick Cellerier from Paris and Roger Parzybut of Compigne spent three weeks exploring caves of a mostly minor nature in the Chimbu.

Everyone climbed the muddy trail with determination. Heaving himself up over a tangled mass of slippery roots, Xavier took a laboured breath, the straps of his pack straining under the load. Breathing seemed so difficult, in a way similar to the oxygen deprivation experienced by high altitude mountaineers. The humidity of the jungle had this effect on the explorer, experienced or otherwise; it was almost suffocating and a far cry from the bracing atmosphere of Europe's alpine karsts.

With Pomio several hours behind them the French cavers, guided by Mike, floundered through the torturous landscape, a stifling hothouse that strangled their innermost fears and banished all thoughts save those of the journey's end. Flailed with barbed vines and reeking in perspiration, they trudged grudgingly towards the interior of the island, often sinking in vile ooze well above their knees, gaining ground, but ever so slowly. The winding trail formed the only tangible point of reference in that hot house with no horizon.

To each of them, the sound of boots sloshing through the jungle mud had an almost hypnotic effect which seemed to lure them ever deeper into the accursed forest. It was effortless under the circumstance for the imagination to fly off at a tangent, seeking a mental escape at least from that very *fait accompli...*

Where would mankind be without the benefit of curiosity or a sense of wonder? The view that the world no longer holds any surprises would be as incorrect as the notion that, apart from the inner space of man's consciousness, there are no frontiers left to explore. But where else, except New Guinea, could one hope to find leathery winged foxes and tree kangaroos, or forests so damp that shrimps find life in the moss? Is it any wonder, in a land where grass can grow to three times the height of man, that rats reach the size of domestic cats...?

A machete ringing in the undergrowth dragged Xavier back to the immediacy of the moment. Stopping in his tracks, he took another mouthful of water from his canteen. It was warm. He lingered on the moment in a pensive mood, careful not to lose a single precious drop of the liquid...And after all those wondrous discoveries, what other revelations await the latter-day adventurer? Why, the megadoline of course!

Nare lay 40 kilometres to the northwest at the eastern limit of the Nakanai Mountains, bordering the Iso River canyon, which separated this range from the Kol Mountains and Wide Bay further to the east. Several years before, Alex Brown, a caver from Queensland, had sighted this mighty chasm whilst taking part in an aerial fly past for the Australian Ora expedition. A yawning hole piercing jungle and mountain had opened beneath their wings. Through rising vapours he had perceived a dim vision of another world – or was it a nightmare more akin to an abyss than hell itself?

A swiss caver descends into Minye, 410 metres deep.

Mists swirl across the Hindenburg Wall as Steve Worthington sorts out rope on a ledge during the climb to Era Tem.

At the Turbine,
the Yu Atea tumbles into a rift the width of a telephone kiosk.

BENEATH THE CLOUD FORESTS

In 1978, a partial descent of Uli Mindu held the promise of a higher entrance to the Atea system on Legari Mountain. In 1982 the shaft dropped into a large chamber and the cave bottomed out at just under 200 metres.

Dvorâk Hall and the beautifully decorated New World Series were discovered in the Atea by British caver Tony White while waiting for water levels to subside in the Ship Canal.

The resurgence of the Nare River seen from a helicopter flying along the Isis Gorge.

Giant tree ferns in the dense jungle near the Dalum efflux.

A burial cave visited by the Swiss in the Southern Highlands.

173

Speleifilm Enterprise/Gérald Favre. Previous page: Jean-Paul Sounier

The Minye River efflux at Tuke.
Previous page: The bottom of Minye megadoline viewed from -200 m.

Circling lower for a better look, the depths revealed a whitewater river twisting through the sub-bush like a tormented albino serpent roaring furiously at its confinement, trapped in limbo twixt the halls of Lethe and the living green purgatory above. It begged the question: what manner of living creature could hope to survive in those alien depths?

After several days on foot the Frenchmen at last reached the village of Nutuve at the start of their three-week sojourn in the mountains. Nare was by then within striking distance, though still an hour and a half trek away. Mike was astounded by the French approach to expedition caving: each man shouldered all essentials for the duration of his stay in the mountains, including his caving gear. They did not employ helicopters, nor did they rely on native porters as many expeditions before and since have done. Their technical ability, too, was beyond reproach and impressed Mike to the point of admiration as they efficiently rigged the mighty collapsed shaft.

The elliptical doline of Nare, fully 200 by 100 metres across, took several hours to safely equip for the descent. All the while the ever-present roar of the Ire River rising from below was a constant reminder that this was no Sunday afternoon picnic in the Loire countryside. The prospect preyed on the conscience, winkling out personal weaknesses and underlining any doubts about the folly and vanity of man's aspirations to tame the elements.

The actual rope descent of 217 metres proved longer than any pitch yet descended in the country, the shaft widening out at the base into a bell-shaped room. Its shape and a 40-metre-high talus slope at the bottom provided positive evidence of its origins as a true cavern once roofed over in the past. Over time, erosion and piecemeal breakdown brought the ceiling too close to the surface to withstand the strain and collapse became inevitable. In both directions the architecture of Nare was on a scale the explorers had never before witnessed. The shaft merged into moss-tinted porches, dripping wet and resembling the wrecked gothic arches of some colossal cathedral (see fig. 23).

The megadoline of Nare, measuring 238 m at its lowest point and 330 m at its highest.

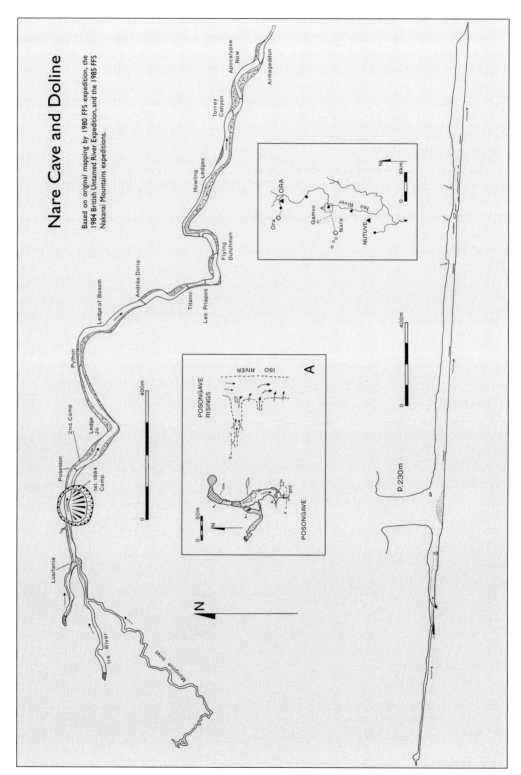

Nare Cave and Doline

Based on original mapping by 1980 FFS expedition, the 1984 British Untamed River Expedition, and the 1985 FFS Nakanai Mountains expeditions.

Fig. 23) Nare Cave and Doline

Downstream, it was impossible to follow the right bank of the river. Crossing the Poseidon Tyrolean with the aid of a rope gave the awestruck group tentative access to a shingle bank in a 30-metre high canyon. This unlikely beach was followed until it too ran out a few minutes later. It was an atmospheric spot; a companion standing nearby had to shout fit to burst his lungs just to make himself barely heard. Spray and mist veiled the air, making it difficult seeing into the receding gloom, where white-capped waves assimilated into a blackness that beckoned in an alluring yet somehow threatening manner. The river stretched from wall to wall, contained and yet unrestrained, casting a metaphoric gauntlet at the feet of mankind in all his insignificance.

The current and sheer volume of water made further progress decidedly unappetising and, for the moment, impossible; upstream was little better. After only 200 metres they were once again checked by the speed of the river. After this brief yet audacious flea jump into the unknown, Nare, the "untamed river" was to remain so for the time being. By Saturday, November 17, they had shifted camp 18 kilometres west, to the collapsed aven shaft of Minye and a rendezvous with the malevolent spirit Tuke.

Two days' preliminaries could not have prepared them for this moment. It was early morning and the atmosphere in camp was electric. Frédéric and Daniel had already spent the whole of the previous day fixing ropes on the drop, employing 400 metres of line and many deviations. Everything had been checked and double-checked. At last they were ready to commence the descent.

To say the entrance of Minye was spectacular would be a classic of understatement. At the rim it measures 450 metres across, reducing to 350 metres at its base 410 metres below. On this basis the calculated volume of 26 million cubic metres easily makes it the largest known doline on the planet. It speaks volumes on the nature of this rugged island that such an amazing hole could have escaped attention until as late as 1968 (In fact, most of the central Nakanai remained unexplored until around 1926).

First down Minye was Daniel, followed 20 minutes later by Mike Bourke. The pitch initially consisted of a series of near vertical descents through bush (see fig. 5). For the most part, the rock was too rotten to safely take anchor bolts or pegs, so the rope had been tied off where possible to convenient shrubs. On this section the caver was completely absorbed into the jungle that covered the walls and, under the circumstances, abseiling could be accomplished only by resorting to use of the machete, a hazardous practise requiring unerring concentration to avoid disaster.

The final drop of 75 metres hung well clear of the rock for most its distance and gave a bird's eye view of the violent river below. Near the equator the sun is directly overhead at noon; long before then the huge doline was illuminated in all its splendour, which perhaps contributed to Mike's heightened sensation of exposure. He was using a borrowed French Petzl descender and had until then experienced no problems.

The roar from the river was indescribable. Glancing down, he could see it being swallowed by a vast downstream cavern. He continued the descent with growing apprehension as he realised he was travelling far too quickly for safety. Mike found the Petzl device more difficult to control than the Australian whaletail descender. Scrub clinging to the rock walls whipped by with the quickening pace. He reacted badly, at first applying hand pressure to the rope. This briefly regulated his rate of descent but things then went badly wrong. Snap went one shrub, then another as branches scraped and lashed him while he gathered speed. Plant debris fluttered down to a floor that was rushing up to meet him at an alarming rate.

He knew then that he had precious little control over his destiny, he was dropping out of control. With only 15 metres to touchdown, the branches of a sizeable tree growing on a scree slope slowed his fall. He crashed through it, snapping off a number of limbs – fortunately none

A French caver begins his descent into Minye.

Jean-Paul Sounier

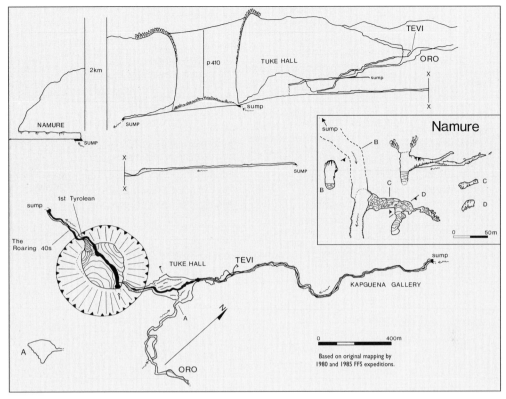

Fig. 24) Minye

of his own – and landed amid a shower of brushwood and leaves. His landing was fairly gentle, but he had severely burnt hands despite having worn protective gloves.

By the time the first aid kit arrived and Xavier was able to treat Mike, he was suffering mild shock. His right hand was the worst affected: the whole palm by then had become one huge blister 4 centimetres high. A bivvy was set up beneath a convenient overhang and Mike was assisted into his sleeping bag. There he remained over the following 24 hours. Given any other circumstances, Mike might have been amused at the notion of warming himself on a merry crackling campfire, surrounded by exotic plants...400 metres below ground. As it was, his French companions went on to explore and map a most unusual cavern, leaving him to contemplate many times over how he would manage the return to the surface.

From beneath the west wall of the shaft a flow estimated at 30 cubic metres per second surged powerfully from a siphon pool with a strange bluish tint. The Kanue River then followed a boisterous course through the interior forest of the doline, and at the far side disappeared again in a series of white-flecked rapids down a passage at least 90 metres high. The river occupied the full width of the downstream canyon. This and the heavy flow put paid to any thoughts of following the cave in that direction.

Climbing cautiously around the upstream sump, the cavers gained access via a steep ledge to a wide gallery fringed with arborescent ferns and mosses. In a short distance the streamway suddenly opened out into the spacious Tuke Chamber, a cavity so vast that the walls remained invisible (see fig. 24). A voice echoed in the dark, "Over here, this way!" Gripped by exploration fever they leapt eagerly forward, passing an inlet streaming from a roof which soared upwards beyond the range of their caplamps.

The serpentine gallery continued through beautiful forests of calcite encrustations. After several hundred metres they were faced with an airspace reducing to 10 centimetres and were obliged to swim. Luckily the ceiling soon lifted as they entered a more chaotic section at a lofty canyon. They plunged through flooded rockmills and, climbing two waterfalls, entered a wide meandering section of cave. The passage gradient eased and soon the stalactites disappeared, replaced by a tortuous route through rockfalls. The water could be heard grumbling between boulders somewhere beneath their feet, and after two and a half kilometres they found themselves on a mud flat preceding the final sump. It marked the end of a fine passage.

Back in the doline, it was the moment of truth for Mike as the time came for the return to the surface. As it happens he was able to operate his jumars with his heavily bandaged left hand; his right one by then was totally useless. He made a tandem ascent, with Daniel leading up the rope. This took three agonising hours in passing changeover points and knots, with help being administered by his French friend. With commendable patience those remaining below waited for their turn to ascend, the last out detackling and not surfacing before 9:00 p.m.

After these exciting developments, December saw the centre of operations for the French team switched to the New Guinea mainland. At the same time, three other French cavers from Toulouse were investigating some cave sites in the Mapos and Finschhafen areas of the Morobe Province after having explored caves in the Kiowa catchment of the Chimbu.

The team spent the first two weeks on the mainland looking at the caving potential of a remote plateau on Mt. Bangeta (4,127m), again in the Morobe Province. They then crossed the mile-high Kassam Pass to Kainantu in the Eastern Highlands to jointly explore caves there with local expatriate cavers. The Mt. Bangeta massif separated the Finisterre and Saruwaget Ranges from the Cromwell Mountains, all three forming part of the precipitous Huon Peninsula. Despite the great relief, the results of this reconnaissance, like all previous ones, proved disappointing. Out of over 20 sites investigated, the deepest cave was a mere 19 metres; by small compensation it did rank as one of the highest in the southern hemisphere.

The Eastern Highlands proved a welcome contrast, not only to the speleological desert of Mt. Bangeta, but also to the inhospitable jungles of New Britain. Gone was the oppressive humidity, replaced by an almost temperate, springlike climate that was cool at night and pleasantly hot by day. The dense forests were replaced by extensive grasslands, developing cattle country where the landscape was dominated by soaring ridges, stands of graceful casuarina trees that sighed in the indolent breeze, and hilltop clusters of thatched native huts.

At the turn of the century the beauty of this region belied the treacherous nature of its inhabitants. This is Kukukuka territory, where the first government patrols had often been received with bull roarers and a flurry of barbed arrows. Now the influx of whitemen did not provoke such a reception, but enabled the continued exploration of a few cave systems that were beyond the resources of local cavers. Barananomba Cave, for instance, was a twin entrance river system located in the upper Ramu catchment near the Yauna Mission station. Earlier that month, at the end of the Hole in the Wall expedition, Norman Flux and Noel Plumley had partially explored this with Francis Pusal (later Minister for Minerals and Energy). Norman joined the French team in pushing the system a week later.

From the four-metre high entrance of Barananomba, a rift passage led its jagged way down through a sporting series of small waterfalls with intervening plunge pools. Some short climbable cascades followed, then after an 11-metre drop the cavers entered a dismal canal where the passage was almost filled with water. While swimming through the gloomy continuation Frédéric Poggia had his life shortened by ten years when, to the amusement of the others, he mistook a floating log for a crocodile!

Beyond the canals the roof shot up and shortly a dry inlet entered on the left from the second entrance at Anuntina. Rumour had it that inhabitants from the nearby Swiss mission had, with minimal equipment, explored the cave from this entrance to the junction with the active passage. Beyond the confluence the cave assumed generous proportions with more cascades. At -130 metres the character of the cave suddenly changed. The team explored a more confused area to the final sump, a dark pool complete with a flotsam of dead trees.

The Obura patrol post is located about one and a half hour's drive southeast of Kainantu, in spectacular country overlooking the Lamari River, itself a feeder of the much larger Purari. Despite the limited lateral displacement a number of limestone beds offered scope here for well developed caves. With the extra manpower on hand it was an opportune moment for exploration.

Yunamare formed part of a promising multi-entrance system with a potential vertical range of 300 metres. The cave was well known locally and in 1963 had been used to dispose of the bodies of three murdered villagers. Earlier in 1978, Mike Bourke and John Webb had turned back after reaching a depth of 50 metres. Mike had returned with Allan Goulbourne and followed the cave downstream, adding a further 77 metres to the vertical depth, and finding a human skull at the base of the second pitch. Now Mike, Daniel Martinez and Xavier Goyet continued the exploration. In total they descended seven pitches to a terminal pool at minus 156 metres. They also made the first descent of the other major entrance to this important system, the Oravanana sinkhole. Here they descended eight verticals into a roomy but flood prone streamway, surveying the cave to where the roof plunged into a pool at -190 metres. They followed an upstream continuation for 15 minutes but declined to force a restriction through to its inevitable connection with Yunamare.

Thus after two months in the field (or rather the bush) the French team returned to their homeland suitably inspired, having seen and been impressed by the huge doline caves of New Britain and experienced first-hand the problems of following their rivers. Useful work was concluded elsewhere and the groundwork laid for those who were to follow. The mighty underground rivers remained a tantalising challenge to those brave enough to take up their lead.

SWISS ACCEPT PNG CHALLENGE

The logistics involved in preparing for a full-scale expedition was to prevent the French from returning in 1979 as planned. At the end of June that year however, a Swiss group arrived in Port Moresby led by Gérald Favre, a caver and film maker from Geneva. The young team intended to continue where their counterparts had left off, and had set themselves a number of scientific and sporting objectives both in New Britain and on neighbouring New Ireland.

Notwithstanding the problems they experienced in recovering their equipment from customs, they decided to carry out a two-week reconnaissance into the Nakanai Mountains with the limited supplies at their disposal. Gérald hoped this would at least allow them to acclimatise and

The Dalum River near its efflux.

help in locating major objectives seen on the aerial photographs. Principal among these was the Kavakuna Doline (see fig. 5). Lack of time had prevented the French from reaching this the year before and there was every prospect of entering a major river system.

Once in Pomio they had little difficulty recruiting sufficient porters for the carry to Olaipun, a village located slightly east of the Matali River gorge. This was the last habitation before entering the featureless tracts of virgin jungle heading northwards into the mountains. By July 11, they had established a staging camp seven kilometres from Olaipun on the trail to Kavakuna. Here their problems began, for the wet season was upon them in a land where the mean annual rainfall is measured in metres.

Despite the appalling conditions they were determined to locate Kavakuna; unfortunately none of the local tribesmen knew of such a place. Due either to the presence of evil spirits or simply the lack of desire or need, villagers rarely if ever strayed far into the uncharted interior, except to hunt. Wild pig and cassowary were much sought delicacies; the plumes of the bird of paradise were also highly prized for headdress decoration.

The bush seemed to become thicker with every passing hour. Pushing on a further four kilometres they found themselves wandering through a confusing region. Compasses and altimeters were of no use and they had little idea where they were. The daily rains were relentless and their position seemed beyond hope. Gérald decided to turn back but had not gone far when a timely break in a forested ridge enabled them to fix their position from a feature identified on their aerial photographs. The decision to continue northwards proved fortuitous for, more by luck than judgement, they eventually struck the doline of Kavakuna at a tangent.

Even before the jungle fell away at their feet, the sound of a large river drifted up through the trees. It took them an hour to circumnavigate the rim of the crater and find a route down. The east flank was steep but, debris strewn and well wooded, allowed them to reach the underground Matali at its foot 370 metres down without ropes. What hand of nature could create such a fearful void? Their gaze was drawn irresistibly to a verdant gallery out of which the 20-metre wide river leapt in one great bound – a mighty waterfall indeed – to be swallowed by the most violent sump pool imaginable.

The air was riven by a maelstrom of spray vapours, whipped into a frenzy by a dozen conflicting winds. Together with the awesome rumble, this created the combined effect of descending into some infernal cauldron. The cavers could do little to satisfy their desire to explore the unknown caverns backing the cataract, yet it took every effort to tear their eyes away from that forbidding scene. But lack of equipment and disagreeable weather prompted their early return to Rabaul and a move to more hospitable regions. It was time to rethink their strategy.

On July 24, the Swiss cavers' equipment at last received clearance by the port authorities. After a rest period in Rabaul, Gérald and his team departed for Kavieng and the easily accessible regions of the Lelet. Three years had passed since the Australian expedition explored this plateau; even so, Lemerigamus Cave was still wide open and the Dalum efflux offered scope for tracing an extensive resurgence cave deep beneath the mountains.

Camp was set up close to Sunamokola Cave and over the following two weeks the explorers prospected west for several kilometres beyond the limit previously reached by the Australians. Though they found several new cave systems, major development continued to elude them, the most important work undoubtedly being the exploration in Lemerigamus. This was concluded over two separate trips.

The pitch that had stopped the previous explorers proved to be a 15-metre fall into a plunge pool. At its base, the continuing cavern fell to two metres in height. Pleased to be exploring new cave at last, the team pushed on in anticipation, wallowing through mud and water in passages displaying rounded, phreatic sections sometimes partly blocked by clay deposits. An eight-metre drop preceded a couple of easy short climbs then the cave returned to its former character of tight meandering canyons similar to the entrance passages (see fig. 18).

They shuffled along, rigging two more pitches. Suddenly the passage floor disappeared and the cavers found themselves perched in the ceiling of a huge chamber; their exclamations echoed in the blackness. Rigging the drop with a 15-metre rope, they abseiled into the bouldery wastes of the Lakuna Chamber, hopeful of reaching greater depths towards Dalum. The dome-shaped cavern measured 50 metres in diameter and was floored with angular blocks that were a devil to cross. At the lowest point – some 203 metres below the entrance – the stream played hide and seek between rocks then was lost forever where a fracture zone had created a weakness along its west side. Lemerigamus was finished.

A palm-fringed coral strand fronting an azure Pacific is the stereotyped conception of the tropics. After a spell in the jungle, it was a temptation difficult to resist. An added attraction was of course the Dalum resurgence. This represented the principal outflow for the entire Lelet Plateau and had only partly been investigated. It clearly offered considerable scope for major

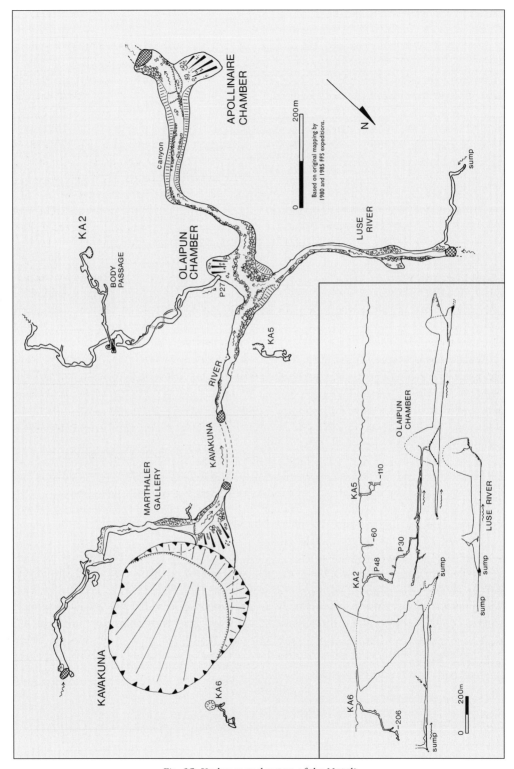

Fig. 25. Underground system of the Matali

extensions. Several obvious points of emergence presented themselves where the flow adopted a braided pattern rather like a river delta.

Two entrances were found to give access to a waterlogged labyrinth aligned principally along an east-west suite of joint-controlled rifts. For most of its length it was more meaningful to speak of water depth rather than usable airspace, and the explorers found it an exhausting business manoeuvring themselves along narrow rifts and arched sections of passage above deep water. It was impossible to determine exactly where the main flow entered the cave in the many flooded channels, one of which was guarded by a large green python.

On August 15, the exploration at Dalum was terminated with a little over one kilometre of passage surveyed. This in itself had proved a difficult task, and the team was unable to reach a conclusion in most of the restricted leads. A week later, scientific members of the expedition had completed their field studies and returned to Europe, leaving a depleted group for the return to the Nakanai. The team then comprised Gérald Favre, Rosemary Emery, Rene Marthaler, Christian Rufi, Marianne Mariettaz as well as Julius and Martin, two native guides from Olaipun village. After an attack of malaria, Marianne had to make an early return to Rabaul for treatment.

From their camp near the Kavakuna entrance the team carried out a number of investigations. Firstly, they had hoped to enter a high-level fossil series from a hole seen above the downstream sump. It took the explorers three spray-lashed days of aid climbing to overcome the 30-metre overhanging wall, only to enter an alcove where the jetsam of previous floods had collected. After a failed attempt to reach the massive Luse Doline (four kilometres to the northwest), lack of time dictated that they focus their effort on their remaining two objectives.

While some of the group was climbing the wall of the huge doline, others descended a hole previously located beside the track in a small depression only half an hour from the camp. There was nothing astonishing about this discovery, it being merely one more undistinguished cavity amongst the many lurking in the doline karst. But there was one difference: though the Swiss team did not realise it yet, the minuscule entrance would be of major significance in the exploration of the underground course of the Matali River.

The small hole, Kava Martel,[1] consisted of a series of pitches descending in the manner of the restricted systems of England's Yorkshire Dales, through sharp limestone in a semi-active flood prone passage. After rigging four short drops the Swiss team was forced to turn about at the foot of a spacious 48-metre shaft, where a trickle of water chattered away through a restricted outlet. The total depth reached was little more than 100 metres.

After their first week in the Nakanai, the team was joined by Franc Malecker, a geology student from Yugoslavia. Conditions on the plateau were still very wet but some of the team decided to enter the cave despite the risks. On Friday, August 31, Franc and Gérald descended into Kavakuna Doline and negotiated an eight-metre climb up the left wall of the cascading river. This took some time under incessantly dripping overhangs, but eventually they stepped into the wide mouth of the upstream riverway (see fig. 25). For the first 50 metres progress was unimpeded thanks to convenient ledge forming the near bank of the river. It was not long however before it was necessary to install a tyrolean line to facilitate crossing the Matali, at a point estimated to be seven metres wide. It was a bright sunny day and, because the doline intruded rather than dropping vertically into the riverway, some sunlight penetrated to this point, making rigging quite pleasant.

They crossed successfully after several abortive attempts to lasso a boulder at the far side. With the rope secured, Franc pulled himself across commando style using his hands and feet,

[1] *Named after the famous French speleologist.*

A caver is dwarfed by the Matali River cascading from the upstream entrance of Kavakuna.

and explored a short way upstream. Once he established that passage was possible he rejoined Gérald and the two returned to camp to plan their assault.

Early the following morning the two again entered Kavakuna and continued exploration beyond the tyrolean. Water flow was still very high, but despite this they managed to follow the passage for about 100 metres. Using a quantity of pitons, traverse lines were installed to aid their progress along the fissured walls. They encountered and safely passed a short waterfall, but then reached a point where the river spanned the full width of the passage. Lacking more gear, they exited the cave.

Sunday dawned with that grey-green hue that makes one day little different from any other in the twilight world of the equatorial forest. Gérald wished to rest so Franc descended the doline once again, accompanied by Christian, Rene and all the paraphernalia required for an extended stay below ground: ropes, bolts and food supplies. They hoped to complete the exploration this trip, so surveying and photographic equipment was also backpacked into the cave. At 8:00 a.m. they entered the upstream gallery and quickly reached the limit of the previous day.

Climbing and traversing above river level took them 300 metres in from the entrance waterfall. Here they were forced to quit when the river divided, each branch welling up from an impassable sump where the roof dived into the water. The cave was mapped and derigged as they returned downstream, tired but satisfied with their achievements. Unknown to them heavy and persistent rain had been falling for some time. This only became clear when they noticed that some of the rocks used as stepping stones on the way in were by then awash. It was about midnight when they reached the tyrolean.

Christian was first across, taking with him a sackful of equipment. To recover the rope after everyone had crossed, it was re-fastened as a double line passing through a loop secured to a boulder on the far bank. Franc belayed himself then tested the line, but it was too slack. Christian spoke little English and Franc understood even less French, so he asked Rene in English to relay to Christian in French that the line needed tensioning.

Rene shouted across the passage but the noise of the river made it impossible for them to convey their wishes. Lamps were by then fading fast; in the gathering gloom, the high humidity and spray filling the riverway made it difficult to see the far side. Franc bellowed at the top of his voice but Christian did not seem to hear. By then Franc's light was reduced to little more than a glimmer, so he set about giving it a fresh charge of carbide. As he did so Rene clipped himself via a snaplink to one line and with a jammer on the second rope, set off hauling himself across the river with a hefty pack.

"Rene, the rope is not tight enough!" implored Franc. "You'll get wet!"

Rene ignored him or perhaps never heard, for he continued to edge his way across the line. Everything went well until, a metre or two from dry land, he lost his hold on the rope. He splashed into the river but, held to the second rope, soon had his hands and feet back on the tyrolean.

"Leave the sack!" yelled Franc, but even if he could have heard, it was impossible for Rene to discard his pack because of the way it was slung around his shoulder. He fell into the water again and, though held by his harness, was fighting desperately to regain his grip on the rope. Constantly buffeted by the river, he was clearly becoming exhausted as he struggled to keep his head above water. Waves kept washing over him. Christian attempted to pull Rene into the bank but was unable to do so because he was firmly held by his jammer to the main rope. The situation was serious.

Cautiously entering the water, Franc tried lifting the ropes to hold Rene clear of the water but this was not possible either. At the far bank Christian loosened the rope in a desperate bid to allow Rene to be carried with the current downstream and into the side. By then Franc managed to pull his companion clear of the water and get him to dry land, some five to ten minutes after he had fallen into the river. Franc could detect no pulse, and Rene was no longer breathing.

Franc immediately set about administering CPR. His acetylene lamp went out, leaving him only a feeble electric light to see by. Christian set off out of the cave to raise the alarm while Franc continued for an hour trying to revive his friend. He noticed the river was rising again so with considerable effort, he dragged Rene to higher ground where, exhausted, he fell on top of him and slipped into a haunted sleep.

At length Franc awoke with a start and renewed attempts to revive his friend. What time was it? Where were the others? In desperation he shouted at Rene to breath but knew inwardly that it was hopeless. Just after 9:00 a.m. Gérald arrived in the cave with Julius and the tyrolean was re-secured. It transpired that in the dark Christian had become disorientated in the bush and failed to find camp until dawn.

Early on September 4, the base radio at Pacific Helicopters in Rabaul crackled into life. Captain Gareth Bean picked up a message requesting assistance. He took off immediately, arriving at the doline to find the cavers had cleared an area of bush part way down the forested slope of the doline. In a remarkably brave act Captain Bean manoeuvred his machine 200 metres down into the hole. With rotors whirling dangerously close to the trees and the down draught flinging brushwood wildly in all directions, the landing was aborted as too fraught with danger. He returned to Pomio intent upon making a second attempt early the next day.

After the 1979 disaster, helicopter pilot Gareth Bean manoeuvred his craft into the forested pit of Kavakuna to recover the remains of Rene Marthaler.

By morning the weather had deteriorated. Heavy rain was falling in grey sheets and dense cloud shrouded the ridgelines of the mountains. Amazingly, the pilot relocated the doline without much difficulty and in a further display of courage flew down the doline, picked up the hapless caver's remains by net sling and returned with Christian and Gérald to Pomio. Without delay they departed along the coastline to Rabaul. The poor conditions dictated that they fly quite low and slow as they frequently encountered rain squalls.

As they crossed the estuary of the Isis River about 20 kilometres east of Pomio, the rain became torrential. Gareth decided to make for the beach where he intended to put down and await a break in the weather. By then the wipers could no longer cope with the rain hammering noisily upon the windshield. Suddenly there was a total loss of visibility. No mayday was possible, for almost simultaneously there was a loud report as the machine hit the sea and turned on its side, settling gently into two metres of water.

Everyone was quickly out of the craft and sitting on the cabin while it rolled in the swell. No one was injured, but the chopper was extensively damaged. They swam ashore and Gareth raised the alarm at the nearest plantation. Later that afternoon they were picked up by the Assistant District Commissioner who took them by motor launch back to Pomio. Meanwhile the remainder of the team had arrived after walking out of the mountains.

It was not until the next day that the evacuation was completed by a second helicopter, flying via Pomio to Rabaul. A day or so later a CAA investigator was paddled out to the crash site by dugout canoe. He leapt over the side to inspect the wreckage. As he bobbed about in the warm sea he asked some of the villagers to enter the water to assist him. Everyone shook their heads in stubborn refusal. It was some time afterwards that he discovered the reason for their reticence: the previous night they had apparently seen a large estuarine crocodile patrolling the site.

It is so often the case that pioneering is interwoven with stirring accounts of courage and determination in the face of adversity and, sadly, the ultimate sacrifice must sometimes be paid in the quest for knowledge. The Swiss team was unfortunate. Being strongly motivated by the discoveries of others before them, they were keen to explore the underground course of the Matali to conclusion, and they acquitted themselves admirably under the most trying conditions. The disaster marked the end of the Swiss expedition and closed the pages on one of the most poignant chapters in the history of New Guinea speleology.

MATALI SUCCESS

In mid-January, 1980 an 11-man French team returned to the caves of New Britain. All hand-picked by the FFS, they had within their accumulated experience undertaken pioneering work in many far-flung corners of the world and were all experts in one field or another. Included among them was Dominique Boyer, an ecologist from the Ardèche, and Jacques Orsola, a caving instructor from Lyon known to his friends as "Rusty" because of his bright red shock of hair. Joining the team was Jean Delpy alias "Nanou," who hailed from Toulon and once in the mountains Dr. Jean-Marie Flandin would attend to their medical needs.

When the original request for applicants had been circulated over 50 expedition hopefuls had responded. Serge Fulcrand and Jean-Paul Sounier were chosen for their climbing ability and good all-round experience respectively, Gérard Bouteiller for his reputation in rope handling. Serge and Gérard Cazes came from the south of France and shared a mutual passion for bull fighting. At 23 years, Cazes was the youngest of the group. With Serge and Dominique he was responsible for expedition photography.

Jean-François Pernette, a 25-year old speleologist from Bordeaux, was appointed leader of the venture, perhaps (so he thought) because they were unable to recognise in him any other quality. He was often thought of as something of the lady's man, as he was well spoken and carried himself with the slight air of an aristocrat. He was a highly respected caver with many deep exploration firsts to his credit, especially in the Pyrénées.

Completing the team and perhaps acting as a stabilising influence for the whole group was Christian Rigaldie and Richard Maire, the "old men" of the expedition at 29 and 30 years respectively. Richard was a geomorphologist attached to the Scientific Commission for the French Caving Federation and had an abiding interest in anything remotely connected with limestone. Of course he knew something about the area from the reconnaissance two years earlier. He was a wiry sort of person; Christian on the other hand was possessed of a strength of character which made him a powerhouse below ground. The expedition received the enthusiastic support of French industry and their President, Valéry Giscard D'Estaing, kindly agreed to act as patron.

Upon arrival in the Papua New Guinea capital of Port Moresby, the members were faced with many frustrating hiccups with immigration and delayed forward flights. Even worse, the provincial government for East New Britain voiced its objection to cavers returning to the Nakanai region. In the aftermath of the Kavakuna disaster the year before they simply had no desire to witness a recurrence of events. Denis Viart, the cultural attaché and French Ambassador to Papua New Guinea, stepped in to argue the cavers' case, and with some persuasion the administration relented. After eight days of sorting out formalities, they departed from Moresby on January 25, for the journey by plane and motor launch to Pomio on the south coast of New Britain.

A cable awaited them: "Carbide on *Santa Theresa*. Stop. Will arrive 8 Feb. Pomio. Stop." None of this solid fuel for their headlamps had been brought from Europe for the simple reason that it was a prohibited substance; besides, Mike Bourke had purchased a 100-kilogramme supply locally on their behalf. Fortunately a small cache left behind by the Swiss the year before would allow limited exploration to take place until their own supplies arrived. Three days later they were heading for the village of Olaipun, stepping-off point for the central Nakanai.

The humid conditions in this part of the tropics helped breed lingering sores and New Britain was certainly no exception. They overnighted at Olaipun where Jean-Marie, the doctor, felt obliged to hold a surgery for the benefit of villagers needing treatment. A wayward looking moustache imparted to him the distinct look of a fakir. It was a repeated source of amusement for his team mates, who could never work out whether it was this or the whiteman's medicine which most worried the people. The villagers all called him the *"masta em i long-long"* (crazy white man) anyway for wanting to go down holes in the ground, which simply added to their suspicions that somehow there was an ulterior motive for their unhealthy interest in caves.

The following morning they succeeded in employing ten porters for the carry north. As it happened this was to be the largest number of helpers they would be able to muster during their stay in the region. At the earliest opportunity the caravan, together with two guides, Martin and Joseph, struck out on the six-hour march to the proposed site of their advance camp, the Kavakuna Doline. Each of the cavers carried a pack weighing between 23 and 30 kilos. They were quickly absorbed into the wall of jungle which encroached upon the village from all sides. Next came the rains, followed soon afterwards by the leeches. It was a great relief that these never reached sufficient numbers to become traumatic, yet even so in the weeks ahead, at least one person awoke to find one of the loathsome creatures sucking at his eye.

Eventually the vague trail terminated close to the rim of the crater. With evening approaching an air of urgency prevailed while an area of bush was cleared and the camp hurriedly built. As the final glimmer of day was extinguished their accommodation was complete, a plastic roofed hut without walls. The porters were paid off and all excepting Joseph and Martin returned to Olaipun. As darkness closed in the nocturnal wildlife broke into song. They knew then that the expedition truly had begun. It was 6:30 p.m. and after their first day in the forests, those new to the tropics were by then swinging in their hammocks, thankful for a well-earned night of rest on the eve of their initial encounter with the megadolines they had heard so much about.

WILD RIVERS "Я" US

At first light the camp buzzed like a disturbed ant-hill as two teams enthusiastically prepared to go underground. The disappearance of the Matali at Kavakuna was intriguing. About three kilometres to the southeast the river was suspected of appearing again at the head of a precipitous gorge that wound its way down to the coast by Pomio. That there had to be another way into the downstream course of that underground river they had no doubts.

Jean-Paul Sounier, Jean Delpy, Jean-François Pernette and Gérard Bouteiller began a detailed investigation of KAII. This was the system discovered and named Kava Martel by Gérald Favre's team the year before. The entrance was indistinguishable from countless similar holes on the plateau, simply a tiny black space overhung with lush growths at the base of an equally minuscule depression. Entry was effected by squirming on one's belly. Sweeping accumulated forest detritus to one side, they crawled forward with helmets scraping the low, jagged ceiling and at last entered a roomier section.

From the beginning the cave was noticeably similar to the well-watered systems for which Britain is renown, but fortunately in this case it was quite dry. Each explorer wore only a caving suit over shorts and a cotton shirt, yet the high temperature of 20 degrees meant they were soon perspiring intolerably. A succession of generously proportioned shafts descended in rapid succession through sharp limestone to a depth they guessed to be around 150 metres. Jean-François unclipped from the rope after abseiling a grand 48-metre shaft. "Rope FREE...free...," his shout echoed up the pitch.

His companions soon joined him and together they watched the trickle of water as it vanished into a narrow calcited fissure, splashing into a pool two metres below. The latter appeared to run into a tight bend. With hammer in hand Nanou attacked the restriction with vigour and after a while was able to slip gingerly down the uninspiring slot. Several minutes came and went. All his companions could hear was the sound of splashing and banging, and the grunts and curses of their friend as he demolished further projections. The hammering stopped and, for a moment...silence. "Hey it continues, come on lads!"

Jean-Paul discarded his rope bag and entered the bottleneck, grateful at least for the chance to cool off. He wallowed through the pool, mouth trailing in the murky water that lapped the scalloped walls of the confined tunnel.

While his team-mate negotiated the low crawlway, Jean-François was struggling to get his load clear of the tight slot. With one last concerted effort he kicked at it with both feet and to his surprise the bag shot through, landing in the pool below with a splash. "Shit. Watch out!" There were sounds of a scuffle and more curses. The resulting wave had almost swamped Jean-Paul who was still flat-out in the passage ahead. This incident highlighted what each had been secretly

French cavers crossing a river in New Britain.

considering: should there be a cloudburst on the surface, they would be caught like rats in a watery trap.

Body Passage continued low and miserable for 50 metres before allowing any respite. Nanou was still in front when the splattering of water ahead announced his arrival at a new pitch. With some difficulty he fixed an anchor bolt for the rope and abseiled down into the unknown. The others soon joined him 30 metres below and they explored a narrow canyon leading swiftly downwards with the occasional short drop. They were then following a respectable stream, which led in time to a more spacious, well-decorated tunnel, the Malogue.

They guessed by then that they were approaching a depth of 300 metres. It was at least six hours since they had entered the system, so they unanimously called it a day. It was an opportune moment to turn around for ahead was another low section developed along a horizontal bed in the strata. They retreated up the ropes, finding the watery restrictions even more awkward in reverse.

Back in camp the others related how they had explored Kavakuna beyond what had clearly been a sump during the Swiss visit. After crossing the river three times, they had pushed on upstream until stopped momentarily by a seven-metre cataract. Serge had managed to bypass it with a superbly placed route up an exposed wall, eventually reaching a true sump after adding 300 metres of new passage.

The next day, Christian, the two Gérards and Jean-Marie descended the KAII system (see fig. 25). At Jean-Paul's previous limit they forced a way through the low passage to enter a confusing maze of passages that revealed several promising leads. To their chagrin none of these continued far, and they were about to pack in for the day when an excited call from Jean-Marie announced he had found something. From a banking he had climbed to examine a decorated alcove where he could look along the flat roof of the chamber. It was festooned with a forest of fragile soda straw stalactites that gave the impression of an inverted fakir's nail bed. But something else riveted his attention. From a nearby niche an enticing breeze blew from between a grill of stalactites.

Crawling forward expectantly for a few body lengths, he was surprised to emerge in a passage several metres high, the Gallery of the Fool Joggers. The formations through which he had just passed were dulled by comparison to those now confronting him. The passage was literally jam-packed with a fabulous display of concretions in every conceivable size and form. Tall pillars supported the roof. There were cascades frozen in mid-leap and stalactites that resounded like tubular bells when cautiously struck. There were long ones and short, others twisted into grotesque forms, even curtains of a delicate translucence through which the light from a lamp shone like streaky bacon.

Almost with reluctance Jean-Marie left the grotto behind, setting off at a trot down a roomy cavern with his comrades close on his heels. Along the passage chuckled a small stream, merrily wending its way between banks of shingle and silt. But what was that noise? They stopped and listened, then suddenly above their own panting they could all hear it, a muffled rumbling somewhere ahead. No, it was impossible. Even given the acoustics of the cave, a brook so small could not make such a din. "How could it be?" they wondered.

Madly optimistic, they cut a dash down the wide passage, the black space just in front growing larger and more menacing. Suddenly at their feet appeared an enormous abyss. They stopped but gravity took hold of the stream as it leapt out into space, exploding into myriad starlike droplets that sparkled in the beams of their lamps until lost in the boundless night of the cavern. Somewhere below – a long way below – the murmurings of an underground river gave hint of the fate awaiting the immature tributary.

It seemed the passage had burst out high in the side of a cavern of mammoth proportions. It was quite impossible to see walls or roof, let alone determine the bottom of the void. Whatever awaited them sounded colossal, yet for the time being they could only speculate on the unknown. With no more rope left they had no option but to retreat to the surface. Back at camp the jubilant team recounted their fantastic journey.

The next day, Jean-Paul, Gérard Bouteiller, Rusty and Jean-François rigged the new drop. A few metres down Gérard found it necessary to deviate to one side in order to position the rope safely clear of the waterfall – a flood was always uppermost in their minds – and after 30 metres the descent landed on the apex of a debris cone. Only one wall of the Olaipun Chamber was visible (the one they had just descended) but this was lost in the darkness somewhere high above them, doubtless supporting some distant vaulted ceiling.

Stumbling down a scree slope brought them 50 metres lower to the banks of a huge river. White-capped rapids, wave upon wave, stretched away in both directions. There could be no doubting they had reached the Matali beyond the downstream sump of Kavakuna. But what measure of success was it? The rapids tearing by seemed terrifying in the gloom of the cavern and Jean-François doubted that they could ever continue. Frustrated, they returned the way they had come.

Almost as if the elements were marshalling all their might against the intruders, that night their rudimentary camp was hit by a ferocious storm. For hours on end thunder claps shook the ground and lightning transformed the jungle into a scene from a Hammer horror movie. Torrential rain pounded the flies and freak winds uprooted trees on the edge of Kavakuna, some crashing down uncomfortably close to their flimsy shelter. Coinciding with the death of one forest giant, a large beetle – more like a flying fortress than an insect – chose that very moment to seek refuge in Dominique's wiry beard, soliciting a scream out of all proportion to the size of the unfortunate creature. It was some minutes before the others, still cowering in their beds, calmed down sufficiently to realise that a tree had not fallen on the camp.

A remarkable peace ushered in the dawn. They awoke from the vestiges of a fitful sleep to sunbeams slanting across their beds. The air was already hot and, but for the drone of insects, strangely calm. Over breakfast they recounted the previous violent hours and discussed their hopes and fears for the downstream river cave.

With carbide stocks seriously depleted Serge, Jean-Paul, Richard, Nanou, Gérard Cazes and their leader went back into the river cave. The last two were given the unenviable task of mapping Body Passage, while the others meanwhile descended quickly to photograph the huge new chamber. Although dangerous, exploration of the river was just too much of a temptation to resist. Though it seemed to them that the flow through the chamber was far greater than that in Kavakuna, they could not see how this was possible. Some way upstream they were surprised to find the current less violent. At that point several large angular boulders broke surface providing a possible ford. The usually cautious Serge announced that he would try to cross the river by leaping between these; tying on a lifeline, he prepared himself for the hazardous task.

The first two jumps of around one and a half metres each were accomplished uneventfully, but left him teetering precariously on a rock shaped like a gable. His position looked frightful. Shouting for more rope and balanced on the point of the boulder, he hesitated for a split second, then sprang into the air. He managed it amid sighs of relief, landing somewhat ungainly on the third boulder. After a short wade he was safely across. Those watching from the bank let out a rousing cheer.

The roar of the river almost drowned their jubilation. Despite the communication handicap, a tyrolean line was soon installed and the others joined Serge on a wide cobble-strewn terrace. A short way downstream this narrowed and as they turned a right hand bend, slipping on loose scree, they picked their way down to the water's edge.

"Look at the river!"

"Well, what about it?"

"It's going the opposite way!" Sure enough, though they were travelling downstream, the water was flowing toward them. Reality dawned a few minutes later when it occurred to them that in the vastness of the Olaipun Chamber they had failed to notice another major inlet joining the Matali from the northwest.

To begin with they traced the Luse River along a magnificent gallery flanked by shingle banks, sparkling wetly in their lamps. In places these deposits were cemented with hard calcite out of which arose mammoth stalagmites in their hundreds. Some of these presided sentinel-like over nests of exquisite cave pearls. Further on, a large tree wedged incongruously between stalagmites gave brief hope of perhaps emerging into daylight at the base of a large and hitherto unsuspected doline. It was not to be, for like the main branch, the Luse River also terminated in a siphon pool. It was perhaps just as well, they mused, for how would they have found the way back to camp through the trackless bush?

Downstream from the Olaipun Chamber the waters of the Matali and Luse combined in an estimated flow of 20 cubic metres per second. The aggressive waters had carved out a canyon of more than generous proportions. The river swirled around a left-hand bend and in so doing dashed against the far wall, hissing and flinging spray into the air. The passage groaned and in a cavalcade of whitewater challenged the cavers to carry on. They had now reached a depth of almost 400 metres. With the sides of the cave by then vertical and featureless, further progress was – for the time being at least – beyond their available resources.

After the first month carbide stocks were virtually exhausted, so everyone returned to the coast for some rest and recuperation. At Pomio news reached them that a ship had run aground off the coast of New Ireland and the *Santa Theresa*, carrying their precious supplies, had altered course to answer the Mayday. With little chance of receiving their carbide before February 14, it was suggested they examine surface features further afield while Jean-François, accompanied by Jean Delpy, left for Rabaul to see what could be done about their supplies.

The Matali rumbled through an impressively confined canyon, one of several carrying the monsoon rains from the Nakanai Mountains into the Solomon Sea. Relative to its depth the walls were so narrow in places that to fly up it by chopper was both an exhilarating and harrowing experience. It was to give full measure of excitement to Serge and Jean-Marie, who had volunteered to enter the gorge the hard way: straight down by rope. To reach the resurgence involved a 400-metre abseil down the headwall of the jungle-covered ravine. Part way down this Serge received the fright of his life when he came eye-to-eye with an large serpent coiled on a ledge near the rope. And in what had become a recurring theme on caving expeditions to New Guinea, the doctor was obliged to sew himself after a self-inflicted wound with his machete.

The river outflow opened into the gorge as an 80-metre high keyhole fissure divided into two levels by a gigantic chockstone. The upper entrance, 30 metres in diameter, gave access to a series of airy traverses and climbs above the fast-moving river. When the ledges ran out and the cave continued, they thought it far too risky to follow it further – but not before an attempt by Serge almost ended in disaster.

The remainder of the group returned to base several days later after having located and mapped the Luse and Poipun dolines. The latter was situated in territory once again considered by the local villagers to be the abode of evil spirits. It was also known as Totung Tu, after a hunter who it was said had fallen to his death during the Second World War. Impressive though both of these holes were in terms of their respective volumes, they were of little speleological interest.

An even larger depression had still to be reached at Wunung, situated in very remote country midway between the Galowe and Wunung rivers and at least two week's walk west of Jacquinot Bay. Other minor discoveries in the vicinity of Kavakuna included two potholes designated KA4 and KA5, both explored to conclusion at depths of 204 and 113 metres respectively.

At long last all the expedition supplies were finally on hand and the focus switched once again to the KAII system. A determined group descended with climbing gear, grappling irons and an inflatable boat, in the event the downstream riverway yielded some frenetic exploration. But the cave was not going to give in easily: six tyrolean crossings had to be made before the system could be fully explored. In a passage at least 100 metres square they succeeded in securing a rope across the river by hurling a grappling hook behind a rock. Once safely across, the team continued downstream with little difficulty, though it was nowhere to have a slip.

A wall fell vertically into the tortured river, above which an exposed traverse line took them to some narrow ledges. Their hopes finally faded in a blank wall soaring high above them in a defiant challenge to the rock climbers in the party. Standing on a tiny spray-lashed ledge, they surveyed the scene before them, haunted by the increasing suspicion that a great void lurked just ahead. The river was deafening as it plunged about two metres to spend itself in a pool of relative calm. Here it gathered its power before rushing impetuously through an area of terrifying rapids. They considered their next move.

It was Serge once again who took the initiative. Just as he was about to take the plunge, Jean-Paul and other members of the upstream party approached. They could see the caplamps of their friends ahead like fireflies in a unique but alien tableau, tiny pinpoints of light lending scale to the immensity of the huge cavern.

Wearing flotation jacket and flippers Serge lowered himself into the dark water, the dinghy suspended from his harness. He launched himself into the flood, propelling the wildly gyrating craft with all his might. As expected, the current lessened in mid-channel but there were a few anxious moments when, just as he made it to the far side, the river engulfed him. A little shaken, he dragged himself clear and was soon able to secure a rope for the remainder of the team. As one-by-one they balanced across the aerial tyrolean, the lights of their companions on the near bank cast enlarged shadows down the cave, to be overwhelmed by the brooding darkness ahead.

Traversing brought them shortly to a steep wall of shattered rock. The violence of the river beneath them permitted progress in one direction only: upwards. Serge took the lead, climbing on delicate holds. He gained a slope and as the gradient eased, pure white stalagmites loomed out of the darkness. Suddenly they realised they had indeed entered a vast hall. Still climbing to the right they were by then 100 metres above river level, and yet looking in that direction the chamber roof continued to rise. This gave some idea of the immensity of the downstream canyon, though it was impossible to glimpse its roof.

The explorers regrouped in the vast chamber to congratulate each other on their success. They decided to name it after Guillaume Apollinaire, a French poet of aristocratic Polish descent who had led the avant-garde in Parisian literary circles through the turn of the century. After a reflective moment or two they considered the downstream continuation. A 30-metre high blank wall formed a barrier between the explorers and whatever lay beyond, but by then everyone had had enough for one day and made their way back to the surface.

On the final trip two days later, a team consisting of Jean-Marie, Bouteiller, Gérard Cazes, Serge, Jean-Paul and Jean-François bottomed the cave at 459 metres, taking 17 hours to reach a terminal pool just 100 metres beyond the Apollinaire Chamber. Here the Matali River slid powerfully into a large and evil-looking sump.

BEAUTY AND THE BEAST

On the surface, explorations continued within the constraints of the tortured landscape and almost impenetrable bush. On March 5, Jacques Orsola and Christian Rigaldie, after prospecting some time along dry streambeds, came upon a vegetated creek 45 minutes from camp. This they followed to the entrance of Liklik Vuvu, a cave located some distance from the main trade route linking Pakia to Pomio.

A high rift was followed to where it could be seen developing into a steeply descending canyon. At this point they returned for reinforcements, safe in the knowledge that they had made a significant discovery. In all, five trips were necessary to complete the investigation and survey the extensive labyrinth of galleries. It was a pretty cave, lacking the technical nature of KAII and decorated throughout with pristine grottos reminiscent of scenes from Helm's Deep[2]. Liklik Vuvu was the sort of find that made all previous disappointments and hardships fade from memory, vindicating all their efforts, agonies and discomforts.

...The light from Dominique's lamp painted wavering shadows among the columns and stalactites. He sat absolutely spellbound by the beauty of the scene before him; a petrified forest, yes, unyielding like its counterpart hundreds of metres above, but in this case white rather than green, crystal rather than living wood, and lacking those loathsome bloodthirsty leeches. Stalagmite bosses, some linked to the ceiling of white tracery to form colonnades, vied for attention with dripstones and intricate protruding forms. From above, many gangly growths hung among groups of stalagmites like plump dwarves in white, pointed hats marching to work through a fairytale wood made of candy trees.

Words fail explorers when faced with such marvellous works of nature. But, one might ask, why must we make odious comparisons, or try to measure or belittle such gems? Is it not enough simply to be present and for a brief measure of an equally short lifetime become absorbed into – and content with – the realm of natural creations? Who could wish for more...?

Some two kilometres to the north of Liklik Vuvu was another major cave referred to as Bikbik Vuvu. This had been found at the beginning of the expedition from an obvious linear feature on the aerial photographs. Without tackle the cavers had been unable to act upon their urge to instantly explore. Now there was no excuse: a camp was established nearby and over the space of a week Bikbik Vuvu was to provide some snatched moments in a unique system.

On the photographs it had appeared like the serpentine course of a large river ending at a black dot assumed to mark the position of a shaft or large cave mouth. In reality a surface gorge eventually went to ground and the cave consisted of its subterranean continuation, made passable by virtue of the prevailing dry season. It was clear that when the seasonal rains came the cave would almost certainly be a death trap for anyone unfortunate enough to be caught below.

Apart from the occasional rockfall in the entrance ravine, exploration provided few surprises until they reached a depth of 240 metres. Here the gradient increased in a passage made notable for its many blind pits, holes scoured out of the riverbed by the mechanical action of trapped boulders rolled about by the river. The French called them giants kettles, or *marmites*, though they are usually referred to in English as rock mills. The Crucible in the Atea Kananda is an impressive example.

After descending into these blind pits the cavers found themselves having to climb several metres up the far side, an exhausting process which to their consternation had to be repeated several times down the cave. The physical aspects of negotiating these barriers – some quite dry, others containing deep water – was comparable to that experienced by Martel and others in the early 1930s during the epic exploration of the famous Padirac system in France.

Thankfully the rock mills ended and the more sedate Eel Gallery continued with a further 60 metres of walking, as far as the shore of a wide lake. This they crossed by inflatable raft to reach twin sumps, giving three kilometres of sporting caving and a depth of 414 metres, making it the third deepest system in the country. Reflecting on their good fortune that the cave remained inactive during the dry season, they could only imagine what the place might be like when the monsoon arrived. It was not a prospect to dwell upon. The cave everywhere bore evidence of the violent floods which tear through the passages, and in some places large trees were jammed high in the roof. From the tide marks they observed, flow levels at such times were estimated to increase to as much as 200 cubic metres per second.

---

[2] *Inspired by J.R.R.Tolkien's novel Lord of the Rings.*

Nare Doline

AN AUDACIOUS LEAP

With expedition supplies dwindling it was time for the assault on Nare, the final and perhaps most daunting objective of the expedition. It was also the most remote of all the doline avens that the French had come to explore, located 40 kilometres north of Pomio and nearly three hours walk from Nutuve, the nearest habitation.

After their achievements along the subterranean course of the Matali, Jean-François Pernette and his team attacked Nare full of optimism. Richard Maire and Christian Rigaldie were given the task of rigging the entrance pit. The tree chosen for the main belay shook alarmingly under Richard's weight but the rock (where it could be seen for the jungle mantle) was so poor that it left them no alternative. As he continued down, there was an almost continuous avalanche of rocks, earth and even whole banana trees that clattered their way to the bottom.

After an intoxicating descent involving 17 deviations and rebelays, the team was able to step onto scree angling down to the river. Covered in mud, brushwood and forest ants they set off to explore, though it was still necessary to cut a path within the interior jungle, amazingly even thicker below than on the surface.

Following the true right bank, they could only progress about 120 metres before they were faced with a featureless wall. Across the river was a wide beach of cobbles and larger boulders, and they chose to attempt a crossing at an area of calmer water below a cascade. At the third try they succeeded in lodging a grappling hook behind a boulder. Trusting that it would hold fast, Serge hauled himself hand over hand along the line flat out in a dinghy and lined from downstream. In no time at all he had easily crossed the river.

Their celebrations were short-lived, for only 180 metres further they were faced with a repeat of the process. Huge waves lurched over submerged obstacles, crashing down in violent stoppers with an explosion of spray, counter eddies and foaming water. The river thundered like a stampede of crazed white horses galloping into the deepening night of the damned. One would have second thoughts about crossing such an obstacle on the surface, let alone over 300 metres below ground. The swirling waters groaned into the unknown with a noise that was unnerving. Boulders could be heard colliding in the current; spray was flung everywhere, filling the air with an all-embracing mist that reduced visibility practically to zero. Despite their initial victory there was a natural reluctance to ride this subterranean rodeo; but nothing ventured…the passage continued.

Once again Serge bravely rode the white horses, balanced precariously in a dirigible ducking stool masquerading as a dinghy. The river asserted itself and he proceeded to enact an Eskimo roll, but with one subtle difference: he no longer had a boat, his trusty steed was by then galloping away into the darkness towards…no one knew. Even the resurgence for the Nare was still only a question mark on the map.

"Pull! Pull!" he yelled fit to burst his lungs. To lifeline from upstream would have been fatal. Instead, making their way along the stalagmite-strewn banking, his companions played him like a salmon on a line, hoping the current would do the rest. Luckily he was projected back to the bank which, as it happened, ran out only a few metres beyond. It was not simply a case of lifelining as with normal caving, for there was certainly nothing orthodox about the Nare. To haul in from upstream would result in certain drowning despite the use of buoyancy vests. In most cases the topography of the cave passage would preclude any practical assistance other than holding the "victim" on a lead. This time they had won the day, but what about next time? Next time? Of course, they had still to gain the far bank…

This was their first encounter with the Nare. It was more difficult than they could have imagined, despite being conditioned by the findings of the reconnaissance and their experiences from the previous weeks. Not even Jean-François could have foreseen the problems of following the river; if he had, it would have made little difference for a caver does not willingly suffer defeat. With explorations of this nature, when faced with obstacles never before encountered in a cave, new methods must be devised and alternative techniques evolved by trial and error; one could not simply give in.

If the comparison to a rodeo seems a little bizarre, some of the applied techniques were more so. River crossings invariably demanded a tyrolean line. Of course someone must be the first across to fix and tension the main rope. Various methods were employed – usually involving some maniac throwing himself in and floundering to the far side or slinging a grappling hook across to the far bank. When all else failed the explorers resolved to gain the far bank by using a lasso, perhaps a rope weighted with a carabiner or chockstone, in the hope that this would lodge in some crevice and remain there long enough for some brave soul to make the hazardous traverse. Another technique involves the "trail ferry," which allows the person making the first crossing to drift with the current while held on a rope. A pendulum manoeuvre on the water surface in theory then projects the explorer in an arc to the far bank.

This time they had lost the dinghy, some rope and a little pride; but more important, the trip nearly ended in disaster. Back in camp there was an air of despondency at their failure, and one point worried them: through the gloom of the riverway, they thought they had seen another bend just ahead. If this was the case and if they were forced by the nature of the passage to cross the river every 100 metres, they doubted they could ever fully explore the system.

The following day a fresh team went down. After negotiating the Poseidon Crossing Jean-Paul climbed a wall to gain a ledge. He set off along this, but after a mere 20 metres came to a halt. He scrutinised the rapids below him with a mixture of wonder and fear. They appeared impossible; however, abseiling down to water level for a closer look, he spotted a possible traverse line just clear of the waves. At length he was able to step from Ledge Jo onto another terrace and around a left bend. It had taken five damp hours clinging to the wall to gain 100 metres of passage. The river wound its away into the darkness like a snake coiled and ready to strike. The inevitable happened only 350 metres ahead: the bank ended and in front of them lay 15 metres of whitewater hell, the Python Crossing.

The following morning another group made its way to the limit of the previous day. They stood for half an hour spellbound by the atmosphere of the place. It reminded Jean-François of the large halls of the Gouffre de la Pierre-St. Martin in his homeland. Twin waterfalls cascaded from an invisible ceiling and had with time built up large domes of calcite in the riverbed. They hoped to use these as a means of crossing.

The first to try in a madly bold attempt was Jean Delpy. After a first successful jump he faltered, then leapt. A split second later he was in the water, still clinging to the rope, only his helmet appearing now and again as he fought desperately to gain the side. Somewhere a sub-merged rock enabled him to drag himself from the water, at which point those lining him allowed the trail ferry principal to carry him, spluttering, back to the shore.

Some time was spent examining the far side with a powerful torch. At length they retraced their steps to where the river slowed a little. They tried a grappling iron. The first reached the far bank but slipped back into the river where it lodged for good. Some large stal bosses inspired the use of the lasso. The rope was cut and a large loop tied in the end of the line. It missed its mark at the first attempt then jammed, perhaps on account of the knot. The team set a second line using some nuts as a weight and, using both lines, eventually fastened a tyrolean crossing. Their reward: an eight hour headache and a further 100 metres progress along the riverway. A ledge could then be seen high up the wall, but of course it was on the far side.

Over the next couple of days they traced almost 300 metres of riverway by rigging three more perilous tyroleans: the Andrea Doria, the Titanic and Les Priapes (see fig. 23). They were then faced once again with the inevitable river crossing. The day before, Jean-François had spotted a bridge spanning the canyon high up in the roof. This was to prove the key to gaining the far bank.

The Flying Dutchman was without doubt the most spectacular tyrolean yet, the explorers having to cross commando style whilst dangling dangerously 30 metres above the raging riverway. Traversing along a section beyond the Flying Dutchman, the river squeezed into a narrow channel leading to further exposed sections for a few hundred metres. Here they found themselves up against yet another formidable stretch of whitewater. The Torre Canyon crossing was followed soon afterwards by the Les Nutuvians, before the Nare showed its true colours at Apocalypse Now.

Thus on March 28, after a dozen trips lasting as much as 20 hours each, they halted at a depth of 400 metres and two kilometres from the entrance shaft. Faced with rapids judged to be quite impassable, downstream exploration was abandoned and the passage photographed, surveyed and detackled. No less than 11 tyrolean lines had been installed and more than 1,150 metres of rope employed. Further work included making a film for the French television station Antenna 2. Although the only records broken concerned the volume of the caves, the size of the rivers and – ironically – slowness, the French explorations marked the beginning of a new era in cave exploration. Despite their good fortune, it was to be a further three years before French cavers returned in strength to the antipodes.

There were no expeditions in 1981 but there was some activity by a dwindling number of expatriate cavers. On January 2, Mike Bourke, Lex Brown and Tony Stearns, a Californian, descended Berema Cave in the Chimbu and found the terminal lake had dried up. Pushing on beyond this, they explored the system to conclusion at a depth of 120 metres. In March, Mike Bourke visited the Mapos Caves at Snake River; at Easter Graham Lash, Neil Ryan, Allan Goulbourne and Martin Richardson climbed Mt. Kaijende in the Enga. Neil returned in November with Roy Berger to look for caves, and so ended one of the quietest years for cave exploration, soon to be followed by one of the most productive.

In March 1982, Neil Hickson and Carol Clayton returned to the Iaro River Cave with Robin Field, who had also visited it late the previous year. On both occasions no new finds were made and progress along the river passage not attempted. The Easter period also saw something of a reconnaissance to the Ular Plains, a high altitude region of the Huon Peninsula. The area in which caving potential was assessed was located at 2,400 metres and bounded by the Cromwell Range to the north and the Mongi River to the south. Though little was found, good depth potential warranted further study.

Although these two trips marked a rather disappointing beginning to the new year, the events that were to follow were to make it one of the most fruitful in New Guinea caving history. The two main expeditions – a large scale one from Australia and an American-led venture, between them discovered almost 70 kilometres of new cave or extensions to existing systems, and length and depth records were to be broken yet again.

Rolan Eberhard entering the Atea Kananda.

Brian Evans

Chapter Eight

MAMO KANANDA

During the post-Atea period world depth statistics had remained in an almost continual state of flux, with one group after another jockeying for the prestige of becoming the world's deepest cavers. Shortly after returning from New Britain in 1980, Jean-François Pernette and a Franco-Spanish team had ended a ten-year quest for the elusive underground St. Georges River in the Pyrénées. In a steeply descending pothole called simply BU56 (later named La Puerta de Illamina), they succeeded in reaching a depth of 1,195 metres, making it the world's fourth deepest system at that time. Subsequent explorations would take the depth to 1,408 metres.

Earlier that same year news filtering through to the caving press hinted of a new Soviet threat to the West in the shape of the Snezhnaya Cave. This was found in 1971, high in the Bolshoi Caucusus and quickly took its position in the league tables, shaking French dominance of the 1,000 metre plus club. During the winter of 1979-80 a team of Moscow speleologists, spending a total 86 days below ground, had explored the cave to a depth of 1,280 metres, placing it firmly in third position.

Not wishing to be outdone by any foreign upstarts, the French launched into a flurry of activity. A meticulously planned expedition by members from the Spéléo Club Vulcain of Lyons supported a dive in the terminal sump of the Gouffre Jean Bernard. This produced yet another world depth record of 1,455 metres. In other areas of the world, cavers were anything but idle. In the Gouffre Mirolda a depth of 1,100 metres had been reached, and the next year a group of British explorers from Oxford University reached 1,139 metres in Pozu del Xitu in Spain's Picos de Europa.

Of course the country most likely to upstage the Gauls was Mexico, where since the late 1960s a persistent bunch of vertical cavers from the States had been steadily working away at the incredible vertical complex of Sistema Huautla. Continued exploration here will eventually set the stage for a total depth of 1,639 metres, if it can be linked with its presumed resurgence at Peña Colorada.

When the Atea expedition dispersed in 1978, Hadia Yaneabogairi had reached a depth of 200 metres and over eight kilometres length. It was quite modest by world standards, yet within this distance so many unexplored leads remained that there was no doubting the Australians would return. The only questions were when, and who? "When" more or less worked itself out as 1982. This was the earliest practical date for a return, considering the logistics of planning what was to become one of the largest expeditions of its kind ever organised. Of course it was infinitely desirable that their period in the field coincide with the so-called "dry season" in the Muller Range, falling between June and August.

Chopper pad at Kananda Pugwa before the porters cleared the sight, ...

Despite the pessimistic geological reports (which in previous years had undermined the enthusiasm of some vertical cavers), many suspected that beneath the plateau at Mamo, a major cave system would in time be found. Moreover, with all the news of world depth records flying around there was renewed hope – among some Sydney cavers at least – that in the Muller, perhaps, they were at last on the threshold of a deep cave which would push New Guinea (and Australasia) into the spotlight of world caving.

Faced with such a challenge it was not surprising that the "who" quickly gelled into a pre-dominantly Australasian mix with a cast of thousands – well, 59 to be precise. Since the expedition was to be spread over a two month period with people variously participating for all or only part of the duration in the field, leadership of this large-scale influx of explorers and scientists was vested not in one person, but a collective.

Alan Warild, Tony White and Steve Bunton were a pretty tough bunch whose outdoor experiences were manifold. Tony had been involved with both the British expeditions of 1975 and 1978, and had made important contributions to the Atea trip in 1978. He was a particularly diligent cave surveyor and photographer as well as a reasonably accomplished rock climber. Modestly describing himself as a short, overweight, balding wimp, Steve too had a wealth of experience to offer, gained in New Zealand, Great Britain and elsewhere. He had successfully climbed New Zealand's Mt. Cook and Mera Peak (6,162m) in Nepal, in themselves no mean feat.

What goes up must go down as they say, and Alan was just as happy below ground as he was trekking over the snowy wastes of some remote peak. In fact, to some he seemed a likely contender for the title of Australia's caving machine. Standing just short of 180 centimetres and

…and chopper's first landing at camp.

weighing 60 kilos, he was superbly fit with a fanatical capacity for caving. Completing a foursome was that doyenne of antipodean expedition caving, Julia James, architect and driving force behind the three previous Muller expeditions. She was able to draw upon a constellation of experiences and skills gained in caves the world over.

Handling the planning at the New Guinea end of the operation was Neil Hickson, a somewhat assertive caver regarded by some as an aspiring hard man with experience of deep caves on both sides of the Pacific, in Mexico and in New Zealand. At the time of the expedition he was living and working as an accountant in Mount Hagen and therefore well placed to look after expedition logistics there. Between them all, they possessed a formidable store of caving expertise.

Helicopters were the preferred choice of transport for both personnel as well as the four tonnes of supplies; they were cheaper and less troublesome than local tribesmen. Employment of the Duna was mostly restricted to support for the advance party, some remaining afterwards to service camps and act as guides. Up to a dozen were eventually retained in this capacity; some of them such as Kerupa were "old hands" from earlier trips.

By late June, Steve Bunton and the advance team of six had trekked in to establish lines of communications. It was also their responsibility to set up camp and construct a new helipad by the entrance to Mamo Cave. They found that in the intervening years the forest had enacted a remarkable process of reclamation, winning back what had been relinquished to the temporary gains of the cavers. The landing pad at the Atea site and most tracks – except those regularly in use as native hunting pads – required some work with a bush knife to clear the mantle of regrowth.

The noise of the cicadas rose to an ear-rending pitch as other creatures of the twilight joined the chorus. It set the teeth on edge, as does metal grating upon metal. In the tropics the transition from twilight to total nightfall is rapid, and in 20 minutes it would be dark. It was the same each evening as countless insects, some probably unknown to science, announced the imminent arrival of dusk. Then, just as suddenly as it had begun, darkness brought an abrupt end to the din and an uneasy hush fell upon the jungle. The performance was as regular as clockwork, almost making timepieces unnecessary in the tangled heartland of this green wilderness.

Beneath the protective overhang of a sizeable cave mouth a campfire crackled merrily, shooting out searching tongues of flame that cast a halo of orange light. Here at the meeting place of two worlds, a group of figures huddled around the embers, contemplating the weeks that lay ahead. In their glowing expressions an observer might have detected a hint of optimism or maybe the mixed emotions of hope and fear: hope of exploring a cave deeper than any other, fear perhaps of the unknown or of returning to civilisation at the end of a once-in-a-lifetime experience.

A loud crack and a shower of sparks from the fire momentarily interrupted the cavers' talk of the Iguanodon and the Sacking of Rome. This was no history lesson on the fall of ancient empires and equally extinct saurians, but an animated discussion on the passages found four years earlier beneath their feet. The Sacking of Rome was an especially well decorated gallery leading off from the Iguanodon, one of the largest chambers so far found beneath the Muller Range. Over a meal of bully beef and instant mash their aspirations were given an airing suitably tempered by anxieties, while behind them on the rough cave walls the flames projected enlarged shadow pictures that flickered and danced like sentinel spirits of the underworld the cavers were about to enter.

From the outset the plan had been to divide expedition manpower between several widespread camps, each in theory having its own leader. Should the discovery of a deep going cave dictate such a move, the venture could focus all of its resources on any one objective. The organisers believed this approach would achieve greater flexibility while giving a broader spectrum of meaningful results to the scientific programme. Individual groups would enjoy a certain amount of autonomy and still benefit from central logistical control.

As with previous expeditions the Atea camp was again chosen as the centre for the whole operation. Instrumental in this decision was the lingering hope that untold depths might still be reached beyond the Ship Canal. Single side-band radios were to provide their sole link with the outside world on a twice daily basis.

In early July they began moving supplies and personnel from the roadhead at Koroba. While some participants enjoyed the journey "tourist class" – on foot over the steep Anu Pass and on through Geroro – the remainder passed through the idyllic Lavani Valley and its contrasting world of yanks in shiny construction helmets. While awaiting their lift on a *mixmaster bilong Jesus* ("helicopter" in Melanesian pidgin), the cavers enjoyed succulent T-bone steaks in air conditioned comfort while watching, appropriately enough, a video of Jules Verne's *Journey to the Centre of the Earth*.

Up at the Mamo camp there was no mistaking the sound of an approaching "mixer." The distinctive *thwack, thwack, thwack* grew louder even though the source of the noise remained invisible due to the serried trees fringing the doline. Then with a high-pitched whine the chopper was suddenly overhead, the pilot banking his craft dangerously close to the tree canopy. A starburst of sunlight bounced from the windshield as he circled around then angled down towards them, skilfully settling his machine onto the platform of felled logs beside the doline.

Mark Wilson climbs out of the Satrurn 5 entrance of Mamo.

Mark Laurendet near one of the jungle-covered entrances at Mamo.

Dirk Stoffels with leeched eye.

Mark Laurendet in the Roaring Eighties.

Australian Mark Laurendet negotiating a duck in the Backyard, a passage in Mamo Kananda leading directly from the expedition camp established beneath its overhanging entrance.

Dirk Stoffels in one of the outflow caves of the Atea system.

Mark Laurendet in a outflow cave of the Atea system.

Dirk Stoffels

Brian Evans

Surface travel between the Mamo camps, as elsewhere in New Guinea, was anything but leisurely.

First pitch down Kananda Pugwa below camp chamber.

Space Oddity, Kananda Pugwa.

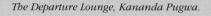

The Departure Lounge, Kananda Pugwa.

Stream entrance at Kananda Pugwa.

The Yu Atea cascading into the Atea Doline.

Porter wearing a bird of paradise that had been shot that day.

Mamo 4 camp in 1982.

While the chopper was kept ticking over with one skid balanced precariously on the pad, out leapt Helen Turton and Graeme Smith into a storm of twigs and leaves whipped into a frenzy by the fierce down-draught. The supplies were bundled out and seconds later the pilot was up and out of sight, the sound of his machine fading on a barely noticeable breeze. There were flights the following day but bad weather then forced the pilot to return to base before completing the shuttle. As a result some of the Mamo personnel and most of their supplies – 1,200 kilos in all – were marooned at the Atea camp. It was three days before camp necessities for the Mamo team could be backpacked the five kilometres up to the plateau. Until then no one would know if Julia was correct in her assumptions about the potential of Hadia Yaneabogairi.

It was frustrating for those left at the Atea to know that the Mamo campsite was only one minute flying time to the west; they were faced with making the journey on foot, and four gruelling hours would be needed to cover the same distance over the muddied trails. Tales were legion of boa constrictors that could drop unannounced from the trees and crush a person to death: three coils was all it took, so rumour had it.

The comfort of those who had to face these horrors, real or imagined, was assured upon arrival. The well appointed campsite provided beds, a shower, latrines and a kitchen complete with tables, chairs and shelving, all of course fashioned from readily available bush materials. The camping cave, Hadia Nduhongairi, was both spacious and dry, protected from downpours by the east-facing overhang of its roof. From here they could enjoy an unimpeded view of their temporary home, a forested depression. Hardly a Gold Coast resort but then beggars can't be choosy.

The passage receding into the hill behind the camp became known as the "Backyard" and was the source of a small misfit stream. Under normal circumstances this chuckled merrily along a channel carved through collapse debris for 250 metres before vanishing down an obscure hole in the floor. A few metres nearer daylight, in fact quite close to the camp kitchen, was a narrow unexplored fissure between boulders. Although highly significant, no one at first gave this a second thought. However, as the dry season was coming to an end later into the expedition, those in camp were to discover the unpredictable nature of the backyard stream when they had to rescue buckets of jelly that had been left in pools to set!

While team members were coming to terms with life at the Mamo camp, Al Warild, Anne Wright, Mark Wilson and Stefan and Rolan Eberhard were choppered directly into a remote clearing high on Mt. Legari. They had with them rations to last one month, 500 metres of rope, a two-way radio and high hopes vested in the unknown depths of a large black hole (see fig. 9). Due to their isolation – some 15 kilometres to the northeast of the Atea base – and an unfortunate breakdown in communications, they were to remain out of touch with their colleagues for the entire first month of the expedition.[1]

The Eberhard brothers were Tasmania's latest up and coming hard man act, having many fine vertical performances to their credit, especially in the Junee-Florentine region. Indeed Stefan was credited with having single-handedly revitalised the flagging Tasmanian caving scene. Only a few weeks before coming to New Guinea he had discovered and explored a cave called Ice Tube, clinching a new Australian depth record of 345 metres.

By comparison Mark Wilson was a youngster but very strong and fit. He was to demonstrate competence in his approach to caving and, capitalising on the experience he gained, would later shine on Al Warild's expeditions to Mexico. Anne Wright was one of four geologists taking part in the Mamo trip. She had been a leading light in organising some of the Nettlebed Cave expeditions in New Zealand. If she had one overriding trait it was being terribly talkative, though indeed she meant well.

The Black Hole was one of the goals that had come to symbolise all that the Mamo expedition stood for, and a picture of its impressive, rock-rimmed maw had been used in the promotion blurb sent to sponsors. The hole had been seen once, from a helicopter flying over the region a few years before. The only other holes known to offer similar spectacular entrances were Nare in New Britain, Hoya de la Luz and a few other dolines near Xilitla in Mexico and some large pits in Venezuela. With over two vertical kilometres of virgin limestone between the Black Hole and any known outflow, it was no surprise that the Eberhard brothers chose to join the Mamo team. Like other vertical caving participants they had quickly grasped the implications of a major break-through on Legari. As it happened, the Black Hole was not all it had seemed, and over the space of four weeks they faced many hardships with little reward for their troubles, but more about this ill-fated patrol later...

At the Mamo advance base the initial team of ten soon settled into a routine of exploration, simply walking into discoveries with startling ease. It was unusual in fact if a returning party was unable to report extensions of at least a kilometre. The main cave was characterised by extensive horizontal development, and camp cuisine by limitless attempts to make a mouth watering dish from canned dog. Some even resorted to flavouring meals with kerosene during their fruitless attempts to encourage flames from a pile of damp kindling!

[1] *The radio failed after three hours and though it was repaired a week later, it was too heavy to carry and was left behind.*

Stalactites decorate Roll-a-Go-Go, one of many fossilized phreatic conduits in Mamo Kananda.

In 1978, as many as eight distinct levels of cave development had been identified. If this was not bad enough for those who were trying to unravel its geomorphology, very soon during the first week an entirely new horizon was revealed midway between Siltstone Blues and the trunk route at Mainline. The cave was turning into a confusing labyrinth with open passages being found faster than they could be mapped (see fig. 19). During a nine-hour trip with Barry Were and Ian Westwood, Steve Worthington revisited Bloody Him, one of the first really good leads in the cave. Half a kilometre of tortuous twisting rift terminated at an aven that later was connected to the surface. While retracing their steps however, Steve poked his head into an insignificant looking hole. This led up a fossil inlet and, via some fairly straightforward climbs, to a major junction. As time was pressing, they went no further that day.

Returning the following morning and turning left at the junction, they wandered into the spacious gallery of Roll-a-Go-Go. This they eagerly traced for nearly two kilometres, all of it in easy, walking-size passageways displaying an arched cross-section in places decorated with a wealth of speleothems.

While this was taking place someone had a closer look at the fissure near the campfire. After dropping a series of pleasant pitches in clean, sound rock, they suddenly found themselves on familiar ground, back in Siltstone Blues. Access into the system by way of this new route, almost direct from camp, had the advantage of being a quick alternative to the original thirty-metre shaft of Hadia Yaneabogairi. The latter was reached via a horrendously filthy overland trail, so not

Ian Westwood using a Michie phone at the helipad.

surprisingly the new way in became preferable, although the original shaft was left rigged as part of a flood escape route via the Sacking of Rome and Mainline.

The entrance to Leaptover, as the direct route became known, was so close to the camp mess that those returning to the surface at the end of a long, hard day were often treated to enticing aromas of curry, or pancakes and syrup wafting several pitches down into the cave on the aspirating air current. The height of luxury for exiting cavers in Leaptover was to contact camp and order a hot shower and a brew for their imminent arrival. This was made possible over the Michie phone[2], installed during the first days of the expedition.

The ethos of surveying discoveries as they took place was standard procedure on all Australian expeditions; however, in this instance the more passage they found and painstakingly mapped, the more the convolution of interconnected fossil galleries, streamways, avens and pits simply added to their confusion. Moreover, as the length of the cave grew, some passages were "lost" and subsequently rediscovered on more than one occasion.

Accompanied by Mark Laurendet, Steve Bunton pushed the Backyard inlet, scaling the terminal cascade with the help of a tree trunk and a couple of rock anchors. Clad only in sandshoes, swimmers and T-shirt, Steve bravely gargled his way through two low airspace sections (duck-unders, as they are more commonly known) to be rewarded with a further waterfall beyond. This inlet later yielded another of the 24 entrances that eventually were found to lead into the labyrinth. Elsewhere in the cave, Kraftwork, Superglue and Supertramp were discovered, the latter eventually being recognised as a higher level of the Cooks Tour circuit explored in 1978.

Both Kraftwork and Roll-a-Go-Go represented major fossil trunk routes, each holding the key to countless more kilometres of new cave. As a measure of the system's complexity, no less than

---

[2] *A single wire telephone devised by Neville Michie of theSydney Speleological Society.*

Ian Westwood and Steve Bunton in the Ship Canal (Atea Kananda).

40 leads were plotted during the ten hours spent exploring Kraftwork. Early on Thursday, July 15, two teams entered the cave to follow up those active passages leading on from there. Graeme Smith, Mark Laurendet, Dirk Stoffels and Helen Turton entered the Roaring '80s streamway where a ten-metre waterfall was recognised as a major feeder into Cooks Tour. Meanwhile Roy Winstanley, Barry Were and Steve Bunton were looking at a similar passage off Kraftwork. One chamber revealed the sad remains of a bandicoot, while an aven prompted the tongue in cheek name Whirling Person when a large flake unexpectedly parted company with its host wall as Steve was attempting to climb it. The impromptu flying lesson resulted in a six-metre fall. Though potentially serious, this incident fortunately resulted in nothing worse than a severely bruised arm. Exploration continued regardless.

In the hope of finding the feeder stream for the Backyard, Barry Were, Steve Bunton, Steve Worthington and Beruwi, a Duna tribesman, began a surface traverse the following Saturday. Hidden in the rugged bush country to the northwest of camp, a trio of strong streams were found to channel through the jungle in miniature canyons. It was patently clear that the combined flow was far too large to be the Backyard creek. Instead the explorers had stumbled upon the first of the fabled sinking streams, seen on aerial photographs as early as 1973 but believed by many to be the figment of the cartographer's imagination.

The three streams united at an 80-metre plunge down a sheer sided doline. A tubular entrance of handsome proportions could be seen piercing the north wall part way down, while below this both up- and downstream portals beckoned elusively from behind a mantle of vegetation.

The next day Steve Bunton and Steve Worthington returned to this promising site and were rewarded with a roomy passage heading off into the great unknown. Surveying as they went, they were delighted to run out 50-metre tape legs as they plunged through deep pools in leaps and bounds. Eventually they halted at Spring Creek where a series of clean, wet shafts proved

The Atea camp during the '82 Australian expedition.

remarkably devoid of suitable natural belay points. They had to turn back but were pleased nevertheless, for in four hours they had mapped 384 metres. On a later visit these shafts were found to drop into Cooks Tour via Hoth, a superb pressure tube with many sporting cascades and swims. It was named after the frozen planet in the film sequel to Star Wars.

As the cave grew in length over the first three weeks of the expedition, the system's greater significance and complexity demanded a more appropriate title. The many leads which remained when the cave was vacated four years earlier simply multiplied with every turning. Both Hadia Nduhongairi and Hadia Yaneabogairi ("cave where we are" and "cave over there" in the Duna tongue) were a bit of a mouthful, so the cave was unanimously renamed Mamo Kananda. It sounded like an exclamation – Mamo Kananda! – a sort of Melanesian "Eureka!" Perhaps this was appropriate, for in Hadia Yaneabogairi the Australians had, without realising it in 1978, stumbled upon a discovery which was to provide the major surprise of the New Guinea caving calendar. The cave was growing daily into a vast three-dimensional maze underlying just one small corner of the forested plateau. Considering the latter has a total area of around 100 square kilometres, it was more than the imagination could cope with to consider where the cave might ultimately end.

While the Mamo team was rolling back the frontier of caving, a large group remained at the Atea. Some Sydney cavers still courted hopes of greater depth and had designs on the section of cave beyond the known end of the river-way. The deepest point at Winchester had only been quickly looked at once on the previous expedition. With this in mind an eight strong team set off rigging float rope through the swims in the Ship Canal, as had become standard procedure. The conditions were ideal for pushing on down the river-way, a drought having produced a generous two metres of airspace in the ducks where in the past there had been just a few centimetres.

Heaped upon nearby ledges, colonies of freshwater crabs looked on with indifference as the rubber-suited intruders drifted silently by. Unfortunately little progress was made beyond the previous terminal point; the sole find here added a pitiful 20 metres to the total depth. Their failure to discover anything more significant was not for want of trying, and the modest extension was hard won after forcing a tortuous route down through the jammed boulders forming the floor of the chamber.

During another visit Susan Laidlaw and Neil Hickson supported Allistair MacIntyre in a close encounter with the Penstock (see fig. 11b). Allistair was a well built ex-riot cop from London who had been forced to take early retirement after receiving a missile in the eye during the Brixton disturbances. He had joined the venture as part of the advance team. He was a pretty tough type and not easily ruffled. Secured with a lifeline to his ankle, Allistair allowed himself to be swept into the violent sump pool for a short way before being dragged back to safety. And just to prove how much he had enjoyed it, he went in a second time! It was a heroic but desperate attempt to find a passable outlet.

Success was limited elsewhere. The Spanish Inquisition provided a more direct route between the New World Series and the south-trending Austral. A difficult aid climb by Ron Levy, Rauleigh Webb and Jeff Crass eventually paid dividends in 300 metres of beautifully decorated galleries out of Hidden Inlet. But it was the opposite extremity of the system where perhaps the most significant discoveries came.

Brian Evans, Jane Dyson, Dave Martin, Bryan Cleaver, Peter Nieuwendyk and Terry Barr set up a rudimentary camp deep in the Yaragaiya, a series of galleries beneath the Yu Dina Valley, some 14 hours caving from the entrance. In six days at this remote site the group met with mixed fortunes, failing either to find a new upper entrance or to reveal a link with the underground course of the Yu Dina. The latter was known to drain to the Nali resurgence via an independent course not linked with the known Atea system. In spite of this there were some compensations.

On the return journey downstream, a careful search of the roof levels along the Ugwapugwa Streamway revealed a new high-level solution network. The Ant's Nest yielded almost two kilometres of new galleries, and added 40 metres to the vertical range of the system. The team thought that further finds must ultimately be within their grasp, but dwindling rations merely reinforced their growing urge to see daylight. Back on the surface they made plans for a return but this never eventuated, as enthusiasm was usurped by the exciting developments taking place at Mamo. Although Mamo was a great pull, the Nali Gorge still could not be ignored. It had been visited by the previous two expeditions and its steep headwall partially explored. At the base of this, the Yu Atea emerged to become the Nali River, a tributary of the Strickland, which flowed off into the Papuan lowlands before meeting its confluence with the mighty Fly.

A previous helicopter reconnaissance had given a tantalising glimpse of what appeared to be a sizeable horizontal slot headed by the 200-metre vegetated cliff. In the first weeks of the expedition, discoveries in the Atea had fallen well short of expectations and there was a strong urge to explore other avenues. The "hole" at the Nali might simply have been a shadow, but they were haunted by doubts. The existence of a fossil outflow was a possibility too good to be discounted.

After emerging from the Yaragaiya camp Bryan Cleaver, Peter Nieuwendyk and Dave Martin, assisted by Kerupa their Duna guide, hacked a switchback trail through dense undergrowth from the Nomad River trade route to the brink of the Nali scarp, in the vain hope of assessing the terrain below. Compasses were of little use, but Kerupa was possessed of an uncanny sense of direction in the bush. Although the postulated cave could not be seen for the thick vegetation and swirling mist, a suitable takeoff point was located for what they thought would be a long abseil. They then returned to base to make plans.

The route back to the Nomad trail proved a nightmare, and was so precipitous in places that Kerupa's dog had to be carried or manhandled up numerous climbs. Two days later Ian Miller and Dave Martin joined Peter and Bryan for the abseil into the Nali, using two thirds of the available 550 metres of rope on the steep descent.

After abseiling down through tangled lianas and scrub they made a final landing on a slope flanking the cliff face. The air was still and humid, pierced only by the occasional *wauk, wauk, wok, wok, wok* of some bird. By late afternoon the explorers had emerged from the enchanted world of the rain forest into more or less open bush country for their first view of what was undoubtedly a hole. Crossing a landslide, they reached the wide cave mouth with relative ease. Nightfall was by then fast approaching so they sought a suitable campsite, leaving exploration for the morning.

Ngoma Kananda offered the prospect of a bivvy, yet it was less than ideal: some of the rocks forming the floor had the distinct appearance of not having long been detached from the roof. They prudently chose the eastern side of the entrance in which to bed down, just beyond the drip line. Here the rocks looked less fresh, having gathered a soft veneer of moss.

After rising full of enthusiasm they began mapping their find. The cave was simply one large chamber hollowed out of the cliff by solution, and subsequently modified and enlarged by the gradual collapse of walls and roof. The effect of this process had created a more or less domed ceiling, at its maximum some 50 metres high. A survey loop of 865 metres took them right around its perimeter and eventually back to daylight. The only water they found during this traverse had been near the rear of the cavern, where a tiny stream splashed from a crack in the wall to vanish amid the chaos forming the floor.

Brian Evans arrived around noon and together they followed a side passage that quickly ended in a choke. Although they were quite impassable, a cool wind blew from between the boulders, a sure sign of larger caverns beyond. The team took photographs and completed the survey detail before bedding down for a second night in the spirit lands of the Nali.

Dawn arrived bright but uncomfortably humid. From their bivvy in the entrance, the cavers could look across the treetops, in places glistening with the floss-like communal webs marking colonies of gregarious *Cyrtophora* spiders. Another interesting feature of the Nali Gorge was a precipitous bluff around which frequent mists created an effect resembling one of those classic karst scenes depicted in Chinese art. They decided to have a look. Bryan Cleaver briefly surveyed the wooded heights of China Buttress then carefully picked his way up and soon vanished from view. Reaching a rocky terrace at a higher level, he stumbled upon another cave whose railway tunnel proportions came as quite a surprise. Though he should have returned there and then for support, the lone explorer was seduced by the receding darkness. He hadn't gone far however, when he was obliged to take to the water. He was joined eventually by the others and they progressed until stopped by a pitch. There was no way forward without more equipment; another night in the gorge was inevitable before they could return to base for tackle. Sleep was fitful and their dreams were haunted by things that went bump in the night, and the slow, deliberate flapping of some mystery creature that repeatedly came and went until daybreak.

With more rope and augmented by the arrival of Barry Were, Tony White and Steve Worthington, a full exploration and survey at Pimbiraga Kananda was underway. To all outward appearances the cave was a flood overflow conduit for the Nali, but whether it was fed by the Yu Atea remained a matter for debate. There was also the question of where exactly any floodwaters

Dirk Stoffels crunches numbers in camp on an early model Sharp PC-1500 computer.

might enter the cave, though understandably no one wished to be present to learn the answer. A large aven was thought likely. In the final computation Pimbiraga Kananda was just short of two and a half kilometres in extent with the nearest point in the Atea – the Austral Series – still a long way above.

On July 17, an appeal for more cavers at the Mamo camp brought reinforcements in the shape of Nick Hume, Ron Levy, Lloyd Hitchins and Rauleigh Webb, swelling the number in camp to fourteen. Three days after they arrived, dawn broke at the Atea base and all hell seemed to let loose. At first, those in camp thought perhaps the military choppers were the start of an Indonesian invasion. The air shook and eardrums popped as two Iroquois landed, each in turn disgorging copious quantities of rum and canned delicacies, followed by Peter Passmore, Mick Fry and Karen Gamble, three sociable types from the Royal Australian Navy Caving Association.

Cavers at the Atea Kananda were now making ever lengthier expeditions for precious little reward. As a result, more cavers departed for the expanding frontier of Mamo Kananda where discoveries were continuing with the same remarkable ease. At the end of each day everyone eagerly queued up to process their survey notes, reducing data to coordinates and plotting them with a PC1500 computer and printer unit donated by Sharp Industries.

By this time the system was approaching 18 kilometres in length. Some descended to take photographs and surveying continued as usual, though still the system confounded them with its intricacies. Cooks Tour was probably the most mapped section in the whole cave, being repeatedly rediscovered and surveyed by those whose grasp of the system was less than perfect. Following a few scares with flood pulses a 2:30 p.m. curfew went into effect on all passages likely to be affected. This was mostly adhered to, although one or two exceptions very nearly resulted in disaster.

Barry Were looks down the pitch taking the sinking stream that leads into Kananda Pugwa.

During the last half of July two important passages were found, Geronimo and Delusions of Grandeur. A week or two later, the former proved to be part of a safe alternative to the risky traverse of Rinse Cycle and Cooks Tour. Its discoverers (Rauleigh, Graeme and Ron) had named it Geronimo after a curious formation they found there. Delusions of Grandeur was stark by comparison. Mark Laurendet, Ev Tulp and Dirk Stoffels first entered this spacious passage floored with block fall after pushing a lead trending north from the Sacking of Rome. It ended with three promising waterfall leads, one at the northern end, falling seven metres into a lower level. As the team had been underground for six hours, those virgin depths were to remain unknown until another day; indeed, it would later prove to be an important find.

Ever since the first Muller expedition in 1973, the streams shown on the maps as sinking in the southeastern corner of the Mamo Plateau had been a source of wonder. Having already found one major stream sink and answered the vexing question of whether or not they flowed, Barry Were, Ian Westwood and Rauleigh Webb were making a systematic exploration of the dense bush country slightly north of camp. Assisting in this were two Duna tribesmen, Beruwi and Kalawei. It was Wednesday the twenty-first, a memorable date for some.

Starting from a waterfall seen the previous weekend they proceeded upstream. Arriving at a junction, they took the right hand smaller branch, turned northeast along the true right bank and then south 15 minutes later. At this point they could hear the unmistakable sound of falling water ahead and somewhere below. Scrambling down breaks in some siltstone bluffs, they passed a waterfall where a stream vanished into a debris-choked swallet. A few minutes away the water reappeared briefly before sinking again into a walking size cave.

Frustrated by the lack of lights, they had to abandon thoughts of glory and begin their surface survey back to camp. Suddenly a yell from one of the Duna up ahead brought Ian running to investigate; however, he almost fell through the scrub cover spanning a large 50-metre-deep pit. To both his horror and delight, he found himself teetering on a moss-bearded log spanning the abyss…creaking. After he had recovered from the sudden shot of adrenaline he could barely contain himself with the prospect. The sound of a large stream drifted up from below.

Early next day Steve Worthington, Rauleigh and Barry descended into the new sink and explored a complex of entrances. From one of these they literally ran along an enlarging passage to where the strong flow was lost in a chaos of rocks and decaying tree trunks. Beyond this the passage continued 12 metres high and wide to a wet mud slope strewn with logs. Above and beyond this a strong air current drew them forward into a cave of increasing size. Proceeding three abreast suddenly they popped out in a passage of aircraft hanger proportions with pale daylight streaming in from the right. They picked their way over and around boulders; in this direction, the passage grew even larger until eventually it emerged in a huge vegetated doline, for all the world like a vast picture window opening into Eden.

Left from the point of entry a descending boulder floor terminated in a deep pitch. Rocks cast down this clattered for four seconds before striking bottom, indicated by a wonderful echo. The team decided that the obvious promise of Kananda Pugwa ("Big Cave" in Duna) should be left as a going concern for the arrival of the second month team. This large new cave was not visited again during two weeks of consistently dry weather, the irony of which was soon to become apparent.

BAD JU-JU ON LEGARI MOUNTAIN

Back on Legari Mountain, the team was making poor progress, being stricken with a run of bad luck. Three hours after being dropped on the mountain, they had finished the so-called Black Hole. It had not been the "bottomless" pit originally seen from the air, but instead ended 102 metres down in a lush interior forest complete with a resident tree kangaroo. Disappointed, the cavers decided to look further afield, knowing that a colossal shaft hailed yet from somewhere out in the bush. That night the radio failed to work and no contact could be made with Atea base. Perhaps this was just as well, for Al Warild and his team might have been chagrined if they had been aware of the choices facing their colleagues.

At the opposite end of the range was Uli Mindu, the deep unfinished shaft with a six-second drop partially explored by Tony White and Rudi Frank on the 1978 expedition. Between the helicopter drop zone and this promising hole, the aerial photographs showed a string of scrubby clearings dotted with depressions (see fig. 9).

Camp had been set up on a grassy knoll, a simple A-frame covered in polythene. A cache of supplies was left here and on Saturday, July 10, the team set off south, hacking through forest that resisted the sharpest of machetes. Progress was painfully slow, with a daily average of a kilometre or less. To make matters worse the only caves they found were muddy and uninspiring. Several days removed from their supply dump they passed through a third glade, finding more short caves. Track cutting continued.

In pouring rain and depressed by clouds that crept in among the ranks of moss-covered trees, they blazed a trail, keeping where possible to clearings, otherwise following the forested ridgelines clear of the doline country. The lack of going caves was a serious blow, and it was estimated they were only half the way to Uli Mindu. By this time they were sufficiently isolated from camp to warrant relocation. Al and Anne had discovered a convenient rock shelter on the edge

Mamo 5 camp in the Kananda Pugwa entrance.

of a huge depression, and the whole of the next day was employed forward loading some of their gear and rations to this site. It was dry, and the remains of firewood and charcoal pointed to its regular use by indigenous hunters.

Sharing the lugubrious accommodation with some especially voracious fleas meant that sleep was fitful despite the rigours of the trail. This was the least of Al's worries. While around the campfire one night, Mark had received a burn when he accidentally stepped into a billy full of boiling water. His ankle came up in a huge liquid filled blister and cast serious doubts on the future of the patrol. While Mark remained immobile at the cave the others continued cutting track. On the 17th, Alan came across a stream cave that was so nasty they were all relieved when it had the decency to end at a sump 200 metres in.

A week passed and Mark's ankle showed some improvement. They had endured persistently atrocious conditions for several days when they staggered into a large clearing at an altitude of 2,835 metres. This was maybe a kilometre in length with low, frost-shattered limestone cliffs taking minor streams. At its southern end was a small lake above which they found the overgrown site of the old 1978 camp. All about the scrubby slopes ranks of stumpy cycads marched downhill like triffids seeking refreshment at the shore of some extraterrestrial watering hole.

The trail to Uli Mindu proved elusive and despondency once again descended upon them. Al and Anne left the cave shelter in the morning and spent a fruitless day searching for the deep shaft. Meanwhile Mark remained out of action. Early the following day they set off again, this time packing rations for three days. At the same time Stefan and Rolan were despatched back to their first camp to make radio contact with the Atea base, advise of Mark's accident and collect additional supplies from the cache. By 7:00 p.m. they had still not raised the Atea at the prearranged transmission time. Overnight temperatures at Camp One fell below zero that night and a frosty dawn greeted them with 25 millimetres of ice on nearby pools. It was a sluggish start that morning. When they arrived back at the rock shelter they found Mark in much better spirits, his leg thankfully free of infection and on the mend.

It was Saturday, July 22, when Uli Mindu was at last located. With a third staging camp soon established nearby, the team was able to turn its attention to this magnificent shaft. Standing on the forested brink of Uli Mindu, the cavers belayed and lowered a 200-metre rope into the consuming darkness, each individual warming to the prospect of some good caving at last.

Threading the line through his descender, Al proceeded down, rigging a rebelay at a small inclined ledge after 55 metres. Another bolt proved necessary after a further 40 metres, then with a free hang assured, they dropped spider-like to the floor and landed in a huge rockfall chamber with no apparent way on. Unwilling to admit defeat, they tried forcing their wretched bodies down holes between the boulders but all ways were barred. Sadly, they added only a few precious metres, making a final depth of 200 metres.

RETREAT FROM LEGARI

With the conclusive end of Uli Mindu went their last hope of a major discovery. It would hardly have made their frustration any easier to bear had they known that Uli Mindu bottomed out the same day that the impressive entrance to Kananda Pugwa was discovered. In any case, they had all had quite enough of life on Legari Mountain.

Camp was struck and they trudged back to the site of their second staging camp, Anne spraining an ankle en route. Adding insult to injury, they found that the camp had been visited by uninvited "guests" and some supplies and equipment were missing. The Australians in 1973 had been warned against the Bogaiye, a local nomadic tribe with lingering cannibal tendencies. The Hewa also ranged over a wide expanse of the Southern Highlands, though they were mostly confined to the wild hinterland along the east side of the Strickland Gorge, and between there and Lake Kopiago to the north of Mamo. On occasions though, the Hewa had been known to travel as far afield as the Mullers.

In the early 1930s, young *kiaps* were warned, "don't get etten bi the natives," before setting out on first contact patrols into potentially hostile territory. Given the eating habits of many potholers, most of whom are always ready to try anything once, this warning today might easily have been reversed! Whether the mysterious raiders had been the Hewa or any other nomadic tribesmen they were unable to say, but if they were still around they remained inconspicuous – though in the dense bush at the best of times it was easy to attach substance to fleeting shadows.

After almost three weeks in the field, a much improved Mark accompanied Al back to camp one to pack gear in readiness for a later helicopter lift. Their jaded fortunes received yet another setback as the campsite was being cleared. Rubbish burning got out of control, incinerating half the clearing, the food and some of the gear; even worse, the radio batteries were destroyed.

Some of their equipment was later salvaged from the creek where it had been thrown in a panic to save it from destruction, but now all hope was gone of making contact with Atea. The latter was an estimated week's walk away, and now completely without radio they were all very conscious of their isolation. Two days later they began the long walk out to Atea base. This in itself developed into an epic. On the first day Al injured his shoulder with a machete, then after losing their bearings while searching for the valley carrying the Yu Dina, they were forced to spend a waterless night on an exposed ridge.

The dense bush seemed endless. After a further two difficult days they had no real idea of their position. They climbed a ridge in the hope of fixing their position but there was nothing but a rolling "ocean" of trees. After thrashing through dense bamboo thickets and pandanus they suddenly intersected a well-worn track. Then around lunchtime they were amazed to meet Ian Miller and John Wyeth bound for the Hegaibagu area. It was a relief to be told they were only about an hour and half from Atea base. With visions of hot showers and a good solid meal, they said their farewells and went their separate ways; Al's group staggered into camp exhausted, with barely an hour to nightfall.

The Legari team soon found that while they were in the field there had been an expedition policy change. Cavers had pushed the Atea to its limit, or so it would seem. Little had been found at either extremity of the cave and the Nali had not revealed any "backdoor" into the system. The small party Al and his companions had met on the trail were heading for Hegaibagu and the unfinished Uli Eta Riya found in 1978 and still going when vacated at minus 200 metres. But it was in Mamo Kananda where their best chances now lay.

By the time Julia had arrived for the beginning of the second month leadership patterns had become well entrenched. While much had been achieved in her absence, it was perhaps inevitable in organising such a large group of essentially free spirits that some friction would result. The odd personality clash had not been unexpected but, like the Legari team, everyone soon forgot his hardships. Any differences of opinion amongst expedition leaders were eclipsed by the growing conviction that Mamo Kananda was certainly no ordinary cave.

By July 26, Julia James, Tony White, Susan Laidlaw and the navy cavers had arrived at the Mamo Kananda camp. The system had by then reached a length in excess of 20 kilometres and showed little sign of ending. A few days later Tony descended with Trevor Worthy and Rauleigh Webb in an effort to clear up a few question marks in the passage confusion south of the Cooks Tour and Rinse Cycle area. They descended via Uli Kendi, the cave of the leeches. It was not the most popular entrance, various people having suffered from leeches in their eyes, mouths and noses. The pit dropped the three explorers into the phreatic conduit of Roll-a-Go-Go, where at the foot of the pitch were several outlet passages. In the course of 11 hours below ground they shuffled around in ever decreasing circles, never quite knowing exactly where they had been, or for that matter where they were at any one moment.

While his companions attempted to make some sense of these passages, Rauleigh left the group and wandered off down another promising lead. Unknown to him this had been briefly looked at earlier by Roy Winstanley. Sensing Rauleigh was onto something good the others caught him up after a couple of minutes, and together they followed the gallery for about half an hour, noting several side passages. Ignoring these in favour of what seemed to be the main way on, they suddenly became aware they were following a single set of ghostly footprints left in the silt. The mysterious "Man Friday" had seemingly vanished into thin air since the tracks suddenly ended. Naturally they continued, tracing an obvious draught. Not far up the way they encountered an awkward looking free climb. Tony managed to pass this and the others quickly joined him in a gallery where masses of decomposing swiftlets' nests littered the floor ahead of them. At one point they narrowly missed treading on one occupied nest in the middle of the passage. A solitary egg had rolled out onto the gravel, at once prompting a name for the find, Raiders of the Lost Egg.

A few metres further, the way on ended at a "window" into a huge shaft with a pale glimmer of daylight penetrating from a long way above. At first this was thought to be the newly discovered 100-metre pothole they had called the Wankabater, which dropped into Cooks Tour, but during a descent the following day it turned out to be Uli Kendi, reached by yet another new route.

Mamo Kananda was proving every bit the fine cave that the optimists had hoped for. It was Indiana Jones country, only this time for real. New leads were being found almost faster than they could be explored. As a result the naming of its principal features became an almost manic exercise in the rhetoric. Imaginations were allowed to run riot, as reflected in the labels pinned to the multitude of new passages. High and Mighty, Power in the Darkness, the Outer Limits and Blows Against the Empire were inspired examples in the best traditions of the celluloid heroes.

Though exploration fever gripped all who descended into Mamo Cave there was also much to do on the surface. Another camp was constructed within the entrance chamber of Kananda Pugwa, nicknamed the Departure Lounge. This was made ready for the fresh wave of explorers whose arrival was imminent. Julia had organised a helicopter lift for fresh personnel and additional supplies up to Mamo, yet dismissed Steve Worthington's request for a few minutes of chopper time to carry out a much needed air reconnaissance.

The shuttle was planned for early on August 1st, but as it happened poor weather meant the flight was delayed for three days. By this time the decision had been taken to move the entire expedition over to the two Mamo camps, where with so much going cave it made little sense to remain at the Atea, now increasingly subject to the law of diminishing returns.

At 6:30 a.m. the Atea base – and 15 minutes later the Mamo camp – resembled ant-hills poked with a stick as the helicopter buzzed overhead. Several loads of supplies began arriving at both Mamo camps, while at the same time the air lift brought in members of the second month team and back-loaded those now leaving who were quick enough to scramble up to the helipad. For a few moments, mayhem threatened to descend upon what was a complicated logistical exercise not helped by heavy cloud build-up over the mountains.

When the third load had been dropped at the Hadia Nduhongairi campsite Tony White, Steve Worthington and Steve Bunton leapt aboard. Giving the pilot instructions, they set off north and northwest of camp for a fly-by. Although this controversial reconnaissance only lasted six minutes, it was to provide valuable data on the local geography. The antagonists subsequently incurred the wrath of Julia for interfering with her meticulously calculated air schedule. Upon completion of the Mamo shuttles, and after refuelling at Koroba, the pilot returned to Atea base with more expedition members. Unfortunately the pilot had left his cargo net back at base and Al Warild and Ian Miller, who were waiting, had to stash the supplies for Hegaibagu in the passenger cabin. They leapt in and with these lifted off.

When John Wyeth and Ian Hickson had reached the campsite at Hegaibagu on foot a few days before, Jeff Crass had informed them that Allistair MacIntyre and Peter Ruxton were down Uli Eta Riya from which they later surfaced to announce they had pushed it to a conclusion at 205 metres. Despite this premature end to one of the expedition's best prospects and the obvious attractions of returning to Mamo, the team opted to remain at their remote but relatively comfortable bush home.

Over the following week they were rewarded with further discoveries in Sunrise Cave (Kanada Heiowa Heia) which to their delight proved a much more interesting system than the 1973 reports had them believe. They were also well positioned to make a dash to the Yu Balalo, a remote river sink 15 kilometres northwest of the Atea. On the 1:250,000 series geological maps, the Blucher Range sheet showed the surface course of the Yu Balalo as continuous, yet the aerial photographs suggested otherwise.

Cumulus was rapidly gathering over the plateau when, within minutes of leaving the Atea base, the chopper carrying Al and Ian put down at Hegaibagu. With a sense of urgency the supplies were pushed out and while Ian Miller remained in camp, Rucko and Ian Hickson joined Al in the helicopter and they plotted a course for the Yu Balalo. The sink was located without too much difficulty, and after circling the site once, the pilot deftly settled his machine onto a large boulder in the riverbed beside the sinkhole. Al jumped out to take a quick look at what appeared to be a 30-metre deep shaft swallowing a sizeable flow. From the air an abandoned sink with a promising walk-in entrance was also visible nearby.

Afterwards, Peter Ruxton was dropped off back at Hegaibagu while the others guided the pilot to the drop zone on Legari to recover gear left there by Al's four-week patrol. Some time later Ian Miller heard the chopper returning overhead but the weather by then had closed right in and prevented it landing again. The pilot could no longer see the campsite so he banked away east as cloud billowed up the dry valley.

At a little after noon the last flight had left Koroba carrying Dave Waters, Brian Carter and Henry Shannon. They just made it into Atea base after a harrowing journey skimming the tree tops among shifting cloud. At the last minute, spotting a tree or other unlikely landmark that only he recognised, the pilot dived through a break in the cloud cover and there below them was the landing pad.

On August 9, Ian Miller, Allistair MacIntyre, Jeff Crass and a porter set off to join Rucko, who had been cajoled into a ground reconnaissance of the Yu Balalo. He had left with three Duna carriers four days before. About mid-morning on the second day out they met Rucko returning. He related how after several days cutting through trackless jungle, they had set up their flies beside the sink. By this time rations had been almost exhausted. While waiting for the expected arrival of supplies and caving equipment, their camp meantime was inundated when heavy rain caused the river to rise by five metres. A mutiny flared up among the Duna, who were unhappy at being so far out of their familiar hunting grounds. They wished to leave and whatever was said there was no way they could be persuaded to return.

And so the chance to investigate this exciting karst feature was lost; in fact, it was not until 1983 that anyone made it to the site equipped for exploration. At Easter that year, Neil Hickson, Carol Clayton and a Chimbu man acting as porter took a chopper in from Tari and spent four days at the site. The Balalo fell 20 metres into the sinkhole; however, a pitch to one side led via a descending passage back beneath the waterfall. Following a downward route through a tangle of washed-in logs, Neil was faced with a vicious reduction in passage size. The river was lapping the roof here and further progress looked decidedly unhealthy. All thoughts of heroics finally evaporated when Neil discovered that the river reappeared again only about 200 metres below the sink.

WET SEASON MAYHEM

After the August 4th helicopter lift, there were 18 people in camp at Mamo Kananda and four less at Kananda Pugwa. The going cave at the latter tended to overshadow recurring problems with the porters and cavers soon settled into a system. The daily routine here was invariably heralded by the reveille-like call of "pogs up" at some unearthly hour of the morning. It was then a mad scramble through the boulder field of the Departure Lounge to reach the kitchen before all the porridge was snaffled.

During the next three days Kananda Pugwa was explored beyond the Departure Lounge, down two pitches and forward along a spacious dry gallery with some gypsum deposits. In turn this ended where a third pitch pierced the roof of a large black void. Some of the team were fans of the game Dungeons and Dragons and so Dragons Reach seemed an apt name for the new chamber. It was appropriate for what turned out to be one of the largest cavities under Mamo.

Across and upwards from their point of entry into Dragons Reach a major inlet entered between boulders, and at the lowest point of the chamber plunged noisily down a wide cleft, the Edge of the World. Luckily they could rig a dry shaft bypass nearby. On the next trip this was found to drop into a high canyon streamway heading southeast then north, with short climbs and pools carved through clean washed limestone. The Fruit Loop was to give a taste of things to come, when around a few bends the main stream was rejoined where it crashed in as a powerful waterfall. A pile of water-dappled boulders had collected where Dragons Reach intruded into the lower passage.

The many sporting cascades and plunge pools downstream from Fruit Loop were an inescapable feature of the high vadose canyon, providing some magnificent caving. But the cave had yet to fly its true colours. The writing was on the walls as it were, for these were scoured clean by the floods that regularly bored through the cave. The weather was by this time changing, with rainfall arriving earlier each day.

On August 6, a team comprising Julia James, Neil Hickson, Tony White, Rolan Eberhard and Al Warild headed off into the new downstream lead, named for obvious reasons Thunderush. After rigging a few short drops, Julia and Rolan decided to head off out while the others pushed on down the steeply inclined passage. When the rope ran out at another shaft they had by then reached a depth approaching 400 metres. As they surveyed back upstream, they were unaware that rain had been falling for most of that afternoon. Thunderush was about to live up to its name.

By 9:00 p.m. those below noticed the water was rising. Forgetting the survey, they made their way against the increasing current back to the boulders where the main river descended from Dragon's Reach. They found Neil, who had gone on ahead, sitting on a ledge clear of the rising stream; Julia and Rolan were waiting for them at the head of the next pitch. They climbed this with some effort, but together they made it through the Fruit Loop and into the safety of the large chamber. By then clear of the main flow, they each surfaced, knowing that this time they had been lucky.

The next day was triple cause for celebration. Everyone had gathered at the Kananda Pugwa campsite for Julia's birthday, for which an enormous chocolate covered spotted dick had been provided. Mamo Kananda too had almost reached 30 kilometres in length and seemed certain to overtake the Atea, while the new stream cave gave every indication of going deep. Though there were now only two more weeks left, these last precious days were to provide some first-class caving and further moments of anxiety as the wet season was ushered in with dramatic consequences.

Everyone was gripped by the urgency of exploration, and a certain amount of friendly, inter-camp rivalry tended to lend impetus to further discoveries. The increasing risks from descending these flood prone passages meant that while underground everyone had one ear cocked for the first hint of an approaching wave of water, and half a mind perhaps on the consequences of being caught out.

While caving continued, logistical support for the team was never idle. As was the case with most indigenous employees on New Guinea caving expeditions, the Duna were tireless workers, acting as willing guides and track cutters, or maintaining a steady supply of camp essentials such as firewood. This of course left the cavers free to concentrate on exploration. Now as the end of the expedition rapidly drew near it was all the more important. The Duna, however, were reluctant to carry firewood far, which meant that trees were often skilfully felled directly into the doline overlooked by the Kananda Pugwa entrance camp. Here they could then be split and dried on the spot, at leisure, and with the minimum of cartage.

On one occasion, a falling wood giant suddenly crashed to the ground without so much as a "Timber!" There was nothing unusual in this, except that the camp toilet sat in a vulnerable position on the flanks of the doline. The resulting draught blew the polythene cladding off the superstructure, but fortunately no one was sufficiently constrained to have been in residence at the time. Most people remained in excellent spirits with humour (no matter how warped) never far from the surface. One person remarked that a trip to the "dunni" was the most hazardous aspect of the whole trip, someone indeed having sprained an ankle after falling out of it!

Many more new leads paid handsome dividends for their discoverers, but those first entered on Sunday, August 8, were arguably the most significant. After plotting on the survey plan it was clear that the end of Delusions of Grandeur deserved further attention. Consequently Ian Westwood and Stefan accompanied Mark Wilson, Dirk Stoffels and Mark Laurendet for a "look-see." The last three entered the Eiger Connection, a hitherto unsuspected link between Delusions of Grandeur and Kit Canyon.

A marked feature of the Eiger Connection was its profusion of gypsum. This is one of the least common cave deposits and usually occurs in the form of either flowers or needles. Its origin owes much to the presence of pyrite, a sulphide of iron. When this oxidises it produces sulphuric acid. Reacting with calcium carbonate, the acid in turn forms calcium sulphate, or gypsum. In Mamo Cave, it was found in the form of sand-like deposits which in the Eiger Connection was piled in large drifts and covered footholds on the climbs rather like powder snow. Following the passage called for exploration techniques something akin to winter mountaineering.

While others floundered through the pseudo-alpine landscape, Stefan and Ian tackled the undescended seven-metre pitch previously noted at the northern end of Delusions, landing in an entirely new active passageway. First looking upstream, they passed a side passage with a daylight aven, and were eventually stopped by a waterfall below which a number of logs suggested the proximity of another open entrance. Mapping 400 metres back to the pitch, they headed out after nearly eight hours underground. Because of the train of events elsewhere, five days were to pass before the importance of this streamway became known.

DEEPER STILL

A 9:00 a.m. start saw a large team descending Kananda Pugwa to continue pushing. Dave and Carey Barlow, Ed Garnett and Shane Wilcox followed the upstream lead out of Dragons Reach, as Tony White, Al Warild, Rolan Eberhard, Neil Hickson and Barry Were reached the previous downstream limit in Thunderush. Roping down a series of pitches and cascades in a well-watered vadose trench, they came at last to a 12-metre drop into a deep pool. Ahead was a complex oxbow which allowed some respite from the water; however, the latter was met again shortly in a narrow but high canal where swimming was unavoidable.

The aptly named Icy Armpits lured them on into a spacious tunnel which gave the impression it might never end. Just when things were looking good, they were stopped by the inevitable muddy sump. While the remaining three started surveying back, Barry found and managed to scale an obscure climb. Neil joined him at the top and through a squeeze in a rock pile they popped out into a larger, high-level conduit floored with mud. At a drop, they had to kick steps down a slope to regain the main stream.

Neil was far from happy with the flood-prone appearance of the passage so he retreated for the surface. Below, there was now a change of character in the continuing cave. The Doldrums was a nightmare, with wet mudbanks reaching ominously towards the roof either side of the passage. Between these the stream flowed silent and sluggish, and they could well imag-

Paul Dyson descending a tension traverse in Thunderush, Kananda Pugwa.

ine floodwaters slowly filling the passage to the ceiling; however, they had no desire to be around to observe this for themselves. Neither Rolan nor Tony were feeling well at this stage, and since three people were needed for mapping, a coin was flipped to decide who stayed. Tony lost and Rolan headed off out. The depleted party then headed back down the cave, knowing that they were already pushing their luck with the afternoon curfew. They turned around and began mapping from a lake that Rolan had reached. At the canal sections Barry was sat on a rock when the water level suddenly rose up his leg.

It was time to move. However, when they reached the bottom pitch of Thunderush their rope could not be seen for a mass of whitewater. It was obvious they would be going no further in that direction. Having left their retreat too late, it seemed logical under the circumstances to continue surveying, for the time being at least, while waiting for the floods to subside.

On the surface their absence was not discovered until the early hours. In fact the Barlows, Ed Garnett and Shane Wilcox were trapped also, somewhere in the upstream passage out of Dragons Reach. They had entered the system at 7:00 a.m. but, like those lower down, had simply pushed the boat out too far. Cavers at both camps were put on alert.

After leaving Dragons Reach, Shane and his companions had explored some good streamway before the flood struck. They sat it out for four hours in a gypsum-lined gallery above a waterfall until Ed noticed a slight drop in the stream. Lured into attempting their escape, they set off downstream only to find the water rising again. Progress was then made even more hazardous by the fierce current so to safeguard their passage, Shane banged in some doubtful pegs and they roped down the rapids, looking for another dry spot in which to wait. In desperation, they chose a windy ledge about two metres above what they hoped would be the high water mark and, wrapped in space blankets, they shivered a further 11 hours before an exit was possible.

Although those marooned below Thunderush had been luckier in finding a relatively comfortable bivvy, they had to ration their limited amount of food and carbide. It was to be 56 long, cold hours before they next saw the light of day. To conserve carbide Al, Barry and Tony had sat most of the time in total darkness. Attempted sleep was haunted by all manner of sounds and imagined voices. A rescue team descended early on the tenth, two days since the cavers had entered the system. As a safeguard against further flooding, high-level traverse lines were installed throughout the risky sections below Dragons Reach.

At about 9:00 a.m. approaching lights in the darkness signalled the arrival of Steve Worthington, bringing food and drinks and the news that over 60 millimetres of rain had fallen in two days. The trapped explorers began the long haul out, meeting other members of the "rescue" team further upstream. Finally they surfaced a little after midday, somewhat ragged but at least under their own steam: once again the cavers had had a lucky escape.

Friday the 13th was hardly the most auspicious day on which to explore potentially lethal caves; indeed, there were those in both camps who suggested – quite seriously – that everyone should remain on the surface. In light of the events that followed, perhaps they should have taken heed of the advice. But there again, the dramatic developments of the day might have had a different turn of fate. Moreover, some were still recovering from the previous night on sultana wine, cracked open to celebrate a new Southern Hemisphere length record of 34 kilometres.

With rainfall becoming ever more unpredictable, the curfew was becoming ineffectual. When the heaviest rain of the expedition made its way into Mamo Kananda, it had cavers everywhere scurrying for safety. With perhaps more people underground on that day than at any other time it is all the more remarkable that there were no disasters. Several parties were indeed lucky to escape with their lives, including one at either end of the Cooks Tour – Rinse Cycle floodways.

Stefan had returned to the downstream continuation of the Wish You Were Here streamway entered on the previous Sunday. With him went Jeff Crass and Mark Wilson. Another pitch was soon reached where a traverse out gave them a dry hang for seven metres. There was another drop then a pleasant, descending stream passage thought perhaps to be the source of the water in the White Grunt, an upstream extension of Far Away. Two days earlier Cathy Giles and Trevor Worthy had with Stefan explored the White Grunt for 1,170 metres during a 15-hour sortie.

Rain once again came early on that eventful Friday, and by mid-afternoon a flood pulse came racing down the streamway that was subsequently to bear the date's name. Having just negotiated a low section that would be sure to sump, Stefan's group retraced its steps, just making it back through the low bit of Friday the 13th as the water rose to the ceiling. This perhaps is the only known instance when a flood could be said to have benefited cave exploration, for while sitting in an alcove waiting for the water to subside, Stefan noticed a dry side passage. After walking a short distance along this he turned back when stopped by a vertical drop. The importance of this would soon become apparent.

Exploration was now feverish. Al Warild, the Barlows and Shane Wilcox picked up the gauntlet in Kananda Pugwa. From the previous limit of the Doldrums a steep mudbank led upwards into Silent Running, a quiet passage floored with deep silt. Increasing in size all the while, this burst out unexpectedly into the vast boulder wastes of Space Oddity. The true dimensions of this immense chamber could only be sensed, as it was almost impossible to determine its size within the limited range of their caplamps. They surfaced, having failed to locate the

Tony White climbing in Dragons Reach, Kananda Pugwa.

continuation of the river, but very fortunate not to have been caught by the floodwaters that had created so much mayhem for their colleagues in Mamo Kananda. And still there were more discoveries.

The Saturday following the flood scares was noteworthy for one discovery in particular. Steve Worthington descended to survey a lead out of Siltstone Blues. As it happened, Trevor Worthy, Cathy Giles and Steve Bunton were also following up a similar development off Rinse Cycle. Part way through the passage the two parties met and accused each of being poachers. It transpired that they had each found the same lead from opposite ends and it was only then that the importance of their discovery dawned. The Fire Escape as they called the new passage, provided a link with Geronimo, giving a safe, quick exit route that avoided all the flooding horrors of the epiphreatic passages between the Iguanodon chamber and Cook's Tour. This was an ironic turn of events. When Al, Julia and Neil had been surprised by the 1978 flood in Rinse Cycle, they could have avoided their extended stay below ground. If they had in fact climbed the passage wall opposite the alcove in which they sought refuge from the rising waters, they would have found the safe route through Geronimo!

The next morning Stefan returned with his brother Rolan and Ian Miller to their downstream limit in the Friday 13th passage and here made the suspected link with the Screaming Frog area of the cave. He remembered the dry side passage – Faith – and the pitch down which he had gazed (see fig. 19a). This was only four metres deep and was soon rigged and descended. A crawl led off immediately. This soon opened into a much larger fossil tunnel terminating at a shaft with a three-second drop. This was a totally unexpected development since the passage proved to be

Rauleigh Webb

Crossing a log bridge en route out of Mamo.

heading downstream in a different direction from all others in the system – interestingly enough, towards Kananda Pugwa. On the way out Stefan slashed his hand quite badly on a sharp flake, and the infected wound subsequently prevented him taking part in what was possibly the most vaunted event of the whole expedition.

Rolan, Steve Worthington, Trevor Worthy and Ian Miller hurried back in the next morning and pushed on down Faith Passage with ropes for the new pitch. At the same time, Al Warild and Rauleigh Webb had just completed an aided climb to a flood inlet passage high in the south wall of Dragons Reach. A passage here took them to the base of a high aven. Reality dawned as those above were just lowering their rope to hear euphoric shouts arising from the depths. The system was instantly 528 metres deep with a length approaching 50 kilometres. It was cause for celebration yet there was still much to do.

On the 17th Alan and the Eberhard brothers made one final trip to the bottom of Kananda Pugwa to survey Space Oddity and detackle the pitches. There was much evidence of the previous floods, foam everywhere and debris in high places; even the footprints of earlier teams had vanished. Though they found nothing new, even as the pull-out got underway discoveries were still being made in many obscure parts of the system and on the surface.

During the final week a new direct trail was pioneered back to the Atea base. En route Julia and Henry Shannon discovered the deep pit of Malemuli, another sonorous hole only 20 minutes from Mamo camp. This was explored by Al, Rolan and Peter Dyson over two days and proved to be a fine shaft system descending to a sump at an ultimate depth of 420 metres.

Perhaps the most tantalising discovery of all was that made at the eleventh hour by Rauleigh Webb, Murray Little and John Wyeth. They had already surveyed a kilometre of new passages which they named Silent World, when at one point they stumbled upon a new pitch. They were astounded to peer down into a vast hall that they thought to be Dragons Reach, but since they had no tackle with them they were unable to descend and confirm this.

The successful Muller '82 ended then, with the explorer perched on the brink of that mysterious void and his shout trailing into the unknown, "AIYEeeee…" When it was plotted on the computer survey, expedition members learnt that the system had reached a length of 53 kilometres, rocketing it to the eleventh longest in the world. Moreover, the "new" chamber was clearly some distance from where it should have been, if it was indeed Dragons Reach. Rauleigh left the Mamo Plateau along with everyone else, frustrated by this conundrum: Was the large black space the true or false Dragons Reach? The caving world would have to wait the next phase of exploration to learn the answer.

Chapter Nine

ARMAGEDDON AND BACK

P.S. *Wouldn't mind looking up on Kaijende sometime. Any takers?* – This recondite postscript ended a letter dated November 1980 from Neil Ryan in Papua New Guinea to his old friends Donna Mroczkowski and Neil Montgomery, then living in the States. It was the catalyst that set the ball rolling for Neil's involvement in yet another caving crusade to Papua New Guinea. As so happened, Neil's associates in Sydney were at that time also planning the fourth Muller Range Expedition, and so a choice presented itself: join them, or have more than just a look at Mt. Kaijende.

In fact the British team en route to Telefomin in 1975 had first drawn attention to this virgin area. Anyone who has flown west from Mount Hagen to destinations like Lake Kopiago and Oksapmin, would have immediately been struck by the dramatic nature of the intervening Enga province. About half an hour into the flight, a strange and beautiful landscape unfolds beneath the wing-tips; on one side the bleached cliffs of the McNicol Range, on the opposite Mt. Kaijende soars impressively straight out of the forests, reaching a height of 3,748 metres. The jewel in the crown here is the labyrinth of weather-honed pinnacles and soaring arêtes, the centrepiece of a massif known to the local Tibinini people as Asenda. When seen piercing early-morning clouds, these features are not unlike the impressive limestone spires that in northern Sarawak extend through the tree canopy for a 100 metres or more from the forested slopes of Gunong Api.

The Enga province and the Mt. Kaijende massif are situated within the orogenic belt of the central mountain chain, characterised by highly folded mountains that have been deeply dissected by aggressive rivers. Mt. Kaijende apart, the limestone plateau reaches high points in the neighbouring peaks of Mt. Leiwaro (3,415m) and its neighbour Mt. Togopipi (3,646m). The whole area covers a hundred square kilometres or more and gently dips to the northwest. Apart from the pinnacle karsts, other obvious features of the region are the scarps that tower above the Tibinini Valley.

In many respects Mt. Kaijende is a unique mountain, until 1981 unclimbed and certainly uninhabited, though the local population has hunted the surrounding forests from time out of memory. The topography invites superlatives, for it is as strange and fantastic as any on earth. For this reason alone, cave explorers could be excused for anticipating that the scenery below ground would be every bit as stunning. There are other attractions too: in the Pacific-Asian region true alpine flora exists only in the high mountains of New Guinea. Here we find the endemic cushion plants and hardy grasses, along with gentians, buttercups, fuchsias, violets and other tropical variants of their distant European cousins. The sub-alpine forests also form the lofty habitat of the superb ribbon-tailed astrapia and other exotic bird species.

Needless to say, Mt. Kaijende was to prove a fascinating alternative to the more predictable physiographic model of the Muller Range. Given a preference then, it is little surprise that Neil

Aggressive rainfall has carved out vicious pinnacle karst high on the flanks of Mt Kaijende.

The Mt. Kaijende expedition had thirty members, from the USA, Australia, Switzerland, England, and Papua New Guinea.

opted to participate in the American expedition, if for no other reason than that Kaijende would provide the singular opportunity to study an equatorial alpine zone.

Initial research suggested that depth potential was considerable, with relatively straightforward access via the Highlands highway. The proposed target area, for instance, was less than two days' walk from the airstrip on the Porgera River. However, once away from this corridor of relative civilisation, the difficulties of travel would be compounded. The Spaniards had in 1978 attempted to reach the high karst region, but failed after running out of time. Patrols which had succeeded were brief and of limited benefit. Neil Ryan, Allan Goulbourne and Kevan Wilde at some stage had each visited Mt. Kaijende, though in each case their patrols had failed to reveal any promising cave features.

Following the 1977 reconnaissance, Kevan had concluded that the main plateau and north-eastern flank of the central massif held the best prospects for discoveries. It was said to rival the Huon Peninsula for the greatest limestone relief. Despite the disappointment of the initial probes, expedition planners in Los Angeles pored over maps and drew up their strategies regardless. Cavers all over stateside were contacted, and when the 1981 International Speleological Congress was convened in Kentucky, target areas had been pretty well identified and interested cavers forged into some semblance of a coherent team.

By December that same year Neil Ryan and Roy Berger made a further reconnaissance, using a chopper to gain access to an area of interest east of the mountain. Neil had also made what was believed to be the first ascent to the main summit. Once again the findings were disparaging, yet the dramatic photographs he sent back to the organisers ensured that enthusiasm never went off the boil.

At last a committed team of 29 was assembled, made up principally of 17 cavers from the States, four from Australia, two British and a Swiss group of six. They decided that the optimum period in which to field their trip was between June and August the following year. This meant they would be running more or less concurrent with the Australian explorations in the Muller Range 100 kilometres west-southwest of there.

By June the advance party was ready to move. This included Urs Widmer of Switzerland, Donna from the USA, Judith Bateman and Phil Toomer from "down under" and the two Brits, Dave Elliott and Paul "Sedbo" Seddon, a director of the British company manufacturing Troll Outdoor Equipment. At the time, an election was in progress and the Hagen-based helicopter company Rotawork was engaged in the collection of ballot boxes from remote villages and outstations. By virtue of this happy circumstance, the expedition was able to obtain transport for its cargo and the advance team at below the counter prices. This saved a great deal of time and was just one of many ways in which Neil Ryan was able to use his local contacts to smooth matters along.

The end of the first week in July saw the main body of the team leaving Mount Hagen town bound for Porgera. One group embarked upon the eight-hour journey by Toyota 4x4 pickup. It was to provide a memorable introduction to New Guinea, a highlight being when they drove through the front lines of two opposing Mae Enga factions who were settling a tribal dispute. An official-looking type was standing in the road brandishing an automatic weapon. He stopped them to offer a cautionary note, though his main concern seemed not so much to be for their safety, as to ensure that warriors abided by the rules of engagement! *Em tasol, pasin bilong Niugini* [1].

They proceeded through the skirmish with a mixture of wonder and alarm as blackpalm arrows whistled overhead or bounced off the cab roof as one group, seizing the initiative, used

---

[1] *"The way of things in New Guinea" (pidgin).*

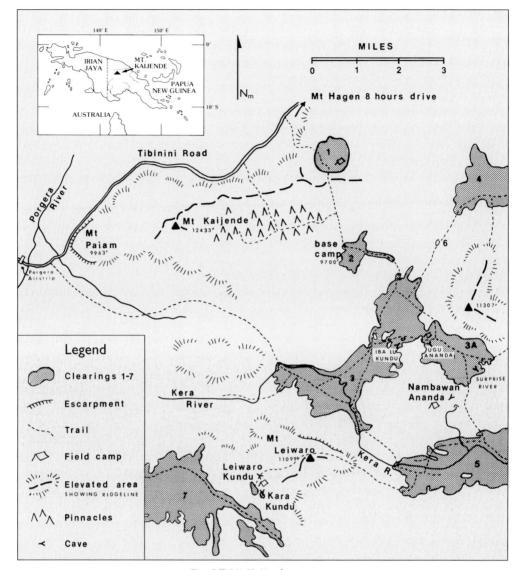

Fig. 26) Mt. Kaijende area map

the vehicle as a moving shield. Yes indeed, the Kaijende trip was certainly going to be different from the usual run-of-the-mill caving expeditions.

Another valuable liaison was forged with Graham Campbell, a Scot managing the Placer Mining station just outside Porgera. Gold had been discovered in the diorite intrusives that occur in the region, and Placer had been established many years before as a prospecting station. The team spent a night of hospitality with Graham discussing the aims and aspirations of the expedition and examining the 40 kilometres of core samples that the company had amassed.

The team explained to their host that their chosen goal was an extensive region immediately to the east, containing seven grassy clearings, the largest of which was 12 kilometres long (see fig. 26). Though tree cover in these glades amounted to a few cycads, Graham was quick to point out that they must not be beguiled into assuming this made travel any easier than in the forests enclosing them. Seen from altitude the grasslands appeared like neatly manicured bowling greens, but in reality were dominated by swordgrasses *(Miscanthus)* and the razor sharp "kunai," of which the most common, *Imperata cylindrica,* can grow to two or more metres in height.

Placer Mining was only ten kilometres from Mt. Kaijende, yet when the team departed on Thursday, July 8, and began the trek to base camp, they found that true to Graham's word, overland travel was anything but straightforward. The surface everywhere was riddled and pock-marked with a covert network of deep grykes, potholes, stream channels and sinkholes, all hidden beneath a mantle of vegetation – with sometimes dire consequences. The difficulties of the trail were temporarily relieved by a touch of humour part way into the second day of the trek, when they came upon a notice erected by the advance party. It read, "no food or services for next five kilometres."

When they arrived at base camp later that afternoon they discovered the notice was not entirely in jest, for the facilities had indeed yet to be completed. The main hut occupied a slightly elevated position at the edge of a clearing, overshadowed by an area of limestone spires imme-diately east of the principal summit. Though it was to provide every amenity one could expect given the isolation, construction work had been set back several days. Problems had begun when a group of passing hunters set light to the surrounding grasslands. What turned out to be a local form of amusement caught the cavers unawares, destroying some group and personal

Noel Sloan and Peter Keller exploring Ugu Ananda, Clearing IIIA, Mt. Kaijende.

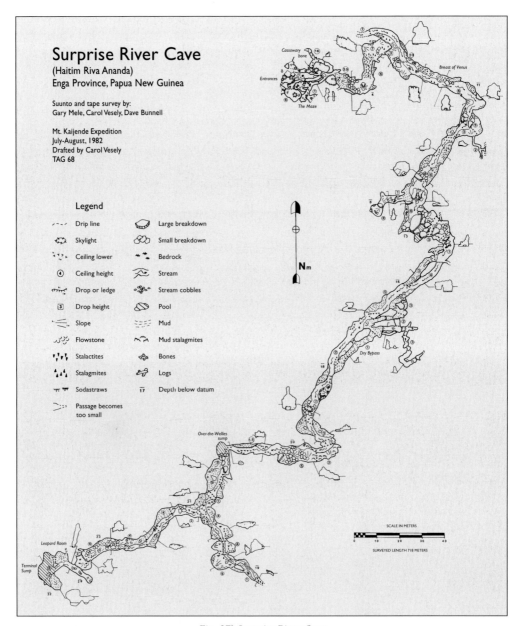

Surprise River Cave

(Haitim Riva Ananda)
Enga Province, Papua New Guinea

Suunto and tape survey by:
Gary Mele, Carol Vesely, Dave Bunnell

Mt. Kaijende Expedition
July-August, 1982
Drafted by Carol Vesely
TAG 68

Legend

~~	Drip line		Large breakdown
	Skylight		Small breakdown
	Ceiling lower		Bedrock
	Ceiling height		Stream
	Drop or ledge		Stream cobbles
3	Drop height		Pool
	Slope		Mud
	Flowstone		Mud stalagmites
	Stalactites		Bones
	Stalagmites		Logs
	Sodastraws	17	Depth below datum
	Passage becomes too small		

N m

Cassowary bone
Entrances
The Maze
Breast of Venus

Dry Bypass

Over-the-Wellies sump

Leopard Room

Terminal Sump

SCALE IN METERS
0   10   20   30   40
SURVEYED LENGTH 718 METERS

Fig. 27) Surprise River Cave

gear, the first aid supplies and a stretcher. Because of this turn of events base had been relocated in the next glade to the northwest, away from what they realised was a well-used hunting trail.

While some concentrated on finishing the camp that first week, others began prospecting for likely holes. By the start of the third week their initial eagerness was somewhat jaded, for without exception all the caves found were small; shafts developed in sharp limestone simply closed down into suit-wrecking, impenetrable fissures. These initial finds were confined to the immediate environs of base camp, one of the first being a beautiful little cave named Liklik Ananda.

Top and bottom: Surprise River Cave, Clearing IIIA, Mt. Kaijende.

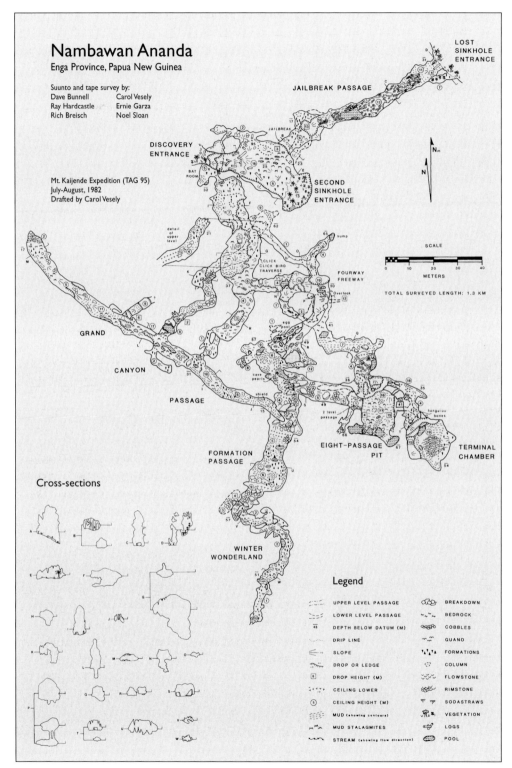

Fig. 28) Nambawan Ananda

A day or two later a party comprising Neil Montgomery, Ray Hardcastle and Graham Camp-bell headed off to examine a clearing southeast from base. They returned after finding Ugu Ananda, where a powerful stream entered an imposing entrance 15 metres in diameter. Despite its auspicious beginning the cave quickly sumped. However, Louise Hose suggested that the geology might be more favourable if they shifted the focus of attention further in this direction.

Over the following two weeks there were renewed problems with itinerant tribesmen and their pyrotechnic tendencies. One conflagration had to be fought all day to prevent it engulfing base camp. Nevertheless another three kilometres of cave was by then mapped. Garry Mele, Carol Vesely and Dave Bunnell discovered Surprise River Cave and were rewarded with almost a kilometre of refreshing streamway that was both sporting and beautifully decorated (see fig. 27). As underground leads nearer to base were gradually exhausted, people began searching further afield to explore the remaining clearings and the dense bush country separating them.

Vegetation showed marked changes due to the dramatic climatic conditions wrought with altitude; it had no doubt evolved in response to the extremes of intense diurnal heat and the subzero conditions prevailing by night. Though the forest remained dense, gone were the lianas and pandans, the dreadful vine bamboos and epiphytes of the mid-mountain forests. These were replaced by tougher sub-alpine forms. Higher still, the cycads (tree ferns) were abundant as were hardy ericas and dwarf rhododendrons.

The explorers stumbled upon an abandoned bush hut which everyone thought would form an ideal site for a field camp. It was situated on the crest of a hill several days hike from base. While out tracing an old hunting pad in search of a reliable water supply for their new base, Ernie Garza came across an interesting sinkhole hidden in the bush between two of the clearings, one and a half kilometres southwest of Surprise River Cave. He returned with Carol Vesely, Ray Hard-castle and Dave Bunnell, and the 20-metre deep doline was rigged with a wire caving ladder secured to a sturdy tree. Ray then lifelined Carol to a debris cone, which she reached only by dint of a deftly wielded bush knife. The others joined her among a collection of decaying logs, and to-gether they thrashed around in the dense growth. A cave mouth beckoned on the east side.

Soon finding themselves in a chamber, they saw a vague green light ahead of them, stream-ing in from another doline apparently intruding into the cave. In the left-hand wall two other black spaces stared at them. The most intriguing was a four-metre diameter passage, almost closed off by a row of stalagmite columns. This feature prompted the name Jailbreak. Only a few metres beyond the stals a pitch dropped them into a north-trending trunk route originating from yet another entrance, the Lost Sinkhole. Retracing their steps to the chamber, they ex-plored the second exit. As they followed this to the left it doubled back beneath the entrance and down a mud slope, to where a passage floored with rocks turned off, again to the left. A few metres of narrow draughting rift opened suddenly at a chamber with a crystal pool and many roosting bats. Two ways from the Bat Room led eventually to Fourway Freeway, beyond which the system grew more complex.

Though most of the cave systems so far found had proved of limited extent, many had compensated for this deficiency with a profusion of calcite decorations. Those discoveries paled into insignificance by comparison to this cave, Nambawan Ananda, in which the explorers mapped at least a kilometre of the most exquisitely decorated galleries over the next two days (see fig. 28). This new system alone made the expense of the journey from the States worthwhile. The explorers were simply lost for adjectives that would adequately describe the pristine beauty garnered in the Winter Wonderland; The Pearl Palace, too, astounded them with its golf ball sized cave pearls, the paragon of all that is worth preserving in nature's dominion. As a measure of the cave's charm, Dave Bunnell and Ernie Garza spent five hours bent over cameras recording the detail of just 30 metres of passage! At a little over a kilometre, it remained for some time their most extensive find.

While revelling in the delights of Nambawan Ananda the cavers were having recurring problems with their lamps. Their capricious behaviour inspired Ray Hardcastle to formulate his theory that four carbide lamps represented "critical mass" as far as caving trips were concerned. For instance, up to that number there could be times when all would function, but above four there can never be a moment when all work together. Such is the fickle nature of the caver's acetylene lamp.

When it was clear that the reliability of their lamps was beyond redemption, and with low carbide stocks threatening their being stranded underground, they surfaced to a dinner that they enjoyed with an air of optimism. Afterwards slumber came peacefully to the riveting lullaby of countless frogs. Mindful that expedition time was advancing, they did not wish to remember that all too soon they would have to return to jobs and other commitments back home.

LEIWARO KUNDU

Scrutiny of the aerial photos by those remaining back at base led to much speculation. Some tantalising dolines high on the neighbouring peak of Leiwaro offered their best, albeit last, chance of following a cave deep. Located in remote country some ten kilometres distant, these depressions were at such an altitude that it fuelled hopes that any caves there would have remained clear of the debris and mud that blocked many of the holes at lower altitude.

Halfway through the expedition an attempt to reach this area met with failure when they tried wading along the Kara River to avoid cutting track. Two of the Swiss team, Ursi Sommer and Philippe Rouiller,[2] had in the interim picked up a vague trail heading roughly in the right direction. After several tiresome days they finally made it to the summit and were then within two kilometres of the holes marked on the photos. After a return to base for help they departed again on Thursday, August 5, accompanied then by Rich Breisch and Peter Bosted, each staggering beneath overloaded backpacks.

Using a staging camp beside the Kara River they could establish a forward base the next day on a ridge about one and a half kilometres southwest of the Leiwaro summit. With precious little daylight remaining Philippe and Ursi attacked the dense scrub with their machetes to reach a prominent doline at the head of a shallow syncline valley. There appeared to be no cave leading off from the foot of this, so they retraced their steps in torrential rain, arriving back at camp bedraggled and despondent.

The next morning dawned clear with the promise of dry weather for the weekend. While their Swiss companions checked for holes further along the ridge, Peter and Rich returned to the original doline. Philippe's trail took a precarious footing along the edge of an overhanging cliff forming one side of the doline. At the base of this Pete thought he could see a hint of darkness between the trees, or was it simply a shadow? Cautiously clearing a route down for a closer look, Pete slithered to the base of the 30-metre bluff. Sure enough, the black patch expanded into a broad cave mouth through which he stepped from the warm sunshine and herb-like aromas of the scrub into a twilight world filled with the sound of running water. Almost at once he found himself in a 12-metre high vadose canyon with a moonmilk column over three metres across. It was pleasantly cool and the urge to explore was irresistible.

[2] *Sadly Philippe met with a fatal canyoning accident in 1990.*

BENEATH THE CLOUD FORESTS

Sunshine in Clearing II, Mt. Kaijende, Enga province.

First light and a cold morning feeling in the cloud forests, Mt. Kaijende, Enga province.

As base camps evolved, so did their construction and the time and effort it took to build them.
Top: Kure cutting the first grass at the base camp site. Right: Planting a post by "jumping force". Bottom left: After the floor is finished, the poles for the roof are set. Bottom right: Tying down the saplings with vines. Page 251: Top: Putting in a floor. Middle: Main gathering hut and stockroom viewed from the helipad. Bottom: Peter Keller and Philippe Rouiller covering an almost finished sleeping hut with a tarp.

Page 250 and 251: Urs Widmer

The Mt. Kaijende expedition had several purpose-built structures, including the eating, gathering and working hut, a stockroom and kitchen, three sleeping huts, and an outhouse.

The chopper made about 15 trips in two days to bring all the equipment to base camp from Worawari.

Noel Sloan exploring "Stream Cave", one of the many caves of Clearing III, Mt. Kaijende Expedition.

A gallery in Ugu Ananda, before and after a flood pulse. Note the high water mark.

Carol Vesely at "Jailbreak" in Nambawan Ananda. Top: Noel Sloan in Surprise River Cave.

The blue plastic of the camp in Clearing I stands out in a "forest" of fern trees. Mt. Kaijende, Enga province.

The muddy jungle path between Clearings I and II.
Right: Fires set in Clearing II by members of the Enga tribe threatened to engulf the camp.

A much stronger inlet entered not far beyond the column and joined a stream that had carved itself a meandering route through dark calcareous marls. This made for slippery going over the next 300 metres, whereupon the impure beds ended and the water took an impetuous leap into space. Rich joined him there and together they peered longingly over the edge. The drop appeared to be about seven meters, the falling stream drawing their eyes downwards to where it appeared to flow off down a roomy continuation.

Back at the undescended drop the next day, a length of Bluewater was quickly belayed. Descending in turn, Peter and Philippe dashed off along a passage carved in clean scalloped limestone trending down dip to the east. An increasing volume of water was fed by no less than 18 tributaries. This made the many cascades, short free climbs and plunge pools a sporting feature of the system. As they were perhaps half expecting, they reached the inevitable sump barring the passage, but all was not lost. Philippe displayed his climbing prowess by shinning up into a muddy alcove 12 metres above. Still higher, an overhang partially obscured his view of what he thought was a continuing rift. In a strenuous and fully committed move he managed to haul himself over the calcite bulge and squeeze through a narrow vertical cleft. Almost immediately he found himself in a chamber full of pretty dripstone deposits: more important though, he regained the stream beyond.

The camp at Leiwaro.

Back in camp they decided to call the going cave Leiwaro Kundu after the host mountain. Convinced that at long last they had a major find on their hands, Peter and Rich were dispatched to base the next day to break the news, seek additional rations and recruit more manpower. Philippe and Ursi stayed behind to begin mapping. After a 16-hour trip they regained the surface, cold and tired but pleased to have surveyed almost one kilometre of fine passageway. Later that afternoon they investigated some of the other caves that Rich and Ursi had found further along the ridge.

When they returned to camp they found this restocked with some welcome supplies, and Peter Bosted and Alan Williams sitting around the campfire. No more reinforcements could be expected since another party that had set off to assist had been delayed: Jim Pisarowicz had stumbled into a crevice in one of the glades, injuring his leg seriously enough to warrant helicopter evacuation.

It is sod's law that on most overseas expeditions the finest discoveries are always made at the eleventh hour, as the end nears and with enthusiasm flagging, usurped perhaps by debilitating illness or the growing desire to return to civilisation. Leiwaro was no exception. Time was now of the essence as the needs of exploration pressed with increasing gravity.

The next morning two separate teams entered the system and began surveying leapfrog fashion. Nowhere in the cave did they see signs of fossil development; the cave throughout displayed one linear active system, fed by many tributaries. The narrowing passage now maintained an almost constant width of three metres. Combined with this reduction in size, the aqueous nature of the cave passage and the lack of any dry bypasses made for strenuous caving. The impervious marls seen in the upper reaches of the cave outcropped occasionally at depth but of speleothems, only a few delicate straws were present. In places flowstone deposits on the walls restricted progress and only increased their difficulties on the return. Passing a 15-metre drop they were pulled up soon by yet another large cataract. Having used the last rope some way back they could only retreat, safe in the knowledge that they had at least another half a kilometre of new passage under their belts.

Over the following few days the cave continued to descend but with a shallower gradient. Pools became ever more frequent and deeper, until eventually Ursi and Philippe turned around at an obviously deep plunge, not wishing to suffer the serious consequences of flooded dry suits. They explored several side passages on the way back, reaching daylight after having spent 20 hours underground. The system was now 250 metres deep.

They took a well-earned rest the next day. The unrelenting rigours of Leiwaro Kundu meant that a trip to the end and back had become an epic test of stamina, due to the constant immersion and many cascades that had to be free climbed. Peter Bosted and Alan Williams pottered about together in nearby sinkholes, soon locating another new cave. This was only followed as far as the first pitch though the howling gale blowing up it urged an early return.

The next day Alan had to leave for base, but Peter and Philippe returned to the draughting cave and splashed down an exciting stream passage similar in character to Leiwaro Kundu. They were pleasantly surprised, when after 700 metres their cave joined the latter, emerging unexpectedly through a 30-centimetre hole half full of water.

By then the Leiwaro camp was dangerously low on food. No longer expecting any reinforcements, they decided upon an all-out push down Leiwaro Kundu. Ursi and Philippe descended and explored beyond the ominous pool that previously had stopped them. Further drops were encountered where they exhausted all available rope and even resorted to the use of six-millimetre slings they carried in their packs! In a marathon 25-hour trip they finally turned around after reaching a depth of 330 metres. At this point, running water could distinctly be heard beyond a "sump" pool, while a tantalising gale blew from a nearby side passage.

Following the successful evacuation of Jim, the team on Leiwaro Mountain was joined by Karlin Meyers and Paul Morrill, who had arrived there to help explore Leiwaro Kundu. However, by then the system had been derigged. With only two expedition days remaining, they entered another new cave that Peter had found. Kara Kundu began as a four metre wide, eight metre high meandering canyon leading off from the foot of a rather undistinguished depression. For the first hundred metres or so a narrowing passage descended steeply and became increasingly muddy as far as a series of short rope pitches. Much dripstone formation adorned the walls hereabouts and provided belays for the drops – in each case, a less than substantial stalagmite. One of these promptly broke off as Karlin's weight was taken by the rope, allowing him an unaided six-metre descent to the floor. Luckily his only injury was a badly bruised heel. Exploration continued, though somewhat subdued.

Peter and Philippe resumed the survey in Kara Kundu the following day while Paul pushed on ahead of them down the steeply dipping cave. A mixture of narrow meandering canyon was punctuated by large collapse chambers. They stopped mapping at a depth of 130 metres when they met a jubilant Paul returning from his reconnaissance below. He reported having climbed down a further series of short pitches totalling 100 metres in depth covering an estimated half a kilometre. The cave had picked up a sizeable stream and at the furthest point the cavern was becoming appreciably larger.

All good things come to an end, and in the case of expeditions to such idyllic locations, all too soon. It was marred or coloured – depending on the individual viewpoint – by a further spate of tribal conflict, grass-fires and magnificent mornings. The Kaijende team may not have discovered caves equal to those found elsewhere that year, but, when regarded simply as a preliminary investigation of a speleological unknown, the expedition was considered to be an unmitigated success. In an ideal world everything would proceed according to plan, but consider how tedious life would then become. By their very nature caves surprise and also deceive. If some of the caves fell behind expectations, others such as Nambawan Ananda were impressive beyond words. And the environs of Mt. Kaijende certainly compensated with the stunning beauty of its landscapes, its misty dawns, dewy spider webs and its striking flora and fauna.

Though the discoveries lacked extensive passages or grandiose chambers, in this case small was definitely beautiful. The intricate and varied forms of concretions, for instance in Nambawan Ananda, provided hours of painstaking camera work for the photographers in the group. Moreover, when the efforts of mankind are scrutinised in detail, individual contributions to our overall knowledge rest on the resources, manpower and enthusiasm of those who came before, for the benefit of those who will follow. This is the essence of true pioneering. In this respect, if the two cave systems of Kara Kundu and Leiwaro Kundu can be linked beyond the terminal sump of the latter, then this may yet prove to be a cave of international calibre.

The bon camaraderie of this – and indeed all – caving expeditions in PNG, is yet further vindication of the well balanced disposition and underlying good humour that makes up a speleologist, whatever his nationality or calling in life. Even the team doctor, Noel Sloan, in retrospect saw the funny side of the moment he ate some maggot-infested peanut butter.

RAIN DAMPENS JAPANESE HOPES

Apart from the two international expeditions of 1982, the remainder of the year was relatively uneventful from the caving standpoint. August 1982 witnessed the arrival in New Britain of a group of seven Belgians from the Spéléo Club de Schaerbeek. Inspired by the film *Apocalypse Now*, they headed northwards into the Nakanai Mountains. However, due to budget constraints they confined their activities to the Nutuve area, where they made a tourist descent of Nare. It would appear that they had a rough time of it in the forests. Discoveries made elsewhere in the vicinity were minor, the most significant being the 70-metre deep Kelapaie close to Bakuria village, two kilometres northeast of Nutuve.

Since independence in September 1975, government insistence on the employment of local people over foreigners meant that the expatriate caver population had gradually diminished. A small group of local cavers, including Bernard Pawih, were reasonably active on Bougainville due largely to the driving force of Hans Meier. But on mainland New Guinea the only other recorded caving in 1982 took place in the Eastern Highlands. Over several months Mike Bourke visited Barananomba Cave with Henry Shannon, Frank Caines and Paul Sinclair.

The following year too was quiet, with only one small reconnaissance team from the Kansai University Exploration Club of Japan. They visited the Hanoi area of the Southern Highlands, finding around 20 smallish caves. Neil Hickson and Carol Clayton also visited the Yu Balalo Sinkhole (see previous chapter). Atsuo Tanaka, an "old boy" of Shizuoka University, wrote of his

During the second half of their stay, the Franco-Swiss team filmed some breathtaking cone karst landscape in the Southern Highlands Province.

lone travels to the Solomons and New Britain.[3] Though his visit does not constitute an expedition, he does nevertheless record the existence of a few small caves.

Exploration started to pick up again in 1984 with four international expeditions. A large team of British cavers arrived to take up the challenge of Nare, a Franco-Swiss team visited New Britain to produce a film featuring the megadolines, and two more groups arrived from the "Land of the Rising Sun." The first of the these teams was drawn from Meiji University. After failing (due to political reasons) to have plans approved for an expedition into Irian Jaya, a group of six cavers instead headed for the Lavani Valley area. Although they covered much ground during their six weeks in the field, their lack of research had them arriving during the monsoon season, a common mistake. Another factor that limited the team's effectiveness was the high cost of employing 30 native carriers and two guides. This put a heavy burden on their finances, some 1,500 Japanese yen per porter daily.

Using Egele village as a staging point they began the westward trek toward the Lavani, site of their first camp after nine kilometres on the trail. Nearby a 150-metre deep shaft was descended by Iwama but although the hole began impressively enough at 30 metres wide, it simply narrowed in with no obvious outlet from its foot.

Upon entering the Lavani Valley the team divided at Gwali, the largest village. One party headed for the more remote Emama Valley further west, while the second group continued south toward its other main objective, a huge doline located beneath the 2,830-metre Mt. Bongoneheli, a ten kilometres trek from Gwali. The Queen of Sava failed to smile on their optimistic little band however, for investigation of the doline found no water and even worse, no caves. The remainder of the team returned with similar disappointing news, having failed to locate the huge sinkholes in the Karius Range to the west of the Emama Valley. South of Mt. Karoma (3,629m) the Emama River goes to ground beneath a massive white cliff, a site first visited in 1978 by Rob Kay and the late Bruce Unger during the Atea expedition. At that time the pair were unable to penetrate the underground system due to the heavy flow.

Cutting down on the number of porters and leaving behind all nonessential supplies, the Japanese set out again on March 18 for a second attempt to reach and hopefully explore this impressive sink. Once again high water levels were to prove problematic and prevented them, like their predecessors, from entering any passage that may exist beneath the main sink.

A major cave draining the Lavani and Emama valleys was predicted as early as 1973 when an expedition to the area was first considered. Common opinion then believed that subterranean drainage from these valleys provided the source of the Tumbudu River at Harerage some 20 kilometres distant, but it is equally probable that the sinks feed the Yogona River only ten kilometres away. In each case the depth potential is less than 1,000 metres. The Japanese group obviously hoped to gain entry to the cave system carrying that flow, but in the event were prevented from doing so for the reasons already outlined. Their report makes an interesting account and, reading between the lines, we can deduce that they grossly underestimated the difficulties of overland travel. [4]

In March a Franco-Swiss filming expedition flew to New Britain with the aim of producing a film that would highlight the extraordinary karst features of the Nakanai Mountains, namely its huge dolines. Leading the venture was the Geneva film maker Gérald Favre, assisted by his wife Rosemarie, Pascal Perracini from Lausanne, Martin Figère of Lunel and Jean-Jacques Delannoy

---

[3] *A Mysterious Land, Melanesia.*   [4] *Japan Caving, Vol. 17. No. 1-2 (Nov. 1987).*

from Grenoble. The team also included Richard Maire of Verchaix, the karst geomorphologist who had been a participant on earlier French trips.

Aided by a helicopter, they undertook a number of explorations. At the Namure resurgence of the Minye system the river passage was known to terminate in a large sump. At a higher level however, they explored a fossil gallery until the presence of large green python curtailed further progress. The team then trekked overland to Minye where Richard had hoped they could penetrate the downstream passage.

In 1980 they had been without suitable equipment. This time, with a number of grappling hooks at their disposal, they were pushed for time and the difficulties of original exploration while film-making proved too much of a burden. As a compromise they rigged the tyrolean across the Kanue River to gain access to the upstream Gallery of Kapguena. The old rope from 1978 was still in place, bearded after six years with pendulous growths of moss. They illuminated the heights of Tuke Chamber with flares, but even with these it was difficult to gain a true concept of the size of this vast hall.

After vacating Minye they flew to the Kavakuna Doline and gained some dramatic footage with a helicopter journey along the Iso River canyon, searching the steep walls for resurgences. They saw a likely contender for the Nare outflow where a large river emerged from a high bluff and in several plumes cascaded majestically into the jungle below.

But perhaps the most exciting site of all was noted to the southwest, within the verdant depths of the Galowe River gorge. Both Gérald and Martin were filming as the helicopter flew over an albino "serpent" threading its course through the dense forest. This emerged from a magnificent resurgence – possibly the world's largest – and was believed to drain the vast unexplored plateau situated between the Galowe and Wunung canyons. A few kilometres east, cavers had yet to feast their eyes on perhaps the largest known doline at Wunung. Poor weather prevented Gérald and his crew locating this, and after three hours precariously skimming the treetops (at 5,000 French francs an hour), they had to call off the search.

For the second half of their stay in the antipodes they switched their focus to the mainland, where they flew into the green mosaic of mountains comprising the Southern Highlands Province. Their pilot was captain Gareth Bean, who in 1979 had provided logistical support for the ill-fated Swiss expedition. He thrilled them with the manoeuvrability of his Hughes 500. While the cavers filmed with the cabin door removed, he banked effortlessly through gorges and flirted with the tree-clad limestone arêtes. Pimaga village provided a suitable landing ground where some time was spent exploring. With the aid of a kayak they ran some good footage in a cave carrying the full flow of the Mubi River. The previous December, Gérald and his wife had also made a limited investigation of this and the picturesque Lake Kutubu area three hours trek west of there.

Once back in France the film *Megadolines* was presented at the September film festival in La Chapelle-en-Vercors. Considering the hardships endured by the team and the undoubted quality of the production, they found it hard to accept not receiving the smallest acknowledgement for their effort. Instead, the French television company Antenna 2 carried off this most prestigious award.

Before the year was finished the Nakanai Mountains again became the focus of overseas cavers. On September 5, the Japanese newspaper *Asahi* carried a feature by Sumio Kondo accompanied by an aerial view of the Minye Doline. It announced the imminent departure of an eight-man team and plans to explore this New Britain river cave. Sumio's team arrived two days later and headed directly for the mountains with the intention of producing a film for the Japanese media. They remained in New Britain until October 15, during which time they explored Kavakuna and partially descended nearby KAII, though they made no new discoveries and Minye was not descended.

THE UNTAMED RIVER

The French explorations in New Britain that took place in 1978 and 1980 were followed closely by Dave Gill and a small group of experienced English speleologists. Dave was highly respected within British caving circles and had been around some time, leading or taking part in many major explorations both at home and abroad. He was a wiry sort of character, an electrician by trade, balding with a ragged moustache that gave him the appearance of a South American gaucho. He was the sort that was always ready to take up a fresh challenge.

Having laid his hands on a copy of the French reports, Dave leafed through these, feasting his eyes on their accounts and photographs. The exploration of Nare made gripping fireside reading, coloured with such exciting notations as "the roar is almost terrifying" and "in just a second a powerful wave washed him out of the boat."

The very nature of the Nare system fired the imagination. The Tuttering Hand Traverse, The Flying Dutchman and Howling Ledges was graphic terminology for the ultimate in speleological difficulty. Contrary to what one might expect, such nomenclature inspired rather than deterred hopeful followers of the French pioneers. Their's was an audacious stab in the dark which with perseverance had paid off; yet when face-to-face with such an adversary even they were defeated, forced in the end to admit they had reached their limit. Apocalypse Now, they believed, was the end of the Nare; could anyone do more? The British picked up the gauntlet, determined that they should.

The Untamed River Expedition began, as indeed had many similar British ventures, with a fag packet sketch and a few pints of ale in a Yorkshire Dales pub. It had flared into existence from a spark of an idea kindled by Mike Boon two years before. Boon had gained some memorable experiences, not all of them pleasant, in the large river caves of western Guatemala and the Yochib system of Chiapas, Mexico. He was inspired by the brassy success of the French in Nare and intrigued by its challenge. He began touting for support for an expedition.

In the summer of 1983 he visited Britain to discuss plans with Dave Gill and other interested parties. As preparations went ahead there were conflicting views on finances and the make-up of likely expedition teams, Mike preferring people whom he knew personally. Consequently when it came to the crunch the following year Mike was unable to participate. Manpower was eventually drawn almost exclusively from two British caving clubs from the Derbyshire county, the Eldon and Hyperion.

At 42 years, Dave Gill was what some might consider old for a potholer, but this in no way deterred him nor did it prevent the Royal Geographical Society from making the expedition one of its flagship ventures. Dave was appointed leader and they soon received the enthusiastic support of industry, including British Airways who agreed to fly out the whole team, gritty underpants and all. The expedition was to be fielded with a budget of £ 60,000 sterling. When it became clear the trip was definitely on, the team embarked upon a vigorous training programme involving whitewater familiarisation at Swallow Fall in North Wales. Despite this and the availability of the French accounts, no one really knew quite what to expect.

In the 1930s much of central New Britain was restricted territory. Inhabiting this region were the Mokolkols, a fierce nomadic tribe much feared throughout the Nakanai Mountains, even as far as the southern littoral fringes. They had a habit of bearing down on unsuspecting villages with long-handled axes (their preferred weapon), wreaking mayhem, then disappearing just as suddenly into the thick tropical jungle. Today, due to the need for a cash economy, outsiders are more welcome among the Nakanai tribes, though the population is sparse and it is never an easy matter to raise labour for carrier lines. In this respect the British were fortunate.

It transpired upon arrival that Lord Shackleton, the expedition patron, was by happy circumstance also the chairman of Conzinc Rio-Tinto. This company was prospecting the area and a helicopter was being used to make regular flights into the interior forests, shuttling geologists into field camps. They readily agreed to provide use of the chopper as and when schedules allowed. It was an act of generosity that saved Dave's team a great deal of time and money.

Despite their turn of fortunes the venture might have miscarried right at the outset. One day Bill Wineburge, the CRT pilot, took Steph Gough and Dave Gill on a flight over the Nakanai Mountains in search of possible drop zones. Intrigued by Nare, Bill flew his craft into the gaping shaft, and with considerable daring descended to the point where his white knuckled passengers could peer directly into the river passage. This demonstration of skill almost met with grief when vibrations from the helicopter triggered an avalanche, sending rocks and trees trundling into the depths, just a little too close for comfort.

When you are sitting astride five tonnes of supplies and equipment in near 100 percent humidity, swatting mosquitoes that land hopefully on your tender pallid skin, only then does the reality of the moment sink in: the expedition really has begun, the inevitable can be delayed no longer. That was at shore base three weeks earlier. Now, after at least 100 hours hauling tacklebags in one of the most fantastic river passages imaginable and after rigging literally thousands of metres of ropes and climbing aids, Dave Gill and his team stood in Nare at the

Dave Gill

The loan of a G.Q.Defence compressed air grapnel launcher was to ease progress of the British team along the Nare riverway.

French impasse of 1980 (see fig. 23). They were two kilometres from the entrance and a world removed from civilisation.

The final stretch of river-way leading to the French limit had been remarkably simple. After much precarious climbing and uninviting river crossings Tim Allen, Des Marshall and Alan Gamble had reached the seventh French tyrolean, named the Torrey Canyon. By wading with the aid of boulders that broke the surface of the river, they gained a ledge at the far bank. This was the departure point for an 80-metre traverse along the wall, the Dirty English Sneaky Bit, which effectively bypassed the next two French crossings to arrive at Apocalypse Now.

During these first two weeks rigging the cave, the long prussik back to the surface, repeated at the end of each day's push down the river-way, had begun to tell on each member of the group. It took over an hour per man to climb out using jammers. To avoid this the camp had been relocated at the foot of the great shaft, though the noise of the river was so bad that everyone had to wear ear plugs around camp.

One evening as they sat around the camp fire, a tree lost its fight with gravity and fell down the pit, tearing out several others en route. With a clatter of stones, earth and branches, it landed dangerously close to camp. The night before, a rockfall had nearly killed Des Marshall as he lay in his hammock. As he rolled out of bed and tumbled headlong down the slope towards the ferocious river, his mates – lying in bed with ear plugs fitted – were unaware he was in danger. Following this second incident, nerves were strained to breaking point. Des threw in the towel and headed out, while Dave thought it prudent to shift camp to somewhere safer, this time to a downstream site beyond the Poseidon Tyrolean. Confined between rock walls the roaring of the river was even more unbearable, but at least they were protected from further avalanches by the solid roof of the downstream portal.

On December 3, Dave stood on the riverbank surveying Apocalypse Now. They had high hopes of spending the Christmas period back on the coast, but for the time being that pleasant prospect seemed about as remote as the moon. In front of them was a 20-metre wide stretch of water, infinitely less welcoming than the warm Pacific surf. The Ire River, as untamed as ever, foamed and danced ferociously down a cascade that seemed to scream back at them with the words of Dante: "abandon all hope ye who enter." It was indescribably appropriate. They almost gave up there and then. Perhaps it really was the limit? Jean-François Pernette was a much revered speleologist with many premier explorations to his credit. If his elite team had reached their limit, what chance had anyone else of going beyond the impossible?

Cavers of course are nothing if not resourceful: the impossible today is commonplace tomorrow. In the rock climbing fraternity a revolution in techniques has lately seen dramatic feats of endurance, and today we see its parallel taking place underground. What once seemed out of the question simply becomes another exciting challenge for the next generation, and changing attitudes as much as anything can decide the outcome of an expedition. Dave's party retired to discuss the best way of overcoming the obstacle.

The solution was to prove quite simple, if not a little fraught. Two days after they had first reached Apocalypse Now a team of five returned to the fray. They were Alan Gamble, Tim Allen, Des Marshall, Steve Dickinson and of course Dave Gill. Four hours after setting out they again stood before the monstrous rapids. They spent ten minutes sweeping the river and far shore with a powerful Techna lamp, watching and trying to "read" the water. How were they going to cross? Three options presented themselves: to make a dangerous boulder hop across the river, the largest gap of three metres being slap bang in the middle of the fiercest rapids; to make a

In Pavie the British found the major source of the Ire underground river seen in Nare, flowing at an estimated 10 cumecs.

giant downhill leap from a tall boulder where the passage narrowed some way upstream...or bring in the heavy artillery. The GQ Defence Company had loaned them a grapnel iron launcher specially developed for the marines. With compressed air as a propellant, this could fire a carbon fibre grapnel about 80 metres. It had been used with success on the Andrea Doria Tyrolean earlier.

The second course of action seemed the more attractive. Held on a safety line, Tim Allen eyed the river from his precarious perch on a boulder. Taking a moment to compose his thoughts he launched himself, and seemed to be in the air for an eternity until...he landed miraculously unscathed on the far side. He was followed by Allan Gamble. Cautiously they edged downstream along the far wall, sodden by the spray from huge waves that thrashed around close beside them.

Tracing the large passage steeply downhill they arrived at a point where the roof lowered and the walls were only five metres apart. They halted at a possible traverse line, beyond which the river-way swung around a left-hand bend. After that it was anyone's guess what happened. The noise was terrific, but the thought of reversing the leaping manoeuvre uphill seemed an unattractive prospect. It would be virtually impossible, so they rigged a tyrolean a little way downstream.

This spanned 23 metres and, once tensioned, allowed the remainder of the party to cross without incident.

Once everyone was across they examined the water-level traverse. Under any other circumstances it would have been simplicity itself; but here, lashed by spray from the worst whitewater any of them had ever seen…suffice to say there would be no margin for error. Tim set off slowly, installing runners as he went. He placed a bolt at an overhanging calcite wall while waves, deflected by submerged obstacles, flew in all directions with a deafening boom. While each of his companions looked on with heart in mouth he disappeared from view beyond monstrous waves. He appeared momentarily then vanished again, only this time around a corner, the flame from his carbide lamp now and then backlighting the violent scene. Some 20 metres from base the half-submerged ledge petered out. The Nare was finished.

They each took turns to look. The cave confronting them reduced to two metres across with a ceiling just a metre above their heads. They were lost for adequate words for there was nothing in the cavers' vocabulary to describe such a place. It was hardly a sump, simply an airspace that was repeatedly closed off by waves as 20 cubic metres of wild water groaned into the constriction each second they stood there. It was a conclusive end to a magnificent cave: Armageddon in no uncertain terms.

The remainder of the month was taken up photographing and derigging the river-way and entrance shaft. While this was proceeding other discoveries were made nearby. A half-hour walk up the dry riverbed running past the base camp was Kille, a large rift dropping into a series of pitches developed entirely along a fault. This ended all too soon in a sump at a depth of 260 metres. On December 10, Ken Kelly, Tim Allen, Des Marshall, Jim Hook and Dave Sims left for Ora village, taking with them Camillus, a local guide. That same day Rod Leach found the entrance to Pavie and Bogalave-Gouvi; however, due to work elsewhere it was not until the middle of January that exploration could begin.

Ken's team was unable either to reach the obvious cave at the Ora outflow, or progress any further downstream in Ora Cave than Mike Bourke's party in 1972 (see fig. 8). Everyone eventually returned to shore base for the festive holiday celebrations and a chance to unwind and recuperate, after which most had to return to England. This left a much-depleted team consisting of Steve Dickinson, John Salmon, Tim Allen, Dave Gill and Rod Leach.

The search for feeders of the upper Nare River began. A JetRanger helicopter was hired for a half-hour in order to restock Nutuve village for the remainder of their stay. Later, an abortive attempt to locate resurgences in the Isis Gorge spotted a very large entrance in the forest on the return flight. Meanwhile at Bogalave-Gouvi, the explorers found the entrance passages extremely depressing, a flood prone place of grey corroded stalactites. It was no place to dally, even without the repulsive pink leeches and large black spiders. Downstream of the twin entrances a combination of shafts coalesced at the Bloodsucker Passage, a continuation with a shallower gradient but littered with stinking guano and flood detritus. Beyond a seven-metre pitch with a nearby inlet, the cave became friendlier, with further cascades and clear pools, until at Plasma Pot the stream took another impetuous leap into space.

What at first seemed like a colossal void was tackled in two drops totalling 49 meters. Loose rock demanded extra care and the roof…well, the passage was so large that it was mere guesswork how far above their heads it really extended. Descending last, Rod settled for a smoke while waiting the return of the others who had shot off ahead. Before too long a light in the distance announced their return. The Anaemia Series had apparently led to two sumps, one at 163 metres and a second and larger one at the true bottom of the cave, 173 metres below the entrance. They would not be reaching the upper Nare River that way.

On January 12, Tim, Dave and Dickie began exploring Pavie, which began as a dry canyon entered some two kilometres northwest of Nare. This they traced to where it fell into a sizeable rock-rimmed doline. A three-metre drop through a vegetated gully led to a traverse to a tree. Belaying a second rope here allowed them an easy abseil to a large boulder. Placing a bolt here, they dropped another pitch into a dry plunge pool. Having run out of rope, they turned around at a large shaft that merged into a downstream portal at 50 metres depth.

Tim and Dickie returned four days later with a 46-metre length of 9-mm rope and shortly found themselves exploring an inclined gallery. The occasional scramble over jumbled boulders was followed by a narrowing of the passage leading to a 14-metre drop at Swift Chamber. Beyond this was a climbdown into a blind pothole, the Marmite, which provided some entertainment for the climb out. At this point, they became aware of the distant grumbling of a large river. There was a sudden longing to rush ahead, but the limestone was razor sharp and overhanging. With care, Steve eventually made it, followed as quickly as possible by the others. Dave brought up the rear; from the rock-mill the way ahead turned sharply east and he could hear the whoops of excitement from those ahead.

Within a few paces he arrived at the lip of another drop. In their eagerness to see the river, the others had already dropped the easy 23-metre pitch and were calling for him to join them. At the bottom they met the river flowing left to right down a superb 15-metre square passage. This was estimated at around ten cumecs. They had clearly found the major source of the Ire River seen in upstream Nare, though reduced in volume. Pavie was a fine discovery that provided another piece to the Nare hydrology puzzle. It was to take them until the end of the month to complete the exploration of almost two kilometres of river passage reaching a depth of 261 metres. This involved a number of daring crossings: the Beever Brook Tyrolean, Swan Dyke, the Long Jump, San Ferry Ann and Serpent's Tail Tyrolean.

APPOINTMENT WITH A KRAKEN

Though a number of other worthwhile discoveries were made, the finest and most important was undoubtedly Gamvo. Its large arched entrance lurking in the forest was first seen from a helicopter on January 7th. At a later date a track was hacked to the entrance with the help of Camillus, but due to their commitment in Pavie it was not investigated until well into the second week of February.

Tim and Steve arrived at the impressive 50-metre-high mouth, the focal point for two normally dry river channels. A short sortie into the entrance was soon halted by a deep pitch around 40 metres across that seemed to echo endlessly when stones were cast down it. Unaccustomed to such intrusions, a number of large fruit bats began wheeling noisily about the roof. Satisfied with what they saw, the cavers surfaced to steady rain and with help from their guide improvised some accommodation. The rain had become torrential when they descended again an hour or so later, clad in full caving gear and armed with a bag of rope.

What was in effect a single 100-metre shaft could be split safely into several drops, each blessed with a refreshing plunge pool. Thirteen rebelays were required before they were satisfied with their rigging. After descending three of the pitches a shout from Steve, who was some way above, announced the arrival of a flood pulse. Anticipating that there would be a delay before the *marmites* on each ledge filled and overflowed, Tim drilled a hole for a hanger and descended the next pitch of 36 metres. Around a corner he was stopped by a further drop, below

Impressive formations in Gamvo Cave.

which he imagined he could just hear a river. They hurried back up the ropes, surfacing after nearly five hours underground.

Cammilus was despatched to the Nare base for more rope. When he returned just before lunch the next day they eagerly set off down again, soon reaching the undescended shaft. Apart from the chance of flooding a further hazard on the entrance climbs were some nasty-looking hairy spiders infesting the ledges. Needless to say, handholds were carefully inspected before being used. No one knew if the creatures were venomous, but they didn't care to find out, given their isolation from proper medical care.

Dropping the new pitch led to a point where a small river emerged from between boulders obscuring a wide bedding. Anticipating greater things they splashed along the stream for 150 metres in a beautiful passage floored with gour pools and a medley of sporting cascades terminating at the Aquabat, a short but very aqueous pothole. Their rope was only just long enough, so they adopted a technique whereby they abseiled off the end of the five-metre line, then made a lunge for the side. It was all very sporting and gave them a taste of the excitement to come. A further 600 metres of sporty cascades took them to the aptly named Edge of the World pitch, where the water plunged at least 16 metres over a flowstone formation spanning the full passage width. It

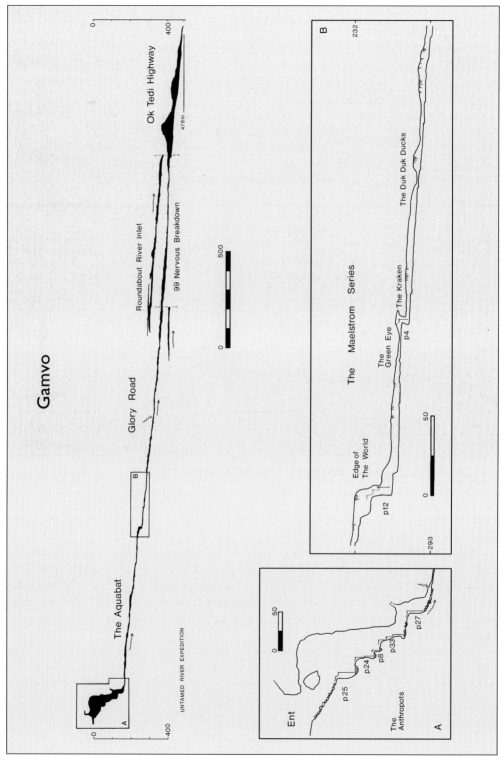

Gamvo

The Aquabat

Glory Road

Roundabout River Inlet

99 Nervous Breakdown

Ok Tedi Highway

478m

UNTAMED RIVER EXPEDITION

The Maelstrom Series

Edge of
The World

The
Green Eye

The Kraken

The Duk Duk Ducks

p12

p4

Ent

The
Anthropots

p25

p24

p8

p33

p27

Fig. 29) Gamvo

Thundering waterfalls in Gamvo Cave.

marked the beginning of the Maelstrom Series, where over the next few days the cavers encountered a whole gamut of watery perils (see fig. 29).

The next day the original two explorers descended with John Salmon. They overcame The Edge of the World without difficulty, a short descent beside the cascade allowing them to lasso a calcite boss on the left wall. This enabled an exposed traverse prior to a final drop through heavy spray. Another traverse along an overhanging wall took them around the deep pool below before they gained the relative calm of the continuing passage. It was an exhilarating piece of caving but Gamvo had yet to play its ace.

Some short waterfalls were followed by easy scrambles ending suddenly in a long and obviously deep canal. Being a salmon by name meant that the others looked upon John as their official expert in a wet spot. Pushed to the front, he proceeded to swim along the narrowing passage, ever mindful of the perfect head-sized airspace just in front. Its shape and size combined with the colour of the water gave it the resemblance of a sinister green eye. He contemplated changing his name as he approached the draughting orifice. It looked horrendous; the sound of rushing water coming from the other side sounded like the roar of some ravenous monster awaiting an approaching meal.

Once through the Green Eye the explorers faced an even worse continuation. The noise of the stream was deafening and with spray everywhere, all they could make out was a great deal of fast moving water as the entire stream was swallowed by a horrendous cascade. The Kraken was an intimidating obstacle, first attempted by Tim who became pinned against the right-hand wall below by the force of the water. It was almost impossible to reverse from this position without assistance from above, and in the process he almost drowned. After a further attempt he returned to announce he had reached what he took for a sump.

While the other two searched for a bypass John fed himself to the Kraken and disappeared from sight. He returned shortly and announced he had found the way forward. A series of lowering arches with minimal airspace represented Gamvo's last-ditch attempt to foil the intruders. It signalled the end of the Maelstrom Series, beyond which the going became easier in a passage that gradually grew in size.

The Glory Road seemed to go on forever. It was a handsome passage crammed full with every conceivable variety of cave decoration. The kilometres slipped by almost unnoticed as they negotiated sporting cascades and plunge pools displaying a remarkable turquoise tinge. Eventually the stalactites gave way to a region of cavern breakdown and here a major inlet crashed in from the right. The combined flow of about five cumecs slid noisily over a six-metre drop and into a turbulent pool before roaring off along a canyon 60 metres high and almost as wide, carved through black limestone.

They estimated they had by then covered nearly ten kilometres since leaving the ducks and were starting to wonder where the cave was taking them. Dare they hope that Gamvo would rejoin the Nare beyond Armageddon? The passage by then had developed a terraced cross-section that greatly aided exploration with its many convenient ledges; nevertheless, extra caution was needed wherever they were forced to cross the river. They were considering the logistics of exploring the cave beyond its link with the Nare, or the possibility that it might pop out in the side of the Isis Gorge, when the Ok Tedi Highway slid silently and swiftly into a commodious sump pool.

Well impressed with their discovery the party turned around and headed for the entrance, checking inlet passages as they went. They were all thoroughly exhausted when they gained the surface 12 hours after entering the cave. And what a magnificent system!

Further trips were launched to survey and photograph the cave and explore its inlets. In total, Gamvo was pushed for six kilometres (rather than the imagined ten) to a depth of 478 metres. It was a spectacular cave, made all the more enjoyable on account of the way it was explored: by a small, fast-moving team. The passages proved a delight to follow with a minimum of fright factor, and were a welcome contrast to the siege tactics employed for both Nare and Pavie.

It was the end of February by the time they had completed their work in the Gamvo system, and with the rainy season practically upon them, they commenced the pullback to Nutuve. By the second week of March, all the remaining equipment had been shuttled to Gonaile shore base from where it was to be shipped to Rabaul by motor launch. It was in many respects a time of sadness to leave such a tropical paradise. But before they said their final farewells, they spent a few days on the north coast at Kimbe.

For the return to Gonaile, a chopper was chartered and they flew back via the Whiteman Ranges, hoping to catch a glimpse of some very large dolines spotted on the air photographs. These were easily located on account of their size but there was no sign of sinking rivers or cave entrances. Unknown to them, a large French team was in the forests below eyeing the chopper with suspicion. They were by coincidence finding and exploring some impressive river caves beneath those very same dolines…

A caver begins the ascent of the 230-metre free hanging entrance shaft of Nare.

Large chamber in Pavie Cave.

Exploration of the beautiful Gamvo Cave was sometimes tempered by obstacles such as The Kraken,
where the river leapt over a gour dam.

The French declared Apocalypse Now the "end" of Nare, but British cavers rose to the challenge, in 1984 exploring one more bend to be halted by Armageddon, where waves closed the continuing airspace.

The Python tyrolean was the second of eight river crossings rigged before the end of Nare could be reached.

The Ire river has carved itself an impressive course of colossal tunnels in which the noise of whitewater rapids necessitated use of ear plugs.

Inspired climbing in 1985 allowed French cavers to progress along the roof of Minye's downstream river passage. Over 35 belay points later, they passed the Roaring '40s but after one more tyrolean they reached a sump at minus 473 metres.

With an estimated normal weather flow of 1-2 cubic metres per second the Manicouagan Waterfall formed a major obstacle to the exploration of Guimbé.

The Green Lake Chamber (Salle du Lac Vert) at -1155 m in Muruk Hul.

Chapter Ten

DEEP NAKANAI

In early 1985 Julia James and a team of four speleologists from Sydney were invited to carry out the first investigation of caves in the Lukwi Valley. This formed a part of the feasibility study being undertaken by Ok Tedi Mining on a proposed tailings dam site. The all-expense paid trip came out of the blue with a phone call from Geoff Francis on January 2. At the time Geoff was working for the Geological Survey of New Guinea and had been approached by Ok Tedi consultants seeking expertise in the field of speleology. It was not the first contact between Ok Tedi Mining and cavers; the company had sought their advice during a previous survey and British cavers had been welcomed at its Tabubil base in 1975 and 1978. Given the rarity of the attractive proposal, it was only natural that Julia should grasp the hand of opportunity.

Accompanying Julia were Bernard Pawih, a karst geologist with the Geological Survey, Mark Bonwick, Dave Martin, Peter Nieuwendyk and Graeme Smith, the last three having been participants on Julia's earlier Muller trips. The area under scrutiny centred upon the catchment of the Ok Ma. This bisected the Warre Limestone formation around 15 kilometres to the southwest of Tabubil in the far northwest corner of the Western Province. It was about one day's trekking from the Ok Arem area explored by cavers in 1978.

Although the Ok Ma was a relatively minor tributary of the Ok Tedi, itself only a feeder for the even larger Fly, it had nevertheless carved itself an impressive canyon prior to its confluence some ten kilometres upstream of Ningerum. During ten days of field study over 200 karst features were investigated, including 15 caves. These were all explored to the east and west of the Ok Ma Gorge, within a bed of limestone 60 to 85 metres thick. Although the Lukwi karst was relatively minor compared with other areas throughout the country, many of the caves displayed well-formed passage sections, as in Ok Mi Cave and Column Cave. Others too, had quite extensive lateral development, the longest being Ok Bedda Cave (460 m) and Swiftlet Cave (610 m). Though the study provided a unique opportunity to explore a completely new lowland karst region, the area offered little prospect for significant discoveries.

The Lukwi studies were in fact the precursor to an exciting year of exploration that would make 1985 one of the most successful in New Guinea. This was entirely dominated by French cavers: indeed, if we were to look in retrospect at the 1980s as a whole, we might view them as the French decade of discovery in the antipodes. While British and Australian cavers took the lead in China, Sarawak and mainland New Guinea, a French group cast its eyes longingly towards the island of New Britain, one of the larger satellites of the New Guinea group. Both China and Indonesia were heavily populated and politically delicate. By returning to New Britain once again, the French could expect exciting caving in remote and little known regions and in 1985, there was certainly everything to play for. During Christmas the previous year a joint Australian and New Zealand team had extended the Nettlebed Cave in New Zealand to almost 21 kilometres.

In so doing they had clinched a new Southern Hemisphere depth record of 725 metres, systematically explored upwards from the resurgence.

Once more the latest French expedition was being funded by the FFS. In the spring of 1983 it held a pre-expedition meeting in Saint-Martin-en-Vercors, a picturesque venue attracting about 40 cavers hopeful of being selected. Though the organisers were meticulous to the finest detail, having topographical and geological maps on display as well as reports from previous expeditions, it was the images of colossal jungle-fringed pits, dizzying gorges and ferocious subterranean rivers that sold the idea of New Britain to the assembled throng.

The Commission des Grandes Expéditions had in fact sent out a prospectus through the FFS publication *Spelunca*, inviting likely candidates both from the domestic front and from French Canada. A twin-tiered venture was being proposed, in reality two separate expeditions targeting areas at each extremity of the island. Once they set foot ashore, each group would be independent and would spend three to four months in the field, overlapping during the months of February and March. It was fortuitous that the gathering was attended by a handful of veterans of previous New Guinea campaigns. Indeed it was due in no small measure to the input of Jean-Paul Sounier, Serge Fulcrand and Christian Rigaldie that the proposed expedition would not be venturing into completely unknown territory.

The megadoline of Minye in the central Nakanai Mountains was to be a prime target for the first group, the Papou team. East of Pomio, around the Galowe gorge, and also in the Whiteman Range a further 200 kilometres west, were two remote and completely untouched karst regions where deep caves could be anticipated from the geological maps and photos. These would be the objectives of the second group, the Niugini team.

A group of 25 cavers was selected, including 27-year-old Laure Garibel from the Moselle, the first woman ever to take part in a French overseas caving expedition. They would be joined also by Pierre Bergeron of Montreal and a Polish student by the name of Ryszard Knapszick. Though the venture possessed no hierarchy as such, the circumstances dictated that, being the most experienced in New Guinea conditions, Jean-Paul, Serge and Christian would tend to pull the strings in the field. It transpired from the Vercors meeting that each participant would have to dip into his or her pockets to the tune of 12,000 French francs. In fact, by the time the expedition departed Paris at the end of December 1984, individual contributions had inflated to around 28,000 francs, the equivalent of 2,800 pounds sterling.

WILD WATER IN MINYE

By January 9, seven members of the Nakanai team had left the golden strands of Jacquinot Bay and taken the devious trail to Nutuve village, the remainder going with the supplies by air. Due to language difficulties the helicopter pilot misunderstood the cavers' instructions and inadvertently landed them in the village of Kapguena, instead of at Tuke much further to the north. En route, however, they carried out an aerial survey of the Galowe gorge and the huge doline of Wunung, the latter measuring at least one kilometre across.

A villager named Tom was employed as guide, but later that same day an attempt to porter camp supplies the remaining six kilometres to Minye had to be aborted when a violent thunderstorm swept the mountains. For those whose lot it was to make the journey in on foot, Nutuve represented perhaps the last concession to civilisation in the remote interior of the island. Apart from the radio, its sole means of contact with the outside world was its jungle airstrip, but more often than not this was rendered inoperative by the village pigs that frequently dug up its surface!

Since the first French expeditions to New Britain a number of logging companies had begun operations in the area, and by 1985 rough roads were gradually radiating east from Pomio and northwards in the general direction of Nutuve. The cavers were able to utilise these though they did not extend far inland and in keeping with most logging tracks, the conditions under foot were precious little better than the jungle trails.

For Jean-Paul and Christian it was all familiar ground. The equipment and rations might have gone on ahead by chopper shuttle, but the overland group was under no illusion as to what the forthcoming weeks would bring. Once the loggers' "roads" were left behind the difficulties began. The British in 1975 had found the use of knee-length gaiters indispensable to prevent abrasions to the lower leg. In the first two days fatigue and dehydration took their toll on the French team and, as they had for some reason spurned the use of gaiters, leg wounds were soon infected. Quick to sense the arrival of fresh supplies, the leeches too put in their first of many appearances.

Three days after leaving the coast everyone had made it to Kapguena, and with the whole team assembled at last they set about building and organising a camp. The site chosen was only 20 minutes from Minye, in a fairly exposed position on a ridge at an altitude of 1,000 metres. This overlooked a clear running creek fringed with palms that in another place and time would have been considered heaven on earth. Though somewhat basic, this plastic roofed shelter was over the coming weeks to take on the importance of a jungle Hilton.

Three days later, with work on the base completed, they could at last get down to the real business of exploration. It was almost a month since they had left the temperate climate of Europe and six years since French cavers first ventured into this beautiful but harsh equatorial wilderness. This time the French hoped to trace the subterranean Kanue River to its outflow at Namure, a distance of perhaps one and a half kilometres separating the two known points.

Tuesday dawned hot and sticky as usual. Pierre Bergeron and Didier Faust began the descent. This took eight hours of dangling Tarzan-like on a rope, with hundreds of metres of humid air beneath their feet. Eighty deviations were needed to rig the great drop for a safe descent. Even so, Didier very nearly missed his 24th birthday when he mistook his rope for a liana while wielding his bush knife to clear a way down through the initial vegetated incline.

The base of the great pit bore the ubiquitous scars of rocks that had tumbled down into the depths, along with trees that had tried (and failed) to survive too near to the edge of this frightful abyss. To hang about too long was to court injury or worse from falling missiles, so as a matter of urgency they sought safety in the downstream portal. It was no mean feat to reach this on account of the dense interior forest and huge piles of scree and debris that had collected from above. Finally a team was assembled at the 1984 downstream limit.

The next day, secured by a length of 8-mm Kevlar rope, Bruno Théry took to the waves, riding what may only be described as a water sledge. This prototype device had been developed specially to meet the conditions that would be encountered in the New Guinea river caves. The Australians had designed a similar craft to be built from aluminium reinforced fibreglass. Originally it had been intended for use in the Atea, but the nature of the discoveries in 1978 obviated the need for such a technique. The French sledge was fashioned from an expanded polyester and resin compound, complete with moulded handles for its passenger and a ring at the bow by which the craft could be secured to a grapnel line by snaplink. Using the tried and tested trail

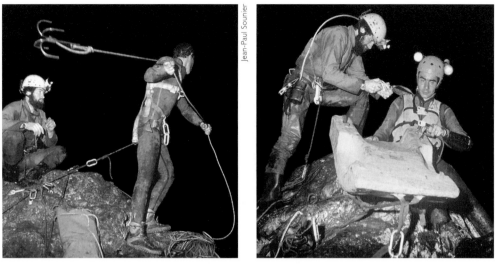

French explorers used a grapnel iron and special sledge to install a tyrolean and cross Minye's underground river.

Downstream in Minye, two tyrolean crossings and a sustained aid climb along the roof allowed French cavers to progress for 200 metres along the 30-cumec Kanue River.

ferry principal, the "victim" lays across the sledge and hangs on for dear life while the current, in theory, propels the passenger across to the far bank.

To their surprise the sledge worked first time, and in a split second a jubilant Bruno dragged himself up onto the far bank, a mass of slippery, water-polished boulders. Once the tyrolean was installed it was a straightforward matter to transfer everyone across the river. Together the team proceeded along the true right bank of a semicircular passage perhaps 20 metres high. They had not gone far when they were halted once again where the river completely occupied the continuing passage. In keeping with those hellish seas that bedevilled mariners at the Horn of Tierra del Fuego, this berserk stretch of water was christened the Roaring Forties (see fig. 24). They could not have chosen a more appropriate name, for ahead of them the passage closed in to some seven metres wide while the cave roof dropped to within a metre or two of the water surface.

The noise was indescribable where the river, possibly as much as 20 cumecs, crashed through the restriction. Was it a sump so soon? The problem in continuing begged the question of what was around the corner. If not a sump then just what kind of a cave were they about to enter? To advance any further their only chance – if hope could be vested in the ludicrous – was to follow a line along the ceiling, literally only centimetres above the infernal waves. To make matters worse, the rock was friable and hardly likely to afford any security to a lead climber.

Back in camp a heated debate ensued. Some wished to abandon exploration there and then, fearing the risks far too great; others took a more optimistic view. Minye presented a unique challenge and some were not easily deterred. They had all come halfway around the world prepared for hell or high water, and if in the event it was to be both... Well, nothing ventured, nothing gained...

While some members of the team scouted around for other caves the next morning, Jacques Bonifacino, Didier Faust, Thierry Krattinger and Pierre Bergeron went back down prepared to bivouac if necessary while a serious attempt was made to pass the obstacle. Didier led off along the roof, slowly advancing metre by precious metre while suspended spider-like in his etriers. It was a dangerous manoeuvre and one never before attempted in a cave. Progress was not made any easier by the rotten limestone or the fact that visibility and communications were impaired by the fine spray veil and the noisy river. Still he advanced and, more important, his belays held. Using every climbing aid at his disposal and lined from the near bank, he distanced himself ever further from his companions who anxiously watched his every move.

Completely out of earshot, the lifeline team kept him on his leash entirely by feel. All the while he tried to concentrate on the task in hand, drilling the next fixing point, switching off his mind to the disturbing fact that immeasurable tonnes of whitewater were racing by each second just a little too close for comfort.

After using more than 35 aid points, Didier at last overcame the Roaring Forties, fortunately without a single mishap. He reached the far side and was able to stand on a small spray-lashed terrace just above the water line. For that brief moment at least, everyone could breathe a sigh of relief. It had taken five days to traverse a mere 30 metres of cave, a magnificent achievement by anyone's standards, but the jubilation was soon to be tempered by what they discovered beyond.

The exploration continued with Pierre and Didier spearheading the small group. It was not long before they could see the passage widening ahead; however, at that point the river was flowing at a steeper angle once again. "It looks possible over here!" bellowed Pierre, spotting a traverse line along the true right bank. Sure enough there was a way, but only 50 metres more were gained before the ledge petered out and they were faced once again with crossing the river. It fell two metres with a deafening roar, underlining the increasingly obvious: Minye was not going to give up its secrets without a battle.

The far bank appeared to be composed of a slope of boulders running down to river level. A grapnel iron was hurled across and when tugged seemed to be successfully lodged between two rocks. The water sledge was employed for a second time. Pierre volunteered for this third hazardous crossing – the Cytrolienne as they dubbed it – fully aware of the danger he was placing himself in. What if the hook at the far side came adrift? Everyone pushed that thought to the back of his mind. If he got into difficulties they would probably be able to hold him on the line rather like playing a fish, but it was decidedly fraught with danger and no one wished to put blind faith to the test.

Held by a lifeline, Pierre gathered his wits as he stood facing the worst whitewater imaginable. After a moment of introspection he gave the signal. In the next instant, as he recalls, "everything happened very quickly. One surge and there I was on the other side." There was no time to be afraid. Once Pierre had made safe his delicate stance, it was merely a case of rigging up a tyrolean as before so the others could join him.

They explored a most formidable stretch of river-way. Initially they were forced to crawl in wet mud along an undercut ledge while constantly lashed by spray from the waves that crashed down beside them. Just when they thought things were starting to get better, the passage closed in again and somehow seemed to stifle the booming of the river. Its note changed to a strange, almost sinister sucking sound as the river angled downwards into a seething mass of foam that marked the end of Minye. That the cave had sumped was a bitter pill to swallow; they had been thwarted after all, despite their heroic efforts.

After their initial disappointment they realised that exploration in Minye was by no means finished. On the maps, they had noticed a sinkhole terminating a well-developed valley half a kilometre to the east of the main doline. In a lone reconnaissance Pat Genuite had succeeded in locating a promising entrance which they decided to call Ora. This was to take two trips to fully investigate.

Several pitches punctuated the sporting cave, which dropped rapidly from the doline base to a depth of 157 metres. At this point a major inlet flowed in from the right. Though small by comparison with the Minye River, the new stream would have been considered of major importance in Europe. Augmented by around 50 litres of water per second, the magnificently decorated streamway continued more or less level as far as a small chamber, after which a six-metre drop led almost immediately to a sump. Above this a fortuitous ten-metre climb provided an unexpected surprise: a balcony overlooking a large black space out of which arose the noise of a large river. It was clearly the Kanue, they thought, and a 50-metre rope descent soon confirmed their suspicions, dropping them into the Salle Tuke (Tuke Chamber), thereby completing a 294-metre deep connection with Minye.

At about the same time that explorations were taking place in Oro, Pat Genuite was jungle bashing with Ryszard Knapszick when they stumbled upon a tiny hole adjacent to the trail linking Kapguena village with Tuke. The unpretentious entrance was situated in a depression where two small streams met. On this first trip they spent an hour and half clearing a blockage and eventually reached a depth of around 70 metres. They surfaced in high spirits to announce another going cave.

Subsequent explorations pushed Tevi down a series of pitches and free climbs that forged a second link with Minye at a depth of 231 metres, joining the Kapguena Gallery a short distance upstream from Tuke Chamber. Strangely, both the 1980 and 1984 teams had missed this important inlet.

Tevi turned out to be a surprisingly aquatic system, for during one trip a sudden downpour sent a flood pulse rushing down the cave, preventing one group from surfacing. They subsequently "enjoyed" a chilly overnight bivouac in Tuke Chamber.

While one team had been tackling the Roaring Forties in Minye, another spent a few days at Tuke. On January 20, Philippe Eté and Luc-Henri Fage explored and mapped the Namure outflow but were unable to find anything that had not been noted in 1984. However, the villagers revealed several other open caves a short walk from the village, including the Gohibe to Tamul through-trip, Kurukulkul, Lakaburo and Tolana. The latter was the most extensive and apparently had been shown to and partly explored by the 1984 *Megadoline* filming team.

The 15-metre wide entrance to Tolana was located in a steep-sided blind canyon a half an hour's walk south southwest of Tuke. This gave immediate access to a large fossil tunnel that appeared as if it would go places. In turn it led into an equally spacious stream passage flowing left to right. This was carrying a moderate flow but unfortunately the impressive cave sumped both up and downstream; in total, the party mapped almost 1,300 metres of delightful cave.

NO SUN AT COPACABANA BEACH

On Tuesday, January 22, the team entered its first major cave. Paulus and Harlus from Tuke were guiding Luc-Henri, Philippe and Jean-Paul Sounier along little-used hunting trails. After proceeding for a while along a ridge forming one flank of a steep-sided valley, the villagers indicated a seasonal streambed below and to their right. On this occasion it was taking only a small flow. Descending to the creek, they traced it through a canyon to a sinkhole with an imposing, 70-metre high entrance. This was one and a half kilometres southwest of Minye and could be clearly seen on the aerial photographs. The three kitted up and entered the cave without delay.

From the base of the surface canyon a high passage festooned with twisted stalactites grew quickly in size as it diverged into the complex Scolopendre Series. After a stretch of gently dipping passage a number of small climbs and *marmites* marked a point where the cave began dropping with greater determination. In places it was necessary to clamber through chaotic areas of rockfall. Shortly they heard a splashing in the darkness ahead, and after passing the source of the noise – a shower-bath cascading from high above them – the galleries coalesced at a pitch of 23 metres. It was by then time to retreat, the first trip having yielded a depth of almost 100 metres.

Guimbé was well developed and though they had a feeling it was going to excel, they had little idea to what extent. It was to take another seven trips into Guimbé to realise its true potential, carry out an accurate survey and photograph the splendid find.

Beyond the first day's limit, the Gallery at the Gate of Ecstasy gave quickly onto the Puits de Nazgul, two more drops of 30 and 28 metres each. These provided additional entertainment in the shape of large, smooth-sided plunge pools. At one especially deep lake they were obliged to take to the steely water by inflatable dinghy. The slow, deliberate sound of paddling was soon replaced by an unmistakable rumbling. They hauled the boat up onto Copacabana Beach, the gravel bank a stark contrast to the golden sands they had left a few weeks before. Here the cave suddenly changed direction and the roaring grew appreciably louder.

Not far ahead they rounded a sweeping bend and passed beneath a high aven where a major stream emerged from a boulder ruckle to their right. This was augmented by a second inlet a few minutes later, the combined flow forming the newborn Irulan River. At that point the water trundled off due west forming a series of exciting rapids. In places the river had carved itself a deep trench; fortunately for the explorers, this was flanked in places by wide ledges which made progress somewhat easier.

The Manicouagan waterfall in Guimbé.

For almost 600 metres the streamway maintained a fairly uniform cross-section some eight to ten metres high and 15 wide, decorated with a profusion of calcite formations. Almost an hour from the beachhead the river became languid and at one point the explorers feared the cave would sump. However, a dull rumbling again announced the approach of more rapids as the cave swung north again along more sporting whitewater sections.

Though the cave still retained its imposing dimensions, the river slowed and again entered a deeply incised vadose trench. Was this merely the lull before the storm? Indeed it was, for the placid section ended, the river quickened its pace and the water took a wild leap into the unknown. The drop appeared to be less than 30 metres and marked a point where the passage had intersected a major weakness in the strata. Cutting back along an obvious east-west aligned joint, the Cascade Manicouagan created a sizeable cavern where it thundered into a large pool below.

Back on the surface, after three weeks at Camp Minye, problems with gradually deteriorating health were intensifying. This was due to an especially virulent form of mycosis which indeed necessitated the evacuation of Luc-Henri. While Jean-Paul and Pierre made a forced march to Pomio to request a helicopter, a team of eight villagers helped stretcher Luc-Henri to Kapguena. From there he was flown to Rabaul where he was hospitalised for ten days before rejoining his companions in Pomio at the end of the first five weeks.

Pat and Ryszard were also immobile for almost a week, and Bruno was suffering from a tropical ulcer. The rigours of the equatorial forest and prolonged exposure below ground had in the end resulted in most of the team succumbing to fungal mycosis, the consequence of having constantly damp feet. The reduced team – at least those who remained half healthy – had little option but to continue the exploration in Guimbé.

Back at the head of the new shaft the explorers surveyed the scene below them. The waterfall was whipping up spray and driving it sideways into the walls of the chamber. By traversing to the right the cavers managed to avoid this obstacle, though lifelines were employed to safeguard the climbers. At the end of the traverse an abseil landed them on a huge, spray-dappled boulder from which they could gaze into the continuing passage. Spacious as ever, the floor ahead was strewn with corroded boulders decked with formations that had formed aeons ago while the blocks were still in situ. Degenerate now, the stalagmites leaned drunkenly this way and that.

Further downstream a splendid ten-metre descent landed them in a lake...*splash*! This was followed by more cascades and the occasional water-filled *marmite*. A vicious lowering of the roof prompted more thought of sumps, and the consequences should a sudden flood pulse bear down upon them. The sombre walls of the continuing passage seemed to absorb the light from their lamps, increasing the feeling that the end was imminent. But once again the ceiling reared up and remained briefly out of sight as they passed beneath a high aven, delivering a splattering from heights only imagined. More whitewater preceded the final straight of 200 metres after which the river was unceremoniously swallowed by the inevitable sump, scummy and final.

Plotting of the survey prompted much speculation as to the cave's ultimate destination. Guimbé had dropped to a final depth of 320 metres and generally trended towards the northwest and the village of Tuke. The River Irulan seemed to possess a greater flow than that seen in Tolana, so it seemed reasonable to assume it would flow not to that cave, but join the Kanue River somewhere downstream of the sump in Minye. The question was purely academic since nothing short of direct exploration or a dye test would furnish the answer.

The conclusion of explorations in Guimbé marked the end of a superb cave system and of five weeks in the mountains. By this time everyone was eagerly looking forward to some rest, to gather their strength and lick their wounds. Apart from the attacks of mycosis which had affected

Jacques Bonifacino fights his way through the jungle and is almost lost in the wall of vegetation as he abseils into Kururu.

most of the team, many also had infected lesions, which for some lasted the entire duration in the bush. Moreover, Pat, Philippe and Bruno had received attention from the *Anopheles* mosquito and were suffering from attacks of malaria.

As had been arranged, the helicopter arrived and in a matter of minutes they were all bathing sore feet in no finer balm than the salty waters of the Solomon Sea. At 30 degrees Celsius the water was almost soporific and a more than welcome contrast to the caves, the parasites and the ever present jungle filth. Yet despite all the trials and medical problems they had every reason to feel pleased with themselves: eight kilometres of new cave had been mapped and a total of 1,000 metres of pitches descended.

Those few indolent days at sea level soon refreshed the parts that no amount of virgin cave passage could reach, and yet further objectives awaited investigation. Time was pressing, and on Wednesday, February 13, the team divided. The plan had been to shift the entire group 200 kilometres west to the Whiteman Range, where they could join forces with the second French team, due to arrive there towards the month end. For financial reasons this notion was abandoned in favour of two nearer but equally promising areas.

While the majority of the team departed for the heights of the Galowe River, Pierre Bergeron, Jacques Bonifacino and a fully recovered Luc-Henri Fage headed off by motor boat across Jacquinot Bay, bound for Meingi village. This was some way down the coast, and formed a convenient departure point for their ultimate destination, the settlement of Siva'Una, perched high above the Melkoi River some way inland. Here at the extreme southwest corner of the Nakanai Range was an entirely unknown karst region with some good-looking pits piercing the jungle.

An enthusiastic welcome awaited them in Meingi, where they were mobbed by many excited youngsters. The village was situated six degrees south of the equator and possessed all the rudiments of civilisation, its own school, and a church, the focal point for a cluster of thatched native huts. Completing the tropical cliché the ubiquitous coconut palms overhung all in gracefully bending groves, their fronds sighing in a warm breeze. Though the teacher had explained the reason for the cavers' presence, the notion of exploring holes in the ground remained a complete mystery to the village people, and no doubt would form a topic of conversation for many weeks hence.

A seasonal four-wheel drive track snaked its way 50 kilometres up into the hills from Meingi, passing through Siv'Una en route to the Au'ula mission station. Unfortunately the absence of a suitable vehicle meant the cavers had to make the journey on foot. After an entertaining overnight stay they departed with three porters, a sufficient quantity of rope and rations to last them ten days. Four uneventful hours later they pulled into Siv'Una red-faced and sweating.

The village was like paradise in comparison to Camp Minye. They were shown to a beautiful house decorated with carved tamburan masks and were impressed with the carefree pace of the life. Here was a richness of natural resources they had not seen in other inland settlements. There seemed to be no shortage of food, with bananas and sugar cane growing everywhere. They saw huge cucumbers, citrus fruits, glossy marrows and succulent tomatoes. Even the village hens, clucking aimlessly about the dusty ground, provided them with an abundant supply of fresh eggs. At an altitude of only 400 metres life here was indeed the closest thing they had seen to utopia.

They began prospecting for caves almost at once. Though the undulating country surrounding the village was pockmarked with depressions, shafts and sinks, lack of time and manpower restricted them to the more obvious. South of the village hospital Luc-Henri investigated the Kusapala sinkhole, where a steep flanked doline funnelled into a ten-metre drop. He negotiated this to a large boulder bridge above a 40-metre pitch taking water. A canyon below fell away steeply and continued with two more drops before closing down at a depth of only 83 metres.

They had more luck in the Melkoi River canyon two kilometres to the southwest, where the villagers showed them a significant resurgence. Unfortunately this was impenetrable but some way above it in a side ravine was a cave entrance emitting a powerful breeze. The Drai Pasis system allowed access through a fossil gallery into an active streamway which sumped at both ends, but not before 1,400 metres of comfortable, well decorated passage was explored.

Just to one side of the four-wheel drive trail, some six kilometres to the northwest of Siv'Una, an impressive shaft called Kururu had for countless generations held the villagers in awe (see fig. 5). The hourglass-shaped pit was indicated to Jacques on February 22, but due to the luxuriant vegetation growing around the rim it was difficult to obtain a clear view into the depths. By sounding the abyss in the time-honoured fashion he estimated the drop to be around 150 metres.

They rigged the shaft the next day and it exceeded all expectations, providing an exhilarating 200-metre abseil. Before landing upon a huge boulder cone forming the bottom, they noted three small inlets pouring from fissures in the walls about halfway down. Four large passages radiated from the base. Upstream, the Phantom River formed a magnificent passage featuring countless rock-mills and cascades, which after about 600 metres divided into a labyrinth of intricate tributaries. At its downstream end the Phantom River terminated in the obligatory sump almost directly beneath the entrance shaft. Continuing downstream from there, two abandoned galleries of quite handsome proportions joined at a large hall, the Aviary of the Flying Foxes, which served as the roost for a large colony of bats. Perhaps 300 metres beyond this the cave ended at another sump with a final depth of 256 metres.

In effect some 35 hours were spent over five days completing the exploration of Kururu and carrying out a detailed survey. This showed they had explored over three kilometres, of which 500 metres remained unmapped. Magnificent as this cave was and, despite the 18 wide-open leads remaining when they eventually vacated the system, the most intriguing questions surrounded the discovery of a troglobitic crab. The specimens were found in a side gallery close to the terminal downstream sump and displayed all the characteristic features of cave adaptation: reduced eyes, lack of pigment and extended, slender limbs. These discoveries, new to science, necessitated the formation of a new family of Crustacea.

CAMP MALPE AND A RECORD

Meanwhile a few kilometres down the coast from Pomio, their colleagues had arrived at Galowe. They learned that Bruno had already departed with eight porters to locate a suitable campsite up river. A colossal resurgence hidden in the deep canyon was thought to form the major source of the Galowe River, first seen from a helicopter chartered the year before by Gérald Favre. It gave an impressive hint of the sort of cave systems that might be expected beneath those isolated forests.

Bruno returned to the coast a few days later after having taken three days to force a trail leading to the Mayang resurgence. More important, he had cleared a campsite at Malpe, a village abandoned, according to informants, at the end of the war in 1945. He believed this would form an ideal base from which they could investigate the surrounding plateaux. On March 6, a team departed full of enthusiasm.

No sooner had they arrived and set up camp than it began raining, and continued without respite for four days. Some of the resurgences within the gorge were examined but none of these revealed any cave passage. It was a testing time for everyone and morale soon sank to its lowest ebb. Mayang was by far the largest resurgence, with an estimated normal weather flow of 30 to 50 cumecs emerging under pressure from between large boulders. If this was not impressive enough, the wet season output was believed to increase fourfold. It drained a vast limestone plateau of some 150 square kilometres in extent, rising to a height of two kilometres. With the outflow at 400 metres this provided scope enough to hide a cave system to match the world's deepest.

With imaginations working overtime they began examining the doline karst of the high plateau. The major breakthrough came on Wednesday, March 6. They had been cutting track on a compass bearing to the southwest of camp when, after three days confined to the vicious bamboo forest, they found an intermittent stream valley. This trended more or less west to east and had been spotted on the aerial photographs. After walking a kilometre down the creek bed they entered a small canyon where Laure, Bruno and Pierre found a shaft dropping perhaps ten metres.

It was almost the end of the expedition and the team was functioning with less than half the available manpower due to injury and illness. People were suffering from sores that would not heal and almost everyone was still troubled by attacks of mycosis. Despite their poor health a team descended the new hole the following morning. It was decided to call the find Muruk Hul after a beautiful cassowary caught that day and later eaten by their guides.

After quickly rigging the entrance, Pierre and Bruno descended to see if the cave went, finding a fall of 26 metres split by a small ledge. Bruno called back for the others to follow on

The Elmira Chamber, Muruk.

down, and together they eagerly explored a further 150 metres, passing a small stream entering from a sump on their left. Cascades followed, then the stream splashed down pitches of 32 and 10 metres. From here the Miriel River turned southwest then west in a classic, joint-controlled vadose passage two to three metres wide. More splendid cascades preceded a pitch into a small lake. By this time the team had already reached a depth of 235 metres and were over the moon at having explored at least a kilometre of fine streamway. Time was advancing so they turned around and made their exit to announce their good fortune.

Though the entrance was located in a dry streambed they were struck by the many tree trunks wedged across bends in the passage and littering the rock mills, unquestionable proof that the cave was subject to severe flooding. Slowly, trip followed trip and the system gradually increased in depth. Beyond the lake that had stopped Bruno and Pierre, the stream took to a passage on the right and vanished into a sump. They encountered water again not far ahead, then negotiated more drops and carefully explored a section of river descending at a 45-degree angle where the roof remaining well out of sight. The streamway eventually ended at the Puits du Visconte, which dropped into a large lake dammed by boulders. A tyrolean traverse was later rigged to make passing this obstacle easier.

Muruk was developing into a fine cave yet amazingly few drops required tackle. Pierre and Ryszard alone then took up the challenge and with more rope quickly reached the foot of the Visconte shaft at minus 405 metres. Then, in what turned out to be a 26-hour epic they added a further kilometre of passage, calling a halt at a depth of 580 metres. On the way in they passed a major tributary entering from the right, naming it the Emeldir River. Downstream from the

Muruk Hul, a spectacular system explored to a depth of over 1,000 metres by French (FFS) expeditions between 1985 and 1988. Right: the Miriel River flows between two walls displaying impressive bedding.

The top of the 12 m waterfall at -568 m, Muruk Hul.

confluence the Galadriel River proved arduous to follow due to its many cascades, plunge pools and small climbs. On the return they found it even more taxing.

Walking back to camp through the dreadful bamboo forest was also slow and punishing, Ryszard's feet being almost raw from infection. Compensations came in the knowledge that they had exceeded the New Guinea depth record, and still the cave continued.

The final team to enter Muruk Hul explored down the impressive stream canyon through more flooded potholes, which were becoming a major feature – and obstacle – of the system. Since the junction with the Emeldir River the roof had never been visible, but now the walls too disappeared as the streamway debauched dramatically into the Elmira Chamber. Here a boulder pile diverted the river along the left-hand wall before entering the continuation. For the next 200 metres the passage gradually reduced in size, and the roof finally reappeared before plunging into a deep sump pool three and a half kilometres from the entrance.

Muruk had proved a superb discovery. Despite their reduced efficiency, the French team had explored and mapped nearly five kilometres of first-class cave. More significantly perhaps, at a depth of 637 metres the cave had overtaken Mamo Kananda as the deepest in New Guinea and displaced Harwoods Hole in New Zealand as the second deepest system in the Southern Hemisphere (see fig. 30).

On March 27, Bruno, Laure and two villagers cleared up a few loose ends and completed the survey of Peleomatana, a kilometre-long resurgence cave found on the edge of the Galowe plateau. This work marked the end of the French expedition in the Nakanai Mountains and, reluctantly (or perhaps with some relief) they packed up and left for the coast. Back in Galowe they celebrated their hard-won success with a feast of pig killed in their honour. Few people had dared or even considered penetrating the inhospitable mountains beyond their traditional hunting grounds, and the village headman, John Kaiopuna, viewed the cavers with open respect.

They had much to be jubilant about. The culmination of two years of preparation had resulted not only in two new depth records, but they had found 32 caverns and mapped almost 20 kilometres of impressive passageways. By the end of March, the Nakanai team was back in France and the cold there merely made it seem as if the experience had just been a dream.

SPIRITS, PYGMIES AND RIVER CAVES

The final phase of the 1985 French involvement in New Britain took the second team to the remote Whiteman Mountains, a range located in wild terrain extending to the north and northeast of Kandrian, administrative centre for western New Britain (see fig. 1). The area comprised some 1,400 square kilometres of unexplored limestone country in which large collapse dolines had for many years been reported to exist. The Australians had had designs on the area and it had only been a serious climbing incident involving Harold Gallasch that prevented a proposed Sydney expedition from getting off the ground four years earlier.

The Whiteman team consisted of a dozen hand-picked speleologists. During late February an advance party of five initially looked at the caving possibilities around Mt. Karoma in the Southern Highlands Province of the mainland. This important karst region is located between the Mullers and the Lavani Valley, roughly in the area that the Japanese had failed to reach the year before. Though there is undoubted potential for the area, the French group produced nothing to inspire the return of the whole team and therefore expedition manpower was focused on New Britain.

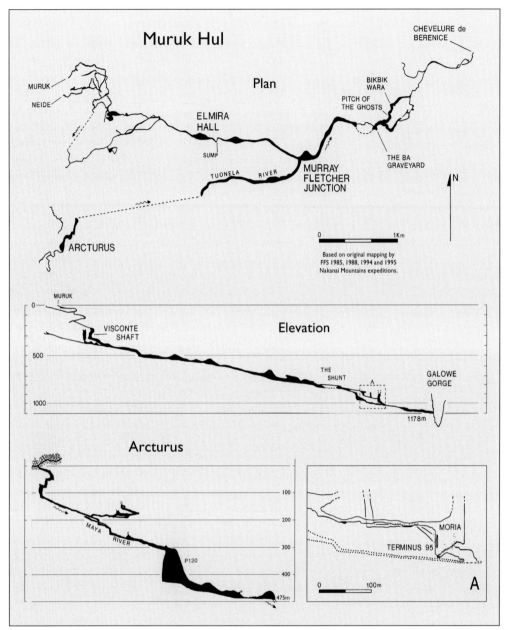

Fig. 30) Muruk Hul and Arcturus

By Monday, March 25, two advance camps were established on the true right bank of the Andru River, over 30 kilometres inland from Kandrian. When they had departed from the coast it had been against all the advice of friends and local people who had some knowledge of the terrain, no matter how meagre. A team of Australian archaeologists had in fact made a slight penetration into the forests to the north and, though having seen some small caves, reported afterwards that overland travel was extremely unpleasant.

The notion of heading tens of kilometres into inhospitable equatorial forests was one that totally perplexed the local townsfolk. More problematic was the *itambus*, which made it almost impossible to recruit guides. The people feared the misty mountains beyond the Andru River, and no one wished to transgress the unknown lands to the north or provoke retribution by angering the spirits of the river, not to mention the monsters that haunted the caves.

The warnings were given in all honesty. They must stay away from a cavern named Warabou, where those unwary enough to enter would waste away slowly until they eventually died from anaemia. And what of Pomogin, the spirit who turned pigs into dogs, or the strange race of hostile pygmies who, according to legends, inhabited a plateau secreted within those remote mountains? There had been no sign of these when the cavers had flown over the area by light aircraft a few days before. Instead they had seen a couple of colossal dolines, each with a whitewater river flowing at its base, all the inducement any caver needed, bad spirits or not.

While successive teams attempted to penetrate the high plateau and find the fabled dolines, others investigated the Andru canyon. On March 26, the entrance to Pomogin was located close to their second camp, and over the following few days they explored four kilometres in this and other resurgence caves close by. The most significant find was Warabou, with an outflow of 6-10 cumecs. Risking death from anaemia the team entered this to explore and survey 350 metres of active and fossil galleries. Contrary to the warnings they did not shrivel up, nor did they meet the huge serpent said to have its lair in the cave.

For almost a week the group cut tracks to the east of the Andru River over successions of heavily wooded ridges, and still their quarry eluded them. Measuring at least a kilometre in length and half as wide, the doline should not have been difficult to locate...that is, but for the forest. When they flew over the great bowl they had also noticed an arched cave entrance at least 60 metres in height. Still the terrain was worse than the imagination could possibly make it; steeper and yet steeper ridges were an inescapable facet of travelling in that tortured land.

On the sixth day they left their second camp with rations for four days, and after once more negotiating the Andru River, continued blazing trails through dense forest to the northeast. All day they had been unable to fix their position due to a build up of cloud that reduced to nil any chances of identifying landmarks. The rains fell with a vengeance, such that they barely improved on the one kilometre a day they had been achieving up to then. Their hopes were momentarily raised when they came to a depression, yet all they found was a small stream. Then, just after 3:00 p.m., they struggled to the apex of yet another ridge and above the noise of the pounding rain they heard – or rather felt – the rumbling of a river.

As they made their way cautiously down the west flank of a depression, the slope grew more and more precipitous, but the roaring of water lured them onwards and down. By good fortune the dense tree cover and an opportune breach in the cliffs allowed them to descend for about 250 metres to reach the river. It was a sight for sore eyes that left them in no doubt that at last they had found the giant doline. The river emerged from beneath a rocky escarpment to one side and, after forming a series of rapids, slid impressively into a sizeable rectangular downstream cave. Above this an even larger fossil gallery stared out from the green-streaked bluffs.

They named the doline Kukumba after a species of bird that apparently frequented the area (see fig. 5). It was a magnificent spectacle. Anyone else would have expressed the volume of this huge cavity as 75 million cubic metres but not the French; they found it more meaningful to consider that if filled with wine, it would meet their nation's consumption for more than a century!

On April 3, they established a bivouac close to the doline to allow a tentative trip into the Arrakis system. They were not disappointed, for this first sortie revealed spacious galleries and a

Several colossal dolines intrude into the Arrakis network of cave passages, as in this photograph of Kukum-bu Doline, showing the upper portion of the downstream portal.

beautiful underground river. Although the latter sumped downstream after only 110 metres, an old entrance above promised a way around this impasse. Moreover, on the north (upstream) side of the doline, they found several abandoned caves hidden in the forested base and sides. These provided a deviation into two kilometres of superb galleries.

Though there were leads to push on all fronts the dreaded mycosis had returned to haunt them, necessitating a return to Kandrian. They were of course two days from camp and needed to move this towards the doline before any serious exploration could begin. But due to ailments, it would be almost another three weeks before they could even think of continuing underground.

Following a period of convalescence at the coast, the team returned inland. By May Day Sunday a new campsite had been equipped and a helipad prepared by the rim of the doline in readiness for the arrival of a filming crew, and also to give some assurance should a serious injury or illness require urgent evacuation. Over the next few weeks the cave very quickly lived up to expectations. Working in relays both up- and downstream, the explorers found altogether over three kilometres of wonderful galleries. At the end of each day the teams returned to camp exuberant with tales of huge halls, 30 metre-square passages, pristine grottos and sporting river-ways.

With Muruk Hul, and now in the new Arrakis system, the French were proving just as the Australians did with the Muller Range: that a concentration of resources and effort into a single area could reap worthwhile dividends. After eight successive trips the length of Arrakis was approaching 12 kilometres. The caving days were becoming longer and more difficult as time

Erich Delnatte/1985 FFS expedition

When a French team first entered the Arrakis system in 1985 they were astounded by the beauty and size of the galleries and streamways.

went by, while those confined to their hammocks due to illness found the excitement almost too much to bear.

In essence the system consisted of sections of large river-way, with here and there much older fossil conduits, long abandoned by the waters that had formed them. In the distant past piecemeal cavern breakdown had begun, and over time had resulted in the formation of shafts and dolines. These broke through between active and fossil levels or connected with the surface to provide convenient "windows" into the complex (see fig. 31). On the upstream side of Kuku-mba the Llombon Gallery provided an indirect route to one such window.

At a crossroads of the main gallery one branch ended in a section of river-way sumping at both ends. Back at the junction however, the explorers noticed a passage some way above in the east wall. Opposite this they followed instead an enlarging tunnel that emerged after 250 metres in a porch looking out into the doline. Returning to the junction and after a relatively easy climb, they gained entry to the high level Awat Gallery, which they subsequently traced for approximately 350 metres. Throughout this length, the passage was characterised by calcite curtains and other magnificent concretions. At one point, due to centuries of flowstone accumulation, the way forward was reduced to a narrow cleft creating a venturi effect on the draught rushing through the cave. Because of this, those negotiating the constriction constantly had the flames of their carbide lamps extinguished.

Passing a small inlet, they shortly came to a devious route upwards through wedged boulders. The way could be determined from the wind and an almost constant stream of cave swiftlets. Scrambling upwards the cavers emerged onto a slope of boulders with a sickly green light streaming down a spacious shaft to their left. Vines hung down the dimly lit grey walls and here

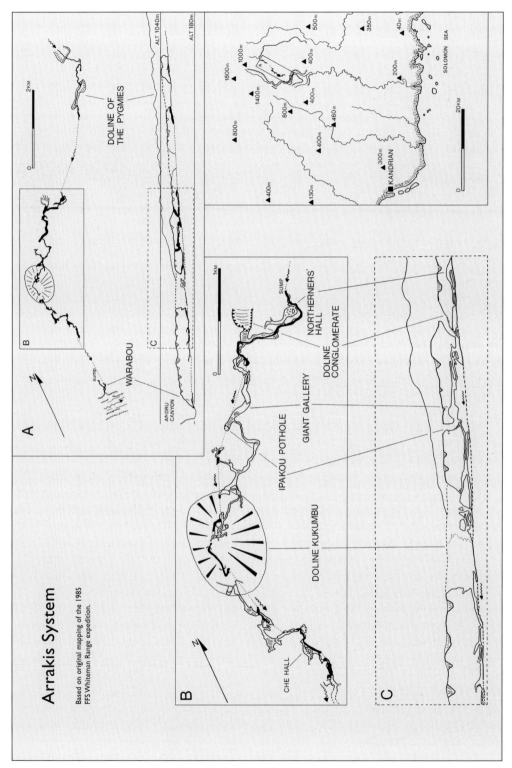

Fig. 31) Arrakis System

and there the boulders were littered with stunted plants. Below their point of entry, a lake at the base of the slope was strewn with forest flotsam originating from the surface 120 metres above.

Beside the lake a calcite ramp allowed easy access to a new gallery 25 metres higher, at a point where an impressive calcite dome occupied the full width of the passageway, here some 60 metres across. The imposing Giant Gallery continued for perhaps half a kilometre with a height that could easily have accommodated the Arc de Triomphe. Formations of every conceivable form were so numerous that there was hardly a square centimetre of bare rock visible. While weaving their way through a veritable forest of columns, they noted at one place a number of calcified bat skeletons. Not far beyond these macabre remains another drop provided a way into a new, lower-level labyrinth beneath the main gallery. From here they were able to explore further meanders of the river canyon.

At one place the *Doline Conglomerate* – similar in both size and nature to Kavakuna Doline further east – had spilled the boulders of its gradual decay into the river-way beneath. The latter continued east and the explorers traced it in a canyon of quite grand proportions for several hundred metres more, before finally halting at a sump chamber where the Arrakis River welled up from beneath the wall. At two points en route it was possible to climb up to the left into the lofty Northerners' Hall (*Salle des Nordistes*).

Exploration was proving slow due to the policy of surveying as they proceeded, and also because of the galloping foot rot that was by then affecting everyone. Yes indeed, life was never dull, even for those laid up in sickness. Their beds were frequently shaken by earth tremors, a constant reminder that they were encamped on the edge of an active volcanic zone. There were other problems too. One day a party had been cut off for a time when a downstream section of the cave flooded. On another occasion, their guide Patrick missed his footing and took a perilous dive from the rim of the doline. He was lucky: grasping a tree six metres below, he escaped with only a fractured sternum.

With the end of their stay in New Britain approaching, a team departed overland to search for another large doline estimated to be seven or eight kilometres further to the north. They had hoped to trace the Arrakis River all the way to this feature, but sumps in the upstream sectors of the system meant they had to sharpen the machetes and head into the forests once more.

On May 16, they at last stumbled into the elongated Doline of the Pygmies. This was about 800 metres long, with both up- and downstream portals providing access to further sections of superb passage. Downstream the explorers passed through a handsome 30-metre square outlet, giving an almost seamless transition from the jungle green to the muted greys of a beautiful, sandy-floored river-way. The water roared off into darkness along a major fracture line in the rock.

After about 300 metres the passage height increased to a respectable 40 metres and was wide enough for eight people to walk abreast. It was gentleman's caving at its best, but short-lived, since the angle of the floor later created a violent current and they were obliged to traverse. A ten-metre waterfall eventually frustrated them where the river plunged directly into a turbulent sump. In the vain hope of bypassing this, they gingerly traversed out along a ledge in the left wall. With the help of a rock projection, they gained a bridge some way above the sump, and from there via another shelf at the far side, they managed to reach another ledge some 20 metres higher. In three successive pendulum manoeuvres it was just possible to alight upon a small bank. The question of a bypass remained since this was as far as they could go without more equipment.

Back in the upstream direction, the way forward was by way of the Moneta Gallery and semi-active passageways. At a major junction the right branch was blocked by a boulder fall, but to the left, going more or less in a westerly direction, an 80-metre long lake provided some sporting caving. After exploring almost one kilometre in a very large tunnel, they finally emerged into the leafy realms of yet another megadoline. The many black pebbles of volcanic rock strewn about the riverbed hereabouts suggested that they were not far from the upper limits of the limestone. In total, they had added another three kilometres to the Arrakis system. By then it had completely vindicated all their hopes, giving 16 kilometres of the most remarkable caving.

When finally drafted, the plan showed that no more than a kilometre separated the downstream sump and the presumed outflow at Warabou in the Andru canyon. Upstream there was still a large gap between Northerners' Hall and the downstream siphon in the Doline of the Pygmies. Clearly there was much more to Arrakis and the chances of finding bypasses to the sumps seemed excellent. With the far upstream limits closely approaching the junction with the volcanic belt to the north, there seems little hope of increasing the vertical range of the system in that direction. But by linking up the known sections of the cave, it may just be possible to clinch the Southern Hemisphere depth record. Moreover, with calcareous strata reaching altitudes of 1,700 metres in those desolate mountains no one was placing bets on where the next French expedition would take place.

Indeed the following year a small French team, derived this time from the Pyrénéen Association of Speleology, returned to the Whiteman Ranges to continue exploration of Arrakis. The four-man team led by Erich Delnatte included Pierre Lefebvre, Philippe Geraud and Philippe Hasson. They spent seven weeks in the area between February and April, and though they failed to find any connection between the three main sections of the system, they did extend it by three kilometres. In addition they discovered and surveyed Wallaby Cave (315 m) and Pleek Lambou Cave (337 m).

CLOSE CALL IN SOUTHERN CROSS

The 1980s were without doubt important years for New Guinea caving. In particular, the catalogue of major French discoveries was certainly impressive, the culmination of a determined effort by committed teams of speleologists. Even so, their success highlighted the need for further work in New Britain. The Arrakis complex and perhaps the Wunung area flanking the Galowe River offered the prospect of a vertical range of at least 1,000 metres. For the time being Muruk stands as a new depth record for New Guinea, but for how long, no one can say.

The continuing decline in expatriate caving activity combined with a lack of foreign expeditions meant that the caving scene was pretty quiet during 1986-1987. In January 1988, Rolan Eberhard from Tasmania had occasion to spend a short time in New Guinea. He visited a well-known hole in Kandrian itself, a site previously called Police Barracks Cave, which proved not to be very extensive. He also prospected around the Kandrian area of West New Britain, and explored and surveyed approximately 130 metre of sporting streamway in Sara River Cave. Though he knew of the French expeditions of 1985, he was not familiar with their findings. Nor it seems was he aware that another major French expedition had already arrived and was about to make significant discoveries in the Nakanai Range.

By the time he had departed for Australia the seventh French expedition to New Guinea was in progress. The 13-man team was once more organised under the auspices of the FFS, with seven of the participants, including one of the two medics, previously having been to New Guinea.

Resurgence and resurgence chamber of Rak River Cave.

Although some small finds were made near Siv'Una, and east of Waterfall Bay at the source of the Rak River (also known as the "Cave at the End of the World"), their principal objective was the plateau forming the southern flank of the Galowe canyon. At depth, they suspected a vast master cave draining the combined waters to the Mayang resurgence. With this prospect in mind they established a camp at an altitude of 1,530 metres, some five kilometres southwest of the 1985 camp. This was to be their operational base for three months.

The Muruk Hul, discovered in 1985, gave them hope that other systems might go considerably deeper, perhaps into the master cave itself. Finding caves in New Guinea has never been easy, and though these karsts in fact promised world-class systems, the same topography that in all probability will eventually reveal such depth continued to hold out against all attempts to find it. In total the team discovered 20 new caves, six of which exceeded 200 metres depth. An astronomical theme held favour and therefore the discoverers mostly named their finds after constellations or their primary stars. Of particular note were Cassiopée, Southern Cross, Aldébaran, Kaïs, Altaïr and Arcturus. With the exception of Altaïr, they were predominantly vertical caves, and indeed Altaïr was explored to a depth of 332 metres.

Cassiopée Cave was one vertical find that gave the impression it might just be the system to lead into the promised land. Its 20-metre-wide entrance was formed along a major weakness in the limestone and was partially obstructed by dead tree trunks that overhung the drop. A rapid succession of pitches, forming a single deep chasm, soon attained a depth of 239 metres, further

A large gallery at minus 420 metres in Arcturus.

sustaining their optimism of greater depth. It was not to be, for after picking up a couple of minor tributaries it promptly levelled out to a sump at an ultimate depth of 280 metres.

On March 9, another group led by Serge Fulcrand dropped the twin entrances of a cave they called Southern Cross. This led into a sporting streamway with many plunge pools littered with washed-in trees. These should have rung alarm bells. The two ways merged just before a 50-metre shaft; from its base the passage continued with further pools and logs, leading to a bedding passage two metres high. At the far side the passage increased in size to the head of a large echoing void.

By traversing out on ledges to one side, the explorers were able to rig their next rope clear of the waterfall, though they received a slight wetting from two minor inlets part way down the 50-metre shaft. Shortly another tributary entered from the roof and the explorers then traced a five-metre diameter tube descending at an average angle of 15 degrees. A feature of this part of the cave was the many cascades and rock-mills which pierced the cave floor. These were tiresome to repeatedly negotiate and made for slow progress. The five-man team had just reached an eight-metre drop overlooking one of these when a sound resembling a drum roll was accompanied a few seconds later by a fierce build-up in air pressure.

The effects of this were noticeable on the eardrums and the cavers experienced a strange sensation in their breathing. Almost instantly the water flow increased from ten litres per second to several cubic metres. Climbing above the rising river, they sought a draughty refuge on a ledge overlooking the plunge pool eight metres below.

About ten minutes after the initial rise in water level the pressure seemed to fall; they deduced from this that the passage downstream from their perch must have sumped. While waiting for the water level to fall, one of them noticed with some unease that the roof above their heads was decorated with fresh green flood debris deposited by an earlier inundation! Two soul-searching hours were spent in that inhospitable place before their predicament eased sufficiently for them to effect an escape. They were lucky that the flood had not been as severe as previous ones. With exploration curtailed, the promising Southern Cross system was left unfinished with a downstream passage four metres wide and five high.

Their finest hour came with the discovery of Arcturus. At 455 metres this was their deepest find and an especially beautiful cave. It was found on the first day of March by Sounier and Citone after nearly three hours in the bush. The small entrance was located to the southwest of camp, partially hidden by tree roots and vines beneath a low scarp. This diminutive hole gave little indication of the first-class cave system waiting below. The duo descended immediately and on that first trip reached a depth of minus 40 metres.

Two more lengthy sorties were required to fully explore the system. At a depth of over 300 metres the explorers had just dropped a 32-metre pitch when they encountered a large black void. After belaying another rope they launched themselves into the unknown. A splendid 120-metre abseil took them to the floor of a colossal vaulted chamber, measuring around 100 by 60 metres. By the west wall the Maya River gathered its strength in a wide lake before flowing off into a handsome gallery. The water wound a way between piles of debris and boulder slopes as far as a second, apparently deep lake. An inlet splashed into the middle, sending ripples radiating outwards across the dark water.

This obstacle dictated an acrobatic manoeuvre along the left bank before the explorers could safely continue dry-shod. After a further 100 metres the river-way entered a wide hall, rumbled along the left wall for maybe 100 metres, then slid into a sump pool with a beautiful green appearance. The floor of the chamber angled steeply downwards to the water line. They searched and searched but there seemed little hope of high-level routes to bypass the sump. Arcturus was quite definitely finished and with it too the last New Guinea expedition of the decade.

In February 1989, Rolan Eberhard returned to New Guinea and took up temporary residence in Goroka in the Eastern Highlands Province. The only other known expatriate cavers present in the Highlands at this time were Neil Ryan and an Englishman named Nick Hawkes. The former appeared not to be actively caving, while sometime during the following month Nick and Rolan took a brief look around the Chuave region and explored Kiren Cave. This had previously been looked at in 1978 by two French cavers, Cellerier and Parzybut. Other caves they briefly examined included Lombila sink, Kirowa and Langamo.

About the same time, Rolan and Nick spent some time locating the entrance of Bibima in readiness for a planned descent later that year. Unfortunately the trip never took place due to a vehicle breakdown on the intended day, although at a later date Rolan made a partial solo descent as far as the second pitch.

In October, Rolan joined the ranks of the few cavers who have seen and marvelled at the huge Iaro River Cave. He took with him Tony Wrightson, a keen kiwi bushwalker. True to form the journey there by road turned into an epic, and although they eventually made it, an early introduction to bush village politics prevented them from entering this promising efflux. With this trip cave exploration in New Guinea was concluded for the 1980s.

The entrance porch of the Chevelure de Bérénice resurgence.

Chapter Eleven

RECORD DEPTH FOR MURUK

During Christmas 1990, a small Belgian group visited a region to the south of the Muller Range in the Southern Highlands province. Two areas interested them, one to the northeast of the Karius Range and a second located slightly east. Pre-trip research revealed many caves in the latter area, but only two were descended but were found blocked at around 50 metres. Although the surface indications were encouraging, further exploration was curtailed on account of a tribal war raging in the vicinity. Combined with illness among the team, this prevented them reaching another perhaps more promising area centred on the Emama Valley, a site examined only once before when cavers Bruce Unger, from the US, and Rob Kay, from England, passed through in 1978.

In April and May of 1993, the French were once again in Papua New Guinea, but this time on a venture jointly organised by Richard Maire and Jean-François Pernette. This eight-man reconnaissance expedition had the remote Great Papuan Plateau as its objective. This is situated in the Gulf Province and extends from the 2,500-metre-high Bosavi Volcano southeast as far as the Kikori Delta. With over 5,000 square kilometres of tangled rain forest, the plateau is completely unexplored and represents one of the last remaining wild places on earth.

Aerial photographs of the plateau revealed a typical karst landscape with many depressions, pockmarked to such an extent that it invites comparison with the lunar surface. Standing out amid this profusion of craters was one colossal doline, which the French called the Gouffre Darai. This measured at least one kilometre in diameter and had an estimated depth of 600 metres, calculated by Paul Courbon from aerial photographs and the angle of the sun at the time of day the photograph was taken. Reaching and exploring this feature was high on the French list of priorities.

The 1993 expedition was a marked departure for the French, who with great success had up to then almost exclusively concentrated their efforts in the karst massifs of New Britain. Back in the 1970s the geographer Professor Williams predicted that the Darai Plateau might harbour a cave to rival the World's longest, but the French soon found that if such a system existed it was to remain elusive. Maybe it was the remoteness of the plateau, or perhaps its savage surface topography; either way they would discover that the plateau was uncomfortably different from the relatively friendly forests of New Britain.

On April 4, the team arrived at Port Moresby's Jackson Airport for a six-week stay in the country's forested heartland. Accompanying Richard and François were Georges Marbach (Jo to his friends), Michel Letrône, Marc Tainturier, Thierry Durantel, Luc-Henri Fage and Jean-Paul Sounier, seasoned veteran of New Guinea caving expeditions.

Flying by Twin Otter, they eventually touched down at Kuri on the banks of the Turama River, which flows from there to the Gawai Mouth on the Gulf of Papua. In Kuri they met Steve Linnel, boss of a locally based forestry company. It was a fortuitous meeting, for the loan of a 4x4 vehicle allowed the team to transport itself and two tonnes of supplies to a base immediately below the southwestern fringe of the plateau. Here they established their camp beside the clear-running Hawoi River, a tributary of the Turama.

Base construction was completed three days later and everyone was as acclimatised as could be given the high temperature and near 100-percent humidity. The team spent a few days picking its way through the matted forest in search of caves. Though travel on foot was no easy matter, it was in fact a walkover by comparison to what they would soon experience. When they found the Hawoi resurgence, a stream with an estimated flow of five cumecs was cascading from a beautiful cave mouth and dashing off downhill between cliffs, eventually to join the Turama.

At first sight the Hawoi resurgence promised extensive cave development, yet reality did not quite match expectations. An idyllic entrance fringed with luxuriant growths led them into a wide river passage and the unknown. Unfortunately the passage terminated abruptly in a deep, blue-green sump pool a mere 50 metres from the entrance. The same occurred with other outflows in the vicinity: all welled up from sumps a short distance from daylight. Shafts too, simply failed to deliver the goods, all terminating in boulder chokes: some wondered whether they should have returned to New Britain.

A STRANGE SAFARI

The first sorties onto the Great Papuan Plateau were enlightening. The Darai Doline was at least 18 kilometres due north of base camp, but centred in what proved to be a green hell devoid of all tracks, habitation and drinking water. On their first day out, the cavers barely managed to progress 450 metres. Every step of the way had to be hacked from a forest more like a fakir's sleeping board – hazardous pinnacle karst swathed in jungle creepers and mosses. Indeed, every tree trunk and liana, all living things, were armed with spines and stings. Tangled vines formed unseen snares and vicious bees attacked with the least provocation. There were countless ants and venomous snakes too numerous for comfort. In short, it was a tropical nightmare.

The next day was little better. Abandoned by their Papuan guides, who simply refused to enter the living purgatory, the scratched and battered group gained an altitude of only 400 metres. In fact, after eight days of thrashing through the bush, they had barely gained four kilometres. The jungle was fighting back! By April 12, it was patently clear that with their current snail's pace it would take at least another month to reach the huge doline, if they were ever to locate it within the dense forest. There had to be a change of strategy.

The leaders decided to have four people air-lifted to the doline by helicopter, no mean feat considering the lack of a safe landing site. In a risky manoeuvre the daring Kiwi pilot held his craft dangerously close to the highest treetops above the rim of the doline. First out onto the skids was Jean-Paul, who calmly fixed his descender to a rope and slid gingerly the dozen metres or so to the jungle canopy, to be promptly swallowed by the chaos of vines, bamboos and forest giants beneath. Luc-Henri followed with camera and a helmet radio. Once on the ground he barely managed to marshal his thoughts and equipment in time to film the three sacks of supplies kicked out of the chopper by Georges. The air-lift was a hazardous operation skilfully performed. The rope was released by remote control and the pilot turned his helicopter to the south.

Jean-Paul and Luc-Henri had an hour in which to create a makeshift helipad before the chopper returned bearing Richard, Georges and the remainder of their supplies. However, to their discomfort they realised that their one axe remained in Richard's sack. Armed only with machetes the two of them set to work like madmen. The clearing was barely prepared in time when a flock of disturbed cockatoos announced the arrival of their team-mates. Hovering close to the trees surrounding the hastily prepared glade, the pilot held his machine stationary while Richard cast out the remaining bags and with Georges jumped out into the clearing. In a matter of seconds the helicopter had vanished and silence reigned: the group faced four isolated days in a landscape quite unlike anything they had imagined.

After establishing a camp on the edge of the doline they cut their way down the steep sides of the cavity. Deeper and deeper they went into a strange world of giant tropical flowers, interlocking vines, epiphytic plants, moss-bearded trees and weird arborescent growths. But it was not the lush vegetation that excited Richard most. Any juxtaposition of karst topography and volcanism is guaranteed a unique situation, and with the dormant Bosavi Volcano only 40 kilometres to the northwest of the plateau, the Darai Doline was to be no exception.

Exploration of the doline floor took three days and revealed a circular vertical fault, or dike. Inside this, the bottom of the cavity was composed of limestone blocks the size of houses. These were actively degrading into dangerous, tottering pinnacles. The scene before them resembled a gigantic conglomerate where breakdown was in places cemented together with hydrothermal concretions. Being a geomorphologist, Richard was in his element and his curiosity was piqued. Examining rock samples, chipping a bit of rock here, a little there, he decided there was something decidedly unusual about the place.

Richard was soon unearthing clues that had him questioning the origin of megadolines. His doubts were vested in the discovery of volcanic outcrops and blocks of hydrothermal calcite. It soon became clear from these that the vast size of the doline could only be explained by large-scale chemical breakdown and solution of the limestone caused by acidic fluids, possibly heated by magma, rising from depths of between 6 to 10 kilometres within the earth's crust.

With a calculated volume of around 150 million cubic metres, the Darai Doline is without doubt the largest known karst cavity on Earth (see fig. 5). This fact is all the more momentous due to the discovery of its volcanic origin, and it would radically change current thinking on the geomorphology of doline formation. Moreover Richard had an interesting notion: because of the circular volcanic intrusion, might the Darai Doline simply be the top of a huge pothole filled with breakdown to a depth of one, possibly even two kilometres? This was something to whet the imagination as the time came to return to base. Perhaps Jules Verne was not far off the mark with his inspired novel *Journey to the Centre of the Earth*.

Back at camp Michel, Jo and Marc left for France, leaving a depleted team of five to explore an area upstream along the Hawoi River. In a 10-hour voyage by motorised dugout canoe they eventually located a cave known as Burufi. A Papuan who had once lived in a nearby abandoned village had reported this to the cavers. Although locals had described it as extensive, the stream cave was explored to an impenetrable boulder collapse only 300 metres from the entrance. A pothole above provided a second entrance via a 70-metre drop.

After the departure of Jean-François, the four remaining headed off down the Turama River to where from the air a river had been seen emerging from a blind canyon. Unable to investigate this due to uncooperative tribesmen, they continued by dugout to the river's mouth, then back up the Kikori river before flying out to Port Moresby.

From a caving standpoint the results of the 1993 expedition were disappointing; however, the exploration of the Darai Doline was a unique experience with a surprising scientific outcome. Two more years would pass before another large expeditions returned to Papua New Guinea.

VOLCANO THREATENS NAKANAI HOPES

Of the outlying islands only New Britain – with its 15,000 square kilometres of doline karst – and the Lelet Plateau on New Ireland offer cavers the chance of winning the caving jackpot. Indeed, after the disappointments of the Great Papuan Plateau, another French team led by Jean-Paul Sounier returned to the Nakanai Mountains with every intention of hitting the big time.

In a 1992 edition of *Spelunca* the FFS presented a resume of its newest project for New Britain, and in this Jean-Paul set out to recruit a suitably experienced team from within his circle of caving associates. Under the banner "Hemisphere Sud, Objectif Premier -1000" the principal expedition objective was to dive the terminal sump of Muruk and push the cave to greater depth, hopefully linking it with the as yet undiscovered resurgence in the Galowe Gorge. Arcturus Cave and the Southern Cross system also gave hopes of perhaps connecting with Muruk from higher up the mountain.

Following the *Spelunca* article, Jean-Paul soon began receiving phone calls and letters from cavers hoping to join the team. The first of these was Didier Sessegolo, a 30-year old cave diver with a reputation more than equal to the aims of the expedition. His many experiences embraced marathon running and cave diving, along with several sorties within the third sump of the Grotte de La Mescla. A photograph depicting the beautiful terminal sump in Arcturus had fired his imagination. Didier was an ideal recruit.

On June 4 Michel Philips contacted Jean Paul. Michel was another experienced man in flooded caves and also had many successful dives under his belt, notably in the Picos de Europa of Spain and within the resurgences of Port-Miou and Bestouan. He was a member of the CRPS (Research Centre for Cave Diving) and was some three years older than Didier.

Almost before he knew it Jean-Paul had a rapidly growing roll call of people wishing to become part of the expedition. Later, on his return from a photographic trip to Corsica, Jean-Paul received a letter from Philippe Hache, a specialist in deep cave systems who had been to the Cigalère and Spain's Sistema del Trave (-1,445 m). Another hopeful was Jean-Paul Blancan, a 42-year old professional diver who had sought his adventures by travelling down the Zaïre River and following the Amazon from its source to the sea. Jean-Paul was introduced to the embryo team as a possible assistant cameraman for the filming crew.

In no time at all the team had expanded into a seventeen-strong group possessing a constellation of experiences in countries as far flung as China, Irian Jaya, Zaïre, Pakistan, New Zealand, Mexico, Peru and Borneo. The team was soon augmented by the addition of Marc Tainturier and Luc-Henri Fage, both of whom had accompanied Jean-Paul Sounier on the 1993 expedition. The eventual make-up of the team included Thierry Baritaud, Pascal Clémot, Hélène Darrieutort (nurse), Fabien Hobléa, Monika Kozlowska (nurse), Guilhem Maistre (a resident of New Caledonia who had participated in the 1988 Galowe Plateau expedition), Christian Tamisier, Denièle Vanhove, the Australian caver Al Warild, and doctor Jacques-Henri Vallet.

Throughout 1993 and late 1994, expedition planning gathered momentum. Then as the projected departure from France approached, Jean-Paul received a fax message from Australia on

September 22, in which Al Warild enquired of planning progress and mentioned almost as an aside that conditions in Rabaul were grim.

Just four days prior to Al's message a series of earth tremors, registering Force Six on the Richter scale, had initiated tsunamis along the New Britain coastline. An eruption of Rabaul's nearby volcanoes had been considered imminent and the town quickly put on alert number three. By Monday, September 19, the evacuation of the area was underway when a little after dawn Matupit Volcano began blowing its top, followed at 7:40 a.m. by the neighbouring Vulcan. As the ensuing eruptions spilled lava down the mountains towards the sea, millions of tonnes of ash and clouds were projected 20,000 metres into the atmosphere, blacking out the sky to the west and southwest or town.

This was a bitter blow for the French team, for it meant they would have to consider using another port of entry for trans-shipping vital supplies, the only possible points being either Kimbe or Kokopo. Despite the threatening news the final phase of the expedition was taking shape, generous sponsorship having been offered from Camping Gaz, Spirotechnique, Sigg, Polartec and Tupperware. The FFS offered its support, the Duchess of Bourgogne had agreed to be patron and Luc-Henri was offered a filming contract with the Gédéon Society.

Sponsorship notwithstanding, at the end of the day each participant was obliged to contribute to the gross budget by 26,000 francs (£ 2,600 sterling). The high personal cost and the problems caused by the volcanic eruptions were, however, just the beginning of their difficulties. These transpired to included an expensive bond for their three month temporary entry permit, exorbitant import duties on their supplies, and seemingly endless red tape and customs problems.

On December 13, Flight PX010 from Hong Kong landed at Port Moresby and out stepped Jean-Paul Sounier to be greeted by Brendan Coombs, an Australian who he had first met during the 1993 expedition. Brendan was joint manager for an industrial equipment company and a distributor for Bauer compressors, one of which Brendan helped secure and deliver for the use of the cave divers. He also arranged the loan of a radio and placed his apartment, office, telephone and secretary at Jean-Paul's disposal for expedition use. Jean-Paul spent a week in the PNG capital making several other useful contacts.

Thanks to the services of the expedition's on-site agent, Wari Vele, custom formalities were completed and the Utilus 10 compressor was safely en route for the port of Lae. Contact was made with the French Ambassador, newspapers and TV. On December 20, Jean-Paul was joined by Hélène, Monika, Jean-Paul Blancan, Marc and Luc-Henri. Guilhem arrived the next day. After another day recovering from jetlag the seven cavers headed for Lae, an interesting flight giving superb views of the precipitous Huon Peninsula.

Upon landing they were astounded by a series of logistical and administrative difficulties. These delays led some to believe that perhaps they might never reach their ultimate destination. Indeed they were able to see in the New Year before any departure for New Britain was possible. Their troubles were soon compounded by the delayed arrival of some of their equipment from Port Moresby. However, after Wari presented the necessary custom documentation everything seemed to be in order.

Finding a suitable boat to ship the expedition to New Britain proved frustrating. The *Waghi* was chartered, but the ship was then forbidden to sailing for safety reasons. Further delays ensued. On January 2, Hélène, Luc-Henri, Jean-Paul Blancan, Guilhem and their leader departed for Pomio by helicopter, leaving Marc and Monika in Lae to harass the authorities, chase up

Unloading expedition gear at Pomio.

supplies and await the arrival of the remainder of the team. Another useful liaison was struck up when they met Murray Fletcher. Murray was employed by a local travel company and proved invaluable in helping sort out lingering customs difficulties. Two days later the remainder of the group arrived and at last the grand plan seemed to come together, until they learned that a port workers' dispute had by then paralysed the docks.

On New Britain Hélène, Jean-Paul, Guilhem and Luc-Henri set off with their Papuan porters bound for Muruk, their aim being to clear the site for a helipad near where their new camp was to be built. In the intervening years deforestation had taken its toll of the rain forests. They learnt that from a point on the coast a little to the west of Galowe, one forestry road wound its serpentine course inland for 13 kilometres to an altitude of 1,100 metres. The abandoned village of Mara was a two-hour walk from the road end, and the Muruk entrance a little over four kilometres as the bird flies. The Galowe "bigman" John Kaiopuna offered to act as guide. Using Mara as a halfway bivouac, he found the way with help from old surviving trail markings and information provided from a GPS receiver and compass carried by the cavers.

Meanwhile back on the mainland the aspirations of their companions were simply to reach New Britain. The following day…by a miracle, the strike was over. After several false starts they finally succeeded in hiring a boat at a cost of 5,800 kinas (approximately £ 2,030 sterling) to take them across the Solomon Sea to New Britain.

The -200 tributary, Muruk.

The Milky Way Gallery in Muruk. Water flows in from Acturus, Andromède, Noria
and other caves as yet unexplored.

314

The Galerie Gigante, a large fossil passage in the Arrakis River Cave.

The beautiful sump pool at minus 455 m in Arcturus prevented French explorers from making the postulated connection with Muruk Hul.

A waterfall at -440 m in Arcturus.

Jean-Paul Sounier

Members of the 1995 French team crunching numbers in camp.

Jean-Paul Sounier

Bat skeletons in the Bat's Graveyard, Muruk Hul.

Photo on this and previous page: Jean-Paul Sounier

The bottom of the Visconte shaft at -394 m, Muruk Hul.
Previous page: Waterfall in the Miriel River section of Muruk Hul.

Dawn broke on January 8th as a dozen expedition members gazed longingly across the beam of the 20-ton fishing boat *Langemak*. The mist had thinned to reveal the distant coastline of New Britain, though heavy cloud shrouded the peaks of the island's interior. In another 12 hours they would be at Pomio unloading their supplies and making preparations for the forward march into those very mountains. After two days at sea, everyone was eager to be on *terra firma* and coming to terms with the Nakanai underground.

A pod of graceful dolphins escorted the *Langemak* as it eased the last few hundred metres toward shore, and an air of expectation gripped each caver. They felt a slight shudder as the vessel came alongside Pomio's small pontoon jetty, and a welcome silence ensued as the engines were cut and shore-bound noises of the tropics took over. There to meet the new arrivals was Jean-Paul's group, having just returned to the coast from the high mountains.

The next morning expedition gear was loaded onto a 4x4 and transported into the village courtesy of the District Officer Charles Pinggah. Nine years had passed since the discovery of Muruk and everyone was eager to know whether the terminal sump was passable. Only direct exploration would answer this and many other questions. Could Arcturus and Southern Cross be connected underground? What was the relationship between these systems and the huge Mayang resurgence? The cavers would spend three months in the field trying to address these questions. It was 9:00 in the morning and spirits were high. Muruk beckoned and there was a record for the taking.

While supplies were still delayed in Lae, the cavers set off to locate a site for the new Muruk camp. John offered libation to the spirits to guarantee everyone immunity from evil in the forbidden regions of the forest. The dry valley leading to the entrance of Muruk was eventually located, as was a suitable location for the camp. John and the porters were then paid, and in the midst of a thunderstorm the cavers accompanied them back to the previous day's bivouac. Later that same night the team returned to Pomio with hope that reveille would be announced by the familiar *thwack-thwack-thwack* of the charter helicopter.

At 6:00 a.m., the new dawn greeted Jean-Paul with silence. At 7:30 he strained for the familiar sound of an approaching chopper. Not a sound. At 8:00 a.m. still nothing…then an hour later he received a radio message relayed to them from Tokua where Rabaul's air traffic had been temporarily diverted. Due to rescheduling of flights created by the volcano disaster, the helicopter was unavailable for the time being.

In the short term this was not seen as a great problem. A team could depart on foot to complete the base camp at Muruk. Jean-Paul also suggested that Marc and Fabien cut a track into the Galowe canyon and search for the Muruk resurgence. In 1988, cave discoveries by the French had been named after the principal stars or their constellations, and in keeping with this convention it was suggested that the resurgence cave, if found, should be named *Chevelure de Bérénice* ("Bérénice's Hair") after a fictional star group in a book by Hubert Reeves.

At the last minute it was decided that Luc-Henri and his film crew would join the search for the resurgence. As it happened his team was already in Galowe village so was ideally placed to film Fabien and Marc in their descent of the gorge. On Saturday, January 14, the unwelcome news was received that Islands Aviation could not provide helicopter assistance until at least the twentieth. A council of war was held. Didier and Christian were to trek back to Muruk with as much rope, bolts and associated gear as they could shoulder and begin rigging the cave. Worse, they would have to be satisfied with minimal rations to last them, hopefully, until the airlift could take place. The enforced idleness was maddening to many.

As far as the team heading for the resurgence was concerned, a shortage of provisions would mean they too would have an early return to shore base, and there was understandable rage at so much lost time. Jean-Paul Sounier endured a miserable week in Pomio mooching around the 2.5 tons of stockpiled supplies, tormented by a feeling of helplessness.

Luc-Henri suggested they might ferry everything to the end of one of the new forestry roads then backpack them to the advance camp by cutting a new trail. Some thought this tactic was bound to fail for three reasons. Trying to find Muruk in the forest from a new direction would be like searching for a needle in a haystack, and travelling in lowland forest regions was at best extremely difficult – Jean-Paul's experiences of 1988 convinced him that the long detour via Mara would be preferable to any attempt at short cuts. Lastly, their supplies in total equated to around 150 porter loads. With ten carriers and a three-day minimum turnaround, not including rest days, it would still have taken over a month to shift the whole load up to camp. There was also the additional problem of transporting heavier equipment like the compressor and dive bottles.

Jean-Paul was still gravely considering their predicament when he was disturbed by the return of Marc and Fabien. They had discovered a large resurgence but were unable to reach what was thought to be an open cave entrance. While some continued to sort out the transport difficulties a small team returned to the canyon to try forcing a way into the cave. With little success, and out of rations, they too returned to Pomio on January 19th. At six the next morning the welcome sound of a helicopter promised that at last exploration of Muruk might begin in earnest.

After innumerable frustrating delays the airlift was finally completed, with nine rotations costing a total 44,000 francs, twice the original estimate. The full team was at last stationed at its new camp, at 1,480 metres altitude in the heart of the Nakanai Mountains. After so many years had passed, Jean-Paul was overcome with emotion at reacquainting himself with the entrance to the cassowary cave. Would his hopes of a depth record be vindicated? Using a GPS, initial investigations showed that the new Galowe resurgence was 200 metres lower than was originally thought probable. They realised then that Muruk had every chance of exceeding a depth of 1,000 metres.

Christian and Didier had made slow progress rigging downstream in the Miriel River passage. Though it was a beautiful streamway, the rock for the most part had proved friable and anchor bolts frequently pulled loose under load. They were surprised also by the volume of water, but with a temperature of 18 degrees Celsius, it nevertheless made the cave quite sporting! The newcomers were at once impressed by the size and beauty of Muruk. After three more rigging trips the awe-struck team finally stood at the impasse of 1985, the sump at -637 metres. It had taken 1,200 metres of rope to come this far!

In the Galowe canyon, the team installed a climbing route and traversed into the cave they had previously anticipated, exploring it upstream to a high point of +60 metres. The cave continued...

SUMP…WHAT SUMP?

On the day of the intended dive Didier Sessegola was confined to camp with an infection, so it was decided that Michel Philips would have the honour. The plan was for Luc-Henri to film the dive while Hélène and Monika, where possible, would act as support team at the dive base. At 10 a.m. on Thursday, January 26 the "support" team entered the cave some four hours after the diver and his sherpas. Everyone in the early team was bearing heavy packs, and passing the many plunge pools, cascades, traverses and pitches would prove taxing. For this reason,

The sump at -637 in Muruk, which stopped the members of the 1985 French expedition.

those in the film crew anticipated they would catch up with the first team by the time they reached the sump.

Five hours after entering the system, the diving team grouped in the Elmira Chamber just 200 metres from the sump. Equipment was meticulously laid out and double-checked, the function of demand valves and cylinder pressures verified. The atmosphere was electric. Jean-Paul, Thierry and Philippe assisted Michel while he methodically kitted up and, bearing two 9-litre Spirotechnique tanks and twin Nordic regulators, he cautiously submerged in the sump pool, laying a 3-mm safety line.

After watching the final flick of fins as Michel disappeared into the gloom, his companions settled down to await his return. Due to bad timing the film crew arrived an hour later. By then Thierry and Didier were both asleep and acetylene lamps were turned down to a mere glimmer to conserve carbide supplies. All was silent but for the chattering of the stream beneath the lofty ceiling. Jean-Paul was running all the possibilities through his mind: did the cave continue beyond the sump or had their friend met with a lonely fate? The tension was palpable. Should someone return to the surface for spare tanks so at least a rescue attempt could be launched? Another hour slipped silently by...

In fact, Michel had with some surprise passed the sump at the first attempt. The dive had attained a depth of only seven metres and surfaced in a wide-open passage after 60 metres length. While those back at the dive base passed the time nail biting or in fitful slumber, their companion was having the time of his life.

After two and a half anxious hours, they noticed a different sound as air bubbles broke the surface of the pool. Everyone was instantly alert to see a dull underwater glow marking the diver's return. Surfacing, an agitated Michel could barely wait to tear off his mask and valve before reporting how he had strolled in wonder down huge river passages. One of them, the impressive Thurecht Gallery, simply increased in size at every bend. Though he had been overcome by the moment, he had realised his companions would be worried and reluctantly turned back where the passage grew to even larger proportions at the Murray Fletcher Junction (see fig. 30).

It was clear that Muruk was merely a tributary into a much more important system, for in the huge vaulted cavern the Muruk stream was joined by the stronger Tuonela River at a depth he estimated to be 870 metres. Jean-Paul was jubilant. With a depth of only six metres, the sump was considered a minor obstacle and clearly the path to the magical 1,000-metre depth was wide open. By 2 a.m. Friday everyone was back in camp in an ebullient mood.

Later that day preparations went ahead for the second dive. Due to ailments both Christian and Didier were momentarily out of the equation. Michel was again to be the lead diver, this time accompanied through the sump by Philippe and Jean-Paul. The following day Fabien and Marc returned to Mara village en route to join Jacques-Henri and Guilhem, who four days earlier had begun the systematic exploration of Bérénice Cave. Early Saturday evening heavy rain began falling and very soon had filled the dry valley leading to Muruk's entrance. By midnight however, the downpour had stopped and water levels fell back to normal.

On the morning of Sunday, January 29, the second diving team entered the cave. Four more tanks were portered to the site but only of four-litre capacity since the sump was both short and shallow by cave diving standards. With a maximum pressure of 240 bars each these were considered adequate to safely carry out four return dives at that depth. Thierry was to accompany the team as far as the sump, but only as sherpa. Additional regulators, four diving suits, spare lamps, sleeping bags and rations were also carried down the cave.

By lunchtime they had reached Elmira Chamber. The sound of the river seemed much louder, an impression perhaps enhanced by the acoustics of the large chamber. After a while Philippe pointed out that the river had indeed risen a metre. He placed a marker on a nearby rock so they could better judge what the water level was doing. It was 6:00 p.m.

After waiting impatiently for another hour they decided to go ahead despite the higher water levels. Pre-dive preparations were made. When all was ready Michel set off into the sump but returned before too long to announce that the increased water flow had reduced visibility to no more than 40 centimetres. Thierry expressed his admiration for their devotion to speleology, wished the divers good luck, and returned to the "comfort" of the Elmira Chamber.

Philippe had already dived. Jean-Paul awaited the OK signal from Michel and submerged, followed soon afterwards by his companion, each firmly gripping the line tracing the right-hand side of the underwater passage. Jean-Paul found himself a little over buoyant and experienced difficulty progressing along the tunnel. To gain the necessary depth, he used his left hand to pull himself downwards and forward, while keeping a tight hold of the line with his other hand. He swam on slowly and clumsily, unclear quite how far he had progressed, and not knowing how much further yet he had to go. To his ears his exhaust bubbles seemed to escape almost explosively.

The more he scraped along the ceiling the more certainly he had to pull himself along the submerged archway. The first shocks on his demand valve were not reassuring, but by then (though he was unable to see) he sensed that he was gradually rising. Suddenly the visibility improved. To his left he noticed the beams from his lamps reflecting back as in a mirror, sure indication that a water surface was close. With relief he surfaced a few seconds later. Philippe was grinning on a nearby rock. Jean-Paul could see immediately that Muruk had regained its handsome proportions, the continuing gallery being 10 metres wide and half as high with a floor littered with boulders of assorted sizes.

Each removed his diving gear and safely stashed it in a higher corner of the gallery. Surveying equipment was sorted and checked; all thoughts of rushing off to explore new ground had to be pushed aside until the passages Michel had found was properly mapped. They pushed on downwards with the combined flow, following the swollen river through more lofty galleries and chambers with an average width and height of 20 metres. In places the passage displayed a perfect semi-circular section. They entered a huge chamber and then followed down smaller passages.

They explored another kilometre marked by deep canals or traverses rigged above the water. Where they encountered more turbulent sections of the river-way, the occasional fortuitous dry oxbow allowed safe bypass. At length they found themselves in a huge hall at least 40 metres wide and over 100 metres in length. On the right a slope of boulders reared up towards a ceiling that remained beyond the range of their lamps. The continuing passage then became a 20-metre diameter tunnel where boulder floors were an ever-present obstacle demanding care and unerring concentration.

THE MIRROR OF GALADRIEL

Still tracing the Galadriel River, they were forced to negotiate innumerable traverses, *marmites*, cascades, climbs and scrambles. At an estimated depth of 847 metres they debouched into a colossal hall where a rumbling in the distance announced that battle with the natural elements was far from over! A wind accompanied the dull roar. At the base of a 3-metre climb they decided to finish mapping for the day, using a large boulder as an obvious survey station. Very soon they discovered the source of the rumbling when their passage was joined by a much larger river feeding in from the right. Murray Fletcher Junction was dominated by a beautiful round lake some 15 metres in diameter into which the new river plummeted 8 metres. Michel proposed the pool be called the Mirror of Galadriel and the continuing river-way was called the Tuonela after the kingdom of the dead in a Finnish mythical saga.

In Tolkein's *The Lord of the Rings* the Lady Galadriel asked the wondrous Frodo and Sam what it was they would wish to see in her magical mirror. Perhaps wishing for such a portent beside his "mirror," Jean-Paul vested his dreams in marching all the way through Muruk to the resurgence. Reflections of the cavers' lamps in the beautiful pool could not convey to them what lay ahead, but with luck and through exploration their hopes would be fulfilled.

And speaking of the resurgence, there was still the question of whether the Bérénice resurgence was indeed the destination for the Muruk River. For this very reason two kilos of fluorescein powder was introduced into the river at precisely 2:12 a.m. As the bright green colour diffused downstream, they hoped that Fabien's team in the canyon had succeeded in placing the activated charcoal detectors in the resurgence.

After peering once more into the depths of Galadriel's Mirror they rushed triumphantly off into the unknown. Only 100 metres from the major junction the cavers came across a small shingle bank that they thought would make an adequate bivouac. By then it was 2:30 a.m. so camp was established and a meagre meal taken. While waiting for the brew water to boil everyone recalled the magnificent adventure the cave had so far provided, each wondering what the next day would bring. By 3:00 a.m., they were in their survival bags taking a welcome nap.

Traversing the river in Muruk Hul at -865 m.

After a fitful sleep they were up by eight the next morning, eager to be off down the new passage. After a hastily consumed breakfast they kitted up and were soon following the left bank of the Tuonela, by then well beyond the limit reached by Michel during his lone reconnaissance. Very soon the river was channelled into a narrow cleft where the current was far too fierce for safe progress. The alternative was an apparently featureless wall. Well…? Philippe found one possible route through the large chamber that was at least 50 metres high. An unstable boulder slope led steeply upwards from the left bank of the river, but to overcome this the self-confidence of a seasoned climber was necessary. They returned to the Thurecht Gallery to consider their options and search for alternative routes.

By negotiating large boulders littering the bank of the river they gained the foot of a 45-degree slope covered in calcite and sand, and after about 50 metres descended again to the water's edge. The continuing bank was very steep, but being determined they reached a ledge about six metres above the river with a blank wall extending above them into blackness. The traverse was tricky for only three metres, but they found solace in a bolt Michel had placed, and the few handholds provided by fissures in the rock. Another anchor drilled in the opposite wall aided the successful river crossing just before the canyon ahead widened in a series of white-water chutes.

At length they reached the end of the large chamber and entered a 20-metre-high and wide continuation. For a while they made excellent progress, following the cave down a northeast trend. They bypassed a lake along its right-hand shore, then easier caving followed as they progressed optimistically from boulder to boulder. A beautiful waterfall bounced seven metres down the left wall from some secretive inlet. They explored another large chamber and came across a 20-metre diameter tunnel that merged 70 metres ahead into yet another widening. Here the Tuonela River tumbled over and among gigantic, pockmarked boulders that all but filled the passageway.

Just when they were becoming accustomed to relatively easy progress Muruk cast another gauntlet at their feet. An immense boulder pile extended upwards to unknown heights on one side, while a seemingly featureless wall overhung them on the opposite. Ahead the river was a seething cataract where it squeezed through a narrowing trench. The light from their lamps was unable to penetrate to the foot of the fall, so opting to try the left side of the passage, Philippe made a tentative attempt on the wall. At the same time Michel returned a little way upstream to see if they had missed anything. When he returned Philippe had gained a roomy ledge.

Michel joined his friend and together they traversed easily to a point where a vicious narrowing of their ledge demanded protection. Placing a bolt, Philippe advanced cautiously along the tiny shelf as far as the top of a slope where he fixed another bolt. At that point Jean-Paul caught up with his friends, attached himself to the rope and took the lead. He shuffled along with care since the few available holds were liberally covered in sand. Gaining a wide shelf he continued a further 40 metres before dropping to the crest of a boulder slope 10 metres below. Joined here by Michel and Philippe they dropped a further 10 metres to find their wall had merged with the continuing narrow canyon. The river at this point was wild. "Where to now?" they all thought.

By chance they could just make out a small gallery at a higher level. To reach this they built a "staircase" by stacking rocks against the wall, and thereby gained the threshold of the passage. Peering over the lip, Michel shouted back that the passage continued. They helped each other up into the tunnel and traced its dry wastes for 30 metres, hoping it might bypass the river-way. Alas their hopes were quickly dashed in a comprehensive boulder choke. The continuing river was, for the moment out of the question, so reluctantly they made their return to the sump, mentally calculating that the magical 1,000-metre depth was now within their grasp.

They ate while they psyched themselves up for the return dive. Philippe then led off with Michel bringing up the rear. Visibility was still practically zero. Once the water barrier was behind them they had still to face 3,500 metres of strenuous caving to the entrance and camp comforts. They picked up Thierry who had been waiting patiently for them in the Elmira Chamber and, after spending 26 hours underground, finally emerged to the aromas of the damp jungle.

Since the cavers' arrival in the mountains the spirits, it seemed, had been angered despite the peace offerings made by their guide John Kaiopuna. Philippe became the latest victim, a white spot on his knee turning into an impressive swelling. Despite his problem he decided he would accompany Marc, Jacques-Henri and Thierry in portering supplies and additional ropes down Muruk for the final push. But by the time they reached the Visconte Shaft, the pain in Philippe's knee had become too much and he was forced to exit.

Jean-Paul was surprised by the number and frequency of medical problems afflicting the team. Since the beginning, there had always been at least two team members incapacitated through illness or injury. To make matters worse, four people had already returned to France. A team of four was placed on stand-by for the push trip, the selection of which would not prove too difficult given the team's reduced numbers: Didier, Thierry, Michel and their leader were to have the honour.

Before the day of the push, they spent some time at Mara village where they learnt from Fabien's resurgence team that the dye test had proved positive. The rapid transit time suggested that in the unexplored section of cave more open passages could be expected. Little did they realise quite how wild the unknown river-way would prove to be. Cavers in Bérénice Cave had explored 800 metres to +104 metres. Initially frustrated by an impressive 12-metre high waterfall, the Cascade Infernale, they had overcome this impasse only after the climbers in the group had drilled and placed 16 expansion bolts in a superb display of determination. When they returned to the surface the cave was still heading into the mountain.

During the dusk walk back from Mara to Muruk camp, bad luck struck once again. In what seems to be a recurring theme where expatriates and bush knives are concerned, Didier inflicting a deep cut in his knee while crossing a ravine. At first, this incident appeared to put Didier out of the push down Muruk, but the lack of other suitably fit and healthy candidates meant that he would descend anyway.

THROUGH THE BAT'S GRAVEYARD

The day of the final push arrived on February 7th. The gear was readied, and after a leisurely breakfast the rising temperature and humidity forced the decision to move by 10 a.m. A half-hour later Didier Sessegola, Michel Philips, Jean-Paul Sounier and Thierry Baritaud descended with 15-kilo packs, including rations to last them three days. With their growing familiarity with the passages they descended almost by auto-pilot, and after 20 hours continuous caving they were gathered at the sump.

The dive proceeded without any difficulties and soon they were back at the ledge reached by the previous team. Didier set off rigging for 80 metres along a miscellany of non-continuous shelves, finally regaining the river at a deep lake. The first attempt to pass this obstacle was repelled. They decided then to camp in the dry gallery found on the previous trip, and the next day use this as the springboard from which to push on downstream.

After breakfast they were quickly back at the water's edge, determined that exploration would only stop when the very last piece of equipment had been used. Altogether they had 250 metres of rope, 50 metres of Kevlar cord, some tape slings and associated bits of equipment, snap-rings, anchors, etc.

Didier loped off downstream with Michel and Jean-Paul following on, surveying. Thanks to Didier they skilfully passed the deep lake without taking a ducking. Beyond this, they bypassed a series of whitewater rapids by way of a ledge on the right side of the passage. Their jubilation was short-lived though, for in a 5 to 8-metre wide section the river leapt impetuously from water chute to chute, forming an angry maelstrom. To proceed in the water was suicidal. The solution was simple but very exposed.

A series of "thin" ledges provided an entertaining traverse, which they successfully protected with a combination of natural belays and judiciously placed anchor bolts. This gained them a few precious metres. Didier by this time was 20 metres ahead of his companions, and the staccato *clink, clink, clink* of the bolting hammer was barely audible above the roar of the river below them.

For some way ahead progress followed in a similar fashion, exposed traverses alternating with the occasional fortuitous shelf. Down to their last 150 metres of rope, they negotiated exposed ledges high above river level. Then Michel discovered 300 metres of small, well-decorated passage (The Shunt) at roof level. As luck would have it, this allowed them to bypass as many metres of rather frenzied river-way. The passage led them finally to a small chamber with a ceiling strewn with slender stalactites. Piercing the floor at this point was a circular 22-metre drop, below which they again heard the river.

In the chamber at the top of the new shaft they discovered several bat skeletons, some partially calcited in situ. Elsewhere Thierry found a dead flying fox. Jean-Paul was encouraged by these finds for it meant that the cave must surely be open all the way into the Galowe canyon. They named the chamber Cimetière des Chauves-Souris (Bat's Graveyard). At the foot of the pitch they found themselves back with the main flow in a gallery 20 metres high and almost as wide. Each was mentally calculating that they must be approaching the magical depth figure: victory was close at hand.

They negotiated more turbulent sections of the river, but before long they left the noise of rushing water behind as they stepped into a slightly smaller passage to the right. They were now unexpectedly following a smaller stream. They passed a beautiful waterfall, the Cascade Probabiliste, and in the Gallerie Mais où Sommes-Nous (But Where are We? Gallery) were soon forced to swim two lakes of about 20 metres each. Thierry, who was in front, shouted back "I found a pitch!"

"How deep?" asked Jean-Paul

"I don't know. It doesn't seem deep."

Standing on the lip their lamps stabbed optimistically at the dark void. Didier was first to the bottom followed by Jean-Paul, Michel and Thierry. In fact the drop was 40 metres and landed them on the edge of a pool in Moria, a large chamber rising up into a lofty aven on its east side. Upstream was well decorated in places, while in the opposite direction the small brook tinkled down a steep slope before sprinkling down an eight-metre overhanging wall. Although they could see a small passage taking the stream below, lack of rope dictated the end of exploration in that direction. With soot from his acetylene lamp Didier wrote on the wall TERMINUS 95.

Back at the foot of the 22-metre pitch they traced the main river through a labyrinth called the Gruyère as far as a very wet 20-metre drop, over which the two to four cubic metres of river tumbled with an angry roar. For a while they gazed longingly into the mysterious depths before turning back for the entrance. They estimated that by then they had reached the depth of 1,141 metres, and had definitely surpassed that of New Zealand's Nettlebed Cave. The cave showed no signs of ending but due to a shortage of rope and time, their unbelievable good fortune for the time being was curtailed. They surfaced after having spent 58 hours underground.

Further trips followed. On February 12, Luc-Henri led a filming expedition as far as the sump. Three days later most of the team had to return to France, leaving Jean-Paul, Didier, Philippe, Pascal, and Danièle. In a further intervention by malign spirits an unfortunate accident on February 21 resulted in both Jean-Paul and Philippe being burned badly by petrol; two days later they were evacuated by helicopter. They spent a whole week in Kimbe hospital recovering from their ordeal, and as a result the remaining expedition time was rescheduled. No more trips were made beyond the sump in Muruk, although elsewhere in the system another kilometre of passage was discovered. Photographic trips wound up the expedition for 1995.

Three years of eager preparations resulted in the 1998 return that the FFS cavers had promised themselves when standing in Moria, the dark chamber terminating Muruk. The expedition once again fielded a very experienced team. In addition to the sixteen French speleologists, the group included the Spaniard Enrique Ogando-Lastra, Belgians Jean-Claude ("Jack") London, Alain Grignard and cave diver Patrick Vanstraelen. An Australian contingent again included Alan Warild, Greg Tunnock and Mark Wilson. The leader was Jean-Paul Sounier, and an even larger diving group was to travel out with them. Together with Patrick this comprised Didier Sessegolo, Thierry Saint-Dizier, Arnaud Guyot and Michel Philips, who had already been through the former terminal sump. The addition of the Australian, Belgian and Spanish contingents imparted an international flavour to the team.

The remaining French participants were Philippe Audra, Thierry Baritaud, Pierre de Coninck, Tristan Despaigne, Georges Marbach, Jérômy Tainguy, Bernard Tourte (Buldo), Corinne Georgeon and Laurent Tondusson. Their medical needs would again be met by doctor Jacques-Henri Vallet and the two field nurses, Hélène Darrieutort and her inseparable friend Monika Kozlowska. The successful filmmaker Roland Théron failed to find a suitable financier to underwrite an expedition film, which in turn resulted in the unjustified fear that it might have a knock-on effect with potential sponsors. More than 30,000 francs was required from each participant and generous sponsorship in both money and equipment was secured from Béal, TSA, Submarine, the Australian Geographic Society, Isotta, Bauer, Spirotechnique and Isotechnic.

The principal aim of this large team was to increase the overall depth of Muruk and making it one of the most exciting through-trips in the world. They intended to dive the terminal sump of Arcturus Cave and hopefully connect the Maya River with the upstream Tuonela, the major inlet in Muruk which Arcturus was believed to feed. They also planned to push the treacherous *Croix du Sud* (Southern Cross) system beyond the limit reached in 1988 and to carry out the first exploration of a large black hole seen in 1985, named the Haricot by virtue of its bean-shaped entrance.

The first of the team to depart left France in early December 1997. Jean-Paul Sounier and Jacques-Henri Vallet arrived in Port Moresby on December 9 to find Hélène Darrieutort already there. Thinking there may still be some lingering logistical setbacks from the 1994 eruption, they were surprised to find that Rabaul harbour had been reopened and their supplies could be routed through the facilities there. In fact the real difficulties didn't begin until their arrival in Galowe on Christmas Day. Attempts to hire porters quickly degenerated into an argument resulting in the local "big men" of the area demanding compensation of 400,000 kinas for access to the mountains. Before the differences were sorted out the heated question of payment had blown up into an aggressive exchange of views involving a schoolteacher from Kokopo, community leaders, forestry workers, a Chinese businessman, the District Officer and the French Chargé d'Affaires for Papua New Guinea. It was finally agreed that the porters would each be paid 8 kinas per day plus food. A week had by then been lost but morale was the highest it had been since their arrival.

The planned departure into the mountains was for December 29. It was about then that they discovered that Cyclone Justine, a side effect of the more comprehensive El Niño weather phenomenon, had wreaked havoc in the forests: bridges had been swept away along the coast and rivers had changed course. Only time would reveal what the consequences were for the underground hydrology.

Finally they departed with six Papuan guides and porters. The trails used three years earlier were all but obliterated as a result of the storm and deforestation by Malaysian logging companies, who were by then working large areas of the mountains. As a consequence it took a great deal longer to locate the entrance to Muruk and Jean-Paul soon regretted not having the benefit of a GPS. The higher they climbed into the mountains the more obvious was the destruction: in places the cavers had to balance precariously along forest giants that had fallen among a tangled melee of scrub and branches. The effects of the storm were visible in every direction.

At last the advance team arrived. The four tonnes of supplies and equipment was brought by helicopter on January 13, and the following day all team members were flown in rather than face

Helicopters were used by the French in 1995 and 1998 to transport gear from Pomio to the Muruk base camp.

the difficult inward march. To avoid having 20 or more people together in the Muruk camp, two smaller satellite camps were established in keeping with other aims. One was established at Mara from which cavers could further explore the *Chevelure de Bérénice,* and a second one conveniently sited to investigate the Haricot Doline. A total of 16 rotations were necessary to complete the airlift.

LE GOUFFRE SAUVAGE

At the outset it took four teams in relays to completely rig Muruk for the big push. The logistics of the latter necessarily dictated a bivouac at minus 854 metres. The first group to penetrate beyond Muruk's sump comprised Jean-Paul Sounier and two of the Belgians, Jack London and Patrick Vanstraelen. They entered the cave on January 21 and again it was a memorable trip through green-blue lakes, huge chambers, past beautiful waterfalls and spectacular river passages. Philippe Hache, Didier Sessegola and Jo Marbach accompanied them to help carry equipment as far as the sump.

The dive proved trouble-free and en route to the "end," dye detectors were placed in the pool at Murray Fletcher Junction prior to a water trace from Arcturus. After a long caving day they finally settled in for the night at the "4-star" bivouac site in The Shunt leading to the Bat's Graveyard. The next day a quick breakfast of muesli preceded an early start at 7:30 a.m. Very soon they had passed through the Gruyère, and Jean-Paul was overcome with excitement: he had waited years for this moment. Before long all three were standing on the edge of the undescended shaft that had stopped them three years earlier. The flames from their lamps gyrated wildly in the terrific draught swirling around the pit.

They thought the apparent abundance of natural belays would make for rapid rigging. Jean-Paul unpacked a rope and some tape slings. A thread belay using two tapes was backed up with a third around a rocky projection. Jean-Paul then set off down through the spray, setting two deviations – the last one on a blade of rock directly over the bottom half of the void – then abseiled into the unknown. After dropping ten metres the pitch demanded some serious thought. It seemed like he was descending into a cylinder of water. After another 3 metres he landed at the bottom without incident but was battered by the gale and drenched by the spray it carried. It was impossible to keep his acetylene lamp alight in the resulting hurricane.

In the glow from his electric back-up lamp he ran downstream almost without regard for his footing in the riverbed. Fortunately the streambed was relatively wide and calm and he had no need to fear the current at that point. Still buffeted by the draught, he fixed a rope through an eyehole and rigged a traverse on a rocky shelf. Like two bedraggled apparitions his companions emerged from the turmoil to join him on the ledge. In an instant the pitch became the *Puits des Revenants* (the Pitch of the Returned Spirits). It signalled the beginning of a much more intimidating stage of the cave, Les Passagers du Vent, on account of the incredible wind that blew along it. There were further surprises to come.

After securing themselves to the traverse line they moved along the wall to a spacious banking. The passage turned slightly to the left beneath a lowering ceiling. Before long the banks gave way to vertical walls dropping into deep water. In an attempt to avoid a wetting they clung to the walls spider-like, but were soon obliged to lower themselves into the river. The roof was by then even closer to the deep green water, and a rhythmic slapping noise ahead suggested they were approaching a sump.

Swimming cautiously forward they suddenly became aware of a muffled rumble. As this became a roar they feared the lake they were in was carrying them toward a deep pitch. Whatever was responsible for the noise was not small. The draught became more of a frenzied wind. Featureless passage sides continued to plunge directly into the lake, but a little way ahead they easily gained the left bank of the passage. Prudence then prevailed for they were clearly heading towards the lip of an abyss.

In front they could see the passage widening, but it would not do to loose a footing and face the consequences of the seething river. The chute of water turned first to the right, then left to become a violent funnel of waves dashing against the ragged walls. At the bottom of the funnel a mass of whitewater foamed against rocks before being swallowed by...well, they were unsure because of the mist-like spray veiling the passage beyond. The effect was both deafening and unnerving. How to proceed was the big question.

The noise and wind made the volume of water falling down the pitch seem doubly awesome. There was no doubt in their minds that Muruk was dealing its ace hand: it was the cave's ultimate barrier in the form of a succession of waves that would ring the death knell for the unwary, the impetuous or the foolhardy. Perhaps it was all three "qualities" that spurred them to action, but what lay ahead? They knew that even as they pondered the obstacle, another team in Bérénice was probably fighting their way upstream to meet them...but what nature of passageways existed in between?

The brief moment of indecision passed, and perhaps motivated by faith, hope and determination they considered their next move. It was no easy decision to make and would have been simpler to just call it a day and return the way they had come, but nothing ventured...

Examining the left wall, it at first sight appeared possible to progress horizontally, then descend from some point further out. Another possibility might have been to descend down the centre of the cataract, but the difficulties would not be diminished, and what of the return? All the holds seemed to disappear further out towards the drop. They vacated their tiny perch but almost immediately were frustrated by a lack of holds. However there was one advantage accompanying the move, for they gained momentary respite from the jet of water ricocheting from the far wall. While Patrick belayed the rope a little upstream Jean-Paul clipped to his harness a miscellany of equipment he thought he might need. He tried in vain to divorce his mind from the difficulties he faced.

Patrick signalled above the noise that the rope was secured and to this Jean-Paul fixed his descender and started moving out. In an instant he was struggling to see the rope through the volume and violence of the water. Pulling himself together he carefully withdrew more rope from the tackle bag slung from his harness, then cautiously moved downwards, installing a rebelay as soon as he could. Aided by these precautions he drew closer to the overflow from the lake, which in his mind's eye he likened to the spout of a giant coffeepot. He was acutely aware that his actions would be the most dangerous moves of the whole trip so far.

In effect Jean-Paul was restrained by the line upstream to which he was fastened through his descender, but for one reason or another he found himself in the swiftest part of the flow with no immediate hope of escaping it! The weight of water was holding him in a dire position. The direction his rope was taking merely compounded his difficulties, reducing his chances of survival: he imagined himself succumbing but banished such a dreary thought to concentrate on his immediate predicament.

Some small foot and handholds caught his eye across on the left-hand wall. These were awash but would enable him to keep his body clear of the worst of the water. He fought his way steadily towards the spot from above but then struggled to find the holds once there. He leaned over at a crazy angle with most of his weight taken by the rope in a crucial move that had him thinking, "one false move and I'm going to drown." Suspended by a single thread, his life literally hung in the balance.

A tiny ledge on the wall no further than two metres below him was level with the overflow from the lake. It disappeared into an overhang and all fissures seemed little more than vertical scratches in the rock. Above, he strained with one arm to reach what he imagined was an eyehole, but which proved little more than a shallow scoop. As luck had it, he located a larger hollow and a possible thread belay. Held by his rope and with a precarious footing, he managed to fix a tape sling through it, then searched urgently for a way to double his security.

At length he succeeded in drilling a hole and fixing an anchor bolt. Reassured, he examined his situation. He found a larger crack and jamming in his right hand as best he could, he installed a length of tape through another thread belay and snapped a carabiner into it. His confidence increased as he transferred his weight to the rebelay. Then taking all his weight on the rope and belays, he let go with both hands and began drilling more bolt holes. The rope in front of him and the spider web of tape slings hindered his movement, but they did at least hold him close to his tenuous perch.

Fixing the spits took several uncomfortable minutes and once more Jean-Paul dwelled on the dangers of making a mistake. With one bolt fixed and an anchor plate in position he clipped into it and was able to relax slightly. However his right leg was cramping up from the constant effort. He was also becoming cold from the infernal wind generated by the waterfall. He cast a reassuring glance at his two anxious friends huddled on their uncertain stance at the far side of the shaft.

Some 50 centimetres from the first bolt he managed to locate a second. He had been a long time in moving toward the overhanging section. At last he secured a third anchor bolt which then enabled him to abseil 2-3 metres to the beginning of the chute. He attempted this move but quickly realised his mistake. To reach the top of the incline he was battered by the waves that licked the walls. His immediate concern was then to backtrack to the relative calm of his previous stance. He knew that to safely progress he must remain clear of the water at all costs.

Trying again, he descended one metre then swung towards the downstream side of the shaft, stretching out at the same time so that he was just able to reach an eyehole. Hanging there a moment allowed him to thread a sling through it, and using this deviation, he abseiled to a point where he could drill yet another bolt. Though he was clear of it, the cascade was bouncing down just a little too close for comfort. The noise was deafening and the draught freezing.

From the new placement he gradually moved obliquely a little downstream clinging to the jagged rock walls eroded by the water. Metre by precious metre he approached a corner closer to the main column of water where the resulting hurricane increased in strength. Another rebelay was found here and, teeth chattering, he let out a few more metres of line from the bag so as not to be restricted in the least by drag when he made his next move. He was still enveloped in spray. While his carbide lamp was working at maximum pressure in a futile attempt to remain alight, his electric backup began functioning in fits and starts. It hadn't worked properly since he had passed through the sump, and flashed on and off like a stroboscope.

He succeeded in overcoming the section exposed to the full fury of the flow, but felt very exposed on the corner. A few metres beneath his feet he could just glimpse the river being swallowed by some unknown tunnel. At the sight of this he realised that the obstacle was all but beaten. Worried by his troublesome electric light he attempted to find another rebelay, but then complete lamp failure plunged him into darkness. In the pale glimmer from his companions' lamps shining down from above, he found and rectified the fault with his electric lamp, and with a new belay fixed he abseiled the last few metres safely to the floor. It had taken him two very tense hours to progress 12 metres down and 20 metres horizontally.

At the base of the Bikbik Wara ("a large volume of water" in pidgin) shaft the team took stock of its surroundings before exploring the relative calm of the continuing river-way. The river flowed swiftly along a roughly circular tube, which they were able to safely follow using convenient ledges above the water. Natural belays allowed the occasional traverse line along the left wall, but they soon reach the end of their last rope. Attached to the final anchor bolt they peered down the river-way. They could not go on without more rope. The river occupied the full width of the passage and was about a metre deep punctuated by swirl holes marked by water of a deeper colour.

The mysterious pathway of unfathomed darkness continued into the unknown. No glimpse of light could be seen ahead of them to suggest they were nearing an exit, no glimmer of lamps from their colleagues was visible downstream. Unfortunately the honour of a connection was not to be theirs, but would be the icing on the cake for the second team into the cave.

Surveying back, they eventually made it to the bivouac site after 18 hours of the most thrilling caving imaginable. They were out of the entrance by mid-afternoon of Friday, January 23, to learn that while down Muruk Buldo and Enrique had overcome the *Cascade Infernale* in Bérénice, having used 200 metres of rope to explore half as much distance. Jérômy and Thierry had followed them and pushed a further 250 metres upstream only to be halted by another waterfall.

While the main group was pushing down Muruk a party of six was actively searching for the Haricot Doline using coordinates worked out while in a chopper three years earlier. These readings were held in doubt once in the jungle since almost a week had by then passed and still there was no sign of the hole. With few days left and all available manpower required for Arcturus, Southern Cross and the Muruk connection, a small sink was eventually located.

The team divided. Philippe Hache and Didier Sessegola explored the hole while the remainder continued searching the surrounding jungle for the Haricot Doline. The passage they were tracing held little interest but to their surprise it suddenly came out into the side of a large black void. Feeble daylight could just be glimpsed at the bottom of the chamber. Descending to the source of the light it dawned on them that by way of a "back door" they had from below in fact found the huge doline they had all been searching for. Unfortunately they had run out of time.

DEPTH RECORD

The three Australians, Greg Tunnock, Mark Wilson and Al Warild, were given the choice of descending Muruk and following on from where Jean-Paul's group had turned around. Travelling in the opposite direction Enrique Ogando-Lastra, Bernard Tourte, Hélène Darrieutort and Michel Philips entered the resurgence and began making their way slowly upstream from the cave mouth.

The Muruk team had been caving long and hard throughout the night and were tired but cautiously traversing high above the rumbling river in a passage four metres wide. They finally used the last of their rope and were about to turn around, when suddenly they thought they could hear voices. At first these were dismissed as figments of the imagination, but while pondering their return upstream they then were in little doubt. A glimmer appeared from around a bend down the passage and shortly they met the Bérénice group heading in the opposite direction. The connection had been forged. It was 21:45 hours on January 25, a time for celebration.

With congratulations exchanged Buldo, Enrique and Michel continued their laborious exit from Muruk, while Hélène returned downstream with the three Australians. The latter team eventually emerged triumphantly from the resurgence into a damp jungle dawn after 20 hours of continuous caving, some 44 hours after entering the top entrance.

Though at the time this could not be verified by reliable surface control, the final depth of the Muruk-Bérénice system was calculated to be 1,128 metres, a little less than the estimate of 1995. Later computations gave a final corrected depth of 1,178 metres. With this the French had completed the exploration of a most beautiful 1,000 metres plus through-trip and Muruk was without doubt ranked among the world's finest cave systems.

By February 12, the expedition pull-out was nearing and as a result, exploration was reaching fever pitch. A choice presented itself: whether or not to split the team to focus some manpower on Arcturus. There was also the vexing question of what happened in the downstream Southern Cross system. Some 1.6 kilometres of new passage had been explored along the Tuonela River upstream of Murray Fletcher Junction, but the greatest surprises occurred in Arcturus. Michel dived the terminal sump and found it to be 90 metres long and 10 metres deep but was halted by a second sump after only 30 metres of open passage. Thierry Saint-Dizier then took up the challenge and passed this second submerged section to reach a third sump. At the outset this formed a descending tube that quickly emerged into a larger space, evidently the top of a large flooded chamber. Though he thought he could see an air surface, the lack of line on his reel forced his return.

Should they concentrate on Arcturus? There were more sumps to negotiate but the increased length and depth of these was an unwelcome surprise. Perhaps a kilometre of new passage remained to be found between Arcturus and the sump terminating the upstream Tuonela, but more flooded sections exist beyond. What about the Southern Cross? This cave was still wide open, still going with a passage five metres high and almost as wide when left in 1988. Did it feed into the huge Mayang resurgence? The possibility of another 1,000-metre deep system, this time carrying a combined flow rate of 20 cubic metres per second, was without doubt one hell of a challenge in anyone's language. With hope of answering this question, the three Australians pushed on down the flood-prone Southern Cross. They explored for 513 metres beyond the 1988 limit and were finally stopped by a sump at a depth of 260 metres.

Picking up the gauntlet, Thierry Saint-Dizier, Jean-Paul Sounier, Philippe Hache and Jérômy Tainguy went down again the next day, packing sufficient gear for one diver to test the sump. During the descent Jean-Paul was impressed by the size of the shafts and passages, but more so by the alarming quantities of washed-in trees heaped up against every bend and restriction. The two 50-metre pitches were especially majestic. Beyond these, the passage continued with a height of 10 metres and half as wide with numerous swirl holes, plunge pools and cascades. But despite its handsome dimensions, Southern Cross was definitely not a place to be caught when the rain was falling.

Without dwelling too long on the incident in question, they silently passed the place where ten years before Serge Fulcrand's party had been caught unawares by a flood pulse. Ahead, the clean-washed streamway eventually lost itself in a large, sombre chamber where mud deposits covered the walls to a height of 10 metres. They found the sump not too far beyond.

Leaving Thierry to kit up, the others began surveying the passages found by their Australian friends. Some time later, they were interrupted by a shout from Thierry. It transpired that the sump was only 2 metres deep and he had emerged after 20 metres into a much wider passage in which he could hear running water ahead. Leaving Philippe and Jérômy to continue mapping, Jean-Paul returned to the sump with Thierry.

A quick decision was made. Because the sump was shallow and quite short they took the calculated risk of sharing the available equipment, one cylinder each, Thierry having the neo-prene top and his comrade the wet suit leggings. Together they submerged and, keeping a close hold of the line, progressed hand-over-hand along the roof of the submerged passageway. Once through they eagerly removed the diving gear and set off to explore. Downstream the widening gallery and approaching noise of a cascade stirred up anticipation. Quickly reaching the source of the noise, they found themselves on the shore of a lake stretching from wall to wall in a chamber maybe 15 metres in diameter. The stream bounced down pale-coloured rocks to the water's edge.

Using their combined lamps they could not make out any continuation at the far side and concluded that the lake was in fact a sump pool. Thierry submerged his lamp into the water and Jean-Paul, divining his friend's thoughts, believed him to be considering a dive. Although Thierry was perhaps the most experienced diver in the group, prudence in the end proved the better part of valour, and so after having found only another 40 metres of virgin cave they returned the way they had come.

In the closing stages of the expedition some other smaller discoveries were made, including two more entrances to Muruk called Neïde and Centaure. The Andromède system, found close to the track between Muruk camp and Arcturus, was thought in all probability to be an inlet into the latter, and was subsequently explored to conclusion at a sump at -169 m.

At last, then, Papua New Guinea had joined the "big cave league," with a secure place on the international caving map. Muruk was not only the deepest cave in the country, but the first system in the southern hemisphere to exceed 1,000 metres. It also represented one of the world's finest through-trips. Though these discoveries may be viewed as a fitting climax to the many difficult years of searching by speleologists, many more questions remain unanswered.

POSTSCRIPT

Two years after the memorable Muruk record a French team once again carried out a reconnaissance in New Britain centred upon two areas recommended by Jean-Paul Sounier. These were the Baraiman Canyon in the Nakanai Mountains and a plateau in the Whiteman Range flanked by the Ayle and Andru rivers to the north of Kandrian township. The group comprised Bruno Fromento, Guilhem Maistre, Patrick Labadie, Gérard Cazes and, mastermind behind the trip, Serge Fulcrand. Both Gérard and Serge were veterans of early New Guinea trips.

Utilising GPS systems and helicopters, they identified caving objectives and evaluated the potential for the year 2001. An area considered most promising was inspected to the northwest of Iombon, where a low-level fly-past pinpointed three deep pits aligned north-south over a distance of 10 kilometres, together with two other promising dolines. Their pilot, Martin Linnix, then took the cavers on a white-knuckle ride along the gorge of the river Ayle in search of likely outflows. The sight of a large resurgence here very nearly paled into insignifance on a flight that aged them ten years with its daring, as the rotor blades whirled so close to vegetation that small branches were pruned!

From the Kandrian zone the cavers moved to East New Britain to examine the plateau flanking the river Ba where this has cut at least 1,000 metres deep into the impressive cleft of the Baraiman Canyon. More chopper induced frights established that resurgences existed both at the foot of the gorge as well as at several levels up its walls. Possible feeders were noted on the plateau above. From the nearest village, Maito, they estimated it would take 12 kilometres of track cutting to gain the heights above the canyon.

Evaluating the findings back in France, the organisers of the reconnaissance decided that the area between the Ayle and Andru rivers would be the theatre of activity for 2001, while the Baraiman Canyon would be targeted the following year. A third expedition planned for 2003 would then, if circumstances required, follow up and capitalise on the discoveries made the year before.

At the beginning of January 2001 a team of eighteen cavers and scientists left France. It was to be the forerunner of a new style of expedition, acquiring all its bulky supplies in Papua New Guinea, taking with it only the specialised caving and climbing gear. The reasoning behind such an approach was that equipment could then be safely stored in the host country for future use by other teams travelling light. They hoped that the new concept based upon lightness would pay dividends once in the field. Each year a new Regional Caving Committee, rather than the FFS, could then arrange its own expedition. Another innovation was the use of an Immarsat satellite phone link with France. Through this means they could relay up-to-the-minute reports of their progress, and update a website specifically set up for this purpose by the FFS.

The team comprised the geomorphologist Hubert Camus, Gérard Cazes, Guillaume Coerchon, Fabrice Fillols, Bruno Fromento, Thierry Gencey, Didier Gignoux, Sebastien Guillot, Philippe

Ratel, Paul Szostak, Pierre Bevengut, Aude Hourtal, Guilhem Maistre, the leader Serge Fulcrand, two medics Raoul Duroc and Jacques Chambard, and two Swiss scientists, archaeologist Roman Hapka and biologist Catherine Perret. Excepting the two Swiss participants, all were members of the FFS and several belonged to French cave rescue teams. Four had previous experience in Papua New Guinea.

The aspirations of this latest expedition were vested in the fact that the extensive Arrakis network of caverns was discovered on the western fringe of the karst plateau they intended to explore this year. This area was in fact only barely investigated in 1985, and again by a small group the following year. It was hoped that on this occasion a similar extensive system might be discovered. In this respect the initial findings were far from encouraging.

Within the first week the previously pinpointed large dolines were found to be completely sealed by boulders. Resurgences too, though they appeared promising from the air, were also blocked by collapse. Disappointed by these results the explorers then began a systematic investigation of sinks and dolines in the vicinity of camp. Again the finds were limited. One promising sink, found on January 27 by Guillaume, Fabrice and Bruno, was called Akhenaton. This dropped via small pitches in pure white, very sharp limestone into a series of small aquatic meanders. Exploration was abandoned at a depth of 200 metres when the risk from flooding became too great. Indeed, there were several skirmishes with sudden floods elsewhere.

Most other sinks and shafts proved either to be hopelessly blocked or descended only for short distances before closing down to impenetrable fissures. The half-way point of the expedition was marked by the departure of Serge, Didier, Bruno and Raoul, and the arrival of Gérard, Roman, Catherine and Jacques. There was by this time a feeling they may return home empty-handed, the first French expedition to New Britain not to find a major cave.

A number of smaller discoveries were made at Pomalngen Hul, which was pushed for 605 metres, and the Lamba resurgence explored for 200 metres. The *Rivière des Hobbits* was 500 metres in extent and Pek-Pek Hull, 250 metres long. The 900-metre labyrinth of Helena Hul surprised them with its 16 entrances, some fossil and others either active or semi-active in nature. Though the system had many pitches and climbs, the total depth was a mere 21 metres.

The finest discoveries were those made at the resurgence of the Ilana River and the sinks of the Omega River that feed it, 1,800 metres and 4,500 metres in extent respectively. This sporting complex provided some interesting caving in a variety of passage types, from boisterous streamways to abandoned galleries that were well decorated in places. Illana was explored upstream to a maximum height of 40 metres above the outflow; Omega ultimately reached a depth of 170 metres.

Although the results paled in comparison to the discoveries of previous years, they had found some 10 kilometres of new cave, included the combined six kilometres of the Ilana-Omega complex. Important biological discoveries were made and, perhaps more important, they had provided another piece in the caving jigsaw of the Nakanai Mountains.

THE FUTURE

The year 1978 saw the French and Australians for the first time tackling the river caves of New Britain and the Atea Kananda respectively. These advances came about not so much due to improvements in technology, but as a consequence of changing attitudes. Only five years before, the exploration of such systems had been considered impossible. These results are to be commended, and in particular the French finds in the Nakanai Mountains, which represented a milestone in underground river exploration. When one considers the nature of the New Britain forest, the rugged terrain and its inhospitable climate, one can only wonder at the impressive string of French successes. Credit must go to the organisers for their boldness and to the participants for their perseverance in the face of untold hardship. An even greater challenge perhaps awaits on the mainland at Tobio, the huge underground course of the Iaro River.

At the time of going to press no less than 29 international expeditions have found well over 200 kilometres of spectacular caves in New Guinea. Some 21 of these systems exceed 300 metres in depth, yet despite these impressive figures, the 60,000 square kilometres of karst has still only barely been scratched. The prospects for further discoveries could not be better, even for groups operating on a limited budget. With excellent road access, the Chimbu Province now offers scope for some very long and moderately deep caves in the Mt. Elimbari region at Chuave.

On the alpine slopes of Mt. Kaijende, Leiwaro Kundu and Kara Kundu have yet to be explored to a conclusive end. The chances of finding a deep system here are thought to be good; if, that is, Kara Kundu can be linked with Leiwaro Kundu beyond its sump. A strong air current in both caves lends weight to the feeling that greater discoveries await just "around the corner." The karst relief of Mt. Kaijende is said to rival that of the Huon Peninsula.

Although much more remote, the Victor Emanuel Range has vast areas of virgin limestone. It gave the 1975 British team one of its greatest challenges. Here the Fault Valley, rising steadily throughout its 23-kilometre length, terminates beneath the remote Mt. Burimsakin in a cirque at an altitude of 3,050-metres. Although overland travel is a nightmare it is believed that here exists one of the best prospects for finding deep caves. On neighbouring Mt. Wamtakin, Owillfore Tem was still going when abandoned at a depth of 200 metres. Further east at Oksapmin, and in the Hindenburg and Muller Ranges, there is still much work to be done.

Of the outlying islands, only New Britain and the Lelet Plateau on New Ireland offer cavers the chance of major finds. A limestone massif of at least 1,000 metres has yet to be exploited in the Baining Mountains of New Britain's Gazelle Peninsula, and a large system remains to be found feeding the huge Mayang resurgence in the Nakanai.

In 2002, a lightweight French team planned to return to New Britain, this time to explore another exciting prospect in the Nakanai Mountains. With over 1,000 metres depth potential, the Baraiman Canyon offers the chance to find another deep system. Aerial reconnaissance in 2000 pinpointed many sinkholes on the high plateau flanking the canyon; flying the chopper through the depths of the gorge revealed large outflows at river level and part way up the cliffs.

The Baraiman Canyon is without doubt an exciting prospect, and while the karst plateaux of New Britain continue to produce dramatic caving, the limestone massifs of the Papua New Guinea mainland have scarcely begun to reveal their hidden secrets. Out there, somewhere, lurks a cave system to rival any the world has to offer. One thing can be certain, however: it will not be revealed easily.

MAJOR CAVING EXPEDITIONS

1965	Australian Star Mountains Expedition
1971	Nanzan University Expedition to Enga and Chimbu
1972	Queensland University Expedition to Ora Doline (New Britain)
1973	Niugini Speleological Research Expedition to the Muller Range
1975	New Ireland Speleological Expedition (Lelet Plateau)
1975	British New Guinea '75 Expedition to the Hindenburg Mountains
1976	New Ireland Speleological Expedition (Lelet Plateau)
1976	Australian Muller Range Expedition
1978	Australian Speleological Expedition to the Atea Kananda (Muller Range)
1978	British Hole in the Wall Expedition (Hindenburg Mountains)
1978	Fédération Française de Spéléologie Reconnaissance Expedition (Eastern Highlands /Mt. Bangeta/New Britain)
1978	Spanish Expedicio Espeleologica to the Chimbu
1979	Expedition Speleologique Suisse en Papouasie Nouvelle Guinee (New Ireland/New Britain)
1980	French expedition to New Britain (Nakanai Range)
1982	The Mount Kaijende Expedition
1982	Australian Mamo '82 Expedition (Muller Range)
1982	Belgian (Spéléo-Club de Schaerbeek) expedition to New Britain
1984	Franco-Swiss Megadoline Filming Expedition to New Britain
1984	British Untamed River Expedition, New Britain (Nakanai Range)
1985	French Antipodes Expedition to New Britain (Nakanai Range)
1985	French Antipodes Expedition to New Britain (Whiteman Range)
1986	French Speleological Expedition to New Britain (Whiteman Range)
1988	French Speleological Expedition to New Britain (Nakanai Range)
1990	Small Belgian group visit remote area between Muller Range and Karius Range
1993	French expedition to the Great Papuan Plateau, Gulf Province
1994-5	French team to New Britain (Galowe Plateau in Nakanai Range)
1998	French expedition to New Britain (Galowe Plateau in Nakanai Range)
2000	French reconnaissance expedition to New Britain (Whiteman Range and Bairaman Canyon of the Nakanai Mountains)
2001	French expedition to Whiteman Range
2002	Proposed French expedition to Bairaman Canyon, Nakanai Mountains

MAJOR CAVES

Deepest:

Cave	Locality	Depth (m)
Muruk Hul	Nakanai Mountains	1,178
Mamo Kananda	Muller Range, S. H. P.	528
Bibima	Porol Range, Chimbu	494
Gamvo	Nakanai Mountains	478
Arcturus	Galowe, Nakanai Mountains	475
Minye	Nakanai Mountains	468
Arrakis	Whiteman Range	468
KAII	Nakanai Mountains	459
Malemuli	Muller Range, S. H. P.	420
Nare	Nakanai Mountains	415
Bikpela Vuvu	Nakanai Mountains	414
Kavakuna	Nakanai Mountains	392
Terbil Tem	Victor Emanuel Range	354
Atea Kananda	Muller Range, S. H. P.	350
Arem Tem	Western Province	334
Altaïr	Nakanai Mountains	332
Camp III Hole	Victor Emanuel Range	330
Leiwaro Kundu	Mt. Kaijende	330
Guimbé	Nakanai Mountains	320
Kanada Heiowa Heia	Muller Range, S. H. P.	314
Uli Guria	Muller Range, S. H. P.	314

Longes:

Cave	Locality	Length (m)
Mamo Kananda	Muller Range, S. H. P.	54,800
Atea Kananda	Muller Range, S. H. P.	34,500
Selminum Tem	Hindenburg Range, W. P.	20,500
Muruk	Nakanai Mountains	17,300
Arrakis	Whiteman Range	11,030
Liklik Vuvu	Nakanai Mountains	6,800
Gamvo	Nakanai Mountains	6,000
Minye	Nakanai Mountains	5,421
Omega	Whiteman Range	4,500
Nare	Nakani Mountains	4,170

Cave	Locality	Length (m)
KAII	Nakani Mountains	3,500
Leiwaro Kundu	Mt. Kaijende	3,500
Guimbé	Nakanai Mountains	2,772
Dolines des Pygmes-Arrakis	Whiteman Range	2,760
Kururu	Nakanai Mountains	2,634
BikBik Vuvu	Nakanai Mountains	2,600
Pimbiraga Kananda	Muller Range, S. H. P.	2,500
Kanada Heiowa Heia	Muller Range, S. H. P.	2,500
Arcturus	Nakanai Mountains	2,425
Pavie	Nakanai Mountains	2,250
Atea Outflow	Muller Range, S. H. P.	2,200
Irukunguai	Porol Range, Chimbu	2,120
Toroku Nantaut	Menetai, Bougainville	1,900
Kavakuna	Nakanai Mountains	1,800
Ilana	Whiteman Range	1,800
Draï Pasis	Nakana Mountains	1,575
Tuweiwu	Obura, E. H. P.	1,525
Kopunei	Manus Island	1,500
Ok Mi Great cave	Ok Tedi, W. P.	1,500
Galué	Nakanai Mountains	1,480
Lemerigamus	Lelet Plateau, N. Ireland	1,300
Oravunana	Obura, E. H. P.	1,300
Antares	Nakanai Mountains	1,286
Southern Cross	Nakanai Mountains	1,253
Pompulyun	Manus Island	1,250
Tolana	Nakanai Mountains	1,236
Bibima	Porol Range, Chimbu	1,220
Dalum	New Ireland	1,200
Gouvi-Bogalawe	Nakanai Mountains	1,200
Nambawan Ananda	Mt. Kaijende	1,200
Capella	Nakanai Mountains	1,165
Altaïr	Nakanai Mountains	1,115
Barananomba	Yonki area, E. H. P.	1,050
Ok Tem	Hindenburg Range	1,040
Grotte Tucana	Nakanai Mountains	1,033
Neïde	Nakanai Mountains	1,015
Surprise River	Mt. Kaijende	1,000
Megadoline Ora	Nakanai Mountains	1,000

CHRONOLOGY OF EXPLORATION

1962   British attempt to organise expedition fails.

1964   Bibima discovered by Fred Parker. First major investigation in Irukunguai Cave.

1965   Team of Australian cavers carry out first exploration of eastern Star Mountains.

1968   Chris Borough and Kevin Read partially explore Minye Doline and its postulated outflow.

1969-70 Neil Ryan begins investigation of caves in Kagua and Erave area. Finds Tobio (Iaro River Cave).

1971   Nanzan University archaeological expedition to caves in Enga and Chimbu regions.

1972   (Apr.) Mike Bourke's reconnaissance to Ora Doline.
        (May) Further explorations in Irukunguai.
        (Aug.) Bibima Cave explored to a sump. Deepest in southern hemisphere at -494 m.

1972-73 Queensland University launch first investigation of Ora Doline.

1973   First Australian expedition to Muller Range. Discover Uli Guria (-314 m) and Kanada Heiowa Heia (-314 m).
        (Apr) Van Watson/Kevan Wilde reach -170 m in Darua Muru.

1974   Howard Beck and Roy Blackham initiate exploration of fossil series in Iaro River Cave.
        (Apr) First reconnaissance to Lelet Plateau, New Ireland.

1975   (Jan) Second Lelet Plateau reconnaissance.
        (Apr) Kevan Wilde and Howard Beck begin two-month reconnaissance for 24-man British expedition.
        Aerial recce of Lelet Plateau crashes in sea.
        (July) First Australian expedition to Lelet Plateau.
        (July) Five-month British expedition to Hindenburg Range. Major find is the 20 kilometres long Selminum Tem.

1976   (Jun) Second Australian Lelet Plateau expedition. Discovers and partially explores Lemerigamus cave.
        (Aug) Second Australian Muller Range expedition. Makes first tentative explorations in Atea Kananda.

1977   Aerial and ground reconnaissance of the Huon Peninsula.

1978   Spanish expedition to Chimbu. Pushes Darua Muru to -234 m.
        A 50-strong team forms Australian Atea Kananda expedition. Atea explored to 30.5 km. Carries out reconnaissance in Lavani Valley. Explores Hadia Yaneabogairi (Mamo Kananda) for 8.5 km
        Five-man British team scales Hindenburg Wall to reach Era Tem. Discovers Arem Tem, Gebemi Tem and others.
        French team to Nakanai Mtns. Partial explore Nare and Minye. Also visit some caves in Eastern Highlands.

1979   Swiss expedition to New Ireland and New Britain. Team bottoms Lemerigamus but disaster strikes when a caver is drowned in Kavakuna.

1980   French expedition to New Britain. Explores Nare for over 4 km to a depth of 415 m. Discovers Liklik Vuvu (-295 m) and Bikbik Vuvu (-414 m). Follows underground Matali river in KAII to a depth of 459 metres.

1982   Fourth Australian Muller Range expedition. At -528 m, Hadia Yaneabogairi (renamed Mamo Kananda) becomes deepest in PNG with length of 54.8 km. Malemuli explored (-420 m). Atea extended by 4 km.
        USA led expedition to Mt. Kaijende. Discovers many pretty caves. Major find is Leiwaro Kundu (-330 m).

1982   A small team of Belgians visit New Britain, making several minor discoveries.
        Japanese team visit Nakanai Mountains.
        (Dec) Gérald and Rosemarie Favre makes reconnaissance in Mubi River region of Southern Highlands.

1984   Franco-Swiss Megadoline filming team to New Britain. Also reconnaissance of Lake Kutubu in Southern Highlands
        Province.

1984   Japanese (Meiji University) expedition to Karius Range/Lavani Valley, Southern Highlands. Restricted by wet season.
        British Untamed River Expedition to Nare. Discovers Gamvo (-478 m), Pavie (-265 m), Killie (-260 m) and Gouvi-
        Bogalawe (-172 m).

1985   First investigation of caves in the Lukwi River area of the Western Province. French expedition to Nakani Range. Major
        find Muruk Hul, at -637 m, a new depth record for PNG. Other finds in Minye. Discovers Kururu (-256 m) and Guimbé
        (-320 m).
        French expedition to Whiteman Range. Discover and explore Arrakis at over 11 km.
        Japanese visit to Kavakuna, New Britain.

1986   Six-man French team extends Arrakis.

1988   French expedition to Mayang area of New Britain. Many discoveries: major find (Arcturus) reaches a depth of 445 m.

1989   Belgian group of cavers carry out reconnaissance in Karius Range, Southern Highlands.

1990   Follow-up Belgian expedition examines two areas east of the Karius Range, but few caves explored.

1993   French team targets Great Papua Plateau in Gulf Province, but few finds materialise. Reaches the huge Darai Doline and
        formulates new theory on the genesis of such gigantic dolines.

1994-95 French expedition to New Britain led by Jean-Paul Sounier. Extends Muruk Hul to inconclusive end at a depth of 1,141
        metres, making it the deepest system in southern hemisphere.

1998   French return succeeds in linking Muruk Hul with its outflow, the Résurgence de La Chevelure de Bérénice (Bérénice
        Cave). The new surveyed depth recalculated to 1,178 m. Sump in Arcturus dived to give new depth of 475 m. Push
        Southern Cross to sump at a depth of 275 m.

2000   Five-man team carry reconnaissance of the Bairaman Canyon, in the Nakanai Mountains, and also an area of the
        Whiteman Range between the Andru and Ayle Rivers.

2001   Sixteen French cavers and two Swiss scientists form expedition to Whiteman Range. Not as productive as previous
        French trips. Many smaller caves explored, including Malalip Hul (-133 m), Rivière des Hobbits (500 m), Lamba Resur-
        gence (200 m) and Helena Hul (900 m). Major discoveries were the Siki River sink (Omega) at 4. 5 km long and 170
        metres deep and the Illan River resurgence at 1. 8 km.

GLOSSARY OF CAVING TERMS

ABSEIL	A means of descending a rope with a variable friction device (see RACK, STOP and WHALETAIL).
AMORPHOUS CALCITE	A colloidal form of calcium carbonate, often cauliflower-like in appearance.
ANCHOR	Artificial belay point, usually a bolt or piton, to which is fastened the rope.
ARETE KARST	A variety of polygonal limestone development often outcropping in narrow, saw-tooth ridges, sometimes in conjunction with pinnacles.
AVEN	A vertical shaft extending upwards from a passage, sometimes carrying water, but not necessarily connecting with the surface. It may link different levels of passage development.
BEDDING PLANE	Passage formed between two near-horizontal beds of limestone.
BELAY	Anchoring point used for ladders or ropes. Also for securing a climber or lifeliner.
BOULDER CHOKE	Mass of fallen boulders blocking a passage.
CALCITE	Most commonplace form of crystalline calcium carbonate, the chief constituent of cave formations.
CANAL	Section of cave passage containing slow moving deep water.
CARABINER (krab)	A metal snaplink used for securing to ropes, anchor point, etc when climbing.
CARBIDE	A carbon compound of calcium supplied in solid pellets. Liberates acetylene gas when exposed to water.
CARBIDE LAMP	Means of illumination using regulated water supply to generate acetylene from calcium carbide.
CAVE PEARLS	Concretions of calcite formed in shallow pool around a nucleus-usually a grain of sand.
CAVERN	Applied commonly to any large chamber, but occasionally to an entire cave system.
CHAMBER	A localised widening of a passage, sometimes on a grand scale.
CHERT	A cryptocrystalline form of silica occurring either in nodules projecting from cave walls, or as pebbles.
CHIMNEY	Ascending rift, free climbable using "back and footing" techniques; i.e., "chimneying."
CRAWL	Passage negotiated by moving on hands and knees, or perhaps flat-out.
CREVICE KARST	Solution enlargement of limestone into fissure up to 20 metres wide. Can be tens of metres in depth (See GRYKE).
CURTAIN	Thin, translucent drapery-like form of calcite suspended from walls or roof.
DESCENDER	See RACK, STOP and WHALETAIL.
DEVIATION	Point where the hang of an SRT rope is moved to avoid rub point, water or loose boulders.
DIP	The angle at which the natural bedding of the strata deviates from horizontal.
DOLINE	A closed depression, formed due to solution or mechanical collapse of underlying strata.
DRYSUIT (Pontonnière)	Rubberised fabric oversuit employing seals at neck, wrists and ankles to exclude all water,
DUCK (Duck-under)	Point at which cave roof momentarily meets a water surface necessitating partial or total immersion. Often used to describe any passage having minimal airspace.
EFFLUX	A cave or point from which stream or river flows.
ELECTRON LADDER	Lightweight ladder made from flexible wire sides on which aluminium alloy rungs are threaded. Usually made in 7.5 metre lengths that can be clipped together for greater length.
EPIPHREATIC	Passage which is only seasonally submerged.
ERRATIC (eccentric)	Formations deviating from the perpendicular.
ETRIERS	Short flexible ladder-like aid used in artificial climbing techniques.
FAULT	A fracture line in the strata, usually accompanied by vertical or lateral displa-cement.
FISSURE	A narrow passage, cleft or rift.
FLOWSTONE	Stalagmite deposit formed on walls or floor of cave by thin flowing film of calcium enriched water.
FORMATION	General term taken to mean any calcite or mineral deposits in cave; i.e., stalactites, stalagmites, gour pools.
GOURS	Pools collected in stalagmite dams.
GROTTO	A well decorated chamber.
GRYKE	A solutional fissure in limestone.
GUANO	Accumulations of bat or bird faeces in tropical caves.
GYPSUM	Cave deposit caused by reaction of calcium carbonate with oxide of pyrites. Commonly found in the form of "flowers" or "needles."

HELICTITE	See ERRATIC.
INLET	Point where a tributary stream enters cave. (see AVEN).
JAMMER	A device used, usually in pairs, for ascending a single rope.
JOINT	A natural fissure in strata.
JUMAR	See jammer.
KARST	Derived from the Slovenian word *kras*, for a limestone area near Trieste. Now universally adopted to describe the world's limestone landscapes.
LIFELINE	Safety rope used to safeguard caver or climber negotiating exposed obstacles, i.e., pitch, traverse or tyrolean.
MARMITE	French term for ROCKMILL, usually of impressive proportions.
MISFIT stream	Small stream, having invaded passage formed and since abandoned by older stream.
NUT	Aluminium blocks of various sizes, commonly hexagon in section and threaded on sling used as a climbing aid by wedging in crack as a running belay.
OXBOW	Abandoned stream channel, sometimes at a level above river that once flowed along it.
PEG or PITON	A climbing aid hammered into cracks in rock. A metal blade formed into an eye at one end to which rope may be attached using a carabiner.
PHREATIC	Geomorphological term for a cave passage primarily formed by solution below saturation level (water table.)
PINNACLE KARST	See ARETE KARST.
PITCH	A vertical descent requiring ladders and/or ropes.
POLJE	Large enclosed basin or valley with no surface outlet.
PORTAL	Term used for entrance of cavern.
POTHOLE (also POT)	Vertical pitch open to surface.
PRUSSIK	Means of ascending a rope using mechanical jamming device.
RACK	A rope descending device in which friction, and hence rate of descent, is varied using sliding metal bars.
RESURGENCE	See EFFLUX.
RIMSTONE POOLS	See GOURS.
RISING	Point where water emerges at surface under artesian pressure.
ROCKMILL	A round pit, or swirl-hole in stream bed, caused by grinding action of pebbles/rocks constantly agitated by moving water.
SCALLOPS	Flow-markings (ripple-marks) on floor, walls or roof caused by water action.
SEDIMENT	Stream or glacial-derived deposits in cave; i.e., sand, mud or silt.
SHAFT	Vertical pot open to surface or forming part of underground network.
SINKHOLE (SINK)	A point of engulfment of a stream or river.
SPELEOLOGIST	Someone who explores and studies caves.
SPELEOTHEM	General scientific term for calcite formations.
SQUEEZE	Restricted section of cave passage or shaft.
SRT	Single rope technique. Method of descending/ascending ropes using jammers/descendeurs.
STALACTITE	Calcite growth suspended from roof.
STALAGMITE	Calcite growth upwards from cave floor or boulders.
STOP	An abseiling device made in France.
STRAWS	Slender, hollow, straw-like stalactites.
STREAMWAY	Cave passage carrying flow of water.
SUMP	Point where cave roof dips below water surface. More prolonged than a duck and usually requiring skilled cave diving techniques to negotiate.
SURVEY	The process, and name for end-product, of detailed mapping of a cave system.
SWALLET	See SINKHOLE.
SIPHON	A term used loosely to describe a SUMP, though not necessarily having any siphonic action.
THREAD or THREAD BELAY	A natural eyehole in rock or space between jammed boulders through which rope or sling may be passed and used as belay.
TOWER KARST	A degenerative tropical karst landscape, forming limestone towers as a result of bedding and rainfall linked solutional breakdown.
TRAVERSE	A means of negotiating a passage at high level by utilising ledges on one or both walls.
TROGLOBITE	Species of animal which spends entire life cycle within a cave.
TUFA	A spongy form of travertine deposited on the surface in limestone regions.
TYROLEAN	A means of overcoming an obstacle (river crossing) by propelling oneself, commando-like across a rope.
UVULA	Complex depressions containing two or more dolines.
VADOSE	Passage formed primarily by moving water above saturation level (water table).
WHALETAIL	A rope descending device devised in Australasia. Works on a similar principal to the rack, but not employing movable friction bars.
WETSUIT	Close-fitting expanded neoprene rubber suit. Warmth is derived from film of water trapped next to skin which quickly heats to body temperature.

GLOSSARY OF LOCAL NAMES

Local names and words	Language	Translation
AFEK	(Telfol)	old woman
ANANDA	(Mai-Enga)	a house
BALUS	(pidgin)	aircraft
BIKPELA	(pidgin)	big, large
BINATANG	(pidgin)	insect
BLAK-BOKIS	(pidgin)	flying fox
BOM-BOM	(pidgin)	a grass torch
BUS ROP	(pidgin)	jungle vine, liana
CUS-CUS	(pidgin)	opossum
GURIA	(pidgin)	earthquake
HAUS SICK	(pidgin)	hospital
HAUS TAMBURAN	(pidgin)	spirit house
HUL-BILONG-STONE	(pidgin)	cave
ITAMBU	(pidgin)	taboo, forbidden
KANANDA	(Duna/Huli)	literally stone house; cave
KIAP	(pidgin)	government patrol officer
KUNAI	(pidgin)	a tough grass (g. Imperata)
MASALAI	(pidgin)	spirit
MIXMASTER	(pidgin)	helicopter
MURUK	(pidgin)	cassowary
OK	(Telfol)	river, water
PIT-PIT	(pidgin)	tall cane grass related to sugar cane
PUK-PUK	(pidgin)	crocodile
SANGUMA	(pidgin)	sorcery, witchcraft
TEM	(Telfol)	a cave or hole
TUMBUNA	(pidgin)	ancestors
ULI	(Duna/Huli)	shaft or pit
WOK	(Faiwol)	river, water
WOKIM	(pidgin)	work
YU	(Duna/Huli)	river

BIBLIOGRAPHY

Antipodes 85, *Spelunca* No. 15. Fédération Française de Spéléologie. (1987).

Audra, P ; Sounier, J-P; et al, *Nakanai, 20 Years of Exploration.* Hemisphere Sud. (2001).

Brook, D. (ed), The British New Guinea Speleological Expedition, 1975. *Transactions British Cave Research Ass'n.* (1976).

Brongersma, L. D., *To the Mountains of the Star.* New York. (1963).

Champion, I. F., *Across New Guinea from the Fly to the Sepik.* London. (1932).

Favre, G.; Chevalley, P.; Bourne, J-D. Papouasie Nouvelle-Guinee. *Stalactite* No. 2/81 1/82.

Gill, D.W. (comp), *The Untamed River Expedition.* (1988).

Hallyer, T., 1965. *First Crossing of the Australia Star Mountains*, manscpt. Austr. Nat. Uni. microfilm PMB83.

James, J. M.; King, R. H.; Montgomery, N. R., Atea Kananda. *Helictite* (1976).

McQuillan, Col., Everest Lies Below. *Walkabout Magazine.* Aug. 1973. p. 58-61.

Pernette, J-F., *L'Abime Sous La Jungle.* (1981)

Robb, M., 1973, The Hindenburg Wall. *Niugini Caver,* 1,no. 1 p. 7-8

Simpson, C., *Plumes and Arrows.* (1962).

Sounier, J-P, *Muruk.* Spelunca Librairie. (1999).

Sounier, J-P, *Nakani.* Spelunca Librairie. (1995).

Souter, G., *New Guinea: The Last Unknown.* (1963).

Speleological Research Expedition NSRE 1973. Ed. J. M. James. Speleological Research Council, Sydney.

Spelunca, July-Sept. 1981, Papua New Guinea. Report of 1979 and 1980 FFS Expeditions to New Britain. (in English)

Steer, G. The Search for the World's Longest Cave (1979). *Geo,* 1, 8-35.

Sweeting, M. M., *Karst Landforms.* Macmillan, 1972.

Waltham, A. C., *Caves.* London, 1974.

Whitmore, T. C., *Tropical Rain Forests of the Far East,* 1975.

INDEX

Sing Sing near Mt. Hagen. Photo: Urs Widmer